The Thinking Reader

James Koobatian
Mt. San Jacinto College

WADSWORTH

THOMSON LEARNING ™

Australia • Canada • Mexico • Singapore • Spain • United Kingdom • United States

WADSWORTH

THOMSON LEARNING

Publisher: Eve Howard
Philosophy Editor: Peter Adams
Assistant Editor: Kara Kindstrom
Editorial Assistant: Chalida Anusasananan
Development Consultant: Jake Warde
Marketing Manager: Dave Garrison
Marketing Assistant: Adam Hofmann
Print/Media Buyer: Robert King

Permissions Editor: Bob Kauser
Production Service: Buuji, Inc.
Copy Editor: Linda Ireland/Buuji, Inc.
Cover Designer: Harold Burch
Cover Image: Guy Billout
Compositor: Buuji, Inc.
Text and Cover Printer: Webcom Limited

Printed in Canada
1 2 3 4 5 6 7 05 04 03 02

For permission to use material from this text,
contact us by
Web: http://www.thomsonrights.com
Fax: 1-800-730-2215
Phone: 1-800-730-2214

Wadsworth Thomson Learning
10 Davis Drive
Belmont, CA 94002-3098
USA

For more information about our products,
contact us:
Thomson Learning Academic Resource Center
1-800-423-0563
http://www.wadsworth.com

International Headquarters
Thomson Learning
International Division
290 Harbor Drive, 2nd Floor
Stamford, CT 06902-7477
USA

UK/Europe/Middle East/South Africa
Thomson Learning
Berkshire House
168-173 High Holborn
London WC1V 7AA
United Kingdom

Asia
Thomson Learning
60 Albert Street, #15-01
Albert Complex
Singapore 189969

Canada
Nelson Thomson Learning
1120 Birchmount Road
Toronto, Ontario M1K 5G4
Canada

Library of Congress Cataloging-in-Publication Data
The thinking reader / [compiled by] James Koobatian.
    p. cm.
   Includes bibliographical references.
   ISBN 0-534-50585-6 (alk. paper)
    1. Reasoning. I. Koobatian, James, 1952–
BC177 .T49 2001
160—dc21   2001026421

For
Sarah, Maxwell, and Spencer

Contents

4. Ben and Jerry's and Corporate Philanthropy   69

5. School Uniforms   79

6. Channel One   93

7. The Tabloids and Checkbook Journalism   114

8. The Bell Curve   131

9. Duty of Care   177

10. The Great Ape Project   189

11. Zoos   211

12. Boxing   225

Preface

Anything can be asserted, almost anything is possible, much is plausible, some is supportable, and very little is provable.

Lloyd R. Cohen, *The Puzzling Case of Jimmy "The Greek"*

To the Student

There's nothing mysterious about good reasoning. If you don't create good arguments now, it's not because you can't, it's because you haven't been taught. *The Thinking Reader* will help you develop the skills you need to identify the structure and quality of arguments. It will also instruct you in how to create good arguments for yourself. There's a logic, a method to identifying and creating an argument, just like there's logic to performing any other specialized activity, whether it's baking, carpentry, fixing broken parking meters, or performing gall bladder surgery. Once you master the process, the particular way you go about identifying and creating arguments, you'll find yourself doing it naturally, and effectively.

What The Thinking Reader *Emphasizes*

You'll notice I've emphasized the role of *definition* and *clarity* in argument—what does a word or term mean, how is it being used, what's the context of the word, do we ordinarily use the word in the sense the author is using it? Often premises and conclusions are not clearly true or false, rather they are just vague or ambiguous, imprecise in what they express. Attention to definition and clarity will increase your ability to assess the arguments of others, and increase the precision of your own arguments as well. I also emphasize the use of *examples* and *analogies*. If you illustrate what you're arguing for (or against) with effective examples and analogies, your arguments will be more intelligible, relevant, and stronger. And if you're effective at assessing the examples and analogies of others, you'll be more effective at assessing the integrity of their arguments as well.

All critical thinking texts and readers emphasize the basics of isolating premises, hidden assumptions, and conclusions, and *The Thinking Reader* is no different in this respect. Additionally, though, the exercises I've fashioned will prod you to not only isolate premises and conclusions, but also assess their significance and relevance. What do you believe is the *strongest* piece of evidence the author gives to support his or her conclusion, and *why* is it strong? On the other hand, there are arguments that are built on *weak* premises, and I ask you to explain why you think they are weak. Examining the integrity of premises and conclusions will take you a long way on your road to skillful argumentation. Last, do the authors reply to objections from their critics? Do they isolate the principal objections to their positions and argue effectively against them, or do they concern themselves with side issues not germane to the central issues being debated?

You need to write papers at the same time you learn to master the structure and skill of argument. Throughout *The Thinking Reader* I've linked these two aspects of argumentation—*outlining an argument* and *putting the argument into essay form*—into the following two-step process.

First, *outline* the argument you're making or analyzing. Here's the argument form we'll use throughout the text, along with a little instruction on how to fill it out.

Issue: *Identify the issue of the argument. Summarize it so you can argue either for or against it.*

Definitions: *Identify and clarify important definitions of words or expressions in the argument so the reader knows exactly what is meant when the terms are used.*

Premises: *Identify the premises of the argument. List the premises, each as a declarative statement, in their most logical order.*

Conclusion: *Identify the conclusion of the argument, and state it in declarative statement form.*

Mastering this form will enable you to grasp the arguments of others and create effective arguments of your own. It's a simple, generic form that will serve you well. But remember, while the form is effective, it's not perfect. The reason for this is it's impossible for *any* argument form or diagram to adequately represent all the subtleties of argumentation. Our language is rich—we employ exaggeration, rhetorical devices, and metaphor; create subarguments; appeal to the sentiments; and so on. Some arguments will lend themselves to outline form more comfortably than others.

As a general rule, to keep your eyes on the prize and not get too involved in the minute details of arguments, keep the following two points in mind when outlining the arguments of others. If the argument is short, strive for comprehensiveness. This way all crucial statements will be present for assessment, and the structure of the entire argument will be evident. For longer articles, it's a good idea to employ the outline in a more economical fashion by restricting the listing of claims to the most significant, leaving out some of the supporting detail in the premises. How *comprehensive* should you be? How much detail should you leave out? There is no single, correct way to determine how much detail you should employ in creating your argument outlines, or to determine exactly what kind of language or terms you should use. The length of the article, the complexity of the material, the amount of knowledge assumed by the author, and the type of language the author employs are only a few important factors that will determine the geography of your outline. The same applies for arguments you compose yourself. Your teacher will counsel you on this important matter, and eventually you will develop a sense for how detailed an argument outline you should attempt, and the kind of language you will use. Once you've completed your argument in this form, you're ready for step two, writing your essay.

Your argument outline is your guide to writing your essay. And since your essay will only be as strong as your argument is in outline form, it's important to list all the crucial claims in your outline, in their most logical sequence, *before* you write your essay. Include only those statements or claims in your essay that you included in your outline. And remember, you're *arguing* here, offering evidence to establish the truth and believability of your conclusion, not writing a story. So avoid including statements in your essay not directly related to the purpose of strengthening your argument.

I've outlined the argument in Sal Marino's article entitled *Chief Executives Are Underpaid* below. (Immediately following the outline is Marino's article.) Throughout *The Thinking Reader* I ask you to outline arguments, and to create arguments of your own using the same model. You can use the Marino outline as a guide when you read the articles and answer the questions in the study sections following the articles. Also, if you glance through the study sections you will notice I've sprinkled additional outlines of arguments throughout the text. I enjoy asking my students to check the accuracy of my outlines of arguments; I encourage you to do the same by checking the ones in this text, and the outlines of your classmates (and don't forget your professor!).

Last, a note on methods of teaching critical thinking, and doing critical thinking. Each teacher (myself included) has his or her own method for teaching critical thinking. But remember: *There are many different, effective ways to teach critical thinking skills.* Further, *there's not one right way to employ your critical thinking skills.* Approaches differ, the goals are the same. When executed with skill, different approaches yield similar results. So whatever method your teacher uses, with a little determination and creativity, I'm sure you will settle into an approach to argumentation you will find both agreeable and fruitful.

Chief Executives Are Underpaid, by Sal Marino

Issue: Whether chief executives are underpaid.
Definitions: Chief executive means the person who has the primary responsibility for running a corporation.
Premises: 1. Professional athletes are paid millions of dollars each year without critical outrage from their fans.
2. Jordan, Stalone, Oprah Winfrey, and Spielberg have unique talents that attract people to pay to see them perform.
3. Their major responsibility is to manage themselves and their unique talents.
4. When Jordan makes a mistake on the court, his blunders may result in a poor shot, a flubbed pass, the loss of a game, or, at worst, the loss of a championship. He still gets his $30 million.
5. Michael and Oprah are being paid for having fun.
6. Compensation packages for CEOs are often depicted as outrageous, inflated, obscene, unconscionable, and undeserved.
7. Bill (Gates) and John (Welch) are being paid to achieve the company's goals and objectives.
8. Eisner, Gates, Welch, and Kluge are expected to create wealth, produce profits, employ thousands of skilled individuals, remain competitive against the world's best competition, and deliver growing value and dividends to their investors.
9. If Gates, Kluge, Welch, or Eisner err, their mistakes affect their

reputations, the thousands of people who work for them, the millions of people who own their stock, and the millions who buy their products.

10. CEOs have more responsibilities than entertainers and sports figures.

Conclusion: Chief executives are underpaid.

Chief Executives Are Underpaid

SAL MARINO

WHENEVER I HEAR A DEBATE about chief-*executive compensation,* I'm reminded of the Arab emir who traveled to the U.S. to have a quadruple coronary bypass performed by a special surgeon. The surgeon was an internationally recognized expert and had performed many coronary operations with extraordinary success. But he was concerned about how much to charge the royal patient. If he overcharged, it might mean unfavorable international press and a loss of goodwill. But if he undercharged, the sultan would feel the operation was not serious enough to require this doctor's special skills. The surgeon consulted his colleagues. He decided to charge $10,000. One of his friends then suggested that he ask advice from a lawyer who specialized in Middle East affairs.

The attorney listened, pondered for a few minutes, and then recommended that the surgeon submit a blank statement with a footnote, "The sultan is wise. He can do no wrong." It was a risky suggestion. It allowed the sultan to determine the worth of the operation. The doctor decided to take the risk. Shortly thereafter, he received a check from the sultan's royal exchequer for $100,000. The doctor was elated. But his euphoria lasted only a few days when he received a blank invoice from his attorney. It had a footnote: "The value of your expert surgical skills is exceeded only by the value of your expert legal advice."

Thousands of words are written each year about *compensation* packages paid to chief executives. Often, they are depicted as outrageous, inflated, obscene, unconscionable, and undeserved. At the same time, professional athletes are paid millions of dollars each year without critical outrage from their fans. Why then shouldn't superstar chief executives earn what star athletes and star entertainers earn?

If Sylvester "Rambo" Stallone is worth $20 million per motion picture, why isn't Michael Eisner worth as much or more as chief *executive* of Disney? If Steven Spielberg can earn $285 million in one year making movies, why should Bill Gates be criticized if he earns as much or more running Microsoft? If Michael Jordan is a $30-million-per-year basketball player, why shouldn't John Kluge or John Welch be $30 million chief executives running Metromedia and General Electric?

Jordan, Stallone, Oprah Winfrey, and Spielberg have unique talents that attract people to pay to see them perform. But their major responsibility is to manage themselves and their unique talents. Eisner, Gates, Welch, and Kluge are expected to create wealth, produce profits, employ thousands of skilled individuals, remain competitive against the world's best competition, and deliver growing value and dividends to their investors.

When Jordan makes a mistake on the court, his blunders may result in a poor shot, a flubbed pass, the loss of a game, or, at worst, the loss of a championship. He still gets his $30 million. If Gates, Kluge, Welch, or Eisner err, their mistakes affect their reputations, the thousands of people who work for them, the millions of people who own their stock, and the millions who buy their products. When viewed in that context, who should be

From Industry Week *247, no. 8 (1998): 22. Reprinted with permission.*

paid more—Jordan and Stallone, or Gates and Welch?

Since becoming chairman emeritus of my company, I see my years as a chief *executive* in a different light and from a new perspective. I find surprising satisfaction in being relieved of other people's stress, pressure, and problems. I can take my own risks and be rewarded for my successes and be held accountable to myself for my failures. I am no longer second-guessed. That's why if I were still a chief *executive*, I'd either demand higher *compensation* or be self-employed.

In other words, I'd rather be a Michael Jordan or Oprah Winfrey than a Bill Gates or a John Welch. Michael and Oprah are being paid for having fun. Bill and John are being paid to achieve the company's goals and objectives. They have too many constituencies and too many people affecting their success or failure.

To the Instructor

The Thinking Reader is meant to be used as a companion with your critical thinking text. You might also find it useful in ethics classes, especially those emphasizing contemporary social issues or issues in communications. It offers articles of varying lengths and levels of difficulty on stimulating subjects. *The Thinking Reader* rejects both the pro/con and pro/con/middle ground formats in favor of including as many articles as necessary to be representative of the issue(s) covered. For example, there may be only two articles on a subject, as in the case of zoos, or there may be as many as ten articles, as with the subject of boxing. Moreover, the study sections are narrower in scope than those found in other readers, focusing on specific issues rather than subjects in general. For example, though the authors of the articles on boxing are a diverse group, ranging from Joyce Carol Oates to the editor of the *Journal of the American Medical Association,* the main issue being debated is the same—should professional boxing be banned? This should keep your students on a narrower argumentative path, no matter what article they choose to study from any section. You may insist that a handful of articles in this text do not contain arguments, at least formal arguments we are accustomed to encountering in readers that teach argumentation. I have included them because they raise important issues, suitable for exercising critical skills about the subjects being debated. In rejecting the pro/con format, I came to embrace a more representative model of how issues are argued.

Some of the subjects in *The Thinking Reader* may be unfamiliar to you. I have strived for interest level, relevancy of subject matter, and readings suitable for identifying and creating argument. I suspect most of you have read your share of papers on gun control. The contents betrays the need for modest occupational revitalization, as well as the pedagogical goal of teaching argument.

In the exercises after the articles, I have used an argument form (Issue, Definitions, Premises, Conclusion) throughout this text that is sometimes used in critical thinking classes (e.g., Richard L. Epstein's "Critical Thinking"). I felt running the risk of using a different argument outline than yours is preferable to no outline form at all. My goal in emphasizing the outline is obvious—to get the students to outline their arguments so frequently that it becomes a natural, integral part of their argumentation process. If you use another method of outlining arguments (e.g., Toulmin), substituting your preference in the study sections should pose no significant hurdles.

Last, I explain in the To the Student section that there are different methods of teaching the skills of critical thinking, and that there is no one correct way to employ critical thinking skills. There are many fine critical thinking texts, and many more approaches to teaching critical thinking. For myself, emphasizing this point with my students has gone a long way toward putting them at ease and encouraging them to be flexible, creative, and confident. I hope *The Thinking Reader* offers you the flexibility you need to teach critical thinking in the way your students will benefit most.

Acknowledgments

The following individuals each contributed to *The Thinking Reader* in significant ways. It's with pleasure that I mention their names and contributions now.

Lydia Herrera-Soren, of the Mt. San Jacinto College Library, for tracking down piles of articles, books, citations, quotations, even people. Whether it was stationary or moving, nothing eluded her grasp.

Bobby Avila, of Mt. San Jacinto College, for sharing his knowlege of chess, articulating its extraordinary heights, and acknowledging its limits.

Peter Adams, Philosophy and Religion editor at Wadsworth, for signing on to the project early and never wavering in his support.

Linda J. Ireland, copyeditor, for magically turning the manuscript into printable form.

The Reviewers for Wadsworth, who labored over the manuscript and offered guidance: David Benfield, Montclair State University; Deen Chatterjee, University of Utah; Blanche Curry, Fayetteville State University; Fred Johnson, Colorado State University; Katherine Katsenis, California State University—Dominguez Hills; Morton Schagrin, SUNY—Fredonia; Mattias Schulte, Montgomery College; and especially Al Spangler, California State University—Long Beach.

My wife, Sarah, and sons Maxwell and Spencer, for allowing me to complete *The Thinking Reader* often at times when we should have been together.

Sarah Feinbaum, my wife, who was instrumental in creating the idea for this book, and for critically evaluating the entire manuscript from genesis to completion. Without her patience, analysis, and encouragement, *The Thinking Reader* never would have been.

With generosity and care they all improved this book. Any shortcomings, as they say, are mine.

Chapter 1

Organ Sales

Background

WITH THE CREATION OF CYCLOSPORINE, the antirejection drug, the success rate in organ transplantation has taken a dramatic turn for the better—patients are living much longer with transplanted organs, and increased numbers of patients are receiving transplants and are being placed on waiting lists. Additionally, numerous transplant centers have popped up both in the United States and abroad to meet the increased demand for transplant therapy. But with the welcomed success has come the need for organs, which are most often in short supply. The reliance on cadaveric donations and organs from living donors (primarily for relatives and close friends) consistently falls short of the need. In the United States there are currently over 69,000 people on transplant lists waiting for organs. In 1999 over 6,000 people died while waiting for organs. The need has stimulated a growing international industry in the sale of organs, the source of which is, almost exclusively, the disadvantaged in need of money and, in the case of China, prisoners who are executed. In England in 1989 a report of a young Turkish man selling his kidney brought the subject to international attention. He was selling his kidney to get money for an operation for his daughter.

Various types of financial incentives have been proposed for legalizing the sale of organs in the United States, both for cadaveric organs, and from individuals who are alive. Such proposals raise challenging ethical dilemmas. In this study section we focus on the proposal to legalize the sale and purchase of organs from live individuals.

Readings

Article 1.1 David J. Rothman is a historian and medical educator. He is the head of the Bellagio Task Force, a group of transplant surgeons, human rights activists, and social scientists working to find a way to stop the practice of organ sales. In *The International Organ Traffic,* Rothman defines the scope and complexity of the international organ trade, and the ethical dilemmas the trade has spawned. He charts a course across continents, conducting interviews and collecting information on hospitals, surgeons, governments, and organ brokers to assess the state of organ trafficking. He concludes that trafficking in organs is thriving, largely unregulated, and carried on pretty much free of public scrutiny.

Article 1.2 Richard A. Epstein is a professor of law at the University of Chicago Law School. In *Sell Your Body, Save a Life,* Epstein argues that we have encouraged people to donate organs for some time, but the availability is never close to the need. People often die or get sicker while waiting for an organ, and kidney patients often spend many painful years on dialysis while on waiting lists. Since it's clear that altruism, or outright donation, has not solved the organ shortage problem, Epstein argues the shortage can be eliminated as we would eliminate any other problem of scarcity: offer cash to increase the supply. His solution is to offer a cash incentive to individuals so they will sell their nonvital organs.

Article 1.3 Janet Radcliffe Richards is a professor of philosophy at the Open University, Milton Keynes, UK. In *From Him That Hath Not,* Radcliffe Richards argues that though we may feel repugnance at the thought of a person selling his or her kidney, this does not necessarily mean we should set about to prevent that person from doing so. When we ban organ sales people in need of organs die, and the vendors, those who would sell their organs, have one less option for their already desperate lives. Rather than banning the business, she argues for regulating it and eliminating the abuses. This, she reasons, would give the vendors the greatest opportunity at maximizing their profit, climbing out of poverty, and managing their circumstances after the sale—not to mention the lives that would be saved as well.

Article 1.4 Leon R. Kass, M.D., is the Addie Clark Harding Professor in the Committee on Social Thought and in the College at the University of Chicago. In *Organs for Sale? Propriety, Property, and the Price of Progress,* Leon Kass is torn between the reality that organ sales save lives, and what he believes endorsing the process will do to us. What does it mean to treat our bodies, ourselves as a commodity? What do we give away or lose when we sell our organs? Is selling our body parts what we want to become? For Kass monetary transactions were never intended to broker our humanity, and the selling of organs brings us perilously close to selling our souls. He argues passionately against adopting the practice of selling organs, yet his comments betray the anguish he faces when confronting solutions that both save lives and press us into ethical territory with few precedents. His opposition is borne from a deep anxiety over where organ sales could take us in the future, as well as his immediate sense of repugnance at treating human flesh as a commodity.

Article 1.5 In *Take My Kidney, Please* Michael Kinsley asks whether our reaction to kidney sales is really more of a reaction to the injustices of daily life. With the sale of body organs, the logic of capitalism and our sentiments collide. Kinsley suggests we should sometimes rely on what our *sentiments* tell us, that capitalism can sometimes take too much of what is important to us if we do not keep its excesses in check.

1.1 The International Organ Traffic

David J. Rothman

1   OVER THE PAST FIFTEEN YEARS, transplanting human organs has become a standard and remarkably successful medical procedure, giving new life to thousands of people with failing hearts, kidneys, livers, and lungs. But very few countries have sufficient organs to meet patients' needs. In the United States, for example, some 50,000 people are on the waiting list for a transplant; fifteen percent of patients who need a new heart will die before one becomes available. The shortages are even more acute throughout the Middle East and Asia.

2   This lack of available organs arouses desperation and rewards greed. Would-be recipients are willing to travel far to get an organ and many surgeons, brokers, and government officials will do nearly anything to profit from the shortage. In India well-to-do people and their doctors buy kidneys from debt-ridden Indian villagers; in China officials profitably market organs of executed Chinese prisoners. The international commerce in organs is unregulated, indeed anarchic. We know a good deal about trafficking in women and children for sex. We are just beginning to learn about the trafficking in organs for transplantation.

1.

3   The routes that would-be organ recipients follow are well known to both doctors and patients. Italians (who have the lowest rate of organ donation in Europe) travel to Belgium to obtain their transplants; so do Israelis, who lately have also been going to rural Turkey and bringing their surgeon along with them. Residents of the Gulf States, Egyptians, Malaysians, and Bangladeshis mainly go to India for organs. In the Pacific, Koreans, Japanese, and Taiwanese, along with the residents of Hong Kong and Singapore, fly to China. Less frequently, South Americans go to Cuba and citizens of the former Soviet Union go to Russia. Americans for the most part stay home, but well-to-do foreigners come to the United States for transplants, and some centers allot up to 10 percent of their organs to them.

4   All of these people are responding to the shortages of organs that followed on the discovery of cyclosporine in the early 1980s. Until then, transplantation had been a risky and experimental procedure, typically a last-ditch effort to stave off death; the problem was not the complexity of the surgery but the body's immune system, which attacked and rejected the new organ as though it were a foreign object. Cyclosporine moderated the response while not suppressing the immune system's reactions to truly infectious agents. As a result, in countries with sophisticated medical programs, kidney and heart transplantation became widely used and highly successful procedures. Over 70 percent of heart transplant recipients were living four years later. Ninety-two percent of patients who received a kidney from a living donor were using that kidney one year later; 81 percent of the cases were doing so four years later, and in 40 to 50 percent of the cases, ten years later.[1]

5   Transplantation spread quickly from developed to less developed countries. By 1990, kidneys were being transplanted in nine Middle Eastern, six South American, two North African, and two sub-Saharan African countries. Kidney transplants are by far the most common, since kidney donors can live normal lives with one kidney, while kidneys are subject to disease from a variety of causes, including persistent high blood pressure, adult diabetes, nephritis (inflammation of vessels that filter blood), and infections, which are more usually found in poor countries. (It is true that the donor runs the risk that his remaining kidney will become diseased, but in developed countries, at least, this risk is small.) The transplant techniques, moreover, are relatively simple. Replacing one heart with another, for example, is made easier by the fact that the blood-carrying vessels that must be detached from the one organ and reattached to the other are large and relatively easy to handle. (A transplant surgeon told me that if you can tie your shoes, you can transplant a heart.)

1. The data is from the United Network for Organ Sharing (UNOS) Scientific Registry, as of July 5,1997.

From The New York Review of Books *45, no. 5 (1998): 14–17. Copyright NY Rev, Incorporated Mar 26, 1998. Reprinted with permission from* The New York Review of Books.

6   Fellowships in American surgical programs have enabled surgeons from throughout the world to master the techniques and bring them home. Countries such as India and Brazil built transplant centers when they might have been better advised to invest their medical resources in public health and primary care. For them the centers are a means for enhancing national prestige, for persuading their surgeons not to leave the country, and for meeting the needs of their own middle-class citizens.

7   In China, more than fifty medical centers report they perform kidney transplants, and in India hundreds of clinics are doing so. Reliable information on the success of these operations is hard to obtain, and there are reports that hepatitis and even AIDS have followed transplant operations. But according to physicians I have talked to whose patients have traveled to India or China for a transplant, and from published reports within these countries, some 70 to 75 percent of the transplants seem to have been successful.[2]

8   With patient demand for transplantation so strong and the medical capacity to satisfy it so widespread, shortages of organs were bound to occur. Most of the doctors and others involved in early transplants expected that organs would be readily donated as a gift of life from the dead, an exchange that cost the donor nothing and brought the recipient obvious benefits. However, it turns out that powerful cultural and religious taboos discourage donation, not only in countries with strong religious establishments but in more secular ones as well. The issue has recently attracted the attention of anthropologists, theologians, and literary scholars, and some of their findings are brought together in the fascinating collection of essays, *Organ Transplantation: Meanings and Realities*.[3]

9   In the Middle East, it is rare to obtain organs from cadavers. Islamic teachings emphasize the need to maintain the integrity of the body after death, and although some prominent religious leaders make an exception for transplants, others refuse. An intense debate occurred last spring in Egypt when the government-appointed leader of the most important Sunni Muslim theological faculty endorsed transplantation as an act of altruism, saying that permitting it was to accept a small harm in order to avoid a greater harm—the same rationale that allows a Muslim to eat pork if he risks starvation. But other clerics immediately objected, and there is no agreement in favor of donation.

10   In Israel, Orthodox Jewish precepts define death exclusively as the failure of the heart to function not the cessation of brain activity, a standard that makes it almost impossible to retrieve organs. The primary purpose of statutes defining death as the absence of brain activity is to ensure that organs to be transplanted are continuously supplied with oxygen and nutrients; in effect, the patient is declared dead, and a respirator keeps the heart pumping and the circulatory system working until the organs have been removed, whereupon the respirator is disconnected. Some rabbis give precedence to saving a life and would therefore accept the standard of brain death for transplantation. But overall rates of donation in Israel are very low. The major exceptions are kibbutz members, who tend to be community-minded, as well as other secular Jews.

11   In much of Asia, cultural antipathy to the idea of brain death and, even more important, conceptions of the respect due elders, have practically eliminated organ transplantation. For all its interest in new technology and its traditions of gift-giving, Japan has only a minuscule program, devoted almost exclusively to transplanting kidneys from living related donors. As the anthropologist Margaret Lock writes: "The idea of having a deceased relative whose body is not complete prior to burial or cremation is associated with misfortune, because in this situation suffering in the other world never terminates."[4] For tradition-minded Japanese, moreover, death does not take place at a specific moment. The process of dying involves not only the heart and brain but the soul, and it is not complete until services have been held on the seventh and forty-ninth days after bodily death. It takes even longer to convert a deceased relative into an ancestor, all of which makes violating

2. Xia Sui-sheng, "Organ Transplantation in China: Retrospect and Prospect," *Chinese Medical Journal,* 105 (1992), pp. 430–432.
3. Edited by Stuart J. Youngner, Renee C. Fox, and Laurence J. O'Connell (University of Wisconsin Press, 1996).

4. "Deadly Disputes: Ideologies and Brain Death in Japan," in Youngner et al., *Organ Transplantation,* pp. 142–167.

the integrity of the body for the sake of transplantation unacceptable.

12   Americans say they favor transplantation but turn out to be very reluctant to donate organs. Despite countless public education campaigns, organ donation checkoffs on drivers' licenses, and laws requiring health professionals to ask families to donate the organs of a deceased relative, the rates of donation have not risen during the past five years and are wholly inadequate to the need. As of May 1997, according to the United Network for Organ Sharing, 36,000 people were awaiting a kidney transplant, 8,000 a liver transplant, and 3,800 a heart transplant.[5] One recent study found that when families were asked by hospitals for permission to take an organ from a deceased relative, 53 percent flatly refused.

13   The literary critic Leslie Fiedler suggests that the unwillingness of Americans to donate organs reflects an underlying antipathy to science and a fear of artificially creating life, a fear exploited, he suggests, in the many Hollywood remakes of the Frankenstein story. Moreover, donation would force Americans to concede the finality of death, which Fiedler is convinced they are reluctant to do.[6] I suspect, however, that the underlying causes are less psychological than social. Americans are unaccustomed to sharing resources of any kind when it comes to medicine. Since Americans refuse to care for one another in life—as witness the debacle of national health insurance—why would they do so in death? Receiving help is one thing, donating it is another.

2.

14   If organs are in such short supply, how do some countries manage to fill the needs of foreigners? The answers vary Belgium has a surplus of organs because it relies upon a "presumed consent" statute that probably would be rejected in every American state. Under its provisions, you must formally register your unwillingness to serve as a donor; otherwise, upon your death, physicians are free to transplant your organs. To object you must go to the town hall, make your preference known, and have your name registered on a national computer roster; when a death occurs, the hospital checks the computer base, and unless your name appears on it, surgeons may use your organs, notwithstanding your family's objections. I was told by health professionals in Belgium that many citizens privately fear that if they should ever need an organ, and another patient simultaneously needs one as well, the surgeons will check the computer and give the organ to the one who did not refuse to be a donor. There is no evidence that surgeons actually do this; still many people feel it is better to be safe than sorry, and so they do not register any objections.

15   One group of Belgian citizens, Antwerp's Orthodox Jews, have nonetheless announced they will not serve as donors, only as recipients, since they reject the concept of brain death. An intense, unresolved rabbinic debate has been taking place over the ethics of accepting but not giving organs. Should the Jewish community forswear accepting organs? Should Jews ask to be placed at the bottom of the waiting list? Or should the Jewish community change its position so as to reduce the prospect of fierce hostility or even persecution?

16   Because its system of presumed consent has worked so well, Belgium has a surplus of organs and will provide them to foreigners. However, it will not export them, say, to Milan or Tel Aviv, which would be entirely feasible. Instead, it requires that patients in need of a transplant come to Belgium, which then benefits from the surgical fees paid to doctors and hospitals.

17   Not surprisingly, money counts even more in India, which has an abundant supply of kidneys because physicians and brokers bring together the desperately poor with the desperately ill. The sellers include impoverished villagers, slum dwellers, power-loom operators, manual laborers, and daughters-in-law with small dowries. The buyers come from Egypt, Kuwait, Oman, and other Gulf States, and from India's enormous middle class (which numbers at least 200 million). They readily pay between $2,500 and $4,000 for a kidney (of which the donor, if he is not cheated, will receive between $1,000 and $1,500) and perhaps two times that for the surgery. From the perspective of

5. According to a recent report on CNN's Headline News, there are only 4,000 livers a year being donated. In response to the shortage, the UCLA Medical Center has developed a procedure for dividing livers taken from the cadavers of donors, so that two recipients can share it.

6. "Why Organ Transplant Programs Do Not Succeed," in Youngner et al., *Organ Transplantation*, pp. 56–65.

patients with end-stage renal disease, there is no other choice. For largely cultural reasons, hardly any organs are available from cadavers; dialysis centers are scarce and often a source of infection, and only a few people are able to administer dialysis to themselves at home (as is also the case in the U.S.). Thus it is not surprising that a flourishing transplant business has emerged in such cities as Bangalore, Bombay, and Madras.

18   The market in organs has its defenders. To refuse the sellers a chance to make the money they need, it is said, would be an unjustifiable form of paternalism. Moreover, the sellers may not be at greater risk living with one kidney, at least according to U.S. research. A University of Minnesota transplant team compared seventy-eight kidney donors with their siblings twenty years or more after the surgery took place, and found no significant differences between them in health; indeed, risk-conscious insurance companies do not raise their rates for kidney donors.[7] And why ban the sale of kidneys when the sale of other body parts, including semen, female eggs, hair, and blood is allowed in many countries? The argument that these are renewable body parts is not persuasive if life without a kidney does not compromise health. Finally, transplant surgeons, nurses, and social workers, as well as transplant retrieval teams and the hospitals, are all paid for their work. Why should only the donor and the donor's family go without compensation?

19   But because some body parts have already been turned into commodities does not mean that an increasing trade in kidneys and other organs is desirable. To poor Indians, as Margaret Radin, professor of law at Stanford, observes, "Commodification worries may seem like a luxury. Yet, taking a slightly longer view, commodification threatens the personhood of everyone, not just those who can now afford to concern themselves about it." Many of the poor Indians who sell their organs clearly feel they have had to submit to a degrading practice in order to get badly needed sums of money. They would rather not have parts of their body cut out, an unpleasant experience at best, and one that is probably more risky in Bombay than in Minnesota. Radin concludes: "Desperation is the social problem that we should be looking at, rather than the market ban. . . . We must rethink the larger social context in which this dilemma is embedded."[8]

20   In 1994, perhaps for reasons of principle or because of public embarrassment—every world medical organization opposes the sale of organs— a number of Indian states, including the regions of Bombay, Madras, and Bangalore, outlawed the practice, which until then had been entirely legal. But the laws have an egregious loophole so that sales continue almost uninterrupted. A detailed and persuasive report in the December 26, 1997, issue of *Frontline* one of India's leading news magazines, explains how the new system works.[9] The legislation permits donations from persons unrelated to the recipient if the donations are for reasons of "affection or attachment," and if they are approved by "authorization committees." These conditions are easily met. Brokers and buyers coach the "donors" on what to say to the committee—that he is, for example, a cousin and that he has a (staged) photograph of a family gathering to prove it, or that he is a close friend and bears great affection for the potential recipient. Exposing these fictions would be simple enough, but many committees immediately approve them, unwilling to block transactions that bring large sums to hospitals, surgeons, and brokers.

21   Accurate statistics on kidney transplantation in India are not available, but *Frontline* estimates that about one third of transplants come from living, unrelated donors; four years after the new law went into effect, the rate of transplantation has returned to its earlier levels. It is true that not every hospital participates in the charade, that the market in kidneys is less visible than it was, and it may well be that fewer foreigners are coming to India for a transplant. But the lower classes and castes in India, already vulnerable to so many other abuses, continue to sell their organs. As *Frontline* reports, many donors who sell their organs do so because they are badly in debt; and before long they are again in debt.

7. *John S. Najarian, Blanche M. Chavers, Lois E. McHugh, and Arthur J. Matas, "20 Years or More of Follow-Up of Living Kidney Donors,"* Lancet, 340 (October 3,1992), pp. 807–809.

8. Margaret Jane Radin, *Contested Commodities* (Harvard University Press, 1996), p. 125.
9. "Kidneys Still for Sale," *Frontline,* 14 (December 13–26, 1997), pp. 64–79.

3.

22   China is at the center of the Pacific routes to organ transplantation because it has adopted the tactic of harvesting the organs of executed prisoners. In 1984, immediately after cyclosporine became available, the government issued a document entitled "Rules Concerning the Utilization of Corpses or Organs from the Corpses of Executed Prisoners." Kept confidential, the new law provided that organs from executed prisoners could be used for transplants if the prisoner agreed, if the family agreed, or if no one came to claim the body. (Robin Munro of Human Rights Watch/Asia brought the law to light.) That the law lacks an ethical basis according to China's own values is apparent from its stipulations. "The use of corpses or organs of executed prisoners must be kept strictly secret," it stated, "and attention must be paid to avoiding negative repercussions." The cars used to retrieve organs from the execution grounds cannot bear health department insignia; the people involved in obtaining organs are not permitted to wear white uniforms. In my own interviews with Chinese transplant surgeons, none would admit to the practice; when I showed them copies of the law, they shrugged and said it was news to them.

23   But not to other Asian doctors. Physicians in Japan, Hong Kong, Singapore, and Taiwan among other countries, serve as travel agents, directing their patients to hospitals in Wuhan, Beijing, and Shanghai. The system is relatively efficient. Foreigners do not have to wait days or weeks for an organ to be made available; executions can be timed to meet market needs and the supply is more than adequate. China keeps the exact number of executions secret but Amnesty International calculates on the basis of executions reported in newspapers that there are at least 4,500 a year, and perhaps three to four times as many. Several years ago a heart transplant surgeon told me that he had just been invited to China to perform a transplant; accustomed to long waiting periods in America, he asked how he could be certain that a heart would be available when he arrived. His would-be hosts told him they would schedule an execution to fit with his travel schedule. He turned down the invitation. In February the FBI arrested two Chinese nationals living in New York for allegedly soliciting payment for organs from executed prisoners to be transplanted in China.

24   China's system also has its defenders. Why waste the organs? Why deprive prisoners of the opportunity to do a final act of goodness? But once again, the objections should be obvious. The idea that prisoners on death row—which in China is a miserable hovel in a local jail—can give informed consent to their donations is absurd. Moreover, there is no way of ensuring that the need for organs might not influence courtroom verdicts. A defendant's guilt may be unclear, but if he has a long criminal record, why not condemn him so that a worthy citizen might live?

25   To have physicians retrieve human organs at an execution, moreover, subverts the ethical integrity of the medical profession. There are almost no reliable eyewitness accounts of Chinese practices, but until 1994, Taiwan also authorized transplants of organs from executed prisoners, and its procedures are probably duplicated in China. Immediately before the execution, the physician sedates the prisoner and then inserts both a breathing tube in his lungs and a catheter in one of his veins. The prisoner is then executed with a bullet to his head, the physician immediately moves to stem the blood flow, attach a respirator to the breathing tube, and inject drugs into the catheter so as to increase blood pressure and cardiac output. With the organs thus maintained, the body is transported to a hospital where the donor is waiting and the surgery is performed. The physicians have become intimate participants in the executions; instead of protecting life, they are manipulating the consequences of death.

26   The motive for all such practices is money. The Europeans, Middle Easterners, and Asians who travel to China, India, Belgium, and other countries pay handsomely for their new organs and in hard currencies. Depending on the organization of the particular health care system and the level of corruption, their fees will enrich surgeons or medical centers, or both. Many of the surgeons I interviewed were quite frank about how important the income from transplants was to their hospitals, but they were far more reluctant to say how much of it they kept for themselves. Still, a leading transplant surgeon in Russia is well known for his vast estate and passion for horses. His peers in India and China may be less ostentatious but not necessarily less rich. They will all claim to be doing good, rescuing patients from near death.

4.

27   The international trade in organs has convinced many of the poor, particularly in South America, that they or their children are at risk of being mutilated and murdered. Stories are often told of foreigners who arrive in a village, survey the scene, kidnap and murder several children, remove their organs for sale abroad, and leave the dissected corpses exposed in the graveyard. In Guatemala in 1993 precisely such fears were responsible for one innocent American woman tourist being jailed for a month, and another being beaten to death.

28   Villagers' anxieties are shared by a number of outside observers who believe that people are being murdered for their organs. The author of the report of a transplant committee of the European Parliament unequivocally asserted that organized trafficking in organs exists in the same way as trafficking in drugs. It involved killing people to remove organs which can be sold at a profit. To deny the existence of such trafficking is comparable to denying the existence of ovens and gas chambers during the last war.[10]

29   So, too, the rapporteur of a UN committee on child welfare circulated a questionnaire asserting that "the sale of children is mainly carried out for the purpose of organ transplantation." It then asked: "To what extent and in what ways and forms do these violations of children's rights exist in your country? Please describe."[11]

30   The stories of organ snatching have an American version. I have heard it from my students, read about it on e-mail, been told about it with great conviction by a Moscow surgeon, and been asked about it by more than a dozen journalists. According to the standard account, a young man meets an attractive woman in a neighborhood bar; they have a few drinks, go back to her place, whereupon he passes out and then wakes up the next morning to find a sewn-up wound on his side. When he seeks medical attention, he learns that he is missing a kidney.

31   Although there have been sporadically reported stories of robberies of kidneys from people in India, I have not found a single documented case of abduction, mutilation, or murder for organs, whether in North or South America. I was in Guatemala in 1993 when the atrocities are alleged to have occurred, and heard seemingly reliable people say there was convincing evidence for them. I stayed long enough to see every claim against the two American women tourists proven false. Nevertheless, as the anthropologist Nancy Scheper-Hughes argues, the villagers' fears and accusations are understandable in the light of their everyday experience. The bodies of the poor are ordinarily treated so contemptuously that organ snatching does not seem out of character. In Guatemala, babies are regularly kidnapped for sale abroad in the adoption market. Local doctors and health workers admitted to me that "fattening houses" have been set up so that kidnapped babies would be more attractive for adoption.

32   But it is extremely dangerous to investigate the adoption racket, since highly placed officials in the government and military take a cut of the large sums of money involved. Moreover, Scheper-Hughes continues, if street children in Brazil can be brazenly murdered without recrimination, it is not far-fetched for slum dwellers to believe that the organs of the poor are being removed for sale abroad. And since girls and boys can be kidnapped with impunity to satisfy an international market in sex, why not believe they are also kidnapped to satisfy an international market for organs?[12]

33   In truth, medical realities make such kidnappings and murder highly unlikely. The rural villages and the urban apartments in which transplants are alleged to secretly take place do not have the sterile environment necessary to remove or implant an organ. Organs from children are too small to be used in adults. And however rapacious health care workers may seem, highly trained and medically sophisticated teams of surgeons, operating room nurses, anesthesiologists, technicians, and blood

10. This and other examples of lending credence to the rumors may be found in the United States Information Agency Report of December 1994, "The Child Organ Trafficking Rumor," written by Todd Leventhal.

11. Vitit Muntarbhorn, "Sale of Children," Report of the Special Rapporteur to the United Nations Commission on Human Rights, January 12, 1993.

12. Nancy Scheper-Hughes, "Theft of Life: The Globalization of Organ Stealing Rumours," *Anthropology Today*, 12 (June 1996), pp. 3–11.

transfusers are not likely to conspire to murder for organs or accept them off the street. Had they done so, at least one incident would have come to light during the past fifteen years.

5.

34   The well-documented abuses are bad enough. Is there some way of diminishing them? The Bellagio Task Force, an international group including transplant surgeons, human rights activists, and social scientists, has made several proposals that might be effective if they could be carried out.[13]

35   Almost all major national and international medical bodies have opposed the sale of organs and the transplantation of organs from executed prisoners, but none of the medical organizations has been willing to take action to enforce their views. The World Medical Association in 1984, 1987, and 1994 condemned "the purchase and sale of human organs for transplantation." But it asks "governments of all countries to take effective

steps," and has adopted no measures of its own. It has also criticized the practice of using organs from executed prisoners without their consent; but it fails to ask whether consent on death row can be meaningful. The association leaves it to national medical societies to "severely discipline the physicians involved." Neither it nor any other medical organization has imposed sanctions on violators.

36   The Bellagio Task Force has posed several challenges to the international medical societies. What would happen if they took their proclaimed principles seriously, established a permanent monitoring body, and kept close surveillance on organ donation practices? What if they threatened to withhold training fellowships from countries which tolerated exploitative practices? What if they refused to hold international meetings in those countries, and, as was the case with South Africa under apartheid, did not allow physicians from those countries to attend their meetings? Why, moreover, couldn't the Novartis company, the manufacturer of cyclosporine, insist that it would sell its product only to doctors and hospitals that meet strict standards in obtaining organs? Such measures would be likely to have a serious effect, certainly in India, probably even in China. But as with the organs themselves, the willingness of doctors to use the moral authority of medicine as a force for change has, so far, been in short supply.

13. D. J. Rothman, E. Rose, et al., "The Bellagio Task Force Report on Transplantation, Bodily Integrity, and the International Traffic in Organs," *Transplantation Proceedings*, 29 (1997), pp. 2739–2745. I am currently serving as chair of the Bellagio group.

Discussion and Assignments

1. In paragraph 14 Rothman discusses Belgium's *presumed consent* law. What is the presumed consent law and how does it function in Belgium? Rothman claims a similar law would probably be rejected by every state in the United States. Do you think he is correct in his assessment? Why or why not?

2. Even though Rothman thinks a presumed consent law won't fly in the United States, try to convince him it can—because it will save lives, it has been proven that it works in Belgium, people can refuse to donate if they want to, the law covers everyone so all can benefit, and so on.

   a. Construct an argument for a presumed consent law in your state using the following argument form: Issue, Definitions, Premises, Conclusion. Remember to use only clear, declarative statements, free of ambiguity or vagueness. I've filled in a few pieces to get you started. Notice I started the argument with the intention of establishing the *need* for a presumed consent law, then moved to offering reasons why such a law will work.

   Issue: Whether it is advisable for Anystate, USA to adopt a presumed consent law in order to increase the availability of organs for transplantation.

   Definitions: (You may want to define *presumed consent,* or *which* organs the law would cover, or . . .)

Premises: 1. There are currently 5,000 people in Anystate on transplant waiting lists.
2. The longer an individual waits on a list, the sicker he or she gets.
3. The sicker an individual is when he or she receives a transplant,
the less likely he or she will survive.
4. Last year 456 people died in Anystate while waiting on transplant
lists because there were no organs available.
5. Many more may have died because they received their transplants too late.
(Keep going!)

Conclusion:

b. Now that you have put your argument into logical form in *a* above, you're
on your way to writing an essay. Using the argument you constructed in *a,*
write a 300 word essay in support of passing a presumed consent law in
your state.

3. Now let's do the same thing as in 2, only this time take the opposing argument.
Someone has proposed adopting a presumed consent law in your state, and you
are opposed to its passage. You need to:

a. Construct an argument against the passage of a presumed consent law in
your state using the following argument form: Issue, Definitions, Premises,
Conclusion. Remember to use only clear, declarative statements.

Issue: Whether it is advisable for Anystate, USA to adopt a presumed consent
law in order to increase the availability of organs for transplantation.
Definitions:
Premises:
Conclusion: We should not adopt a presumed consent law in Anystate, USA.

b. Using the argument you constructed in *a* above, compose a 300 word essay
opposing the passage of a presumed consent law in Anystate, USA.

4. In paragraph 15 Rothman observes that in Antwerp, Belgium, Orthodox Jews
reject the concept of brain death and will not consent to having their organs
removed upon death for transplantation. Rothman raises intriguing questions
regarding their position and the intense debate it has caused within the rabbinic
community. He poses the following:

a. Should the Jewish community forswear accepting organs?
b. Should Jews ask to be placed on the bottom of transplant waiting lists?
c. Should the Jewish community change its position so as to reduce the
prospect of fierce hostility or even persecution?

Select one of these three questions and write a 200 word essay in favor or
against the proposal put forth.

5. An individual rejects the concept of brain death and refuses to donate his organs,
yet he accepts a kidney from an individual who is brain dead (and on a respirator). Can he be accused of condoning murder because he accepts the organ?

6. In paragraph 19 Rothman introduces the concept of *commodification* by way of
a quote from Margaret Radin, a Stanford University law professor. What is *commodification?* What does Radin mean when she says "commodification threatens the personhood of all of us"? Do you agree or disagree with her on this
point?

7. In paragraph 21 Rothman states that the poor and lower classes continue to sell
their organs in India because they are in debt. Apparently the well-to-do don't

sell their organs. Does the fact that only the poor sell their organs and that primarily people of the upper classes buy them suggest anything to you?

8. In paragraphs 22 to 26 Rothman discusses China's policy of selling the organs of executed prisoners to foreigners. According to Rothman's account, what role do Chinese doctors play in the execution and transplantation of prisoners' organs? Why does Rothman object to doctors participating in this way?

9. Rothman claims it may be more likely for a prisoner to be executed in China because of its policy of selling and transplanting prisoners' organs. What evidence does he offer to support this claim? Do you agree with Rothman on this point? Why or why not?

10. In the last paragraph of his article Rothman offers suggestions on how to put pressure on countries that encourage organ sales. One of his suggestions is for Novartis, the maker of cyclosporine, the antirejection drug, to sell its product only to doctors and hospitals that meet strict standards in obtaining organs. Write a 300 word essay for the establishment of a U.S. government policy or law to restrict the sale of cyclosporine to only those countries that abide by strict standards in obtaining organs.

11. What would the consequences be for Novartis if the company were restricted in their sales to India and China? What would the consequences be for the people of India and China? Why should Novartis concern itself with political matters like the execution of prisoners when they are in the business of saving lives?

Imagine you are an executive at Novartis and your company is being criticized for selling cyclosporine to India and China. You need to construct an argument justifying the continued sale of cyclosporine to these two countries. Pick one country and construct an argument for your company's continued sales using the following argument form: Issue, Definitions, Premises, Conclusion. Be sure to use only clear, declarative statements in your presentation.

Issue: Should Novartis continue selling cyclosporine to India (or China)?
Definitions:
Premises:
Conclusion:

1.2 Sell Your Body, Save a Life

RICHARD A. EPSTEIN

EACH PASSING YEAR, public health organizations beg for more people to donate organs when they die. Yet the transplant waiting list continues to grow longer as surging demand outpaces a static supply. Now, Secretary of Health and Human Services Donna Shalala is poised to make the current transplant system even more ineffective. Instead, she should consider a few market-oriented reforms that would make more organs available for transplants.

The federal law on organ transplants stems from a belief that human organs should not be bought and sold. It curtails the supply of this life-saving resource while denying donors any benefits. Some 55,000 individuals anxiously wait for organs on national lists maintained by the United Network for Organ Sharing, a quasipublic agency operating under a federal mandate. Individual organs cannot be "shared," as UNOS's name suggests; they can only be given to one person or another. Since the government has banned markets in organs, UNOS must create its own allocation rules. Until now, these factored in medical compatibility, the severity of the recipient's condition and the locations of the donor and recipient.

At present, organs are collected by local institutions, which get first dibs on them. But new techniques of organ preservation now give cadaveric organs a longer useful life. This emboldened Secretary Shalala to call last month for a single national recipient list under uniform criteria. Organ queues will not longer depend on the happenstance of where a person lives or on how quickly he can fly to some remote transplant center.

But Ms. Shalala's proposed regulation would only exacerbate the grave flaws of the current regime. The comprehensive national list is supposed "to allocate organs among transplant candidates in order of decreasing medical urgency status," so that sicker people get the organs first. This is a risky policy, since extremely sick people have poor prospects even if they receive new organs. A higher survival rate can be achieved by having healthier individuals get transplants, as is currently done with livers (it is harder to quantify the severity of other organs' dysfunction). Ms. Shalala has publicly denied any intention of altering the present practice, but the language of the proposal, quoted above, clearly amounts to a major change.

Ms. Shalala also says that the proposed national regime would remove quirks that benefit some regions more than others, so that patients in Boston will no longer have to wait in longer lines than those in Fort Worth, Texas. But by trying to redistribute the organs more "fairly," the proposed regulations would likely reduce the total number of organs collected nationwide. Fort Worth's short waiting lists stem in part from its successful local LifeGift organ collection program. A centralized system would discourage such ingenuity because the industrious region would not reap the rewards of its labors. Moreover, people are more inclined to donate their organs to benefit their neighbors.

Ms. Shalala's high-minded statements conceal the bitter struggle between local and national transplant centers. The latter have long waiting lists, and therefore will garner a greater share of organs under the proposed pooling arrangements. Already, the keep their supply high, local centers delay reporting their organ inventories until it is too late for them to be shipped out, several doctors and transplant network workers have told me. A fully nationalized system would see an increase in such withholding, jeopardizing the effectiveness of the national program.

All these proposed reforms—now pending in Health and Human Services administrative proceedings—are really beside the point. Ms. Shalala herself observes that "the real answer to the problem of scarce organs is to increase the number of organ donations." Markets know only one way to increase supply: raising prices. But since the government sets the price for organs at zero, shortages will remain and worsen. At the very least, the government should be allowed to pay donors for organs donated upon death, and then allocate the increased supply according to the clumsy UNOS procedure.

But we can do even better at saving lives. Right now, two-thirds of people on the waiting list need kidneys. Kidney transplants from live donors account for nearly 30% of the 11,000 kidney transplants performed in 1996. A price system would not only increase the supply of cadaveric kidneys. It could induce healthy individuals to sell one of their kidneys. Live transplants yield better kidneys because the donor and recipient can be operated on side-by-side on a prearranged schedule. The huge gains to the recipient should dwarf the risks and inconvenience to the donor; cash is the solvent that splits the gain between them. Any non-vital organ, like eyes, could be bought and sold under such a system.

Live donation might create the practical problem of criminals coercing people to sell their organs; the brokers who would run the process would have to institute a rigorous screening process to ensure that live donations are truly voluntary. But the net benefits of an organ market would be great. Fewer patients would spend expensive and painful years on dialysis waiting for kidneys; the pace of improvements in surgical techniques would increase as transplants became more common; and increased safety and reduced red tape would lead to lower prices and broader access. Most important, fewer people would die because of a government-created organ donor shortage.

Discussion and Assignments

1. In paragraph 7 Epstein states, "Markets know only one way to increase supply: raising prices." He then argues that body organs should be treated much like other marketable commodities—chairs, baseballs, automobiles, whatever. Raise the price for the commodity, and the supply will increase. Are you comfortable with regarding body organs as marketable commodities? Why or why not?

2. Epstein argues for the sale of "nonvital" organs, and though he suggests no particular prices for specific organs, he does indicate the government could set up a "price system" to encourage donors. Presumably the government would regulate the sale of organs through "brokers" at prices approved by the government (through laws). If Epstein regards body organs as a marketable commodity—increase the supply by increasing the price—is he consistent in his views when he suggests the government regulate the price for organs? Put another way, why restrict the vendors of organs from setting their own prices?

3. Who would benefit from setting governmental price restrictions on the sale of organs? Do you think it would be feasible for individuals to negotiate the sale of their organs through brokers, newspapers, magazines, infomercials, or the Internet? Or auction organs on a Web site—sellyourorgan.com? Would Epstein endorse such an approach?

4. Epstein refers to individuals who sell their body organs as "donors." In what sense would the sale of a kidney, at a government regulated price as Epstein suggests, be considered a *donation?* Does the type of donation/sale of a kidney advocated by Epstein resemble any other type of donation you are aware of? Does referring to a cash for organ transaction as a *donation* make the transfer of the organ more acceptable, rather than simply referring to it as a *sale?* Do you find Epstein's use of the term *donation* acceptable in the context of everyday use of language? Why or why not?

5. In paragraph 8 Epstein states that any nonvital organ, such as eyes, could be sold under an approved government program such as he proposes. In what sense does Epstein believe one's eyes are "nonvital" organs?

6. Suppose you sell one of your nonvital corneas at age 30 and, as often happens to people, your eyesight begins to weaken as you get older. Added stress on your remaining eye, natural deterioration, the onset of eye disease with advancing age, a little too much unprotected UV exposure, and by age 60, just when you hoped to retire and spend time traveling, you are classed as legally blind in your remaining eye. You find it difficult to get around, and have fallen on public assistance as *disabled.* Is this a reasonable scenario? Would such scenarios affect how you might feel about selling corneas?

7. If Epstein advocates selling nonvital organs, why not advocate selling nonvital limbs as well? In 1998, Clint Hallam, 49, was the recipient of the first hand and forearm transplant. The transplant was successful. In February 2000, Denis Chatelier received the first double forearm transplant in Lyon, France. Limb transplant surgery is expected to become more commonplace in the future. Let's assume for the moment limb transplantation has become a relatively commonplace and successful

operation. See if you can expand upon Epstein's proposal to sell nonvital organs by constructing an argument for the sale of nonvital hands and forearms as well. Use the following argument form: Issue, Definitions, Premises, Conclusion. Remember to use clear, declarative statements throughout your presentation.

Issue: Whether it is advisable for the government to set prices for the sale of nonvital hands and forearms from living people.
Definitions:
Premises:
Conclusion:

8. Would the fact that hands and forearms are visible, whereas kidneys and lungs are hidden, make it more difficult for the public to approve them for sale? Under normal circumstances if a man sells his kidney or lung, others would not know he sold an organ just from looking at him. But if you saw a person missing a hand and forearm, and if such sales were permitted, even encouraged by the state with monetary rewards, would you wonder if the individual had sold it? Do you think this *visibility* factor is of any consequence when approving or disapproving of selling organs or limbs? Put another way, is it OK for the *other* guy to sell his organs or limbs for money as long as I don't have to be visibly reminded of his loss? Does the *concealment* or *openness* of the sale have anything to do with a person's willingness or reluctance to approve of such sales?

9. Opponents of proposals like Epstein's often cite that it's the poor who will sell their organs in the United States, as they currently do in India. Do you believe this would be the case? Does Epstein's argument account for this objection? How important an objection is this to his proposal?

10. What are the two strongest pieces of evidence Epstein offers in support of his argument to allow the sale of organs? In a paragraph for each explain why you think they are strong. What is the weakest piece of evidence he offers to support his argument to allow the sale of nonvital organs? In a paragraph explain why you think it is weak. What is the most important thing Epstein left out of his argument? Explain in one paragraph what it is and why you would have included it.

11. I've put Epstein's argument in a logical form (Issue, Definitions, Premises, Conclusion). Study the argument and discuss with your classmates, in small groups, whether you think I've got it right. Would you change anything?

Sell Your Body, Save a Life, by Richard Epstein

Issue: Whether the government should set prices for the sale of nonvital organs.
Definitions: *Nonvital organs* means any organ you can live without.
Premises: 1.   Each year the demand for organs increases.
2.   Each year public health organizations beg people for organ donations, but the supply remains static.
3.   The current system of allocating organs through the United Network of Organ Sharing (UNOS) distributes organs to the sickest individuals first.
4.   This policy is risky because the extremely ill have the poorest prospects for recovery, and healthier individuals in need of organs have to wait longer, putting them at greater risk.
5.   The latest proposal by Donna Shalala, Secretary of Health and Human Services, to improve the current system of allocating organs would favor national transplant centers over regional centers.
6.   This proposal would, in the end, reduce the number of donations overall, rendering the system even more ineffective

than it already is, putting greater numbers of sick individuals at risk.

7. The answer to scarce organs, even Secretary of Health and Human Services Donna Shalala says, is to increase the number of donations.

8. If the government were to set prices for nonvital organs, there would be an increase in the supply.

9. If the government were to set prices for organs:
   a. There would be improvement in surgical techniques associated with transplant operations.
   b. There would eventually be lower prices and broader access to organ transplants.
   c. Recipients would receive healthier kidneys from live donors.
   d. Fewer people would die waiting for transplants.
   e. Fewer people would spend expensive and painful years on dialysis waiting for organs.

10. A rigorous screening process would need to be initiated to ensure all donations were voluntary.

Conclusion: The government should set prices for the sale of nonvital organs from live donors.

1.3 From Him That Hath Not

JANET RADCLIFFE RICHARDS

1   WHEN THE TRADE in transplant organs from live donors first came to public attention in Britain a year or two ago, what was most remarkable about the immediate response was its unanimity. From all points of the political compass, from widely different groups who were normally hard pressed to agree about anything, came indignant denunciations of the whole business: it was a gross exploitation of the poor by the rich, repugnant in every respect, and should be banned forthwith.

2   This indignation was not, in the first instance, directed at the worst abuses that are now known to go on. Revelations of such horrors as kidney stealing, failure to pay the agreed price, and even abduction and murder, did not appear until later. The trade in organs from live donors was, in Britain at least, universally denounced as unacceptable in itself, and such remarkable concord must seem to suggest that the case for ending it by law is unequivocal.

3   Nevertheless, I want to argue that things are not clear as they may seem. Of course there is something repugnant about the whole business, but it is nevertheless very far from obvious that it should be stopped. If we start not with our own feelings of repugnance, but with the situation of the exploited people on whose behalf we process indignation, the matter begins to look very different, and should at least give us pause.

4   Consider, for instance, the situation of the young Turkish father swept to the glare of British television by the surge of outrage that followed the revelations. He had arranged to sell a kidney in order to pay for urgent hospital treatment for his little daughter. Now presumably the prospect of selling his kidney was, to say the very least, no less repugnant to him than it seems to us; nevertheless he judged this to be the best option available to him. This very fact shows how unspeakably bad the

From Organ Replacement Therapy: Ethics, Justice and Commerce, *ed. W. Land and J. B. Dossetor (Berlin Heidelberg: Springer-Verlag, 1991), pp. 190–96. Reprinted with permission.*

alternatives must have seemed. To forbid the trade, therefore, is to take away what seems the best option open to someone whose position is already so appalling that this *is* his best option. It is to make the worst off worse off still.

5   This is not enough to show that the trade ought to continue, but it does show that anyone who wants to stop it needs to produce a very good justification. If we want to implement policies that cause harm, and especially harm to the worst off, we need to show either that the harm is only apparent, or that it is outweighed by more important considerations. So what kind of justification might be offered?

6   The usual justification we give for interfering with other people's actions is that we want to prevent their harming others. That, however, would be most implausible here. Far from harming anyone else, the father was benefiting his daughter, and probably saving the life of the kidney's recipient as well. (Our desire to protect the poor should presumably not lead us to conclude that the lives of the rich—people like us—do not matter at all.) If we intervene and prevent him from selling his kidney, therefore, we not only cut off what seems to him his own best option and forbid him to sell what is, if anything is, his own; in this case, at least, we also prevent the saving of two other lives. I suppose odd cases might arise in which it would be argued that prospective organ sellers were risking unreasonable harm to other people, but since what the sellers most obviously do is save the lives of the buyers a prohibition would far more reliably cause harm to others than prevent it.

7   Perhaps, then, the idea is to protect not other people, but the would-be vendors themselves. They may be making what seems to them the best choice available, but perhaps we want to claim that they are simply misguided. This idea is certainly more in keeping with the tone of the popular outcry, which does, after all, express indignation on behalf of the exploited victims of the rich. Nevertheless, most people will find this line of argument equally difficult to sustain.

8   In the first place, it obviously runs against the fundamental liberal principle that although people's freedom of action may legitimately be curtailed to prevent their harming others, it may not be curtailed to prevent their harming themselves. Anyone who takes this principle to be absolute, as many do,

must obviously rule out paternalist intervention completely. Even if is argued that some of the potential vendors are being subtly coerced, or are too ill-informed to make rational decisions, the absolute version of the principle can justify intervention only in particular cases. It cannot permit a general prohibition which curtails the freedom of all.

9   Most people probably are less full-bloodedly liberal (or libertarian) than this, and are likely to regard paternalism as justifiable in some cases (such as the compulsory use of seat belts, or the prohibition of drug use). But even they have to confront the problem of explaining why kidney selling is so obviously misguided, and why a benevolent paternalist would prevent it. Of course it is a risky business (as is altruistic kidney giving), and no doubt in many cases, at present, the vendors are making choices they would not make if they were better informed. But there is not the slightest reason to think this must always be the case. There is nothing obviously irrational and mistaken about taking risks. We do not usually regard risking life and health as absurd even for people who are rich enough to have other options open to them: normally we think it entirely a matter for individual decision if people are willing to risk their lives for the joys of rock climbing or for danger money from North Sea diving. It is surely far *more* difficult to see what the desperately poor, who see in selling a kidney the only hope of making anything of their wretched lives and perhaps even of surviving, should be regarded as so manifestly irrational as to need saving from themselves.

10   Of course there is a sense in which some of the vendors are not acting in their own interests; many, like the Turkish man, are taking what risks there are for the benefit of others. It is true that the father would have been greatly distressed by the death of his daughter, but most people would nevertheless count his action as one of altruism, and taken in her interests rather than his own. Even in such cases, however, it is still not clear why a paternalist should feel obliged to intervene. Is it irrational for a man to take risks with his own life to save the life of someone he loves? Should we make a general policy of intervening and insisting on unswerving attention to self interest whenever people are tempted to sacrifice themselves for the good of others? Once again, most people would say not. And anyway, it is quite clear that most of

the people who pose the trade in organs have no such view, since they are the very people who say that only pure altruism can justify organ donation. If the daughter had herself needed a transplant, and the father had offered his kidney, they would have applauded. What difference does it make that there is an extra link in the chain, and that he sacrifices his kidney for money to save her by other means?

11   In one way or another, therefore, most people are going to find it very difficult to justify a general prohibition of organ selling in terms of concern for the well-being of the sellers. Even if they are not opposed to paternalism on principle, as many people are, they still have the problem of explaining why choosing to sell a kidney is necessarily misguided, and why a well-judging paternalist would ban the trade outright rather than intervening only in particular cases.

12   Perhaps, then, we should try an argument based on the idea of exploitation. Poverty may not make people irrational, it may be argued, but it certainly makes them vulnerable to exploitation. We have, therefore, a duty to protect them.

13   No doubt we have such a duty, but if protecting the poor from exploitation is our concern, banning the trade in organs is a very strange way to go about it. An exploiter is typically someone who makes use of the fact that people who are desperately poor will clutch at even the slightest opportunity to improve their situation. Someone whose only alternative is starvation will quite rationally agree to work all day for a loaf of bread, so the exploiter takes the opportunity to get the work done without paying more; someone in grinding poverty may well be prepared to sell cheaply what others would not part with at any price, and the exploiter makes the most of the situation. Now there is of course a sense in which if we intervene to prevent the contract between exploiter and exploited from taking place at all we shall indeed put an end to the exploitation; but only in the way that we should eliminate the miseries of slum dwelling by bulldozing slums, or solve the problem of ingrowing toenails by chopping off feet. In other words, we may end the evil in that particular form, but only at the cost of producing an even worse evil for the sufferers. We may perhaps give ourselves the satisfaction of depriving the exploiters of their ill-gotten gains, or take pleasure

in seeing the greedy rich unable to use their money to save their lives (though it is not clear how we can be entitled to any such satisfaction as long as we go on paying as little as possible for luxury goods made by grossly exploited labourers in the Third World), but we do no good to the exploited. We actually make things worse for them.

14   The simple fact is that there is no short cut to ending what is really evil about exploitation. What makes people vulnerable to exploitation is their having too few options, which mean the only way to improve their situation is to give them more. We can do them nothing but harm by taking options away. The only radical cure for exploitation is the elimination of poverty. Failing that (since we lack either the will or the knowledge to do it), the best thing is not to forbid the trade but to subject it to stringent controls: to organize a system that completely rules out all dealings with donors or organs of dubious origin and profiteering by middlemen, to get the highest price for the organs that the market will bear, to counsel prospective vendors fully about both medical matters and the use of money, and to provide insurance and after care. Provisionally, then, it seems necessary to conclude that this is what we should be doing. We should be eliminating not the trade, but the abuses.

15   It is, however, most important to emphasize that this conclusion is provisional, and to make clear the form this argument has taken.

16   The argument has not taken the form of advocating some controversial moral principle—such as, for instance, the liberal principle that people ought to be allowed to do what they like with their own bodies—and moving from there to the conclusion that there should be a free market in organs. An argument of that kind would be very easy to counter, since anyone who did not like the conclusion could just reject the principle. This argument has been of a different kind. It has worked on the basis of two much less contentious propositions, both of which nearly everyone involved in this debate is likely to accept: that preventing the trade in organs does cause harm, and that whenever some policy has intrinsically bad consequences it must be presumed unjustified until shown otherwise.

17   This is a perfectly familiar idea. It is intrinsically bad to stick needles into a child, and if you announced an intention to do such a thing you would expect to be stopped. On the other hand, you would also expect most people to let you go ahead once you explained that you were bent on nothing more sinister than vaccination, because most people would accept that the expected good justified the immediate harm. In the case of organ selling, however, things seem to be much more difficult. The policy of banning organ sales has several consequences that nearly everyone would accept as intrinsically bad—it limits the autonomy of adults, takes away the best option open to the wretchedly poor, and allows potential recipients of organs to die—but so far no justification has been found for allowing these evils to happen. And by this I do not mean that no one has produced a justification that would convert opponents of prohibition. So far it has seemed impossible to justify prohibition in terms of *anyone's* principles, including those of its most passionate advocates.

18   What the argument does, therefore, is put the onus of proof on anyone who is in favour of prohibiting rather than regulating the trade in spare parts from live donors. It takes the form of a challenge: show that what you are advocating is justified in spite of the harm it undoubtedly causes, or withdraw your objections to the trade.

19   For what it is worth, I rather hope this challenge can be met, since I find the whole business as intuitively repulsive as does everyone else. Nevertheless, once a properly critical attitude is taken to attempted justifications, it is extraordinarily difficult to find any that will fare at all better than the ones already discussed.

20   For instance it is often claimed, as if it were self evident, that the donation of an organ should be altruistic and that it is inherently wrong for it to be a commercial transaction. That of course still does not explain what is wrong with kidney selling when money is wanted for altruistic purposes, and raises again the question of why direct altruism should be acceptable but indirect not. But, quite apart from that, there is the problem of why it is unacceptable to have anything other than altruism as the motive. It may be *best* if a kidney is offered out of love by a relative, but that does not in the least suggest that what is less than best must be wrong. It is best if elderly people are cared for at home by loving relatives, but we are not usually tempted to infer from this that people who have no relatives, or who are not loved by them, should go

without care rather than have it paid for. Some services to other people are performed for love, but many (including virtually all medical services) are paid for, and no one sees any harm in that. If there is a fundamental difference between services and spare parts, what is it?

21   A rather more promising line may seem to be the idea that if some practice is allowed at all, people who do not really want to do whatever it is may be coerced or bullied into it. (This is one of the commonest lines of objection to voluntary euthanasia.) That, however, is true of any kind of freedom, and forbidding something altogether because of the danger of coercion is extremely difficult to justify, because it involves placing a *certain* limitation on the freedom of *everyone* in order to prevent the *possibility* of limitation on the freedom of *some*. If our concern is really to protect people who might be pressed into selling their kidneys against their will, our first impulse should be to institute a careful screening system, and refuse organs from anyone about whose motivation there was doubt. We should resort to an outright ban only after much agonizing, and after careful investigation had shown that allowing kidney trading caused more harm to people who were coerced into it than outright prohibition would cause to people who were prevented from doing what they willingly chose. We certainly have no such evidence yet. And, moreover, even if we had, an argument of this kind could still not be used (as it frequently is) by people who are happy to condone kidney donation by relatives, since within families, surely, lies the greatest scope of all for moral bullying and other assorted pressures. If the willing and the subtly coerced can be distinguished in this context, so they can in others.

22   Obviously it is impossible to anticipate all the arguments that might at some time be attempted, but there is one general matter that needs to be kept in mind whenever proposed justifications are to be assessed, and which should be mentioned in conclusion. It concerns the relationship between the real reason people have for wanting something and the justification they think up afterwards.

23   The fact that people often have their own private motives for approving some policy does not, of course, automatically vitiate the justifications; we may often have selfish motives for wanting something that is perfectly justifiable for other reasons (as when academics and doctors protest against closure of universities and hospitals). On the other hand, it does need to be remembered that people who are firmly convinced of something are often quite extraordinarily uncritical of any argument that appears to support their preconceptions.

24   Now one thing that is quite clear about this kidney-selling issue is that the impulse to ban the practice outright was immediate and strongly felt, and was not at all the result of complicated deliberations. It was from the outset described as repugnant, and when we call things repugnant what we mean is that they produce in us feelings of disgust and revulsion. Strong feelings, however, are not in themselves reliable guides to either rationality or rectitude. Sometimes they stem from good moral impulses, but on the other hand strong feelings rooted in prejudice and superstition, and often superficially rationalized in moral terms, have been responsible for half the evils of history. We have very strong feelings about organ selling, but we must beware of presuming such feelings must have their foundations in morality.

25   I do not doubt for a moment that many of our feelings of outrage in this particular context are indeed connected with the plight of the poor. On the other hand, the foregoing arguments do suggest reasons for doubting that our feelings of repugnance are quite as deeply rooted in legitimate grounds for moral outrage as we may like to think.

We are inclined to say, for instance, that we find the trade in organs repugnant because of the harm it does to the vendors. But if that were really true we should find the idea of making their situation worse by stopping the trade more repugnant still. We should find it even more repulsive that the Turkish father should be forced to keep his kidney and watch his daughter die than that he should sell it and save her, since the first situation is worse for him. It seems, however, that we do not, which suggests that it is the sale of the kidney in itself, rather than the wretchedness of the man who is proposing to sell it, that arouses our deepest feelings.

26   We are also inclined to say that what we find most repugnant about the trade is the abuse and exploitation, but in that case if the trade were regulated and the donors properly paid our feelings of revulsion should go. Once again, it seems that they do not. Most people would probably be even more appalled if the trade were officially sanctioned and

regulated than they are by what goes on now. Or we claim that our feelings of repugnance are caused by the thought that organs should be given for any other reason than love, but if that were so we should find it no more repugnant that a father should sell his kidney to save his daughter than that he should give it to her directly. Most of us find ourselves responding very differently to the two.

27   It seems, then, that our feelings of repugnance are only loosely connected with the moral principles we invoke their justification, and therefore that eliminating the causes of the feelings—whatever those may be—is by no means necessarily the same thing as eliminating what is, morally speaking, repugnant.

28   This is most important, because it suggests one clear advantage to ending the trade that should give us particular reason for suspicion and caution as we consider putative justifications. It seems likely that if we forbid it altogether we shall, for whatever reason, ease our own feelings of disgust. Prohibition may make things worse for the Turkish family and other desperate people around the world, as well as for the relatively rich who will die for lack of kidneys, but at least these people will despair and die quietly, in ways less offensive to the affluent and healthy, and the poor will not force their misery on our attention by engaging in the strikingly repulsive business of selling parts of themselves to repair the deficiencies of the rich.

29   Perhaps, indeed, that may in itself suggest a sufficient reason for allowing the trade to continue. If we are forced to recognize that something we find as disgusting as organ selling provides the best option for the destitute and the only hope for the dying it may help us to keep in mind the need to pursue more radical remedies: on the one hand to increase the effort to find dead donors, and on the other to take the despair of the poor more seriously.

30   But quite irrespective of that rather extreme justification for continuing the trade in human spare parts, one thing does seem to be clear. We must make absolutely sure that there is a better reason than the protection of our own squeamish sensibilities before we rush into legislation whose most striking and immediate effect is—strange as it may seem—to take away, from him that hath not, even that which he hath.

Discussion and Assignments

1. Radcliffe Richards argues that a feeling of repugnance or revulsion (at the prospect of selling a kidney) is not reason enough to support a universal ban on kidney sales. What is her reasoning behind this claim? Do you think a feeling of repugnance or revulsion can be of aid to us in assessing moral dilemmas? If so, in what way? If not, why not?

2. In paragraph 14 Radcliffe Richards argues that taking away the possibility of the poor to sell their kidneys narrows their options, and more options is what they need, not less. To ban such sales, then, may actually *hurt* the vendor. She offers the young Turk in England selling his kidney to get money for his daughter's operation as an example. How strong a line of argument do you think this is?

3. Radcliffe Richards offers several pieces of evidence to support her argument that we should not ban the sale of kidneys. Select the two strongest pieces of evidence and in one paragraph on each explain why you find them so persuasive. Select the weakest piece of evidence she offers to support her argument that we should not ban kidney sales. In a paragraph explain why it is weak. Can you think of anything important, pro or con, she left out?

4. In paragraph 14 Radcliffe Richards argues for not ending the trade in kidneys, but for ending the *abuses* the trade brings. Do you think this is possible? If possible, do you think it would make the organ selling business more acceptable?

5. What would you do to end the abuses in kidney sales (besides banning the practice altogether)? Write a 300 word essay, a proposal to regulate the organ sales industry and end abuses. What would you require or change? What would the changes *accomplish?*

1.4 Organs for Sale? Propriety, Property, and the Price of Progress

Leon R. Kass

Just in case anyone is expecting to read about new markets for Wurlitzers, let me set you straight. I mean to discuss organ transplantation and, especially, what to think about recent proposals to meet the need for transplantable human organs by permitting or even encouraging their sale and purchase. If the reader will pardon the impropriety, I will not beat around the bush: the subject is human flesh, the goal is the saving of life, the question is, "To market or not to market?"

Such blunt words drive home a certain impropriety not only in my topic but also in choosing to discuss it in public. But such is the curse of living in interesting times. All sorts of shameful practices, once held not to be spoken of in civil society, are now enacted with full publicity, often to applause, both in life and in art. Not the least price of such progress is that critics of any impropriety have no choice but to participate in it, risking further blunting of sensibilities by plain overt speech. It's an old story: opponents of unsavory practices are compelled to put them in the spotlight. Yet if we do not wish to remain in the dark, we must not avert our gaze, however unseemly the sights, especially if others who do not share our sensibilities continue to project them—as they most certainly will. Besides, in the present matter, there is more than impropriety before us—there is the very obvious and unquestionable benefit of saving human lives. . . .

From The Public Interest, *no. 107 (Spring 1992): 65–85. Reprinted with permission of the author.*

CULTURE AND THE BODY

. . . Most of our attitudes regarding invasions of the body and treatment of corpses are carried less by maxims and arguments, more by sentiments and repugnances. They are transmitted inadvertently and indirectly, rarely through formal instruction. For this reason, they are held by some to be suspect, mere sentiments, atavisms tied to superstitions of a bygone age. Some even argue that these repugnances are based mainly on strangeness and unfamiliarity: the strange repels *because* it is unfamiliar. On this view, our squeamishness about dismemberment of corpses is akin to our horror at eating brains or mice. Time and exposure will cure us of these revulsions, especially when there are— as with organ transplantation—such enormous benefits to be won.

These views are, I believe, mistaken. To be sure, as an empirical matter, we can probably get used to many things that once repelled us—organ swapping among them. As Raskolnikov put it, and he should know, "Man gets used to everything—the beast." But I am certain that the repugnances that protect the dignity and integrity of the body are not based solely on strangeness. And they are certainly not irrational. On the contrary, they may just be—like the human body they seek to protect— the very embodiment of reason. . . .

II. *Property*

The most common objections to permitting the sale of body parts, especially from live donors, have to do with matters of equity, exploitation of the poor and the unemployed, and the dangers of abuse—not excluding theft and even murder to obtain valuable commodities. People deplore the degrading sale, a sale made in desperation, especially when the seller is selling something so precious as a part of his own body. Others deplore the rich man's purchase, and would group life-giving organs with other most basic goods that should not be available to the rich when the poor can't afford them (like allowing people to purchase substitutes for themselves in the military draft). . . .

I certainly sympathize with these objections and concerns. As I read about the young healthy Indian men and women selling their kidneys to wealthy Saudis and Kuwaitis, I can only deplore the socioeconomic system that reduces people to such a level of desperation. And yet, at the same time, when I read the personal accounts of some who have sold, I am hard-pressed simply to condemn these individuals for electing apparently the only non-criminal way open to them to provide for a decent life for their families. As several commentators have noted, the sale of organs—like prostitution or surrogate motherhood or baby-selling —provides a double-bind for the poor. Proscription keeps them out of the economic mainstream, whereas permission threatens to accentuate their social alienation through the disapproval usually connected with trafficking in these matters.

Torn between sympathy and disgust, some observers would have it both ways: they would permit sale, but ban advertising and criminalize brokering (i.e., legalize prostitutes, prosecute pimps), presumably to eliminate coercive pressure from unscrupulous middlemen. But none of these analysts, it seems to me, has faced the question squarely. For if there were nothing fundamentally wrong with trading organs in the first place, why should it bother us that some people will make their living at it? The objection in the name of exploitation and inequity—however important for determining policy—seems to betray deeper objections, unacknowledged, to the thing itself. . . .

True, some things freely giveable ought not to be marketed because they cannot be sold: love and friendship are prime examples. So, too, are acts of generosity: it is one thing for me to offer in kindness to take the ugly duckling to the dance, it is quite another for her father to pay me to do so. But part of the reason love and generous deeds cannot be sold is that, strictly speaking, they cannot even be *given*—or, rather, they cannot be given *away*. One "gives" one's love to another or even one's body to one's beloved, one does not donate it; and when friendship is "given" it is still retained by its "owner." But the case with organs seems to be different: obviously material, they are freely alienable, they can be given and given away, and, therefore, they can be sold, and without diminishing the unquestioned good their transfer does for the recipient—why, then, should they not be for sale, of course, only by their proper "owner"? Why should not the owner-donor get something for his organs? We come at last to the question of the body as property.

WHOSE BODY?

. . . What kind of *property* is my body? Is it mine or is it me? Can it—or much of it—be alienated, like my other property, like my car or even my dog? And on what basis do I claim property *rights* in my body? Is it really "my own"? Have I labored to produce it? Less than did my mother, and yet it is not hers. Do I claim it on merit? Doubtful: I had it even before I could be said to be deserving. Do I hold it as a gift—whether or not there be a giver? How does one possess and use a gift? Are there limits on my right to dispose of it as I wish—especially if I do not know the answer to these questions? Can one sell—or even give away—that which is not clearly one's own?

The word property comes originally from the Latin adjective *proprius* (the root also of "proper"—fit or apt or suitable—and, thus, also of "propriety"), *proprius* meaning "one's own, special, particular, peculiar." Property is both that which is one's own, and also the right—indeed, the exclusive right—to its possession, use, or disposal. And while there might seem to be nothing that is more "my own" than my own body, common sense finally rejects the view that my body is, strictly speaking, my property. For we do and should distinguish among that which is *me*, that which is *mine*, and that which is mine as *my property*. My body is *me*; my daughters are mine (and so are my opinions, deeds, and speeches); my car is my property. Only the last can clearly be alienated and sold at will.

Philosophical reflection, deepening common sense, would seem to support this view, yet not without introducing new perplexities. If we turn to John Locke, the great teacher on property, the right of property traces home in fact to the body:

> Though the earth and all creatures be common to all men, yet every man has a property in his own person; this nobody has a right to but himself. The labour of his body and the work of his hands we may say are properly his.

The right to the fruits of one's labor seems, for Locke, to follow from the property each man has in his own person. But unlike the rights in the fruits of his labor, the rights in one's person are for Locke surely inalienable (like one's inalienable right to liberty, which also cannot be transferred to another, say, by selling oneself into slavery). The

property in my own person seems to function rather to limit intrusions and claims possibly made upon me by others; it functions to exclude me—and every other human being—from the commons available to all men for appropriation and use. Thus, though the right to property stems from the my-own-ness (rather than the in-commons-ness) of my body and its labor, the body itself cannot be, for Locke, property like any other. It is, like property, exclusively mine to use; but it is, unlike property, not mine to dispose of. . . .

Yet here we are in trouble. The living body as a whole is surely not alienable, but parts of it definitely are. I may give blood, bone marrow, skin, a kidney, parts of my liver, and other organs without ceasing to be me, as the by-and-large self-same embodied being I am. It matters not to my totality or identity if the kidney I surrendered was taken because it was diseased or because I gave it for donation. . . .

The analysis of the notion of the body as property produces only confusion—one suspects because there is confusion in the heart of the idea of property itself, as well as deep mystery in the nature of personal identity. Most of the discussion would seem to support the common-sense and common-law teaching that *there is no property in a body*—not in my own body, not in my own corpse, and surely not in the corpse of my deceased ancestor. . . . Yet if my body is not my property, if I have no property right in my body—and here, philosophically and morally, the matter is surely dubious at best—by what *right* do I give parts of it away? And, if it be by right of property, how can one then object—in principle—to sale?

LIBERTY AND ITS LIMITS

. . . Let us shift our attention from the vexed question of ownership to the principle of freedom. It was, you will recall, something like the principle of freedom-voluntary and freely given donation—that was used to justify the gift of organs, overcoming the presumption against mutilation. . . .

Our society has perceived a social need for organs. We have chosen to meet that need not by direct social decision and appropriation, but, indirectly, through permitting and encouraging voluntary giving. It is, as I have argued, generosity—that is, more the "giving" than the "voluntariness"—

that provides the moral ground; yet being liberals and not totalitarians, we put the legal weight on freedom—and hope people will use it generously. As a result, it looks as if, to facilitate and to justify the practice of organ donation, we have enshrined something like the notions of property rights and free contract in the body, notions that usually include the possibility of buying and selling. This is slippery business. Once the principle of private right and autonomy is taken as the standard, it will prove difficult—if not impossible—to hold the line between donation and sale. (It will even prove impossible, philosophically, to argue against voluntary servitude, bestiality, and other abominations.) Moreover, the burden of proof will fall squarely on those who want to set limits on what people may freely do with their bodies or for what purposes they may buy and sell body parts. It will, in short, be hard to prevent buying and selling human flesh not only for transplantation, but for, say, use in luxury nouvelle cuisine, once we allow markets for transplantation on libertarian grounds. We see here, in the prism of this case, the limits and, hence, the ultimate insufficiency of rights and the liberal principle.

Astute students of liberalism have long observed that our system of ordered liberties presupposes a certain kind of society—of at least minimal decency, and with strong enough familial and religious institutions to cultivate the sorts of men and women who can live civilly and responsibly with one another, while enjoying their private rights. We wonder whether freedom of contract regarding the body, leading to its being bought and sold, will continue to make corrosive inroads upon the kind of people we want to be and need to be, if the uses of our freedom are not to lead to our willing dehumanization. We have, over the years, moved the care for life and death from the churches to the hospitals, and the disposition of mortal remains from the clergy to the family and now to the individual himself—and perhaps, in the markets of the future, to the insurance companies or the state or to enterprising brokers who will give new meaning to insider trading. No matter how many lives are saved, is this good for how we are to live?

Let us put aside questions about property and free contract, and think only about buying and selling. Never mind our rights, what would it mean to fully commercialize the human body even, say, under state monopoly? What, regardless of politi-cal system, is the moral and philosophical difference between giving an organ and selling it, or between receiving it as a gift and buying it?

COMMODIFICATION

The idea of commodification of human flesh repels us, quite properly I would say, because we sense that the human body especially belongs in that category of things that defy or resist commensuration—like love or friendship or life itself. To claim that these things are "priceless" is not to insist that they are of infinite worth or that one cannot calculate (albeit very roughly, and then only with aid of very crude simplifying assumptions) how much it costs to sustain or support them. Rather it is to claim that the bulk of their meaning and their human worth do not lend themselves to quantitative measures; for this reason, we hold them to be incommensurable, not only morally but factually.

Against this view, it can surely be argued that the entire system of market exchange rests on our arbitrary but successful attempts to commensurate the (factually) incommensurable. The genius of money is precisely that it solves by convention the problem of natural incommensurability, say between oranges and widgets, or between manual labor and the thinking time of economists. The possibility of civilization altogether rests on this conventional means of exchange, as the ancient Greeks noted by deriving the name for money, *nomisma,* from the root *nomos,* meaning "convention"—that which has been settled by human agreement—and showing how this fundamental convention made possible commerce, leisure, and the establishment of gentler views of justice.

Yet the purpose of instituting such a conventional measure was to facilitate the satisfaction of *natural* human needs and the desires for well-being and, eventually, to encourage the full flowering of human possibility. Some notion of need or perceived human good provided always the latent non-conventional standard behind the nomismatic convention—tacitly, to be sure. And there's the rub: In due course, the standard behind money, being hidden, eventually becomes forgotten, and the counters of worth become taken for worth itself.

Truth to tell, commodification by conventional commensuration always risks the homogenization of worth, and even the homogenization of things, all under the aspect of quantity. In many transactions, we do not mind or suffer or even notice. Yet the human soul finally rebels against the principle, whenever it strikes closest to home. Consider, for example, why there is such widespread dislike of the pawnbroker. It is not only that he profits from our misfortunes and sees the shame of our having to part with heirlooms and other items said (inadequately) to have "sentimental value." It is especially because he will not and cannot appreciate their human and personal worth and pays us only their market price. How much more will we object to those who would commodify our very being?

We surpass all defensible limits of such conventional commodification when we contemplate making the convention-maker—the human being—just another one of the commensurables. The end comes to be treated as mere means. Selling our bodies, we come perilously close to selling out our souls. There is even a danger in contemplating such a prospect—for if we come to think about ourselves like pork bellies, pork bellies we will become. . . .

III. The Price of Progress

The arguments I have offered are not easy to make. I am all too well aware that they can be countered, that their appeal is largely to certain hard-to-articulate intuitions and sensibilities that I at least believe belong intimately to the human experience of our own humanity. Precious though they might be, they do not exhaust the human picture, far from it. And perhaps, in the present case, they should give way to rational calculation, market mechanisms, and even naked commodification of human flesh—all in the service of saving life at lowest cost (though, parenthetically, it would be worth a whole separate discussion to consider whether, in the longer view, there are not cheaper, more effective, and less indecent means to save lives, say, through preventive measures that forestall end-stage renal disease now requiring transplantation: the definitions of both need and efficiency are highly contingent, and we should beware of allowing them to be defined for us by those technologists—like transplant surgeons—wedded to present practice). Perhaps this is not the right place to draw a line or to make a stand.

Consider, then, a slightly more progressive and enterprising proposal, one anticipated by my colleague, Willard Gaylin, in an essay, "Harvesting the Dead," written in 1974. Mindful of all the possible uses of newly dead—or perhaps not-quite-dead—bodies, kept in their borderline condition by continuous artificial respiration and assisted circulation, intact, warm, pink, recognizably you or me, but brain dead, Gaylin imagines the multiple medically beneficial uses to which the bioemporium of such "neomorts" could be put: the neomorts could, for example, allow physicians-in-training to practice pelvic examinations and tracheal intubations without shame or fear of doing damage; they could serve as unharmable subjects for medical experimentation and drug testing, provide indefinite supplies of blood, marrow, and skin, serve as factories to manufacture hormones and antibodies, or, eventually, be dismembered for transplantable spare parts, Since the newly dead body really is such a precious resource, why not really put it to full and limitless use?

Gaylin's scenario is not so far-fetched. Proposals to undertake precisely such body-farming have been seriously discussed among medical scientists in private. The technology for maintaining neomorts is already available. Indeed, in the past few years, a publicly traded corporation has opened a national chain of large, specialized nursing homes—or should we rather call them nurseries?—for the care and feeding solely of persons in persistent vegetative state or ventilator-dependent irreversible coma. Roughly ten establishments, each housing several hundred of such beings, already exist. All that would be required to turn them into Gaylin's bioemporia would be a slight revision in the definition of death (already proposed for other reasons)—to shift from death of the whole brain to death of the cortex and the higher centers—plus the will not to let these valuable resources go to waste. (The company's stock, by the way, has more than quadrupled in the last year alone; perhaps someone is already preparing plans for mergers and manufacture.) Repulsive? You bet. Useful? Without doubt. Shall we go forward into this brave new world?

Forward we are going, without anyone even asking the question. In the twenty-five years since I began thinking about these matters, our society has overcome longstanding taboos and repugnances to accept test-tube fertilization, commercial sperm-banking, surrogate motherhood, abortion on demand, exploitation of fetal tissue, patenting of living human tissue, gender-change surgery, liposuction and body shops, the widespread shuttling of human parts, assisted-suicide practiced by doctors, and the deliberate generation of human beings to serve as transplant donors—not to speak about massive changes in the culture regarding shame, privacy, and exposure. Perhaps more worrisome than the changes themselves is the coarsening of sensibilities and attitudes, and the irreversible effects on our imaginations and the way we come to conceive of ourselves. For there is a sad irony in our biomedical project, accurately anticipated in Aldous Huxley's *Brave New World:* We expend enormous energy and vast sums of money to preserve and prolong bodily life, but in the process our embodied life is stripped of its gravity and much of its dignity. This is, in a word, progress as tragedy.

In the transplanting of human organs, we have made a start on a road that leads imperceptibly but surely toward a destination that none of us wants to reach. A divination of this fact produced reluctance at the start. Yet the first step, overcoming reluctance, was defensible on benevolent and rational grounds: save life using organs no longer useful to their owners and otherwise lost to worms.

Now, embarked on the journey, we cannot go back. Yet we are increasingly troubled by the growing awareness that there is neither a natural nor a rational place to stop. Precedent justifies extension, so does rational calculation: We are in a warm bath that warms up so imperceptibly that we don't know when to scream.

And this is perhaps the most interesting and the most tragic element of my dilemma—and it is not my dilemma alone. I don't want to encourage; yet I cannot simply condemn. I refuse to approve; yet I cannot moralize. How, in this matter of organs for sale, as in so much of modern life, is one to conduct one's thoughts if one wishes neither to be a crank nor to yield what is best in human life to rational analysis and the triumph of technique? Is poor reason impotent to do anything more than to recognize and state this tragic dilemma?

Discussion and Assignments

1. Kass opens his essay with a discussion of the sentiment of *repugnance,* a concept central to his understanding of organ sales. What does repugnance have to do with this subject for Kass, and why does he regard this sentiment, at least in this instance, as the "very embodiment of reason"?

2. In the section entitled *Whose Body?* Kass states the following: "My body is me; my daughters are mine (and so are my opinions, deeds, and speeches); my car is my property. Only the last can clearly be alienated and sold at will."

   Briefly explain what Kass means by each statement in order to distinguish them from each other.
   a. My body is me.
   b. My daughters are mine (and so are my opinions, deeds, and speeches).
   c. My car is my property.

   Keeping these statements in mind, what is it about the notion or idea of property Kass finds confusing when he applies it to selling one's own organs?

3. In the section entitled *Liberty and Its Limits* Kass contrasts the liberal and libertarian approaches to personal rights and liberties, and warns of disturbing consequences resulting from taking the libertarian approach to liberty too far. Why is Kass so concerned with the limits of liberty as it relates to organ sales? What implications does he see issuing from unchecked liberty? Do you agree with Kass on this point?

4. In the section entitled *Commodification* Kass discusses how things such as love and friendship are "priceless." What does he mean by this? Kass then introduces the *pawnbroker* as an example to further illustrate his point. Why is there such widespread dislike for the pawnbroker? What does this example given by Kass have to do with selling organs? How effective an example is it?

5. Kass further states in his section *Commodification,* "Selling our bodies, we come perilously close to selling out our souls." According to Kass, we lose something essential, very basic to our humanity when we accept the practice of selling our organs. Is it possible to define precisely what Kass means by this statement? What is it we give up or sell? What are the implications Kass claims such sales may hold for the future?

6. In the section entitled *The Price of Progress* Kass recounts Willard Gaylin's scenario of maintaining brain dead "neomorts" as repositories for spare parts, blood, marrow, and other biological needs for the living. Does Kass persuade you the sale of body organs brings us one step closer to Gaylin's scenario? Why or why not?

7. Or might Gaylin's scenario be *desirable?* After all, maintaining neomorts would save lives (and might be cheap, too). Being brain dead, the neomorts wouldn't possess consciousness or feel pain. You might need a bone marrow transplant someday, or a kidney, maybe a cornea, and if every community hospital had a little room off to the side somewhere, just large enough to maintain a few neomorts, then you could rest assured that if you ever needed a. . . .

   a. Construct an argument, for or against, the maintenance of neomorts in community hospitals for use by doctors in treating local patients using the following argument form: Issue, Definitions, Premises, Conclusion. Remember to use only clear, declarative statements in your presentation. And remember to account for Kass's objections to organ sales (and neomorts) in your argument.

   Issue: Whether we should maintain neomorts in community hospitals for the purpose of using them to treat patients.
   Definitions:
   Premises:
   Conclusion:

   b. Now that you have constructed an argument in *a,* use the argument to write a 300 word essay. Remember to use only those statements you used in *a.*

8. How effective is Kass in considering the views of his opponents? Cite specific examples to illustrate how effective he is.

9. What are the two most effective pieces of evidence Kass offers to support his case against organ sales? In a paragraph on each explain why each piece of evidence is so strong. What is the weakest piece of evidence Kass offers to support his case against the sale of organs? In a paragraph explain why the evidence is weak.

1.5 Take My Kidney, Please

Michael Kinsley

Even Margaret Thatcher's devotion to the free market has some limits, it seems. Reacting to newspaper reports that poor Turkish peasants are being paid to go to London and give up a kidney for transplant, the British Prime Minister said that "the sale of kidneys or any organs of the body is

From Time, *March 13, 1989, p. 88. Reprinted with permission.*

utterly repugnant." Emergency legislation is now being prepared for swift approval by Parliament to make sure that capitalism does not perform its celebrated magic in the market for human organs.

Commercial trade in human kidneys does seem grotesque. But it's a bit hard to say why. After all, the moral logic of capitalism does not stop at the epidermis. That logic holds, in a nutshell, that if an exchange is voluntary, it leaves both parties better off. In one case, a Turk sold a kidney for £2,500 ($4,400) because he needed money for an operation for his daughter. Capitalism in action: one person had $4,400 and wanted a kidney, another person had a spare kidney and wanted $4,400, so they did a deal. What's more, it seems like an advantageous deal all around. The buyer avoided a lifetime of dialysis. The seller provided crucial help to his child, at minimum risk to himself. (According to the *Economist,* the chance of a kidney donor's dying as a result of the loss is 1 in 5,000.)

Nevertheless, the conclusion that such trade is abhorrent is not even controversial. Almost everyone agrees. Is almost everyone right? This question of how far we are willing to push the logic of capitalism will be thrust in our faces increasingly in coming years. Medical advances are making it possible to buy things that were previously unobtainable at any price. (The Baby M "womb renting" case is another example.) Meanwhile, the communications and transportation revolutions are breaking down international borders, making new commercial relations possible between the comfortably rich and the desperately poor. On what basis do we say to a would-be kidney seller, "Sorry, this is one deal you just can't make?"

One widely accepted category of forbidden deals involves health and safety regulations: automobile standards, bans on food additives, etc. Although we quarrel about particular instances, only libertarian cranks reject in principle the idea that government sometimes should protect people from themselves. But it is no more dangerous to sell one of your kidneys than it is to give one away to a close relative—a transaction we not only allow but admire. On health grounds alone, you can't ban the sale without banning the gift as well. Furthermore, the sale of a kidney is not necessarily a foolish decision that society ought to protect you from. To pay for a daughter's operation, it seems the opposite.

But maybe there are some things money just shouldn't be allowed to buy, sensibly or otherwise. Socialist philosopher Michael Walzer added flesh to this ancient skeleton of sentiment in his 1983 book, *Spheres of Justice.* Walzer argued that a just society is not necessarily one with complete financial equality—a hopeless and even destructive goal—but one in which the influence of money is not allowed to dominate all aspects of life. By outlawing organ sales, you are indeed keeping the insidious influence of money from leaching into a new sphere and are thereby reducing the power of the rich. Trouble is, you are also reducing opportunity for the poor.

The grim trade in living people's kidneys would not be necessary if more people would voluntarily offer their kidneys (and other organs) when they die. Another socialist philosopher, Richard Titmuss, wrote a famous book two decades ago called *The Gift Relationship,* extolling the virtues of donated blood over purchased blood and, by extension, the superiority of sharing over commerce. Whatever you may think of Titmuss's larger point, the appeal of the blood-donor system as a small testament to our shared humanity is undeniable. Perhaps we should do more to encourage organ donation at death for the same reason. On the other hand, however cozy and egalitarian it might seem, a system that supplied all the kidneys we need through voluntary donation would be no special favor to our Turkish friend, who would be left with no sale and no $4,400. Why not at least let his heirs sell his kidneys when he dies? A commercial market in cadaver organs would wipe out the sale at live people's parts a lot more expeditiously than trying to encourage donations.

The logic of capitalism assumes knowledgeable, reasonably intelligent people on both sides of the transaction. Is this where the kidney trade falls short? At $4,400, the poor Turk was probably underpaid for his kidney. Out in an open, legal market with protections against exploitation, he might have got more. At some price, the deal would make sense for almost anyone. I have no sentimental attachment to my kidneys. Out of prudence, I'd like to hang on to one of them, but the other is available. My price is $2 million.

Of course, I make this offer safe in the knowledge that there will always be some poor Turk ready to undercut me. So maybe, because of who the sellers inevitably will be, the sale of kidneys is by its very nature exploitation. A father shouldn't have to sacrifice a kidney to get a necessary operation for his daughter. Unfortunately, banning the kidney sale won't solve the problem of paying for the operation. Nor can the world yet afford expensive operations for everyone who needs one. And leaving aside the melodrama of the daughter's operation, we don't stop people from doing things to support their families—working in coal mines, for example—that reduce their life expectancies more than would the loss of a kidney. In fact, there are places in the Third World where even $4,400 can do more for a person's own life expectancy than a spare kidney.

The horror of kidney sales, in short, is a sentimental reaction to the injustice of life—injustice that the transaction highlights but does not increase. This is not a complaint. In fact, it may even be the best reason for a ban on such transactions. That kind of sentiment ought to be encouraged.

Discussion and Assignments

1. Kinsley notes that for capitalism, if both parties of a transaction are voluntary participants, they are both better off. Do you think the young Turk trying to sell his kidney was a voluntary participant? In a 200 word essay examine the Turk's behavior in the context of *voluntary action*. Remember to use examples to illustrate your answer.
2. If a man works in an unhealthy coal mine to provide for his family, why shouldn't he be able to sell his kidney, especially when the risk to his health from the sale may be less than his exposure in the mine? In one paragraph distinguish these two situations from each other with as much detail as you can. How are they similar? How are they dissimilar? How persuasive do you find this analogy?
3. Kinsley closes his article with a comment that we might do well in listening to our sentiments when confronted with situations like organ selling. What is the relation he draws between capitalism and our sentiments?

Concluding Questions and Observations

1. If organs are eventually regarded as a kind of commodity and their sale legally supported (even encouraged) by the state, could the state some day *require* the poor to sell their organs for money before they are offered welfare assistance or, ironically, publicly supported medical care? Could the IRS require the sale of a kidney, as it might liquidate an automobile it has seized, for unpaid taxes? Could the courts force deadbeats to sell a kidney to pay child support?
2. Is there any chance the rich or well-to-do might have less interest in eradicating poverty if the state legalized the sale of organs and fixed the price at a level they (the well-to-do) could afford?
3. Michael Kinsley offers an alternative proposal to live kidney sales by suggesting money be paid for cadaveric organs. If money were offered for cadaveric organs, the reasoning goes, organs would be plentiful, and the ethical dilemmas we face with live organ sales would disappear. If not enough people sell their cadaveric organs when they die, simply raise the price until they do. Supply and demand again works its magic. What would the implications of such a program be? Would the program accomplish its desired ends? What about the *means* to achieve the ends? Who would set the prices? Should the sellers be able to set their own prices, as with any other commodity?
    a. Construct an argument for creating a futures market in cadaveric organs. You sell your organs now, and your heirs collect the payment when they

harvest your organs at your death. Use the following argument form: Issue, Definitions, Premises, Conclusion. Remember to use only clear, declarative statements in your presentation.

Issue: Whether it is advisable to create a futures market in the sale of cadaveric organs.
Definitions:
Premises:
Conclusion:

b. Now that you have the argument, put it in essay form. Write a 300 word essay for or against creating a futures market in cadaveric organs employing the argument you created in *a*.

One last thought on this subject: Remember the young Turk (article 1.5), the fellow who wanted to sell his kidney to pay for an operation for his daughter? Would his daughter benefit from a market in *cadaveric* organs? Apparently not. If the young Turk has to wait until he's dead to collect on selling his kidney to pay for his daughter's operation, she may never have the surgery. Was Janet Radcliffe Richards right when she advocated live sales, not cadaveric sales?

4. During a general discussion session at a conference on organ replacement therapy in Munich in 1990, Janet Radcliffe Richards raised an intriguing issue regarding organ sales. She proposed individuals might be allowed to sacrifice their lives, to sell their *vital* organs, such as a liver or heart, so money might be given to loved ones for important things like education or health care. The suggestion drew a response from a doctor that such a practice would be "legalized homicide." Radcliffe Richards responded that such a sacrifice should be called "assisted suicide" and that "A greater love has no man than this that he should lay down his life for his friends." How do you feel about such a proposal?

a. Construct an argument either in favor of or against Radcliffe Richards's proposal that people be allowed to sacrifice their lives by selling their vital organs for family or friends using the following argument form: Issue, Definitions, Premises, Conclusion. Remember to use only clear, declarative statements throughout your presentation.

Issue: Whether it is advisable to allow people to give up their lives by selling their vital organs to get money for family or friends.
Definitions:
Premises:
Conclusion:

b. Now write a 300 word argumentative essay employing the argument you constructed in *a*.

Chapter 2

Chess and Artificial Intelligence

Background

IN 1950 A BRITISH MATHEMATICIAN NAMED ALAN TURING proposed what has become a sort of reference point, a working definition for artificial intelligence, or AI. If you hold a conversation with an entity that is hidden from view, say, concealed behind a curtain, and if you cannot tell the entity you are conversing with is a machine from the conversation alone, the machine would display artificial intelligence. This simple experiment has since been known as the *Turing test*. Interestingly, Turing used the game of chess to illustrate his theory of AI, and in the intervening years chess has played a central, albeit perplexing role in the discussion of whether there could or could not be something called artificial intelligence. The subject made the popular press in two celebrated chess matches between champion Garry Kasparov, widely regarded as the greatest (human) chess player ever, and Deep Blue, an IBM RS/6000 SP supercomputer. The first match was played in Philadelphia in February 1996, the second in May 1997 in New York City. Kasparov won the first match, and Deep Blue won the second. Both matches, especially the second game of the second match, raised intriguing questions about the nature of consciousness, and the potential for machines to think. Were the chess matches fair? Did Deep Blue actually play chess? Did Deep Blue pass the Turing test? Are we on the verge of creating a new kind of intelligence?

After Deep Blue's loss to Kasparov in 1996, the computer's research team went back to work on improving its speed and the size of its knowledge base. They also hired International Grand Master Joel Benjamin to take Deep Blue "to chess school." The result was a much stronger Deep Blue, capable of calculating 200 million positions per second. The program can assess the integrity of the board six moves deep into a game with remarkable exhaustiveness. The computer's program doesn't enable it to recognize patterns or to conceptualize in the way we commonly attribute to humans. Instead, Deep Blue relies on the firepower of hundreds of millions of calculations to assess the board, anticipate danger, and plot attacks. After his loss in 1997, his ego severely wounded, Kasparov issued a winner-take-all challenge to the Deep Blue team (article 4), but they were not interested in a rematch and Deep Blue was retired from playing chess a few months later.

On November 2, 2000, at West London's West Riverside Studios, the often arrogant, always self-assured Kasparov conceded defeat in the 15th game of a 16-game match. The 37-year-old Kasparov, ruled for 15 years until Vladimir Kramnik, a 25-year-old former student of Kasparov's, outmaneuvered his teacher for the title.

Readings

Article 2.1 In *How the Chess Was Won,* Deep Blue's chief designer Feng-Hsiung Hsu points out that Kasparov possesses remarkable intuitive ability for chess, not to mention the benefits derived from 30 years of experience playing the game. But even with all the natural gifts and skill of a champion like Kasparov, when a team like the Deep Blue team comes together with a common goal, they can go beyond the limitations of one human being, even the best there is.

Article 2.2 Glenn D. Klopfenstein is an assistant professor of English at Passaic County Community College and has achieved the rank of *life master* and *expert* by the U.S. Chess Federation. In *Cheating at Chess, 200 Million Times a Second,* he argues that Deep Blue doesn't play by accepted rules of the game, rules humans have long accepted as foundational for a fair game of chess to commence. For Klopfenstein, Deep Blue doesn't really play chess at all, it simply utilizes, or calculates, a vast library of data at an astonishing speed, an unfair advantage not achievable by a human.

Article 2.3 When he played Deep Blue, Garry Kasparov was the top ranking professional chess champion since 1984. In *The Day That I Sensed a New Kind of Intelligence,* Kasparov moves us to the more philosophical concerns of artificial intelligence, offering a tentative appraisal that Deep Blue exhibited a "weird kind, an inefficient, inflexible kind" of intelligence during their first match in 1996. During the first game of their match, Deep Blue made a very "human" move by sacrificing a pawn. The sacrifice set the stage for its first win, and moved Kasparov to ponder the possibility Deep Blue might possess AI.

Article 2.4 After his loss to Deep Blue in their 1997 rematch, Kasparov issued a challenge to the Deep Blue team for one final match. In *IBM Owes Mankind a Rematch,* Kasparov discusses game two, the decisive game of the 1997 match. In this game Deep Blue displayed an uncanny ability to reject short-term advantage, sense danger, and stay focused on long-term results. Kasparov never recovered his concentration during the match after his defeat in game two. The Deep Blue team declined the invitation.

Article 2.5 In *How Hard Is Chess?,* David Gelernter, professor of computer science at Yale University, rejects the proposal that Deep Blue can think, or that any computer or machine could be considered a thinking thing. Gelernter argues that while machines imitate human behavior, and it is likely they will increasingly perform many tasks better than humans, computers are still machines, and machines do not have minds.

Article 2.6 In *Fair Game,* Walter and Bennet Goodman consider how well a computer would fare playing poker. The unusual proposal yields intriguing observations about the nature of human endeavor, motivation, and the operations and limitations of computers. Poker integrates human behaviors like bluffing and reading body language with the mathematical odds of the cards. Moreover, poker players defy logic—one player may raise on a hunch, another may fold even though his or her prospects are good, and another may bet on nothing. There's a kind of anarchic poetry to playing poker, its irrationality being its characteristically human signature. The Goodmans conclude that no computer would stand a chance against the idiosyncratic, human behaviors of a good poker player.

Article 2.7 In *Be Afraid: The Meaning of Deep Blue's Victory,* Charles Krauthammer boldly declares Deep Blue has passed the Turing test. Krauthammer argues that Deep Blue played like a human, even though it came to its conclusions in a different way. He sees this as a monumental advance, and asks why free will could not evolve from silicon, as free will in humans evolved from carbon-based life.

Article 2.8 John Chapman closes our study section with *Man's Brief Reign in the Evolutionary Spotlight.* Published soon after Deep Blue's match victory over Kasparov, Chapman sees man as a brief phase in evolutionary development, ultimately giving rise to electro-mechanical life forms free of the problems associated with the frailties of biology. Chapman claims the most challenging problem out of our reach is the puzzle of consciousness. Once this puzzle has finally been understood, he predicts intelligent, forward-looking, self-directed evolution will predominate, and the human life-form we now possess will be superseded.

2.1 How the Chess Was Won

M. MITCHELL WALDROP INTERVIEWS FENG-HSIUNG HSU

WHEN WORLD CHESS CHAMPION Garry Kasparov abruptly resigned the sixth and final game of his match in May against Deep Blue—a.k.a. the IBM RS/6000 SP supercomputer—a machine finally fulfilled one of the oldest challenges in artificial intelligence. Chess has tantalized computer researchers since the 1830s, when the eccentric English inventor Charles Babbage thought of luring investors to his idea of a programmable "analytical engine" by holding out the possibility of a chess-playing machine. After all, the rules of chess are precisely defined and easy to program, yet they give rise to strategic complexities that challenge the finest human minds. But despite researchers' best efforts, no machine proved able to beat the finest human players. Until Deep Blue.

Ironically, the victory comes when the computer-chess community has long abandoned any pretense of mimicking human thought. Chess masters, like the rest of us, are now known to reason by recognizing patterns, forming concepts, and creating plans—processes that computers do poorly, if at all. Deep Blue, like all the top chess-playing machines since the 1960s, relies instead on brute force—it looks as far ahead as it can at all possible moves and evaluates the strength of each position according to preprogrammed rules. Because of the rule that the faster the computer, the more positions it can search and the better it can play, Deep Blue relies on 32 high-speed processors operating simultaneously, each coordinating the work of 16 special-purpose "chess chips" that run in parallel. This computing firepower enables Deep Blue to evaluate a total of 200 million positions each second.

M. Mitchell Waldrop, author of the bestseller *Complexity* and of a forthcoming hook on the history of computing, recently spoke with Deep Blue's principal designer at IBM, Feng-Hsiung Hsu, about the implications of the machine's victory and its value for other uses.

TR: In February 1996, when Deep Blue was brand new, it went up against Garry Kasparov and lost. Many people felt vindicated—as if that proved the human mind's innate superiority over a mere machine. But now that Deep Blue has won, many feel as if the computer has humbled humanity. Should they feel threatened?

HSU: No. Remember, Deep Blue didn't play chess by itself. Before the match even started, humans programmed the machine to rise to Garry's level. And then during the match we actually went in between games, looked at Deep Blue's mistakes, and adjusted its criteria for evaluating the situation accordingly, so it wouldn't make the same mistake twice. Without that, Deep Blue could not have competed with Garry. So you could say that last year, Garry won one for humanity's past. This year, Deep Blue won one for humanity's future.

TR: How so?

HSU: When Garry plays chess, he is relying on the intellect he is born with, his knowledge of the game, and the experience he has gained from playing both people and computers. This is the old-fashioned way of playing chess; Garry, despite his brilliance, is limited by what is biologically possible. Deep Blue represents any technology that allows us to exceed the limits nature normally imposes on us. Right now we're talking over the telephone: just by shouting I cannot reach you. The principle is the same with chess. Garry may be the top player ever in chess, but while the chess players on Deep Blue's team can't claim to reach

anywhere near Garry's ability, with Deep Blue we exceeded our limits and won.

TR: When you put it that way, the match sounds a little unfair. Garry wasn't playing against one machine or even one person but a whole team.

HSU: But Garry was also part of a team. Between games he would consult with his coach, and even his own chess computer, to find out more about what Deep Blue would do. That is actually a normal part of any master's-level chess match. So you could say that Garry was playing against a computer relying on human power—but Deep Blue was playing against a human relying partly on computer power.

TR: Fair enough. But you could have said that last year when Garry won. Yet this year he lost. What made the difference?

HSU: The most obvious differences are that Deep Blue was twice as fast this year because it had new central-processing-unit chips, as well as twice as many chips designed only for the purpose of playing chess.

But for the match those hardware advances weren't as critical as two other considerations. First, we addressed the knowledge gap. Garry is a remarkable human being, with vast stores of knowledge and intuition about chess gained over 30 years of playing. Last year Deep Blue went into the match as a newborn baby: it had just been built and didn't know much about chess. So afterward we asked International Grand Master Joel Benjamin to come in with us and essentially take the machine to chess school. Actually, we went to chess school and used what we learned to completely reprogram the machine's basic software code and redesign the chess chips to incorporate much more chess knowledge. By this year's match, in Joel's words, Deep Blue had started to play human-level chess.

Second, we addressed the question of continued learning on Garry's part. For a computer scientist, the idea of building a machine to compete with the world chess champion is like climbing Mt. Everest. Unfortunately for us last year, the human Mt. Everest grew 100 feet a day while the match was proceeding: Garry has a human being's ability to adapt to what Deep Blue is doing. We knew that Deep Blue would never be as adaptive as a human, since that's not the way a computer is constructed. But we built software tools that allowed us to go in between the games and adjust Deep Blue's programming much faster than we could before. That turned out to be critical. The situation was like competing in the Indy 500, where you go to the pit stop and use your own high-speed tool to change the wheel.

TR: As you note, Deep Blue isn't as adaptive as a person. You and your colleagues have emphasized again and again that the computer operates by numerical brute force. Why not try to simulate human cognition and adaptability?

HSU: While people are very good at pattern recognition, concept formation, and so on, those tasks are very difficult for computers. Computers can complement humans, however, because they're good at calculations. So from an engineering point of view, if you want to attack chess problems by computer, you figure out how to use the ability of the machine to calculate fast.

The ability to compute quickly is quite useful in many other fields. One application is called data mining. Big organizations use this technique to extract select information from a vast number of details—for instance, businesses employ it to analyze financial markets. Data mining could also help solve a myriad of problems for individuals, such as the information overload people are now experiencing in the wake of increased access to, among other entities, the Internet. Just as we used our special-purpose chess chips to speed up Deep Blue—employing many of them in parallel—we can create computer systems good for data mining the World Wide Web. Such technology could find

and present you with information in a nutshell so that you don't have to spend your whole life surfing the Web.

TR: Wouldn't such a tool reinforce what one might call the "quantification fallacy"—the notion that all judgments and decisions can be reduced to calculations?

HSU: That danger exists. But data mining eventually leads to the discovery of empirical findings and rules, after which people stop to figure out why those exist. In other words, we can use computers to extract knowledge from data, but human beings still have to turn that knowledge into wisdom. That's how humanity progresses.

TR: What's next, now that Deep Blue has beaten the foremost human chess master?

HSU: Deep Blue's basic search blueprint is actually not specific to chess. So we've started looking at other areas such as pharmaceutical research, where Deep Blue could help design new drugs faster. That's important, since if a disease is very deadly and also very contagious, we need to be able to fight it with the best tools we have. Toward that end we are designing a molecular-modeling chip—one that can help predict how a candidate drug molecule would interact with, say, the protein envelope of a virus. We plan to install a number of such chips in a computer next year.

TR: Having come this far with Deep Blue, what would you say would actually constitute artificial intelligence?

HSU: Deep Blue would exhibit real AI if it would not allow me to unplug it.

Discussion and Assignments

1. The interviewer Mitchell Waldrop and Hsu state that computers are poor at mimicking human thought, pattern recognition, and the development of concepts, relying instead on calculating power to solve problems. Contrast what it is that computers do poorly with what it is they do very well. What implications do these strengths and weaknesses have for AI?
2. Hsu has a blunt answer for his interviewer when he is asked what would constitute artificial intelligence. What does he mean by his answer? Do you agree or disagree with Hsu?

2.2 Cheating at Chess, 200 Million Times a Second

GLENN D. KLOPFENSTEIN

HUMANS, TAKE HEART. Sure, Garry Kasparov, arguably the most gifted world champion of chess ever, lost in convincing fashion this month to IBM's supercomputer, Deep Blue (RS/ 6000 SP). But did the machine, with its talented satellite team of programmers and grandmaster consultants, cheat, as Kasparov suggested in his postgame comments? Common sense—something that we should take more collective pride in than we do—would tell us that of course the computer cheated, and, further, that no level playing field has ever existed between man and computer, at least not on the chessboard.

But Kasparov's losing this match, and the wide-ranging philosophical and scientific implications that the loss holds for us—implications that are at this stage probably more symbolic than substantive—should compel us to examine more closely the unfair advantages (in Kasparov's words) that we've been magnanimously allowing the machine to get away with. Perhaps we shouldn't be so nice anymore.

Signaling this change of heart, Kasparov's paranoiac charge that possibly a contingent of corporate-hired grandmasters had assisted Deep Blue behind a curtain during play was, nevertheless, the transparent reaction of a wounded ego. The accusation ("Look at the printouts!" he shouted) was eerily reminiscent of Bobby Fischer's unrelenting paranoia about a Soviet conspiracy to keep him from becoming the world champion more than two decades ago (a paranoia that no one now dismisses as fantasy, in spite of the undeniable manifestations at that time of Fischer's deepening psychosis). The better-adjusted Kasparov most likely will regret his comments when he cools off.

But some of his less caustic observations on the peculiarities of playing a supercomputer deserve to be put in a clear and more accessible light. For these more circumspect remarks of Kasparov's, especially those alluding to the near-impossibility of gaining an advantage, much less holding one's own, in the critical opening stages of a game with a computer, point precisely to just one of the absurd advantages that a supercomputer unfairly holds over a human opponent.

Perhaps the best way to illustrate this is to review the basics of fair play that most humans have religiously adhered to in the modern era of competitive chess tournaments (from the late 1800s, when the chess clock was introduced into serious competition, to the present day). In this context of what a level playing field means in chess, let us then compare how the pristinely amoral computer conducts itself during the course of a game.

The established and general rules of fair play in human chess competition are simple and common-sensical enough. Over more than a century's time, they have helped to foster the misleading myth that it is impossible to cheat at chess, that the game is solely a mental *mano a mano*.

The rules demand that you may not consult with anyone (this would include a computer, these days) during a game; that you may not, in another version of the same sin, secretly refresh your leaky memory by consulting, say, a monograph on a given opening (*e.g.*, "the Nadjorf Sicilian"); and that you may not touch a piece until you are prepared to move it.

Further, each player is accorded equal blocks of "thinking-on-your-own-move" time. Traditionally, in tournament competition, this amounts to 40 moves per two hours for each player, as it did in Kasparov *vs.* Deep Blue. If players abide by the spirit and letter of these rules, indeed, a more level playing field between two opponents is hard to imagine. The better man, or woman, almost always prevails in the long run, hence the utter reliability of class rankings, from novice to master. These are the fundamental rules that have helped to elevate the game of chess to its elite status as "the royal game."

But common sense tells us that chess computers routinely violate every tenet of this fair play. Whether Kasparov's unseemly worries about grandmaster almost-peers-turned-corporate-lackeys illegally helping the team of programmers during play are true or not, the most obvious truth for all to see is that Deep Blue had at its disposal an "in-house" cyberspace library of chess literature that

From The Chronicle of Higher Education, *May 30, 1997, p. B8. Reprinted with permission.*

dwarfs virtually every known physical collection of books on the subject in three-dimensional space. Not only that, Deep Blue's team of hired chess experts made sure that the library was kept up to date, and geared to respond to Kasparov's pet openings.

Beyond this, it can be safely suggested that the supercomputer's infallible memory banks make it possible for it to glean the results of more than a century of chess praxis in the well-charted waters of opening and end-game theory. This was why the disgusted Kasparov proclaimed that he was reduced to playing harmless "crap" in the opening. He had no reasonable alternative. As he well knew beforehand, it was in the infinitely more complex middle-game stage, after most of the pieces and pawns had been moved from their original squares, that his unique genius had the best chance of securing a winning advantage against the brute, calculating force of Deep Blue.

The computer reduces the other major tenets of fair play to absurdity as well. As long as computers play chess, nothing can be done about these unfair advantages, but they are worth mentioning anyway. With the computer's capacity to examine millions of positions per second with breath-taking accuracy, it is, in effect, "touching" as many pieces as it likes throughout the game. Deep Blue has the ability to cheat more than 200 million times per second, a remarkable sleight of hand. So, too, it can cheat time by any mortal reckoning through the sheer speed and accuracy of its calculations. (The odds of a chess master's beating Deep Blue at "speed" chess, which allows each player five minutes per move per game, are slim to none.)

What this all amounts to is that computers *must* cheat—that is, break all the rules of fair play—to humor humans with the illusion that the machine is "playing" a "game." At least the computer must cheat if it is to play the game beyond the level that a 5-year-old could play.

For the time being, while philosophers, ethicists, and other specialists in the field of artificial intelligence debate the larger implications of Kasparov's loss, perhaps we should, like Kasparov, indulge in a little petulance ourselves.

Discussion and Assignments

1. Principal designer of Deep Blue supercomputer Feng-Hsiung Hsu (article 2.1) stated that Kasparov had his chess machine, coach, and others available for consultation between games, and Deep Blue had its team of experts available between games as well. Do you think this would be a reasonable reply to Klopfenstein's claim that Deep Blue had an advantage? Why or why not?

2. Klopfenstein cites several advantages Deep Blue had to prove it didn't play by the rules. Which two pieces of evidence do you believe most strongly support his claim that Deep Blue cheats? In a paragraph on each explain why you think they are strong. Which is the weakest piece of evidence he offers to support his claim that Deep Blue cheats? In a paragraph explain why you think it's weak. Can you think of an important piece of evidence, for or against his case, that he left out?

3. How well does Klopfenstein consider objections to his view?

4. Klopfenstein is arguing to prove there has never been a level playing field when humans meet computers at the chessboard. I've outlined his argument below. Take a few minutes to examine the outline with your classmates. Would you change anything?

Cheating at Chess, 200 Million Times a Second, by Glenn D. Klopfenstein

Issue: Whether computers abide by the rules of fair play when playing humans at chess.

Definitions: *Level playing field* means both contestants abide by the rules of fair play.
Cheating refers to breaking the rules of fair play.

Premises: 1. From the late 1800s specific rules of fair play have been universally accepted by competitors in serious chess tournaments.

2. These long-standing rules ensure a level playing field exists between competitors, thereby ensuring the best person wins the game.

3. The accepted rules require that each contestant:
   a. not consult another person during play.
   b. not consult a monograph during play.
   c. refrain from touching a piece until the contestant is prepared to move it.
   d. be accorded an equal block of "thinking-on-your-own-move" time equaling about 40 moves, at two hours each for each game.

4. Deep Blue:
   a. has a vast "in-house" cyberspace library at its disposal during play, was kept up-to-date by chess experts, and was geared to respond to Kasparov's pet openings.
   b. has an infallible memory that enables it to utilize over a century of chess praxis in opening and end game theory.
   c. has a capacity to examine 200 million positions per second with breathtaking accuracy, the equivalent of "touching" as many pieces as it likes throughout the game.

Conclusion: Chess computers like Deep Blue must cheat, that is, break the rules of fair play, when they "play" chess with humans.

5. a. Klopfenstein makes a strong argument for Deep Blue not abiding by the accepted rules of chess. Can you construct an argument in reply? Give it a try using the same argument form: Issue, Definitions, Premises, Conclusion.

Issue:

Definitions:

Premises:

Conclusion:

b. Now that you have the argument, put it in essay form. Compose a 300 word essay employing the argument you created in *a*.

2.3 The Day That I Sensed a New Kind of Intelligence

GARRY KASPAROV

I got my first glimpse of artificial intelligence on Feb. 10, 1996, at 4:45 p.m. EST, when in the first game of my match with Deep Blue, the computer nudged a pawn forward to a square where it could easily be captured. It was a wonderful and extremely human move. If I had been playing White, I might have offered this pawn sacrifice. It fractured Black's pawn structure and opened up the board. Although there did not appear to be a forced line of play that would allow recovery of the

From Time, *March 25, 1996, p. 55. Reprinted by permission of Time Life Syndication.*

pawn, my instincts told me that with so many "loose" Black pawns and a somewhat exposed Black king, White could probably recover the material, with a better overall position to boot.

But a computer, I thought, would never make such a move. A computer can't "see" the long-term consequences of structural changes in the position or understand how changes in pawn formations may be good or bad.

Humans do this sort of thing all the time. But computers generally calculate each line of play so far as possible within the time allotted. Because chess is a game of virtually limitless possibilities, even a beast like Deep Blue, which can look at more than 100 million positions a second, can go only so deep. When computers reach that point, they evaluate the various resulting positions and select the move leading to the best one. And because computers' primary way of evaluating chess positions is by measuring material superiority, they are notoriously materialistic. If they "understood" the game, they might act differently, but they don't understand.

So I was stunned by this pawn sacrifice. What could it mean? I had played a lot of computers but had never experienced anything like this. I could feel—I could smell—a new kind of intelligence across the table. While I played through the rest of the game as best I could, I was lost; it played beautiful, flawless chess the rest of the way and won easily.

Later I discovered the truth. Deep Blue's computational powers were so great that it did in fact calculate every possible move all the way to the actual recovery of the pawn six moves later. The computer didn't view the pawn sacrifice as a sacrifice at all. So the question is, If the computer makes the same move that I would make for completely different reasons, has it made an "intelligent" move? Is the intelligence of an action dependent on who (or what) takes it?

This is a philosophical question I did not have time to answer. When I understood what had happened, however, I was reassured. In fact, I was able to exploit the traditional shortcomings of computers throughout the rest of the match. At one point, for example, I changed slightly the order of a well-known opening sequence. Because it was unable to compare this new position meaningfully with similar ones in its database, it had to start calculating away and was unable to find a good plan. A human would have simply wondered, "What's Garry up to?," judged the change to be meaningless and moved on.

Indeed, my overall thrust in the last five games was to avoid giving the computer any concrete goal to calculate toward; if it can't find a way to win material, attack the king or fulfill one of its other programmed priorities, the computer drifts planlessly and gets into trouble. In the end, that may have been my biggest advantage: I could figure out its priorities and adjust my play. It couldn't do the same to me. So although I think I did see some signs of intelligence, it's a weird kind, an inefficient, inflexible kind that makes me think I have a few years left.

Discussion and Assignments

1. Kasparov claims he experienced his first glimpse of artificial intelligence when Deep Blue moved its pawn forward to where it could be easily captured. In retrospect, he states this "extremely human" move was not a sacrifice at all. The computer had calculated six moves deep into the game, all the way to the recovery of the pawn. Kasparov goes on to ask the following "philosophical question": "If the computer makes the same move I would make for completely different reasons, has it made an 'intelligent' move? Is the intelligence of an action dependent on who (or what) takes it?"

   a. What does Kasparov mean by this comment?

   b. What role might *motivation* play in understanding Kasparov's question?

   c. If Kasparov were to claim Deep Blue has AI under the stated circumstances, in what way would it differ from other machines or computers that perform programmed functions on cue?

   d. Is Kasparov implying that once a machine calculates at a certain level of complexity it approximates or becomes *conscious*?

2.4 IBM Owes Mankind a Rematch

GARRY KASPAROV

IN THE ARTICLE I WROTE for *Time* last year after my victorious match against IBM's Deep Blue super-computer in Philadelphia, I expressed my surprise and amazement at seeing a new kind of intelligence. I referred to Game 1, in which the computer's decision to sacrifice a pawn, based strictly on the machine's calculations, coincided with what a human would have done using human logic. Thus I stepped into a discussion of whether artificial intelligence has to be an exact copy of human thinking procedures or whether we should judge intelligence by the end result. I viewed the match with an improved version of Deep Blue as an opportunity to study this further—and of course to win a competitive event.

Unfortunately, I based my preparation for this match, played two weeks ago in New York City, on the conventional wisdom of what would constitute good anticomputer strategy. Conventional wisdom is—or was until the end of this match—to avoid early confrontations, play a slow game, try to out-maneuver the machine, force positional mistakes, and then, when the climax comes, not lose your concentration and not make any tactical mistakes.

It was my bad luck that this strategy worked perfectly in Game 1—but never again for the rest of the match. By the middle of the match, I found myself unprepared for what turned out to be a totally new kind of intellectual challenge.

The decisive game of the match was Game 2, which left a scar in my memory and prevented me from achieving my usual total concentration in the following games. In Deep Blue's Game 2 we saw something that went well beyond our wildest expectations of how well a computer would be able to foresee the long-term positional consequences of its decisions. The machine refused to move to a position that had a decisive short-term advantage—showing a very human sense of danger. I think this moment could mark a revolution in computer science that could earn IBM and the Deep Blue team a Nobel Prize. Even today, weeks later, no other chess-playing program in the world has been able to evaluate correctly the consequences of Deep Blue's position.

Also, Game 2 had a very unfortunate finish. Deep Blue held a strategically winning position, but it made a tactical blunder that, if I had sacrificed a piece, could have given me a miraculous escape. But I trusted the machine's calculations, thinking it would not miss such a continuation, and resigned instead.

Game 2 created an enigma for me that I never solved and from which I never recovered. I would like the IBM team to start disclosing the secrets of how they achieved this unthinkable success in chess programming. They claim they developed software that enabled them to change the style of the program in mid-match and the evaluation ability of the machine from game to game. This also is revolutionary, because any change, any tweak in the computer normally needs weeks of testing to avoid potential bugs.

I discovered that I was playing a very flexible, quickly changing opponent with an ability to avoid any mistakes in long-term calculations. My opponent was psychologically stable, undisturbed and unconcerned about anything going on around it, and it made almost none of the typical computer-chess errors.

This machine is not invincible, however, and I still believe that I had a chance of winning, especially if I had prepared myself properly for the match, which was very different in spirit from the match in Philadelphia.

From the opening press conference, I realized that for IBM, this was much more than a scientific experiment. Competition had overshadowed science. It had become a contest about winning and losing. The IBM team was at once a player, organizer, arbitrator and sponsor of the event, which left me at a terrible disadvantage. Whether they intended to or not, they created a hostile atmosphere that was very difficult for me to bear. There was something negative in the air. It was a Deep Blue show, and Deep Blue had to win.

IBM's total control of the site and the playing conditions underscored the vulnerability of the human player. I was the only player in this competition influenced by any sort of negative or hostile atmosphere. I think IBM's unwillingness to cooperate or give printouts of the computer's thought processes harmed that atmosphere. (As of today, I

From Time, *March 26, 1997, p. 66. Reprinted with permission.*

still have not received the complete printouts that I requested.) There were also many minor incidents, starting with the fact that the venue was created for the convenience of the machine—with all these air-conditioning systems and dozens of people serving the machine—not the human player.

I don't want anybody to look at this as an excuse. It's my fault. I accepted the conditions.

Now I would like to look to the future. I think we have to separate science and sport. I believe the IBM team owes the world of chess, and the world of science, a full explanation of how such a flexible machine was developed. They have to make all the scientific data available to allow others to judge their accomplishment.

I also think IBM owes me, and all mankind, a rematch. I hereby challenge IBM to a match of 10 games, 20 days long, to play every second day. I would like to have access in advance to the log of 10 Deep Blue games played with a neutral player or another computer in the presence of my representative. I would like to play it this fall, when I can be in my best form after a summer of vacation and preparation. And I'm ready to play for all or nothing, winner take all, just to show that it's not about money. Moreover, I think it would be advisable if IBM would step down as an organizer of the match. It should be organized independently.

I think IBM was the big winner of this match. It scored many points in advertising and in the stock market. I also think the company owes something to chess. I think it would be great if IBM contributed to chess development; specifically, it could create a scholarship to help talented kids study chess.

I think this match proved that there should be no special anticomputer strategy. To beat this machine, I just have to play great chess. I need comprehensive, bullet-proof opening preparation that checks all sharp lines of play to avoid any flaws—which can be deadly when playing Deep Blue. I need physical and psychological stability, a great level of concentration and a mind free of other distractions to calculate, calculate and calculate.

I think something great is happening. I'm proud to be part of that. But I don't want to be a loser because I'm playing only at 50% of my capacity and 50% of my psychological stability.

If we get this rematch, I'm ready, whatever the outcome, to go to IBM's labs and have a nice talk with the Deep Blue team. But until then, I'm going to treat them as a very hostile opponent, in order to be ready for the toughest challenge of my life.

Discussion and Assignments

1. Kasparov claims the second game of his rematch with Deep Blue was decisive. Why was the game a turning point for Kasparov? What ability did the computer display that made Kasparov think something extraordinary in computer science had been achieved? Does Kasparov offer enough evidence to convince you something extraordinary had occurred?
2. According to Kasparov, why did he lose the match to Deep Blue? Which reasons have to do with skill in playing chess, and which do not? Is it possible to make such a distinction?

2.5 How Hard Is Chess?

David Gelernter

We already knew that computers are first-rate at solving equations, entertaining children, burying friends and enemies under E-mail and doing many other useful chores. They have also been brushing up on their chess. By the end of the second game between Deep Blue and Garry Kasparov last week,

From Time, *May 19, 1997, p. 72. Reprinted with permission.*

it was clear that IBM's extraordinary computer was playing better chess than any machine ever had before. After Saturday's game ended in a draw, the match was still tied at one win and three draws apiece, but technology watchers were pretty well agreed: if the machine doesn't triumph this time, it is likely to triumph before long.

And why bother about the actual date on which the computer finally vanquishes the human world champion? After all, it can already beat you. That in itself is suggestive and important, because no human being can play chess without thinking. And no human could beat the chess champion of the world, even in a single game, without bringing significant intelligence to bear. Shouldn't we conclude that Deep Blue must be a thinking computer, and a smart one at that, maybe brilliant? Maybe a genius? Aren't we forced to conclude that Deep Blue must have a mind? That henceforth *Homo sapiens* will be defined as "one type of thinking thing"?

No. Deep Blue is just a machine. It doesn't have a mind any more than a flowerpot has a mind. Deep Blue is a beautiful and amazing technological achievement. It is an intellectual milestone, and its chief meaning is this: that human beings are champion machine builders. All sorts of activities that we thought could be done only by minds can in fact be done by machines too, if the machine builders are smart enough. Deep Blue underscores the same lesson about human thought we learned a couple of generations ago from mechanical calculators. You can't do arithmetic without using your mind, but when a calculator does arithmetic, we don't conclude that it has a mind. We conclude that arithmetic can be done without a mind.

Winning at chess, of course, is much harder than adding numbers. But when you think about it carefully, the idea that Deep Blue has a mind is absurd. How can an object that wants nothing, fears nothing, enjoys nothing, needs nothing and cares about nothing have a mind? It can win at chess, but not because it wants to. It isn't happy when it wins or sad when it loses. What are its *apres*-match plans if it beats Kasparov? Is it hoping to take Deep Pink out for a night on the town? It doesn't care about chess or anything else. It plays the game for the same reason a calculator adds or a toaster toasts: because it is a machine designed for that purpose.

Computers as we know them will never have minds. No matter what amazing feats they perform, inside they will always be the same absolute zero. The philosopher Paul Ziff laid this out clearly almost four decades ago. How can we be sure, he asked, that a computer-driven robot will never have feelings, never have a mind? "Because we can program a robot to behave any way we want it to behave. Because a robot couldn't mean what it said any more than a phonograph record could mean what it said." Computers do what we make them do, period. However sophisticated the computer's performance, it will always be a performance.

Not so fast, someone might say. The human brain is a machine too. How can we dismiss Deep Blue as just a machine when we don't dismiss the human brain as just a machine?

Because if your brain is just a machine, it's a machine that can do one trick that computers have no hope of doing. A trick that is intrinsic to the machinery, that can't be duplicated onto some other machine, stored on a disc, reworked by smart programmers or appropriated by Microsoft. Because of the stuff it is made of, or the way its parts are arranged, the brain is a machine that is capable of creating an "I." Brains can summon mental worlds into being, and computers can't.

But might not scientists be able one day to build a machine in the laboratory with the same remarkable capacity? I doubt it. But if they do, that machine will be, chances are, an exact replica of the brain itself.

That said, don't sell computers short. What's important about Deep Blue's success is what it tells us about the nature of computer science. We like to think of it as a fast-moving field. In fact, it is plodding but not easily discouraged. In the 1950s, many scientists decided that chess playing was an area in which computers could make rapid headway. Some predicted the imminent coming of a world-champion computer. But the problem turned out to be much harder than they imagined, as did many other problems in artificial intelligence. Outsiders tended to write the whole effort off; computer scientists, they figured, talked a good game but couldn't deliver. The researchers themselves dug in their heels, set to work and produced Deep Blue. Progress has been made on other long-standing problems also: getting computers to translate English into Russian, for example, or to identify objects by sight.

Simulating thought in general, as opposed to solving a particular, sharply defined problem, has proved considerably harder. One of the biggest obstacles has been technologists' naivete about the character of human thought, their tendency to confuse thinking with analytical problem solving. They forget that when you look out the window and let your mind wander, or fall asleep and dream, you are also thinking. They tend to overlook something that such mind-obsessed poets as Wordsworth and Coleridge understood two centuries ago: that thought is largely a process of stringing memories together, and that memories are often linked by emotion. No computer can achieve artificial thought without achieving artificial emotion too. But even in that arcane field, some progress has been made.

The key technique behind Deep Blue is "parallel computing." To solve a hard problem fast, use lots of computers simultaneously. Deep Blue is a computer ensemble: 32 general-purpose computers, each one attached to eight special-purpose processors. Parallel computing used to be (believe it or not) controversial. Some computer scientists were worried that programmers wouldn't be able to manage lots of computers simultaneously. In retrospect, it was a piece of cake.

The more powerful your computer, the more sophisticated the behavior it can imitate. In the long run I doubt if there is any kind of human behavior computers can't fake, any kind of performance they can't put on. It is conceivable that one day, computers will be better than humans at nearly everything. I can imagine that a person might someday have a computer for a best friend. That will be sad—like having a dog for your best friend but even sadder.

Computers might one day be capable of expressing themselves in vivid prose or fluent poetry, but unfortunately they will still be computers and have nothing to say. The gap between human and surrogate is permanent and will never be closed. Machines will continue to make life easier, healthier, richer and more puzzling. And human beings will continue to care, ultimately, about the same things they always have: about themselves, about one another and, many of them, about God. On those terms, machines have never made a difference. And they never will.

Discussion and Assignments

1. What's the distinction between a computer performing or simulating behavior, and a computer that is thinking for Gelernter? What is the relation between emotion, memory, and thought? How do these factors relate to computers and thought?
2. Gelernter claims people often confuse thinking with analytical problem solving. What does he mean by this?
3. When addressing whether Deep Blue has a mind or can think, Gelernter states the following: "Deep Blue is just a machine. It doesn't have a mind any more than a flowerpot has a mind." Let's take this as his conclusion, that is, that Deep Blue does not have a mind (let's leave out the flowerpot). What's the strongest piece of evidence he offers to support his conclusion? In a paragraph explain why you think it's strong. What's the weakest piece of evidence he offers to support his conclusion? In a paragraph explain why you think it's weak.
4. How well does Gelernter consider the views of his critics?

2.6 Fair Game

WALTER GOODMAN AND BENNET GOODMAN

When Microchips Meet Poker Chips

AS FATE PROGRAMMED IT, we learned of Garry Kasparov's loss to Deep Blue while in Las Vegas to audit the 28th annual World Series of Poker. Hardly had the world's greatest chess player fallen to IBM computer RS/6000 SP than 312 of the world's greatest poker players plunked down $10,000 apiece at Binion's Horseshoe to begin a four-day no-limit tournament that would bring the winner $1,000,000.

Even before Grandmaster Kasparov started whining, everybody and his sister had taken to speculating over whether a machine capable of analyzing 200 million chess positions a second is actually "thinking" and so may triumph in other contests that once seemed to require an inimitably human consciousness. But in Las Vegas the poker player's reaction was a horselaugh, directed both at the elitists of the chessboard and the wonks of the computer board.

Granted, chess is the more intellectual, classical, elegant game, definitely more upscale. With all the trappings of royalty and all the trapping of kings and queens, it is a ceremony of aristocratic pretensions that revolutionary theorists have been known to play in jail in interludes between plotting to overthrow the regime. It's a game for the affected and the disaffected.

If chess gets its cachet from the fact that everything is visible, poker gets its appeal from how much is concealed. Chess is a struggle between long-term strategists with perfect knowledge of an opponent's every move if not always his ultimate intentions. Poker is a gamble based on incomplete information, psychological analysis, money management, mistrust of your fellow man, and faith in the cards.

The chess player looks beyond the moment's facts into a distant horizon. The poker player's vision is narrow—in the version of the game played at the World Series, Hold 'Em, he concentrates on just the two cards in his hand and the five common cards on the table. As usually played in more or less friendly encounters, poker is an evening of brief, unrelated battles. Only rarely, as at the World Series, and then only for big-money gamblers, does it extend as long as four days and become a war of annihilation.

There isn't anything elegant about poker; this populist pastime is played everywhere in all sorts of whacky variations for all sorts of stakes by people without advanced degrees, impressive IQS or particularly high brows. Many schools are proud of their chess teams. Where is the school that has ever fielded a poker team?

Yet the laugh around Las Vegas in May was on the chess masters or grandmasters or whatever they like to call themselves, at the news that the world's greatest human player had been brought to a near breakdown by a machine. When Dr. C. J. Tan, the Deep Blue project manager, said the victory "shows what technology can do for man and how far we can take it," to us it sounded like a challenge. Take it to Las Vegas if you dare, Dr. Tan.

The Art of the Bluff

Poker players remain confident that if IBM comes up with a poker-playing computer for the 1998 World Series—call it Deep Red—it would be battered silly by some good old boy with a vocabulary composed largely of four-letter words. Deep Red's problem would not be with the odds on getting the straight or flush it is after. Any machine worth the name could call them up in the flick of a card. But every practiced human player, too, has the odds embedded in his mind; he is more likely to forget his name or anyway his wife's name than those numbers. Yet he also knows that playing strictly by the odds in a serious-money game is an invitation to disaster.

A main challenge for the computer programmers is the bluff, whether carefully set up or hastily improvised, whether by design or by inadvertence or just for the kick of it. A computer can no doubt be programmed to bluff under certain

From The New Leader *LXXX, no. 10 (1997): 7. Reprinted with permission.*

circumstances or at certain intervals or even randomly. But can it conceal its method from players for whom bluffing is mother's milk? And can the machine recognize someone else's bluff? Can it defend itself against the conjunction of money, position, personality, and the constantly shifting tactics of six or seven seasoned opponents?

If the game were made up exclusively of IBM creations, after a few hands each of them could be adjusted to react to the patterns of play already revealed. But what marks the human player at the World Series level is his purposeful unpredictability. He makes deviousness an art.

In deciding whether to meet a big bet from a nonmachine, Deep Red will have to register not only numerical matters, like odds and the sum at stake, but also the player's style, including his weaknesses as disclosed by what the poker fraternity calls "tells." These are the giveaway expressions or gestures or tics that tell whether the big bettor is holding a powerful hand or a worthless one. The best human players can scent weakness in the quiver of the word "Raise!", and once they get a whiff they can be counted on to counterattack with an atomic overraise.

Although the computer is blind to the tells of others, it is itself notoriously incapable of blinking or breathing hard or sweating and so has no giveaway tells of its own. Playing without emotion, it cannot physically reveal its tactics. A further advantage enjoyed by the computer is that it never goes on tilt when disaster strikes. Deep Blue, unaware it had lost the first game to Champion Kasparov, was able to start the second game with its usual matter-of-fact brute power. Once Kasparov lost that second game, he was rattled, as even the most poker-faced poker player may be when he loses a big pot, and that may have had an effect on his later play.

But can anything approaching the top players' astute observation and decisive action be programmed into a computer? Can Big Red be trained to react correctly to the sudden tactical switch or burst of imagination or piece of mischief or show of eccentricity? And how, in competition with players who are alert to every nuance of play, can the computer defend itself against its own built-in rigidities? IBM may be tempted to revert to the famous 19th-century touring chess machine that had a human being inside it calling the moves.

The Defeat of Logic

Playing against amateurs—say, in our Friday game—should be much more rewarding for Deep Red. Given our general frivolity, over the long run a prudently programmed computer would surely prevail. But the programmer would have to resist the temptation to stray from the odds in an effort to meet the oddities of our group; that might end up with Deep Red being consigned to the mental institution that paternal IBM no doubt maintains for overprogrammed computers. Probably by the end of a day's play, Deep Red would have learned not to try to bluff brave Ron and not to fail to bluff prudent Harold. What, though, could the machine do about antic Charles, whose method of play seems to depend on what he has had for dinner?

Our vagaries defy logic. At one moment any of us may bet on nothing; at another we may raise on anything. Or suddenly, with prospects good, we'll fold. To understand our play, you'd have to talk to our analysts. Our strength against the computer, that product of rationality, would be our irrationality. In virtually every hand someone is playing a hunch. You never know; the player never knows. Over time we have figured out how, at least now and then, to assess our friends' behavior even when it is inexplicable. Can the most advanced calculator adapt to spontaneous, sometimes unconscious bets and raises?

If it tried to counter our styles of play, the strictly logical Big Red would find itself treating lunatics as though their actions were part of a grand design or at least as if they made some sort of sense. Simply misreading the cards, as players on our level frequently do, could absolutely confound a machine whose calculations have no place for that sort of human failing. Programmers would spend days searching for the significance of Fred's wishfully discerning a straight where there is merely a pair, or drawing to a nonexistent flush possibility and coming up with a full house.

Which brings us to the matter of luck. Over the long run, granted, the machine, like any sensible player, will do much better than the fish. But on a given day or the few days that make up a tournament, as every exasperated loser can attest, luck often prevails.

In amateur games, at stakes modest enough so that one can afford to hang around for the price of a small bet or two, the looser players not infrequently wipe out those who play by the book. The last card falls and the gent who should have dropped at the start finds he has been blessed against all odds and takes the pot. Unless there is something to Grandmaster Kasparov's intimations of IBM hanky-panky, Deep Red's programmers will not be able to supply their champion with magic cards.

Our advice, then, IBM, is not to load too much into Deep Red. Whatever its mode of attack, it can be pretty sure that most run-of-the-mill players will not even notice, much less adapt to it. Against people like us, its power will lie in its ability to ignore our quirks, to rely on our natural blunders and just play the cards. If it loses a session or three, it won't even know it, and if it stays with us for a few months, it is bound to be a winner.

But come on, Deep Red, all 1.4 tons of you. Come to Binion's next May, put up your stockholders' $10,000 and play with the big boys. Or, if you would prefer to start out with something less daunting, there's always our Friday at-homes, not too far from IBM headquarters. If Deep Red can figure out what shallow Fred is up to, it deserves the name of grandmaster.

Discussion and Assignments

1. What is it about bluffing in poker that makes it difficult for a computer to compete with humans?
2. What do the Goodmans mean when they say the strength of a seasoned poker player against a computer is his or her "irrationality"?
3. What do the Goodmans say about playing the odds in poker? Is it wise to always play the odds? Did Deep Blue play the odds in chess? What does playing the odds have to do with artificial intelligence?
4. A computer can beat the world champion in chess but, according to the Goodmans, can't come close to beating a seasoned poker player at his game. In what way is this comparison instructive with respect to computers and artificial intelligence?
5. According to the Goodmans, are poker players always conscious of their own decisions when playing poker? What implications might this have for the theory of AI? Does their claim have implications for understanding human behavior away from the poker tables? Can you imagine a computer possessing unconscious motivation like humans?

2.7 Be Afraid: The Meaning of Deep Blue's Victory

CHARLES KRAUTHAMMER

What we have is the world's best chess player vs. Garry Kasparov.
          Louis Gerstner, CEO of IBM

WHEN ON MAY 11 DEEP BLUE, an IBM computer, defeated Garry Kasparov in the sixth and deciding game of their man-vs.-machine match, the world took notice. It made front pages everywhere. Great story: BOX DEFEATS WORLD CHESS CHAMPION. Indeed: BOX DEFEATS BEST PLAYER OF ALL TIME. Kasparov is so good that in his entire life he has never once lost a match—and he has been involved in some of the epic matches in chess history, including several Ali-Frazier-like classics with former world champion Anatoly Karpov.

Deep Blue won 2–1, with 3 draws. Nonetheless, the real significance of the match lay not in the

From The Weekly Standard, *May 26, 1997, pp. 19–23. Reprinted with permission.*

outcome, however stunning. Why? Because the match was tied until Game Six and Game Six was decided by a simple misplay of the opening. Kasparov played the wrong move order—making what should have been move 9 on move 7—and simply could not recover.

It was a temporary lapse of memory. (Most openings have been tested so many times by trial and error that there is no need to figure them out during the game. You come in knowing them by heart.) Such lapses are fatal against Deep Blue, however. This brute contains in its memory every opening of every recorded game played by every grandmaster ever. Deep Blue's "opening book" spotted the transposition immediately and pounced. Twelve moves later, his position in ruins, Kasparov resigned.

Blunders of this sort are entertaining and sensational. But they are not very illuminating. The real illumination in this match—the lightning flash that shows us the terrors to come—came in Game Two, a game the likes of which had never been seen before.

What was new about Game Two—so new and so terrifying that Kasparov subsequently altered his style, went on the defensive, and eventually suffered a self-confessed psychological collapse ("I lost my fighting spirit")—was that the machine played like a human. Grandmaster observers said that had they not known who was playing they would have imagined that Kasparov was playing one of the great human players, maybe even himself. Machines are not supposed to play this way.

Playing Like a Computer

What did Deep Blue do? What does it mean to play like a human?

We must start by looking at what it means to play like a computer. When computers play chess, or for that matter when they do anything, they do not reason. They do not think. They simply calculate.

In chess, it goes something like this. In any given position, the machine calculates:

"If I do A, and he does B, and I then do C, and he does D . . . then I will end up with position X."

"On the other hand, if I do A and he does B and I do C and he does not D but E . . . I'll end up with position Y."

Deep Blue, the most prodigious calculator in the history of man or machine, can perform this logic operation 200 million times every second. This means that in the average of three minutes allocated for examining a position, it is actually weighing 36 billion different outcomes.

Each outcome is a new position—how the board will look—a few moves down the road (in our example: X and Y). The machine then totes up the pluses and minuses of each final position (for instance, a lost queen is a big minus, bishops stuck behind their own pawns are a smaller minus), chooses the one in 36 billion that has the highest number, and makes the move.

This is called "brute force" calculation and it is how Deep Blue and all good computers work. This is not artificial intelligence, which was the alternative approach to making computers play chess and do other intellectual tasks. In artificial intelligence you try to get the machine to emulate human thinking. You try to teach it discrimination, pattern recognition, and the like. Unfortunately, artificial-intelligence machines turn out to be a bust at chess.

The successful machines simply calculate. And it is with this kind of calculating ability that Deep Blue beat Kasparov last year in Game One of their maiden match in Philadelphia. It was the first time a computer had ever won a game from a world champion and it caused a sensation.

It happened this way: Late in the game Deep Blue found its king under fierce attack by Kasparov. Yet Deep Blue momentarily ignored the threat (lose the king and you lose the game) and blithely expended two moves going after a lowly stray (Kasparov) pawn. The experts were aghast. No human player would have dared do this. When your king is exposed, to give Kasparov two extra moves in which to press his attack is an invitation to suicide.

Deep Blue, however, having calculated every possible outcome of the next 10 or 15 moves, had determined it could (1) capture the pawn, then (2) bring its expeditionary force back to defend its king exactly a hairsbreadth before Kasparov could deliver the fatal checkmate, thus (3) foil Kasparov's attack—no matter how he tried it—and then (4) win the game thanks to the extra pawn it had captured on its hair-raising gambit.

So it calculated. And so, being exactly right, it won.

No human would have tried this because no human could have been certain that in this incredibly complex position he had seen every combination. Deep Blue did try it because, up to a certain horizon (10–15 moves into the future), it is omniscient.

Game One in Philadelphia became legend. It was a shock to Kasparov's pride and a tribute to the power of brute tactical calculation. But that is all it was: tactics.

Playing Like a Human

Fast forward to Game Two of this year's match, on May 4. This time the machine won but in a totally different way.

It did not use fancy tactics—tactics being the calculation of parry and thrust, charge and retreat, the tit-for-tat of actual engagement, the working out of "If I do A and you do B and I do C, then X." Game Two allowed for no clever tactics. Its position was closed, meaning that both sides' pieces were fairly locked in and had very few tactical and combinational opportunities.

Kasparov had deliberately maneuvered the game into this structure. He knew (from Game One in Philadelphia) that when the armies are out in the open and exchanging fire rapidly, the machine can outcalculate him. He knew that his best chance lay in a game of closed positions, where nothing immediate is happening, where the opposing armies make little contact, just eyeing each other warily across the board, maneuvering their units, making subtle changes in their battle lines.

Such strategic, structural contests favor humans. After all, Kasparov does not evaluate 200 million positions per second. He can evaluate three per second at most. But he has such intuition, such feel for the nuances and subtleties that lie in the very structure of any position, that he can instinctively follow the few lines that are profitable and discard the billions of combinations that Deep Blue must look at. Kasparov knows in advance which positions "look" and "feel" right. And in closed strategic games like Game Two, look and feel are everything.

The great chess master Saviely Tartakower once said: "Tactics is what you do when there is something to do. Strategy what you do when there is

nothing to do." Strategic contests are contests of implied force and feints, of hints and muted thrusts. They offer nothing (obvious) to do. And they are thus perfectly suited to human flexibility and "feel."

Calculators, on the other hand, are not good at strategy. Which is why historically, when computers—even the great Deep Blue—have been given nothing tactically to do, no tit-for-tat combinations to play with, they have tended to make aimless moves devoid of strategic sense.

Not this time. To the amazement of all, not least Kasparov, in this game drained of tactics, Deep Blue won. Brilliantly. Creatively. Humanly. It played with—forgive me—nuance and subtlety.

How subtle? When it was over, one grandmaster commentator was asked where Kasparov went wrong. He said *he didn't know*. Kasparov had done nothing untoward. He made no obvious errors. He had not overlooked some razzle-dazzle combination. He had simply been gradually, imperceptibly squeezed to death by a machine that got the "feel" of the position better than he.

Why is this important? Because when Deep Blue played like a human, even though reaching its conclusions in a way completely different from a human, something monumental happened: Deep Blue passed the Turing test.

The Turing Test

In 1950, the great mathematician and computer scientist Alan Turing proposed the Turing test for "artificial intelligence." It is brilliantly simple: You put a machine and a human behind a curtain and ask them questions. If you find that you cannot tell which is the human and which is the machine, then the machine has achieved artificial intelligence.

This is, of course, a mechanistic and functional way of defining artificial intelligence. It is not interested in how the machine—or, to be sure, how even the human—comes to its conclusions. It is not interested in what happens in the black box, just what comes out, results. You cannot tell man and machine apart? Then there is no logical reason for denying that the machine has artificially recreated or recapitulated human intelligence.

In Game Two, Deep Blue passed the Turing test. Yes, of course, it was for chess only, a very big caveat. But, first, no one was ever quite sure that a machine ever would pass even this limited test. Kasparov himself was deeply surprised and unnerved by the humanlike quality of Deep Blue's play. He was so unnerved, in fact, that after Game Two he spoke darkly of some "hand of God" intervening, a not-so-veiled suggestion that some IBM programmer must have altered Deep Blue's instructions in mid-game. Machines are not supposed to play the way Deep Blue played Game Two. Well, Deep Blue did. (There is absolutely no evidence of human tampering.)

And second, if a computer has passed the Turing test for chess, closed logical system though it may be, that opens the possibility that computers might in time pass the Turing test in other areas.

One reason to believe so is that, in this case, Deep Blue's Turing-like artificial intelligence was achieved by inadvertence. Joe Hoane, one of Deep Blue's programmers, was asked, "How much of your work was devoted specifically to artificial intelligence in emulating human thought?" His answer: "No effort was devoted to [that]. It is not an artificial intelligence project in any way. It is a project in—we play chess through sheer speed of calculation and we just shift through the possibilities and we just pick one line."

You build a machine that does nothing but calculation and it crosses over and creates poetry. This is alchemy. You build a device with enough number-crunching algorithmic power and speed—and, lo, quantity becomes quality, tactics becomes strategy, calculation becomes intuition. Or so it seems. And, according to Turing, what seems is what counts.

From Ape to Archimedes

But is that not what evolution did with us humans: build a device—the brain—of enough neuronal size and complexity that lo, squid begat man, quantity begat quality, reflex begat intuition, brain begat mind?

After all, how do humans get intuition and thought and feel? Unless you believe in some metaphysical homunculus hovering over (in?) the brain directing its bits and pieces, you must attribute our strategic, holistic mental abilities to the incredibly complex firing of neurons in the brain. Kasparov does not get the gestalt of a position because some angel whispers in his ear. (Well, maybe Bobby Fischer does. But he's mad.) His brain goes through complex sequences of electrical and chemical events that produce the ability to "see" and "feel" what is going on. It does not look like neurons firing. It does not feel like neurons firing. But it certainly is neurons firing, as confirmed by the lack of chess ability among the dead.

And the increasing size and complexity of the neuronal environment has produced in humans not just the capacity for strategic thought, but consciousness, too. Where does that come from if not from neurons firing? A million years ago, human ancestors were swinging from trees and composing no poetry. They led, shall we say, the unexamined life. And yet with the gradual, non-magical development of ever more complex neuronal attachments and connections, we went from simian to Socrates. Somehow along the way—we know not how it happened but we know *that* it happened—a thought popped up like an overhead cartoon balloon: We became self-aware, like Adam in the Garden.

Unless you are ready to posit that this breakthrough occurred as the result of some physics-defying rupture of nature, you must believe that human intelligence, thought, self-consciousness itself are the evolutionary product of an increasingly complex brain.

But then if the speed and complexity of electrochemical events in the brain can produce thought and actual self-consciousness, why in principle could this not occur in sufficiently complex machines? If it can be done with a carbon-based system, why not with silicon (the stuff of computer chips)?

An even more powerful mystery about human agency is free will. Yet even here we have an inkling of how it might derive from a physical-material base. We know from chaos theory that when systems become complex enough, one goes from the mechanistic universe, where one can predict every molecular collision down to the last one, to a universe of contingency, where one cannot predict the final event. When that final event is human action, we call the contingency that underlies it free will.

I ask again: If contingency, and with it free will, evolved out of the complexity of a carbon-based system, why not with silicon?

"You Can Never Know for Sure . . ."

On May 4 in New York City, a computer demonstrated subtlety and nuance in chess. A more general intelligence will require a level of complexity that might take decades more of advances in computer speed and power. (Not bad, actually, considering that it took nature using its raw materials three billion years to produce intelligence in us.) And it will take perhaps a few centuries more for computers to reach the final, terrifying point of self-awareness, contingency, and autonomous will.

It is, of course, a very long way to go from a chess game on the 35th floor of the Equitable Center to sharing the planet with logic monsters descended distantly from Deep Blue. But we've had our glimpse. For me, the scariest moment of the match occurred when Murray Campbell, one of the creators of Deep Blue, was asked about a particular move the computer made. He replied, "The system searches through many billions of possibilities before it makes its move decision, and to actually figure out exactly why it made its move is impossible. It takes forever. You can look at various lines and get some ideas, but you can never know for sure exactly why it did what it did."

You can never know for sure why it did what it did. The machine has *already* reached such a level of complexity that its own creators cannot trace its individual decisions in a mechanistic A to B to C way. It is simply too complicated. Deep Blue's actions have already eclipsed the power of its own makers to fully fathom. Why did Blue reposition its king's rook on move 23 of Game Two? Murray Campbell isn't sure. Why did Adam eat from the apple? Does *his* maker know?

We certainly know the rules, the equations, the algorithms, the database by which Deep Blue decides. But its makers have put in so many and so much at such levels of complexity—so many equations to be reconciled and to "collide" at once—that we get a result that already has the look of contingency. Indeed, one of the most intriguing and unnerving aspects of Deep Blue is that it does not always make the same move in a given position.

We have the idea that all computers (at least ones that aren't on the blink) are totally predictable adding machines. Put your question in and you will get the answer out—the same answer every time. This is true with your hand-held calcu-

lator. Do 7 times 6 and you will get 42 every time. It is not true with the kind of problems Deep Blue deals with.

Why? Because Deep Blue consists of 32 computer nodes (of 16 co-processors each) talking to one another at incredible speed. If you present the same question to it a second time, the nodes might talk to one another in a slightly different order (depending on minute alterations in the way tasks are farmed out to the various chips), yielding a different result. In other words, in a replay tomorrow of Game Two, Deep Blue might *not* reposition its king's rook on move 23.

This is not, of course, free will. The machine is not choosing path A rather than path B. But it is a form of contingency—already a qualitative leap beyond the determinism of the calculator—and this is occurring with the computer still in its infancy, barely 50 years old.

To have achieved this level of artificial intelligence—passing the Turing test against the greatest chess player in history—less than 40 years after the invention of the integrated circuit, less than 30 years after the introduction of the microprocessor, should give us pause about the future possibilities of this creation. It will grow ever beyond our control, even our understanding. It will do things that leave its creators baffled—even as Deep Blue's creators today are baffled by their baby's moves.

The skeptics have a final fallback, however. Okay, they say, maybe we will be able to create machines with the capacity for nuance, subtlety, strategic thinking, and even consciousness. But they still could never feel, say, pain, i.e., have the subjective experience we have when a pin is pushed into our finger. No pain, no sadness, no guilt, no jealousy, no joy. Just logic. What kind of creature is that?

The most terrifying of all. Assume the skeptics are right. (I suspect they are.) All they are saying is that we cannot fully replicate humans in silicon. No kidding. The fact is that we will instead be creating a new and different form of being. And infinitely more monstrous: creatures sharing our planet who not only imitate and surpass us in logic, who have perhaps even achieved consciousness and free will, but are utterly devoid of the kind of feelings and emotions that, literally, humanize human beings.

Be afraid.

You might think it is a little early for fear. Well, Garry Kasparov doesn't think so. "I'm not afraid to admit that I'm afraid," said perhaps the most fearless player in the history of chess when asked about his tentative play. When it was all over, he confessed why: "I'm a human being, you know. . . .

When I see something that is well beyond my understanding, I'm scared."

We have just seen the ape straighten his back, try out his thumb, utter his first words, and fashion his first arrow. The rest of the script is predictable. Only the time frame is in question.

Discussion and Assignments

1. Krauthammer claims Deep Blue passed the Turing test (for chess only), that when it beat Garry Kasparov in game two it played with "nuance and subtlety." What evidence does Krauthammer offer to prove Deep Blue played this way? Do you believe the evidence proves Deep Blue passed the Turing test?

2. Krauthammer suggests that since self-consciousness in humans evolved from carbon-based systems, it might also be possible for consciousness to come from silicon-based systems. He further suggests that free will could evolve from silicon-based systems. What evidence does he offer to persuade you this may be possible? Does it seem reasonable to you that silicon-based systems could be self-conscious and possess free will? Why or why not?

3. Is it possible Krauthammer confuses the complexity of a machine with its potential to realize self-consciousness? Put another way, just because a silicon-based machine is complex and makes remarkable moves at the chessboard, does this necessarily mean it might be closer to achieving self-consciousness? Does Deep Blue's defeat of Garry Kasparov incline you to believe it may be possible?

2.8 Man's Brief Reign in the Evolutionary Spotlight

JOHN CHAPMAN

WE'RE BUILDING FASTER, smarter, better computers. Should we worry that our newest creations might surpass us in the next century?

The crowning achievement of evolution on this planet is the human brain. People have taken comfort from the idea that our brains are magically unique and could never be duplicated, never mind surpassed, by machines. However, closer observation of current trends raises some serious questions about that argument.

Human brains are constructed of readily available materials, are confined to a compartment about the size of a softball and are produced according to a blueprint contained in our DNA. Our brain, like our bodies, slowly arrived at its present state through an evolutionary trial and error process. It is conceivable that our design is bumping up against some theoretical optimum, but there doesn't seem to be any evidence of that. It is also unlikely that what we have now evolved to is the best design for our future environment. Evolution adapts to whatever present situation it encounters; it is not forward looking.

It is already clear that computers can compute more quickly and precisely than human minds. But can computers conceptualize? Can they have a sense of self and a will to live? As far as I know, nobody has even remotely approached giving a machine the will to live: My computer is totally unconcerned when I reach for the Power-Off button or threaten it with destruction following hours of unsuccessful attempts to make new software

From The Futurist *31, no. 5 (1997): 68. Reprinted with permission.*

work. On the other hand, computers are progressing rapidly in their ability to conceptualize.

To be able to think, a machine must have a substantial library of concepts and an array of criteria for accessing, applying, and updating them. So far, computers' abilities pale next to what the human mind can do, but milestones are being passed one after another. Recently IBM's "Deep Blue" computer defeated human chess champion Garry Kasparov, and another machine recently produced a mathematical proof of a certain problem that no human mathematician had been able to solve since it was first posed in the 1930s.

Both of these feats, as impressive as they are, still represent conceptualization within very limited domains. However, computers are getting ever more powerful, massively parallel computers are increasingly common, and the techniques for representing conceptual thinking are becoming more sophisticated. In time our creations will surpass us.

The ability to out-compute us, out-think us, and outperform us mechanically still doesn't elevate the machines from being our tools to being our successors at the top of the food chain. For that to happen, the machines would have to have a natural driving force: a sense of self, a will to live, and a desire to perpetuate themselves.

No doubt we will be able to program machines to mimic any of these human characteristics. We will certainly create self-replicating robots, and it shouldn't be hard to program one to beg piteously or attack someone wanting to turn it off. (They already say "thank you" and "have a nice day" with all the sincerity of your average human.) Future machines that learn on their own might initiate projects that spin out of control and become "self-driven," unpredictable, and dangerous. These wouldn't be a new form of life, though—just computer programs gone awry.

When humans finally determine how the sense of self works and can replicate emotions, we will inevitably build robots with these qualities. Human nature seems to dictate that if something becomes doable someone will do it.

What are the prospects of our understanding consciousness, the sense of self, and natural motivation? Unlike conceptualization, computing power, and robotic parts—all of which show trends marching inexorably toward massively capable machines—this last mystery has doggedly resisted our efforts to understand it.

As impenetrable as this final puzzle has proven to be, I can't believe that it won't be solved in the next 25 years. The accelerating pace with which we are unraveling the mysteries of life will sooner or later yield an answer to this one.

In the distant future, the earth may become uninhabitable for us. A collision with a major object hurtling through space could change life as we know it; and the sun isn't going to shine forever. Ultimately, if intelligent life from Earth is to last, it must find additional homes, some in other solar systems.

Unfortunately, the human body is particularly ill-suited for space travel and colonization. Life-support requirements are unwieldy, even in the short run. Creating and transporting a self-contained biosphere for openended survival is no easy task. We simply weren't designed for 100-year odysseys in search of new homes. We get bored easily and have short life-spans, with tendencies to shorten each other's after being cooped up together for too long.

Robot-like intellectual beings, which need little more than electricity to sustain life and can go into suspend-mode for years on end with no adverse consequences, are far better suited to long trips, as well as having a much wider choice of suitable colony sites.

What we are already beginning to see, in our accelerating quest for artificial body parts, is a convergence of man and machine toward a line of bionic humanoids, mechanical beings built around a kernel of biological life. But the bionic humanoid line may be outpaced by pure electro-mechanical "species" because these won't have to contend with the difficult interface between flesh and machinery at every turn. Only if the mystery of the essence of life somehow remains unsolved would it seem likely for bionic beings to prevail.

Any thoughts of man in his present body representing the final form at the apex of the evolutionary pyramid are unrealistically optimistic. The predominantly intellectual evolution that has followed man's ascendancy is about to be followed by a new physical phase in which the preeminent life-form goes from flesh and blood to electro-mechanical. This next stage in the evolutionary process is well under way and will probably displace us in the amazingly short time span of the next 100 years.

Evolutionary mechanisms for mankind are no longer passive. We are now entering the era of forward-looking, self-directed evolution. People want ever more intellectual capacity and to escape the frailties of the human body. And we will achieve those goals, or, perhaps more accurately, the life-forms that we are about to give rise to and that will supersede us will achieve them.

Discussion and Assignments

1. Chapman predicts that "In time our creations will surpass us." What does he mean by this statement?
2. Chapman's claim that our creations will surpass us is based on an assumption that the mystery of consciousness will eventually be understood, and that it will be replicated in electro-mechanical species. What evidence does he offer to support this claim? Do you believe the evidence he offers to support the claim is strong or weak?
3. Does Chapman equate understanding how consciousness functions with knowing the essence of life? Is it reasonable to assume we would know the essence of life once we know how consciousness functions? What implications might this position have for the development of thinking machines?
4. Philosophers have puzzled over the essence of life for thousands of years. And in his great dialogue the *Theaetetus,* Plato tells us the adventures of philosophy begin in *wonder.* If Chapman is correct in his appraisal that we will be superseded by thinking machines in the next 100 years, will there be any room left for *wonder* as Plato spoke of it?

Concluding Questions and Observations

1. Write a definition of artificial intelligence. (Remember to keep it as free of ambiguity and vagueness as you can.) After you've completed your definition, trade papers with a neighbor in class and offer each other suggestions about where you think your definitions can be improved. Last, examine your papers in a small group to see if you can come up with a clear, precise, working definition of AI all of you agree on.
2. Both Krauthammer and Chapman use the evolutionary development of man to argue for the future development or evolution of thinking, electro-mechanical beings. How effective are they in making their arguments from the evolutionary standpoint? In a two-page paper take a pro or con view of the evolutionary aspects of their arguments by comparing the evolution of humans from lower animals with the authors' claims that thinking, electro-mechanical beings will eventually be developed (or evolve) from silicon-based systems.
3. Put the Turing test to the test. Can you imagine a situation where a computer might act or respond like a human, but be clearly only a nonthinking, mechanical computer? Explain a situation in as much detail as possible in a short, one-page paper.
4. Is it possible we may have overestimated the importance of chess and, in turn, overestimated the potential for computers to be self-conscious? Is it possible Garry Kasparov has overestimated the importance of chess? Is it possible the Deep Blue team overestimated the importance of chess? Is it possible Deep Blue. . . .

Chapter 3

Terminator Technology

Background

IN MARCH 1998 THE U.S. DEPARTMENT OF AGRICULTURE (USDA) and the Delta & Pine Land Company (D&PL) received a patent for a method of genetically engineering seeds that, when planted, the next generation of seeds produced at harvest will be sterile. Altering seeds in this fashion prevents farmers from gathering seeds from their crops for planting next harvest. If a farmer wants to plant the same crop again, he or she would have to return to the seed company to purchase more seed. The patent is remarkable in scope, covering all plants and species, including transgenic (genetically engineered) and conventionally bred seeds. The USDA and D&PL named their invention the *Technology Protection System* (TPS) to highlight the need to protect costly new genetically engineered seeds from being taken by farmers around the world at no cost. Critics of the new technology quickly dubbed it *Terminator,* highlighting the seeds' unusual ability to produce plants that produce sterile offspring.

Why would the USDA and D&PL want to create seeds that will produce crops with sterile offspring? Of the many reasons offered, two play a principal role in establishing their case. First, they claim many farmers benefit from costly advancements in genetic engineering of seeds without compensation given to the company that created them. Producing quality genetically engineered seed is expensive. Taking the seed for free is, in effect, the theft of technology. The USDA and D&PL claim there are many negative implications from such theft, such as higher prices paid by farmers in the United States for transgenic seed. Second, since producing superior transgenic seed is costly, the only way research can be funded for other plants is to secure compensation for those seeds already produced. How is a company to create improved varieties of seeds if it's unable to secure compensation from the very people who use them?

Opponents of terminator technology claim terminator seeds could actually end farming as we know it. Most farmers in developed countries purchase their seeds to take advantage of new varieties and to avoid the cost of collecting, cleansing, and storing seeds for future harvests. But poor farmers in underdeveloped countries often cannot afford to purchase seed from seed companies that develop seed. Many of these farmers save seed from each harvest, and trade with farmers nearby and others in their farming region. This practice, carried on for about as long as humans have tilled the soil, is called "brown-bagging"—save the best seed from your harvest, use it again, and trade with your neighbors. Brown-bagging not only offers poor farmers the practical advantage of avoiding prohibitive costs for seed, but also ensures continued biodiversity through the regional sharing of seed. Shand and Mooney (article 3.4) estimate that 1.4 billion people in developing countries rely on brown-bagging for their crops. Critics of terminator technology claim terminator seeds will threaten brown-bagging, and narrow the number of new varieties of plants farmers breed for regional use. They also claim the seeds will create financial dependence of farmers, especially poor farmers in less developed countries, on corporations that will control both research into new varieties of plants and the costs for seed.

Soon after the announcement of the patent, biotechnology and chemical giant Monsanto Corporation set out to buy D&PL (along with the terminator patent) for $1.8 billion. Monsanto is the second largest seed company in the world with revenues in excess of $1 billion per annum. But in the midst of one of the longest corporate mergers in U.S. history, Monsanto suddenly announced it would not purchase D&PL. For over a year Monsanto had experienced intense criticism over its intention of marketing terminator seeds. In an unusual encounter, the president of the Rockefeller Foundation, Gordon Conway, expressed his reservations with the technology in a speech directly to the Monsanto board of directors. In response to growing criticism, on October 4, 1999, Monsanto CEO Robert Shapiro sent an open letter to Conway stating that Monsanto would no longer pursue technologies rendering seeds sterile. In a related development, the Consultative Group on International Agricultural Research (CGIAR), the world's largest international agricultural research network, came out forcefully against terminator seeds in late 1998 by banning seed sterilization technology in its breeding programs.

Though the USDA and D&PL jointly hold the patent on "Terminator," D&PL holds exclusive licensing rights to the invention. D&PL is the largest cotton seed company in the world and holds the largest portion of the U.S. cotton seed market at over 70 percent. Annual sales at D&PL in 1997 were over $183 million. The USDA and D&PL have applied for terminator technology patents in at least 78 countries. The seeds could be commercially marketed possibly as early as 2004. Unlike Monsanto and AstraZeneca, a large UK firm, both of which have rejected commercial sale of terminator seeds, D&PL intends to establish licensing agreements that would market the seeds worldwide. They have spoken of applying terminator technology to staple crops such as rice and wheat, and other "minor" crops like tomatoes. D&PL also plans to apply it to cotton, the crop that forms the financial backbone of the company. The USDA (article 3.1) has stated its intention to make the technology available for public and private research purposes. Additionally, as co-owner of the patent, if terminator seeds are commercialized the USDA will earn a royalty on the sales possibly as high as 5 percent.

Readings

Article 3.1 *Fact Sheet: Why USDA's Technology Protection System (aka "Terminator") Benefits Agriculture* is the USDA's position on terminator seeds. The paper addresses issues such as safety and benefits to farmers, and offers a justification for protecting investments in transgenic seed through the use of seed sterilization technology. In effect, it details why the USDA feels terminator seeds are beneficial for agriculture.

Article 3.2 The Delta & Pine Land Company argues its case for terminator seeds in *Protecting Technology and Encouraging Development.* The article is offered by the company to interested parties as a rationale for its invention of the TPS (Technology Protection System, aka terminator).

Article 3.3 *Advantages of the TPS* is instructive in that it is basically an argument outline of article 3.2, the longer, essay version of Delta & Pine Land Company's position on TPS. Like article 3.2, *Advantages of the TPS* is part of the literature D&PL offers to interested parties to explain its position on TPS.

Article 3.4 *Terminator Seeds Threaten an End to Farming,* from the *Earth Island Journal,* is by Hope Shand and Pat Mooney. Shand is the research director of the Rural Advancement Foundation International (RAFI) and the person who coined the term *Terminator* to identify the USDA and D&PL sterile seed technology. Pat Mooney is the executive director of RAFI. RAFI is an outspoken opponent of terminator and related genetic trait control technologies developed by bio-engineering firms like Monsanto The authors and the *Earth Island Journal* were awarded a Project Censored award in 1998 by the Project Censored Research Group at Sonoma State University for their article. The award is given annually to publications and authors for reporting important news not covered by the mainstream media. It was designated the third "Best Censored" story of 1998 by the group.

Web Based Material

There's an abundance of terminator and related "trait" control material on the RAFI Web site at www.rafi.org. For our section on terminator seeds I highly recommend you access RAFI's critical, running commentary on the USDA's *Fact Sheet* (article 3.1). It's RAFI's point-by-point rebuttal of the USDA's position. The article is entitled *Dead Seed Scroll? The USDA's Terminator Defense,* dated 23/October/1998, and the author is listed as the "RAFI Translator." Duplicate this document from the RAFI Web site and include it as study material for this study section.

3.1 Fact Sheet: Why USDA's Technology Protection System (aka "Terminator") Benefits Agriculture

U.S. DEPARTMENT OF AGRICULTURE

A Discovery to Spur
New Crop Improvement

ON MARCH 3, 1998, the U.S. Department of Agriculture's Agricultural Research Service (ARS)

and Delta and Pine Land Co., Scott, Miss., a major breeder of cotton and soybeans, received U.S. Patent 5,723,765 entitled "Control of Plant Gene Expression." The patent covers technology referred to as a plant "Technology Protection System" (TPS).

Retrieved June 21, 1999, from the World Wide Web: http://www.ars.usda.gov:80/misc/fact.html

TPS uses a genetic engineering approach to prevent unwanted germination of plant seeds. The patent was based on research conducted under a Cooperative Research and Development Agreement (CRADA) between Delta and Pine Land Co. and the ARS. The CRADA was signed in 1993. The ARS portion of the work was done at the agency's Cropping Systems Research Laboratory in Lubbock, Tex.

It should be noted that ARS has entered into more than 825 CRADAs since passage of the Federal Technology Transfer Act of 1986. This act and various other Federal laws—including the Stevenson-Wydler Act of 1980 and the Bayh-Dole Act of 1980, make the transfer of new technology to the private sector and industry a responsibility of all Federal research agencies.

How does TPS work?   Like most genetically engineered plants, TPS plants are transgenic, meaning their new genes come from other species. TPS plants hold three new genes: two derived from bacteria, and one from another plant. The bacterial genes' only function is to help the newly introduced plant gene to work. Before sale, seeds of the plants are treated with a compound that activates a molecular switch in one of the bacterial genes. This switch begins a chain reaction that readies the plant gene for eventual action. The farmer plants the seed and cultivates the crop in the usual manner. When—and only when—the crop's new harvest of seed is almost finished maturing, the new plant gene becomes active. The gene then stops the seed from manufacturing any of the protein it would need to germinate and produce offspring plants.

Aside from the inability of the second-generation seeds to germinate, in all other respects the plants grown from treated TPS seeds should perform normally in terms of growth, maturation, harvest and quality. Also, if seeds of TPS plants do not undergo the seed treatment before planting, the TPS plants produce second-generation seeds that are capable of germination.

What is the commercialization status of the technology and what is the role of the Agricultural Research Service in TPS research?   The discovery of TPS was a joint invention by Delta and Pine Land Co. and ARS, which means each party is a coowner

and may act independently from the other. Furthermore the discovery was made under a CRADA. This law provides that government owned CRADA inventions will be licensed exclusively to the cooperator. Currently the two parties are negotiating a license for the use of ARS' rights to the technology. As these negotiations evolve, ARS will be an active participant in deciding how the technology is applied. ARS' involvement will ensure that the public interest is represented.

It is ARS policy that technology in which it has an ownership interest will be made widely available. Therefore, this technology will be widely available for research purposes by public and private researchers. In line with ARS policy, Delta and Pine Land Co. has agreed to make the technology widely available for sublicensing to other seed companies.

Delta and Pine Land Co. researchers are further developing the technology to ready it for commercial use. However, even the most optimistic predictions estimate that commercial cotton with built-in TPS technology may not be available until 2004.

What are the potential benefits of TPS technology?   Hybrid seeds found in corn, sunflower, sorghum and other crops provide a conventional genetic protection system that allows seed companies to protect their investment in developing and marketing new varieties. But other crops produce seed that can be saved and replanted in the next growing season. Because of this seed-saving practice, companies are often reluctant to make research investments in many crops because they cannot recoup their multiyear investment in developing improved varieties through sales in one year. Farmers will also lose since saved seed has lower seed quality than material developed to meet the standards for certified or commercial markets.

TPS would protect investments made in breeding or genetically engineering these crops. It would do this by reducing potential sales losses from unauthorized reproduction and sale of seed. The knowledge that the seed companies could potentially recoup their investment through sales will provide a stronger incentive for the companies to develop new, more useful varieties that the market demands.

Today's emerging scientific approaches to crop breeding—especially genetic engineering approaches—could be crucial to meeting future world food needs, conserving soil and water, conserving genetic resources, reducing negative environmental effects of farming, and spurring farm and other economic growth. TPS technology will contribute to these outcomes by encouraging development of new crop varieties with increased nutrition to benefit consumers and with stronger resistance to drought, disease and insects to benefit farmers for example.

Limiting the Spread of Genes

A concern has often been expressed that transgenes might escape from genetically modified plants into "wild" populations. The TPS could greatly reduce the likelihood of such an occurrence. Plants that contain active TPS genes can't reproduce. Because TPS is self-limiting, the system cannot be transmitted to subsequent generations of other plants.

What plants will it work with? The patent covers all plants. The genetic molecular switch was originally inserted into tobacco cells as a model for later research. The ARS researchers subsequently inserted TPS genes into cotton cells, which grew into normal cotton plants in a greenhouse.

TPS will initially be used with self-pollinated crops such as cotton, soybeans and wheat. It would generally not be used with cross-pollinated crops such as corn, grain sorghum, sunflower, and canola. These crops usually have hybrid varieties whose seed is not saved because it is not uniformly like the parent seed, which causes yield and quality losses. The TPS system might, however, be used with these hybrids to prevent the spread of novel genes from conventional hybrids into "wild populations." Essentially, the TPS technology gives self-pollinating crops a similar varietal protection to that currently enjoyed by hybrid varieties of cross-pollinated crops.

Commercial production of TPS plants—as with any gene-engineered plant—would require approval by USDA's Animal and Plant Health Inspection Service. Food crops must also conform to rules of the U.S. Food and Drug Administration. These approvals are expected because there appear to be no crop or food safety risks to the new technology. There also appear to be no environmental risks.

Because of the cost of developing improved varieties, it is doubtful if the time and expense would be justified for incorporating TPS into many varieties. Also, ARS has no plans to insert the system into improved plant materials it publicly releases for variety development programs and will continue its policy of an extra level of review for projects utilizing TPS genes. The nonprofit international agricultural research centers breeding programs will probably not do so either. Thus, farmers will continue to have a choice of varieties with and without the TPS.

What are the implications for small farmers in the U.S. and abroad? Small farmers may benefit greatly if the invention stimulates the extension of biotechnology to "minor crops" such as tomatoes. Many minor crops—so-called because they don't occupy a large share of the crop acreage in the U.S. or abroad, even if high-value—are limited by lack of technology to manage pests or produce and harvest the crop efficiently. The private sector sees too low a rate of return to justify the plant breeding research investment in varietal improvement. As a result, growers' productivity—and crop quality—may be lower than their potential. But the new TPS technology could change the equation.

Could the new technology hurt small farmers by ending "brown-bagging," the practice of collecting seed at harvest and bagging it to use as the next year's planting stock? Few U.S. farmers do this; it is much more common in other countries. Countries where brown bagging is common practice will still be able to save their traditional seeds and other public varieties.

Furthermore, loss of cost savings from brown-bagging also must be weighed against the productivity gains to the farmer from having superior new varieties that could increase crop values such as yield and quality, input cost reductions such as for fertilizers and pesticides, and reduce losses such as those due to pests or adverse soils and weather. Raising the economic incentive for minor crop improvement and crop development will raise the rate of return for growers. Market forces will limit the spread of TPS in the seed market to levels that are cost effective. If the cost of the improved seeds does not result in greater value to the producer, there will be no market for the TPS varieties.

Discussion and Assignments

1. Part of the USDA's case for terminator seeds is based on an analogy with hybrid seeds—at harvest hybrid seeds are mostly of inferior quality for planting, and with terminator seeds the harvested seeds are essentially the same, they are *sterile* and unsuitable for planting.

    Is this a strong or weak analogy? Test the analogy by asking how similar or dissimilar the two situations are to each other. What implications can you draw from the similarities or dissimilarities between hybrids and terminator seeds? Why specifically do you find the analogy convincing or not convincing? Does the fact that farmers cannot use most hybrid seed (e.g., hybrid varieties of corn) make the intentional sterilization of seeds more readily acceptable?

2. The USDA claims there are many benefits to terminator seeds. List five specific benefits in declarative statement form, one sentence each. Does the USDA explain how terminator seeds will contribute to these benefits?

3. Are you convinced the stated benefits of terminator seeds are as desirable as the USDA claims? Does it seem reasonable to assume terminator seeds will offer the benefits as claimed? Is it reasonable to assume such benefits must be gotten, if indeed they can be gotten, through the sale and use of terminator seeds? If you believe the benefits of terminator seeds are as desirable as the USDA claims, can you imagine any other way to achieve such benefits without the use of terminator seeds?

4. What is the USDA's position on terminator seeds and small farmers? What is the USDA's position on terminator seeds and poor farmers in second and third world countries? Does the USDA leave anything important out of its argument when considering these two issues? How strong an argument does the USDA offer on terminator seeds, small farmers, and third world farmers?

5. Does the USDA explain why it believes terminator seeds will spur development of new varieties of "minor crops"? Do you find its reasons convincing? Why or why not?

6. Most of the benefits of terminator seeds cited by the USDA, like higher crop yields and conserving soil and water, are needed in third world countries where rural farmers are often poor. But critics claim poor farmers in third world countries cannot buy seed from biotechnology companies because they have so little money. If this is true, do you think it would be any easier for them to buy terminator seeds? Does the USDA address this issue?

7. Does the USDA consider opposing points of view in its argument for the commercialization of terminator seeds? If so, how well does it meet the objections? If not, what objections should it have met, and how should the USDA have met them?

8. a. Construct an argument for or against the sale of terminator seeds. You will end with one of two possible conclusions: (a) The sale of terminator seeds should be allowed throughout the world, or (b) The sale of terminator seeds should be banned throughout the world. Use the following argument form: Issue, Definitions, Premises, Conclusion. And remember to use clear, declarative statements throughout your presentation.

    Issue: Whether the commercialized sale of terminator seeds should be permitted throughout the world.

    Definitions: (At the very least you should be defining *terminator seeds*.)
    Premises:
    Conclusion:

    b. Now that you have an argument, write your essay. Employ the argument you created in *a* in a 300 word essay. Remember to use only the material you included in your argument—if it's important to put a piece of evidence in your paper that wasn't in your argument, go back and put it in your argument in the most logical place.

9. I've outlined the USDA's argument. Examine my work and see if you agree with it. Would you make any changes?

Why USDA's Technology Protection System (aka "Terminator") Benefits Agriculture, by U.S. Department of Agriculture

Issue: Whether the USDA's Technology Protection System (aka "Terminator") benefits agriculture.

Definitions: *Technology Protection System (aka "Terminator")* means the genetic engineering of seeds to prevent the germination of seeds' offspring at harvest.

Benefits agriculture means that farmers will benefit from outcomes such as new varieties of plants that offer higher yields; consumers will benefit from increased food supplies; and the environment will benefit from more effective use of water and other natural and man-made resources (such as pesticides).

ARS stands for the USDA's Agricultural Research Service.

Premises: 1.   Aside from the inability of the second generation of seeds to germinate, in all other respects the plants grown from treated TPS seeds should perform normally in terms of growth, maturation, harvest, and quality.

2.   It is ARS policy that TPS technology be made widely available for research purposes by public and private researchers, and to seed companies through sublicensing agreements.

3.   The ARS will play an active role to ensure that the public interest is represented in how TPS technology is applied.

4.   TPS would protect investments in crop breeding and genetically engineered plants by reducing sales losses through the unauthorized reproduction and sale of seed.

5.   Recouping their investments through sales will spur seed companies to invest in research and development. Anticipated outcomes of new R&D efforts, especially in genetic engineering are:

   a.   increased numbers of plant varieties to better meet future world food needs through increased nutrition and yields.

   b.   conservation of soil and water and the reduction of negative environmental effects of farming.

   c.   conservation of genetic resources.

   d.   spurring of farm and economic growth.

   e.   development of plants that possess a stronger resistance to drought, disease, and insects.

6.   TPS is "self-limiting"; it cannot be transmitted to subsequent generations of plants.

7.   There appear to be no crop or food safety risks to TPS technology.

8.   There also appear to be no environmental risks.

9.   Few U.S. farmers brown-bag seeds.

10.   Farmers in other countries who brown-bag will still be able to save traditional seeds and other public varieties.

Conclusion: TPS technology is beneficial for agriculture

3.2 Protecting Technology and Encouraging Development

DELTA & PINE LAND COMPANY

THE TECHNOLOGY PROTECTION SYSTEM (TPS), developed through the efforts of the United States Department of Agriculture's Agricultural Research Service (USDA-ARS) and Delta and Pine Land Company (D&PL), has received significant attention since the patent was awarded last spring. To ensure the D&PL employees and others in the agricultural industry have accurate information, we have prepared this information on TPS.

Why TPS?

This technology will ensure North American farmers a more level playing field when competing in commodity production with farmers worldwide. North American farmers have been paying for advanced seed technologies for the past several years based upon the value of proven enhancements. Some of these advanced technologies have been pirated into other countries without payments by the farmers receiving the advantages of these traits, creating an uneven playing field.

TPS will also stimulate breeding and marketing efforts in countries which have not benefited from advances currently available in the developed world due to lack of protection of intellectual property. Critics of TPS say the technology will limit choices these farmers have. However, it will actually result in growers, particularly in less developed countries, having more options available to them, including high-yielding, disease-resistant and even transgenic varieties. We expect this new opportunity to present farmers in developing countries with the option of moving into production agriculture rather than their current subsistence farming.

Biosafety Realized Through TPS

Biosafety produced by TPS prevents the remote possibility of transgene movement. There has been some concern that biotech-derived genes might cross to wild relatives. This slight possibility should be prevented by TPS activated plants, as even the pollen, if it happens to pollinate flowers of a wild, related species, will render the seed produced nonviable. In addition, the nonviable seed produced on TPS plants will prevent the possibility of volunteer plants, a major pest problem where rotation is practiced.

Understanding the System

TPS is a transgenic system comprised of a complex array of genes and gene promoters which, in the normal state, are inactive. This means the plant is normal and produces normal seeds which germinate when planted. Seeds carrying TPS produced for sale to the farmer will simply have a treatment applied prior to the sale of the seed which, at time of germination, will trigger an irreversible series of events rendering the seed produced on farmers' plants nonviable for replanting. It's important to note that TPS, like hybridization, will have no effect on the seed product whether for feed, oil, fiber or other uses.

Other Germplasm Protection

While TPS is a first in biotechnology-based germplasm protection systems, there are other means of protecting genetic breakthroughs. The most common type of protection system is hybrid seed production. Although primarily a system for increased yield via hybrid vigor, it is also a protection system. Hybrids are seen in many cross-pollinated crops such as corn, sorghum, sunflower and canola. Reduction in performance and changes from the parent seed lead to little saving of hybrid seed. Farmers, recognizing the value added from increased yields, are willing to buy new hybrid seed each year instead of saving and replanting seed from their previous crop. Their purchase of new seed each year ensures quality and funds new research that leads to new and improved products.

On the other hand, few germplasm protection systems have been successfully implemented for self-pollinated species, such as cotton, soybeans, wheat and rice. The difficulty in producing hybrids, combined with costly implementation and

Courtesy of Delta & Pine Land Company.

poor product performance has kept companies from investing heavily in some of these crops.

Farmers to Receive Choice and Benefits

Farmers will continue to select those varieties which offer the highest returns and most benefits to the farmer. As is currently the case with transgenic varieties, farmers will be able to choose from TPS and non-TPS varieties. It is the expectation of both D&PL and the USDA-ARS that the benefits realized by planting TPS varieties, carrying advanced technology traits, will be significant. Many farmers will be likely to choose TPS varieties when given the opportunity.

TPS Likely to Increase Research

TPS will be broadly available to both large and small seed firms. Because of this, it is anticipated that TPS will encourage increased breeding research in many crop species and geographic areas. Consequently, there should be sizable improvements in technology. Delta and Pine Land Company and the USDA-ARS believe that this is a distinct advantage to farmers because they will have better varieties and transgenics more widely available to them.

Genetic diversity in many important crops is a real concern of both private and public breeders today. There is no correlation between TPS and lack of genetic diversity. In fact, with the increased incentive for many private seed companies as well as universities to breed crops which have not received sufficient attention in the past, it is entirely possible that diversity will increase as breeders focus on providing unique and improved versions of germplasm to farmers.

Timetable for Development

Several years ago, a D&PL cotton breeder and researchers from the USDA-ARS generated the idea for a technology protection system during a casual meeting. With research beginning in 1993, it progressed over the next few years to move the concept to reality. In the spring of 1998, D&PL and the USDA were awarded a patent by the U.S. government. The system is being developed further and we expect that it will be a few years before TPS transgenic varieties are commercialized. Though research is progressing well, there are no TPS plants, nor have there been any TPS plants of any species, growing in a field, anywhere in the world.

Measuring Success

In the end, it is the farmers who will decide if the TPS and other new agricultural technologies have tangible benefits. Seed companies and technology providers are dependent on helping farmers be more successful. If a technology does not bring benefits and increased prosperity to our customers, then they will not purchase the technology. It is in everyone's interest that more choices be available to all of the world's farmers, and the TPS is a means of achieving this goal.

Discussion and Assignments

1. D&PL claims "it is entirely possible that diversity will increase" with the commercialization of terminator seeds. List the evidence D&PL offers to support this claim. Do the claims seem plausible? Why or why not?

2. In the *Why TPS?* section D&PL claims terminator seeds will encourage farmers in developing countries to move from subsistence farming to production agriculture. List the evidence D&PL offers to substantiate this claim. Do the reasons sound plausible? Why or why not?

3. In the section called *Biosafety Realized Through TPS,* what is D&PL's position on terminator seeds pollinating wild relatives? How about a farmer's crop nearby? What would happen to a crop if it were pollinated by a terminator crop nearby?

4. In the *TPS Likely to Increase Research* section D&PL claims the following: "There is no correlation between TPS and lack of genetic diversity." Indeed, D&PL claims TPS may actually increase genetic diversity. What evidence does D&PL offer to support such claims? Are the reasons they offer plausible?

3.3 Advantages of the TPS

DELTA & PINE LAND COMPANY

Advantages of the TPS include:

1. TPS will provide a more level playing field for North American farmers as farmers in other countries will also have to pay for varietal and transgenic traits.
   a. varieties historically have been pirated out of North America
   b. transgenic traits can and have been pirated out of North America
2. Biosafety
   Prevents the remote possibility of transgenic genes escaping into the environment when TPS is activated in the crop plants
   a. volunteer seeds of TPS plants which drop to the ground will be nonviable
   b. TPS pollen which could possibly fertilize flowers of a related wild species near a TPS crop field will produce nonviable seed on the wild plants
3. Increased Returns to Farmers
   Because of the possibility of a return on investment in breeding research, many more improved varieties, in a broader range of crop species, should be available.
   a. in crops which have not been given optimum breeding attention (ex. wheat, rice, soybeans)
   b. in countries in which breeding research has not been at a level proportionate to their agricultural importance
   c. transgenic traits should be more available to farmers in crops and in countries in which they have not been
   d. farmers should be the direct beneficiaries with more improved varieties carrying higher yields, improved quality traits and more and better pest resistance
4. TPS will assist in maintaining the integrity of refugia systems in transgenic fields.
5. Prevention of seed sprouting in the head prior to harvest
6. Genetic diversity may be increased with the increase in breeding efforts among many companies and institutions

Courtesy of Delta & Pine Land Company.

Discussion and Assignments

1. This article serves as a fine argument outline of article 3.2. Notice how D&PL's prior article (article 3.2) follows the main argument points in the outline.

3.4 Terminator Seeds Threaten an End to Farming

HOPE SHAND AND PAT MOONEY

THE 12,000-YEAR-OLD PRACTICE in which farm families save their best seed from one year's harvest for the next season's planting may be coming to an end by the year 2000. In March 1998, Delta & Pine Land Co. and the U.S. Department of Agriculture (USDA) announced they had received a U.S. patent on a new genetic technology designed to prevent unauthorized seed-saving by farmers.

The patented technology enables a seed company to genetically alter seed so that the plants that

From Earth Island Journal *13, no. 4 (1998): 30. Reprinted by permission of the publisher.*

grow from it are sterile; farmers cannot use their seeds. The patent is broad, applying to plants and seeds of all species, including both transgenic (genetically engineered) and conventionally-bred seeds. The developers of the new technology say that their technique to prevent seed-saving is still in the product development stage, and is now being tested on cotton and tobacco. They hope to have a product on the market sometime after the year 2000.

Over the last four years, USDA researchers claim to have spent nearly $190,000 to support research on what the Rural Advancement Foundation International (RAFI) calls "Terminator" seed technology. Delta & Pine Land, the seed industry collaborator, devoted $275,000 of in-house expenses and contributed an additional $255,000 to the joint research. According to a USDA spokesperson, Delta & Pine Land Co. has the option to exclusively license the jointly developed patented technology.

The USDA's Willard Phelps explained that the goal is "to increase the value of proprietary seed owned by U.S. seed companies and to open up new markets in second and third world countries."

USDA molecular biologist Melvin J. Oliver, the primary inventor of the technology, explained why the U.S. developed a technology that prohibits farmers from saving seeds: "Our mission is to protect U.S. agriculture and to make us competitive in the face of foreign competition. Without this, there is no way of protecting the patented seed technology."

USDA stands to earn royalties of about 5 percent of the net sales if a product is commercialized. The day after the patent was announced, Delta & Pine Land Company's stock rose sharply. While USDA and seed industry profits may increase, these earnings come at enormous cost to farmers and to global food security.

USDA researchers interviewed by the authors expressed a strong allegiance to the commercial seed industry and an appalling lack of awareness about this technology's potential effects, especially in the U.S. South.

Impact in the South

Delta & Pine Land Co.'s press release claims that its new technology has "the prospect of opening significant worldwide seed markets to the sale of trans-genic technology for crops in which seed currently is saved and used in subsequent plantings."

Up to 1.4 billion resource-poor farmers in the South depend on farm-saved seed and seeds exchanged with neighbors as their primary seed source. A technology that restricts farmer expertise in selecting seed and developing locally-adapted strains is a threat to food security and agricultural biodiversity, especially for the poor. The threat is real, especially considering that USDA and Delta & Pine Land have applied for patent protection in countries from Brazil to Vietnam.

If the Terminator technology is widely licensed, it could mean that the commercial seed industry will enter entirely new sectors of the seed market—especially in self-pollinating seeds such as wheat, rice, cotton, soybeans, oats and sorghum. Historically, there has been little commercial interest in nonhybridized seeds such as wheat and rice because there was no way for seed companies to control reproduction. With the patent announcement, the world's two most critical food crops—rice and wheat, staple crops for three-quarters of the world's poor—potentially enter the realm of private monopoly.

In May, Monsanto announced it would acquire Delta & Pine Land Company for $1.8 billion. This means that seed-sterilizing technology is now in the hands of the world's third-largest seed corporation and second largest agrochemical corporation.

Monsanto's 1996 revenues were $9.26 billion. The company's genetically engineered crops are expected to be used on approximately 50 million acres worldwide in 1998.

If Monsanto's new technology provides a genetic mechanism to prevent farmers from germinating a second generation of seed, then seed companies will gain the biological control over seeds that they have heretofore lacked in nonhybrid crops.

Nobody knows exactly how many farmers in industrialized countries save seed from their harvest each year. By some estimates, 20 to 30 percent of all soybean fields in the U.S. midwest are planted with farmer-saved seed. Most North American wheat farmers rely on farm-saved seeds and return to the commercial market once every four or five years. Almost all of the wheat grown on the Canadian prairies is from seed produced in the communities in which it is grown. The same is true for lentils and peas.

More Options for Farmers?

Proponents of the Terminator technology are quick to point out that farmers will not buy seed that does not bring them benefits. But market choices must be examined in the context of privatization of plant breeding and rapid consolidation in the global seed industry. The top ten seed corporations control approximately 40 percent of the commercial seed market. Current trends in seed industry consolidation, coupled with rapid declines in public sector breeding, mean that farmers are increasingly vulnerable and have far fewer options in the marketplace.

A new technology that is designed to give the seed industry greater control over seeds will ultimately weaken the role of public breeders and reinforce corporate consolidation in the global seed industry.

Advocates of Terminator technology claim that it will be a boon to food production in the South, because seed companies will have an incentive to invest in crops that have long been ignored by the commercial seed industry. But private companies are not interested in developing plant varieties for poor farmers because they know the farmers can't pay. Existing national public breeding programs tend to focus on seeds for high-yielding, irrigated lands, leaving resource-poor farmers to fend for themselves.

Half the world's farmers are poor and can't afford to buy seed every season, yet poor farmers grow 15–20 percent of the world's food and directly feed at least 1.4 billion people—100 million in Latin America, 300 million in Africa, and one billion in Asia. These farmers depend upon saved seed and their own breeding skills in adapting other varieties for use on their often-marginal lands.

Biosafety Concerns

The seed industry is expected to defend the Terminator technology by arguing that it will increase the safety of using genetically-engineered crops. Since the seed carries the sterility trait, say proponents, it is less likely that transgenic material will escape from one crop into related species and wild crop relatives. The seed industry is expected to argue that this built-in safety feature will speed up biotech advances in agriculture and increase productivity.

Molecular biologists who have studied the patent have mixed views on the potential ecological hazards of the sterility trait. The greatest fear is that the sterility trait from first generation seed might spread via pollen to neighboring crops or wild relatives growing nearby. Some biologists argue that even if pollen does escape, it would not pose a threat. The danger is that neighboring crops could be rendered "sterile" due to cross pollination—wreaking havoc on the surrounding ecosystem. Given that the technology is new and untested on a large scale, biosafety issues remain an important concern.

Reactions to the Terminator

"This is a patent that is too profitable for companies to ignore," says Camila Montecinos of the Chilean-based Center for Education and Technology. "We will see pressure on national regulatory systems to marginalize saved-seed varieties and clear the way for the Terminator. More than a billion farm families are at risk."

"Governments should declare use of the technology illegal," she insists. "This is an immoral technique that robs farming communities of their age-old right to save seed, and their role as plant breeders."

To this, corporate breeders respond that the new technology simply does for hard-to-hybridize crops what the hybrid technique did for maize. Hybrid seed is either sterile or fails to reproduce the same-quality characteristics in the next generation. Thus, most maize farmers buy seed every year.

"Poor farmers can't afford hybrids either," Montecinos points out, "but there's a key difference. The theory behind hybridization is that it allows breeders to make crosses that couldn't be made otherwise and that are supposed to give the plant higher yields and vigor. The results are often disappointing, but that's the rationale. In the case of Terminator technology, there's absolutely no agronomic benefit for farmers. The sole purpose is to facilitate monopoly control, and the sole beneficiary is agribusiness."

Neth Dano of the civil organization SEA-RICE, based in The Philippines, sees a threat to the environment and to long-term food security: "We work with farmers who may buy a commercial variety, but its breeder wouldn't recognize it five years later. Women select the best seeds every year, and, over time, the rice molds itself to the farm's ecosystem. Women also cross the commercial variety with other rice strains to breed their own locally-adapted seeds. The Terminator could put an end to all this and increase crop uniformity and vulnerability. It poses a threat to the culture of seed-sharing and exchange that is led primarily by women farmers."

Terminate the Terminator

At the fourth Conference of the Parties (COP) to the Convention on Biological Diversity meeting in Bratislava, Slovakia, May 4–15, 1998, the Philippine resolution calling for a ban on the technology was supported by delegates from Kenya, Zambia, Pakistan, Rwanda and Sri Lanka. When it was announced on May 12th that the Delta & Pine Land Co. had been acquired by Monsanto, concerns were heightened about the potential dangers of this technology for farmers and food security. The COP has requested that the issue be considered by its Subsidiary Body on Scientific, Technical and Technological Advice (SBSITA).

A genetic technology aiming to sterilize seed threatens to extinguish the right of farmers to save seed and breed new crop varieties, and threatens the food security of 1.4 billion people. RAFI and other nongovernmental organizations are calling for a global ban on the use of Terminator seeds. Both the patent and the technology should be rejected on the basis of common sense, food security and agricultural biodiversity.

Discussion and Assignments

1. Shand and Mooney claim if terminator seeds are commercialized the seed companies will apply terminator technology to nonhybrid crops such as wheat and rice, staple crops for much of the world's poor. And this, they claim, may bring these crops within the "realm of private monopoly." What evidence do Shand and Mooney offer to support such a claim? Is their claim based on any assumptions of how corporations behave? Is this a reasonable claim? Why or why not?

2. Assume for a moment Shand and Mooney are correct in claiming that rice, wheat, and other nonhybrid crops could potentially enter the realm of monopoly control through the commercialization of terminator technology. What are the implications if such a situation were to occur?

3. Critics of Shand and Mooney would no doubt respond that farmers don't have to buy terminator seeds, that if they find terminator seeds are not profitable, or if they can't afford them, then they won't buy them. Farmers would be free to buy nonterminator varieties or to "brown-bag," as they have done for generations—nobody will force farmers to buy terminator seeds. Is this an effective response to Shand and Mooney? How do Shand and Mooney respond to such criticism? Is their response adequate?

4. Shand and Mooney claim the real benefit from terminator seeds are for commercial seed companies because farmers will be forced to return to the commercial seed market each year. Is this a reasonable claim? Why or why not?

5. a. Shand and Mooney claim terminator seeds threaten poor farmers in third world countries and the 1.4 billion people they feed. If these farmers are poor and cannot presently afford seed, according to Shand and Mooney, how can they be threatened by costly terminator seeds?

   b. Could American and Canadian wheat farmers be threatened by terminator seeds? How?

   c. Could consumers in industrialized countries be threatened by terminator seeds? How?

6. Shand and Mooney claim terminator seeds threaten the biodiversity that comes from the sharing and adaptation of seeds to local farming regions. What evidence do they offer to support this claim? Do you think the evidence is convincing? Why or why not? Does the USDA or D&PL respond to this criticism?

7. Do Shand and Mooney consider objections from their critics? How well do they do this, and can you think of any important objections they left out?

8. The USDA is a U.S. government agency supported with taxpayer funds. Do you approve of the U.S. government's involvement in creating terminator technology? Why or why not?

9. Shand and Mooney report in their article that the USDA stands to profit perhaps as much as 5 percent on the sale of terminator seeds through the licensing agreements D&PL establishes. Considering the USDA is a government agency, do you approve or disapprove of the USDA profiting from the sale of terminator seeds? Why or why not?

10. a. Reconstruct Shand and Mooney's argument against terminator seeds using the following argument form: Issue, Definitions, Premises, Conclusion. Remember to use clear, declarative statements throughout your presentation. Note that Shand and Mooney account for some objections to their overall argument. If you include the objections they will make the overall argument stronger. I have included two of the objections in the premises section so you can tuck them into the flow of the argument where they fit best. (Do they consider any other objections?)

    Issue: Whether the commercialized sale of terminator seeds should be permitted throughout the world.

    Definitions: (At the very least you need to define *terminator seeds*.)

    Premises: (A few objections follow to include in your argument to make it stronger.)
    Proponents of terminator technology claim farmers will not buy seed that will not bring them benefit.
    But with the rapid consolidation in the global seed industry and the privatization of plant breeding, the role of public breeders is being weakened, and the options of farmers are being narrowed.
    Proponents of terminator technology claim the technology simply does for hard to hybridize crops what the hybrid technique did for maize.
    But poor farmers cannot buy hybrid seeds, nor could they buy terminator seeds.
    (Keep going!)

    Conclusion: There should be a global ban on the use of terminator seeds.

    b. Now that you have your argument, put it in essay form. Write a 300 word essay arguing for a global ban on terminator seeds using the argument you constructed in *a*. Remember to include only those statements in your essay that you included in your argument.

Concluding Questions and Observations

1. The USDA and D&PL call their invention the *Technology Protection System (TPS)*, and critics call it the *Terminator*. What's in a name? Two names, but they *refer* to the same invention, and the invention means or implies different things to

different people. Does calling the invention *TPS* or *Terminator* prejudice the objective consideration of the invention from the start? Does the *name* of the invention confuse the debate concerning the desirability of the invention? Is *TPS* too vague a name, too neutral? Is *Terminator* too emotive? If you were writing this study section on TPS/Terminator for students to study in college—if you were Professor K—what would you have called the invention, and why?

2. To keep terminator seeds from germinating at harvest, the seeds need to be treated before being sent to farmers to be planted. The seed company needs to trigger a genetic switch in the seeds that will program the plant to bear sterile seeds. Otherwise the seeds will grow as normal plants, bearing seeds that could be saved and planted. The method employed to trigger the genetic switch in the seeds is to soak them in tetracycline, an antibiotic.

   In their papers does either the USDA or D&PL explain the process of treating terminator seeds with tetracycline in order to trigger a genetic switch that will render their offspring sterile? How do the USDA and D&PL address this issue?

3. Let Professor K try out an analogy, then offer your criticisms on how well he does. It goes like this:

   > The large bioengineering seed companies want to function in a fashion similar to the large drug companies. The drug companies get exclusive rights for several years to sell the new drugs they develop. After several years pass, and they have made money on the new drug they have patented, the competition of generic drugs is allowed into the marketplace. The drug companies are given a monopoly on their newly developed drugs from the government so they can recoup their investment and put additional funds into R&D. Otherwise, they would not have enough money to continue funding the development of important new drugs.
   >
   > The bioengineering seed companies want a similar monopoly on the sale of bioengineered seeds so they can accumulate funds for R&D on staple crops, such as rice and wheat, and on "minor crops" like tomatoes. Terminator seeds force the farmer to return to the company each harvest to fund the company's R&D efforts. When new varieties of plants are again developed by the companies, farmers will again contribute to the cycle of funding R&D with their purchase of new terminator seeds.

   How weak or strong do you find this analogy? How similar or dissimilar are the situations? Can our experience with offering drug companies exclusive sales and guaranteed profits on their newly developed drugs tell us anything about the potential marketing of terminator seeds?

4. Is it possible the corporate seed giants could apply terminator technology to all or most of their widely used crop seed to prevent the "unauthorized reproduction and sale of seed"? Is it possible that practically *every* sale of seed could eventually be viewed by seed companies as a *one harvest* sale or crop—even the little pack of tomato seeds you buy to grow on your apartment deck? Or is Professor K just being some kind of conspiracy crank?

5. During the time the Monsanto Company was working out a deal to purchase the Delta & Pine Land Company and its terminator patent, Monsanto decided to review its objective of acquiring the terminator patent and, under heavy criticism, eventually withdrew its proposal to purchase D&PL. During this period Philip S. Angel, a spokesperson for Monsanto, was reported to have said: "we are recognizing now that there is something psychologically offensive about sterilized seed in every culture."

Is it possible that a deep-seated feeling of repugnance or disapproval, a feeling found in many cultures, can tell us something important about the rightness or wrongness of a situation? Or are such feelings misleading? Perhaps the idea of sterile seeds just takes some getting used to. What, if anything, can we learn from the feelings Angel speaks of?

Chapter 4

Ben & Jerry's and Corporate Philanthropy

Background

IN 1978 BOYHOOD FRIENDS Ben Cohen and Jerry Greenfield started an ice cream business in a renovated gas station in Burlington, Vermont. As Ben & Jerry's Homemade, Inc., grew, the founders strived to integrate a commitment to social values into the daily operations of their business. They wanted a socially responsible company, as well as a profitable one. Good business, they reasoned, is not necessarily opposed to responsible social action. In fact, a company can actually *benefit* from it. To this end the founders established a policy of donating 7.5 percent of its pretax profits to charitable causes, mostly community-based projects, many of them related to the environment, children, families, and disadvantaged groups. The company has applied its values-led philosophy to diverse situations. One of the company's proudest achievements is its funding of the Greystone Bakery in Yonkers, New York, where "unemployable" people make brownies for Ben & Jerry's Chocolate Chip Brownie ice cream. The bakery not only serves as a gateway to employment through learning a trade, but it also provides the company with valuable ingredients. Additionally, over 50,000 Ben & Jerry's customers have become members of the Children's Defense Fund (CDF), one of the premier child advocacy organizations in the United States. "Action Stations" were set up in Ben & Jerry's Scoop Shops where customers could call CDF for free on a direct telephone line. The company uses environmentally friendly packaging for its ice cream, and is committed to using milk and cream that has not been treated with the synthetic hormone rBGH.

According to Cohen, business has eclipsed religion and government as the most powerful force in society, and the power business can utilize for the good of communities has yet to be harnessed. When business recognizes its social obligations by giving to communities, it receives in kind through loyalty and increased value through the products it sells. This is what Cohen and Greenfield call *values-led business:* community, centered, environmentally conscious business policies, coupled with returning some of the benefits of business back to communities to make them healthier. More than just saying "thank-you" to communities for their patronage, corporate philanthropy is good for communities, and good for business. Each year since 1989 the annual report of Ben & Jerry's has included a Social Audit, a standards-setting tool and management document that enables the company and shareholders to assess how successful their socially responsible business practices have been. The pioneering practice of making the Social Audit an integral part of the annual financial accounting of the company has acted as a model for other values-led companies.

At the time Ben & Jerry's went public in 1984, the founders informed the business people shepherding the company's transition from private to public that they wanted to donate 10 percent of the company's profits to charitable causes. The unusual proposal became the center of a dispute, and a compromise at 7.5 percent was reached and has been in place ever since. In April 2000 the Unilever corporation bought Ben & Jerry's Homemade, Inc., for $326 million. At the time of purchase Ben & Jerry's donated the largest percentage of profits to charity of any public company. The purchase agreement between the multinational Unilever and Ben & Jerry's requires Unilever to continue the 7.5 percent charitable giving pioneered by the founders. The agreement also includes an unusual provision establishing an independent board to monitor Unilever's execution of the charitable giving provision. The agreement also calls for the company to continue paying a premium for Vermont milk from cows not treated with the rBGH growth hormone. And Ben & Jerry's employees will continue to receive free ice cream every day.

Opponents of corporate philanthropy, like Al Dunlap (article 4.2), claim companies are in business to make money, not give it away. While Dunlap is not opposed to charitable giving, he is opposed to what he believes to be the irresponsible distribution of shareholder funds to charities that have no relation to the purpose of business. If people wish to give money to charitable causes, that's fine, only it should be remembered that giving is a *private* issue for individuals to decide, not the concern of CEOs and shareholders as administrators and owners of a profit-making company.

Yet another perspective on philanthropy is offered by Daniel Seligman who calls into question *all* charitable giving. Seligman argues, we're already giving to charities through our taxes. If you're working and paying your share to the government, you've already made your contribution to charitable causes. Seligman claims the most effective means of meeting the needs of the most worthy charities is through a thriving economy. Because when the economy is strong, there's a better chance the most worthy charities will prosper. What's the solution for Seligman? Don't write a check to a charity; put it in the stock market.

Readings

Article 4.1 Our first reading is from Ben Cohen, of Ben & Jerry's Homemade, Inc. Cohen had been the principal driving force behind the values-led business philosophy at Ben & Jerry's.

Article 4.2 Al "Chainsaw" Dunlap has had positions in large corporations as a ranking executive and CEO, and has a reputation for turning failing companies around by initiating dramatic policy changes, with little sympathy for fired employees. Dunlap has a decidedly negative view toward corporate philanthropy, claiming the dollars corporations donate to charity are taken from the pockets of shareholders. His article is exerpted from his book *Mean Business: How I Save Bad Companies and Make Good Companies Great.* He was the CEO of the Sunbeam corporation at the time his article was written.

Article 4.3 Dan Seligman argues that when people give to charities they may be more interested in the good feeling they get from the act of giving than the results of giving. Giving makes the giver feel good, and that's the primary reason for giving. Further, given the virtues of a strong economy, putting your money in the stock market may be a more effective way of giving than giving directly to charities.

4.1 Is Corporate Philanthropy Fair to Shareholders?

Ben Cohen

BUSINESS HAS A RESPONSIBILITY to make great products for its customers, create economic rewards for its shareholders and employees, and recognize its role in society. Ben & Jerry's mission statement declares a commitment to all three parts: high-quality products, economic reward and social commitment.

Corporate philanthropy is just one part of our social commitment. Our formula for giving creates value for shareholders because it's directly linked to our profitability. Seven and a half percent of our pretax dollars go to employee-led corporate philanthropy. The more profitable we are, the more value there is for shareholders and the more we can give back to the community.

Ben & Jerry's is a successful, growing company because we turn our deeply felt social values into financial value. We've shown that a company can do well by doing good. Our social values, combined with our high-quality products, provide a distinction in the marketplace and create brand loyalty with customers, leading them to choose our products over the competition. This creates more financial value to our shareholders.

If people who have social concerns can buy ice cream from a company that shares those concerns and puts its business power to addressing those concerns, all other things being equal, they will buy ice cream from that company. That's turning values into value.

As well, many investors purchased Ben & Jerry's shares because the company has a social mission alongside its product and economic missions. Our annual meetings draw 3,000 shareholders, who often push the company to higher social standards. They own shares in the company because they know it has a heart and soul and values.

Investors have realized good returns by investing in values-led companies. The Domini Social Index shows that stocks screened for social responsibility outperformed the Standard & Poor's 500 during seven years ending December 1997. During that incredible bull market run, that's saying something about values delivering value.

Our share value has run in up-and-down cycles, not unlike any publicly traded company. However, when we've successfully managed all three parts of our mission—product quality, economic reward and social commitment—we've realized our best growth cycles and share value. The better we perform the more we can give back. The more we give back the more we receive in return, building more value in the company.

From CQ Researcher 8, no. 8 (1998): 185. Reprinted by permission of Congressional Quarterly.

Discussion and Assignments

1. Cohen opens his paper with the claim that business has three responsibilities. Do you agree with him? Why or why not?

2. Cohen claims the profitability of Ben & Jerry's is linked to its social commitment. How is this so? Do you find this claim persuasive? Why or why not?

3. Cohen states that people with social concerns will buy products from companies that share the same concerns, all things being equal with the products. Do you think this is the case? Do you think this is a significant factor in the overall context of individuals purchasing products? How often do social concerns play a part in which product you decide to purchase? Do you think social concerns could play a bigger part in the future?

4. Cohen states that Ben & Jerry's mission statement has three parts: high-quality products, economic reward, and social commitment. The social commitment is built into the company's everyday operations, as well as in its charitable giving. How feasible would it be for other companies to do the same? Can you think of any examples of how companies might exhibit such a commitment?

5. Cohen assumes Ben & Jerry's, and business in general, has a responsibility to society to help make communities better. Do you agree that companies have this obligation? In a 300 word essay make a case for or against companies having a responsibility for contributing to communities to make them better places to live.

6. What are the two strongest pieces of evidence Cohen offers in support of his argument that corporate giving is fair to shareholders? Explain in a paragraph on each why they are strong. What's the weakest piece of evidence Cohen offers in support of his argument that corporate giving is fair to shareholders? In a paragraph explain why it's weak.

7. Put Cohen's argument in the following argument form: Issue, Definitions, Premises, Conclusion. Remember to use only clear, declarative statements in your presentation.

   Issue: Whether corporate giving is fair to shareholders.
   Definitions:
   Premises:
   Conclusion:

8. To what degree does Cohen emphasize the *profitability* of charitable giving for a company, as opposed to making an *ethical* argument that a company has an *obligation* to give? Is his argument strictly a business affair, an argument to convince you that charitable giving is profitable? Or is his argument an *ethical* argument as well, that giving is also *the right thing to do?* Imagine a corporate CEO says his company makes plenty of money and that his company isn't interested in giving to charitable causes. And besides, he's not convinced charitable giving would be profitable for his company as Cohen claims. Is there anything in Cohen's argument—an ethical requirement or justification—that might persuade the CEO his company should give anyway? According to Cohen, does corporate philanthropy bring rewards other than financial ones?

4.2 Excerpt from *Mean Business*

ALBERT J. DUNLAP

IF YOU'RE IN BUSINESS, you're in business for one thing—to make money. You must do everything fiducial, legal, and moral to achieve that goal. And making excellent products that are expertly marketed is the primary way of making money.

Executives who run their businesses to support social causes—such as Ben & Jerry's or The Body Shop—would never get my investment dollars. They funnel a portion of profits into things like saving the whales or Greenpeace. That is not the essence of business. If you want to support a social cause, if you have these other agendas, join Rotary International.

I have no problem with giving. I've left in my estate the largest gift ever to be presented to my alma mater, West Point. And Judy and I give money regularly to hospitals and animal shelters. But it's *our* money, *we* earned it.

Corporate charity exists so that CEOs can collect awards, plaques, and honors, so they can sit on a dais and be adored. But that is not what the shareholder is paying them a million bucks a year—plus stock options and bonuses—to do!

Show me a chief executive who's on five boards and who lends his or her name, prestige, and time to fifteen community activities, and I'll show you a company that's underperforming. A chief executive is paid to run the company. *That's* the CEO's job. Corporations become woefully inadequate when CEOs think they are great social messiahs.

My distaste for corporate giving began as I worked my way up the ladder at American Can in the 1970s. American Can gave away scads of shareholder money. As a representative of the Connecticut-based company, an executive such as myself could have gone to a charity event every night of the week in New York City. It was totally part of the corporate culture.

One day it occurred to me how wasteful this was, and not just from a financial angle. If you went into the city midweek and had to be at work the next morning, you couldn't help but be tired and unproductive—two big fat strikes against the shareholders.

Let's assume that a corporation creates $5 billion worth of value and that its shareholders all sell their stock. If the tax on that increased capital is 30 percent, that's $1.5 billion the shareholders would give to government. Much of that money will go to social causes. Isn't it better for $1.5 billion to go to social causes in that manner than for a corporation to waste its time and resources trying to duplicate the purpose of other agencies?

This policy is no different from the one I enforced with the publicly held companies Sir James Goldsmith and Kerry Packer ran.

Goldsmith, for example, was a most generous benefactor who gave large sums of money to his favorite charities through a foundation. He earned his knighthood for his steadfast devotion to ecology and the environment. But it was his personal money to give, not the investment of his shareholders. He would say to me, "My dear boy, I am going to make a donation of $500,000, but it's my money."

I know people look at me and say, "He's against corporations giving to charity? What a cheap SOB!" But that money is not mine to give. I have no right to give away a shareholder's money, but I have every right to give away my own money.

Whether the United Way or the Red Cross should be supported is a decision that should be made by individuals. Why should the chairman of a company make a decision about the worthiness of a charity on behalf of shareholders? It would be like saying, 'We, the company, know which causes are worth supporting better than you do, so we will make that decision for you."

From Mean Business *by J. Dunlap. Reprinted by permission of Time Books, a division of Random House, Inc.*

Discussion and Assignments

1. According to Dunlap, why does a business exist? How does his view differ from Cohen's view?
2. Dunlap claims corporate charity exists so CEOs can be adored. Do you find this to be a reasonable claim? Why or why not? Does it sound like this is the case with Ben & Jerry's? Even if CEOs are adored, why would it matter?
3. Dunlap claims when companies contribute to charities they are giving away shareholders' money which they have no right to give away. Do you find this objection to corporate philanthropy persuasive? Why or why not?
4. Does leaving a sizable piece of a large estate to West Point after you die, as Dunlap is doing, meet your definition of *charitable giving?* Is this the type of charitable giving Ben Cohen has in mind? Are these two guys on the same page?
5. Judging from Dunlap's argument, what kind of responsibility does business have to society?
6. Dunlap claims when people sell their shares in a company their taxes then go to the government which, in turn, puts the money to work for the benefit of society. What do you find most persuasive about this line of argument? What do you find least persuasive about this line of argument?
7. What are the two strongest pieces of evidence Dunlap offers to support his argument that charitable giving is not fair to shareholders? In a paragraph on each explain why they are strong. What's the weakest piece of evidence he offers in support of his argument that corporate giving is unfair to shareholders? In a paragraph explain why it's weak.
8. Put Dunlap's argument in the following form: Issue, Definitions, Premises, Conclusion. Remember to use clear, declarative statements throughout your presentation.

   Issue: Whether corporate giving is fair to shareholders.
   Definitions:
   Premises:
   Conclusion:

4.3 Is Philanthropy Irrational?

DAN SELIGMAN

AL GORE HAS BEEN GETTING HAMMERED for his cheapskate approach to charity, and it is easy to understand why. On reported income of just under $200,000—a level at which average contributions approach $8,000—Al gave $353 last year. That figure is lower than the average for *all* American households and seems weirdly at variance with a well-advertised social conscience centered on saving the earth and quite a lot more.

You can't resist a certain amount of gloating over Al's treatment by the media, in which "cheap veep" (*U.S. News & World Report*) has been about par for the course. Nevertheless, this could be an appropriate time to make a contrarian statement about charitable giving.

There is an emerging case against it. It begins by noting that the $120 billion or so given annually by Americans is sustained by motives far less

From Forbes *161, no. 11 (1998): 94. Reprinted by permission of* Forbes *Magazine. © Forbes, Inc. 1999.*

altruistic than generally assumed. Furthermore, the money no longer goes primarily to the poor and dispossessed. Charitable giving is still a sacred cause to many because of its centuries-old association with aid to the indigent. That thought is, however, way out of date.

Talk about charity with economists who have given the matter some thought and you will come away with several skeptical questions about giving. Question number one, the most long-winded, asks whether there isn't something profoundly irrational at the core of it all.

We live in a world in which rational people buy no-load mutual funds, use discount brokers and scream if the quote on a stock purchase is an eighth of a point too high.

We take it for granted that rational people maximize returns. Why, then, do they give away thousands of dollars? Since dollars are totally fungible, you can't just say that charity is another realm. The $200 you give to the local symphony instantly wipes out (aftertax) that eighth of a point you possibly saved when you bought $100,000 worth of IBM.

The economists who have written about charity—there are not too many of them—tend to see charitable giving as a form of consumption. This seems somewhat counterintuitive. One would suppose that the beneficiaries, not the givers, are the consumers in a charitable transaction. Yet the economists' underlying thought is clear enough: People gain satisfaction from charitable giving. It makes them feel good, and they tend to consume more of this feeling as their incomes rise. Nobel laureate Gary Becker has written that the income elasticity of demand for giving may be 2.0 or possibly even 3.0—i.e., a 10% increase in income would result in a 20% or 30% increase in charitable giving.

In one sense, this is all perfectly rational. If charity makes you feel better, then you are certainly getting something for your money, and the mystery delineated above—why do penny-pinching investors give away sizable sums to charity?—has been solved. But note a critical detail: If the feel-good test is the one we apply, then charity remains profoundly irrational for those like Al Gore, who evidently feel better when contributing less.

Is it really the case that most charitable giving in the U.S. is driven by feel-good thinking? Apparently so. For an ingenious exposition of the case, listen to Steven Landsburg, an economist at the University of Rochester who is guaranteed to be interesting any time the subject is economic incentives. He elaborated in a January 1997 article in the on-line magazine *Slate*.

His argument centers on a peculiar fact about charitable giving in America. Survey data show something like two-thirds of American households give to charity. About one-quarter of these households give $100 or less. Another one-quarter give $1,000 or more. The average for all givers is around $700, i.e., about twice the cheap veep figure. But here is what's peculiar: The data also show that Americans tend to spread their giving among a number of different causes. The irrationality starts right here, says Landsburg. The efficient giver would not spread his charitable budget over many different causes because (a) recipients gain nothing from being part of a diversified portfolio and (b) the donor would end up giving less than he might to the cause he rates best. In giving, unlike investing, diversifying makes no sense.

But that assumes the donor's main concern is the stated object of his beneficence. If the main concern is, instead, the donor's own feeling of well-being, then it does make sense to diversify. As Landsburg states the choice: "You can puff yourself up with thank-you notes from a dozen organizations, or you can be truly charitable by concentrating your efforts where you believe they will do the most good."

Memorable moment in a recent conversation with Landsburg: I asked him whether he gave to charity himself, and he replied, "I do, and I can't figure out why."

This brings us to question number two: Why should I contribute voluntarily to programs aiding the poor when I am already contributing involuntarily—via taxes—to the government's own antipoverty efforts?

It seems that I am not alone in asking this question. Among economists asking it forcefully is Russell Roberts, a professor at Washington University's John M. Olin School of Business. Roberts has written widely on charity and is especially famous for a paper that appeared back in 1984 in the *Journal of Political Economy*.

The paper illuminates the change in charitable giving that began with the emergence of big government in the 1930s. Until the New Deal, charity was more or less synonymous with helping the indigent. There were endless societies to help the Jewish poor, the Hungarian poor, destitute seamen, husbandless mothers—or just the poor in general. The New York Association for Improving the Condition of the Poor was founded in 1843, and for 96 years it arranged transfer payments from society's winners to its losers. But like countless other charities, this one was undone by the New Deal, which converted transfer payments into a federal government activity.

Roberts' data show that the crucial years were 1932 to 1935. Figures for 120 urban centers in those years show government "relief" payments rising from $315 million to more than $1 billion. In the same period, private funds available for the poor declined from $72 million to $15 million. Private charity targeted on the poor has never recovered. Says Roberts: "It just fell off the cliff."

What took its place? Mainly charity that the middle class identifies with. The single largest category, accounting for close to half the $120 billion of charitable giving, is religion—e.g., contributions to your place of worship. Other heavy hitters are educational institutions, like your college; hospitals and assorted medical causes; museums, symphonies, libraries, parks and zoos.

And now for question number three, possibly the most subversive of all: Is it really clear that voluntary contributions to the nonprofit charitable sector do more for human well-being than investments in the profit-seeking sector? If you have a spare $10,000, are you doing more good by putting it in the stock market or donating it to an average charity?

It is hard to answer the question definitively, but some highly reputable economists share my own unpopular hunch about the right answer. One of them is Donald Boudreaux, who heads the Foundation for Economic Education in Irvington, N.Y. and makes some compelling points. For openers, he observes, the profit-seekers are at least passing the test of the marketplace: They go out of business if people won't put up money for their cars, computers, chardonnay, air conditioners and other known raisers of living standards. The nonprofits never have to pass that simple test and are therefore free to spend billions on dopey programs to raise self-esteem or subsidize bad plays. Yes, yes, the private sector sells cigarettes, and the nonprofits include clearly meritorious public libraries. Still, it is difficult to explain why you should expect a higher happiness payoff on money served up to charities than on money put into the stock market.

Maybe Al Gore is onto something. Even if he can't admit it.

Discussion and Assignments

1. Notice how the structure of Seligman's essay is broken into three sections where he first asks three separate questions, then he answers each question with additional comments. He also has his opening remarks that sets the stage for his discussion. What are his three questions?

2. Seligman uses the words *rational* and *irrational* throughout his essay. Locate where he uses these words. Does he make the meaning of these words clear? Is he consistent in his use of the words? Do you agree or disagree with how he employs these words?

3. Seligman claims the main reason people give to charities is because it makes them feel good, that giving is, in effect, "a form of consumption." What evidence does he offer to support this claim? Do you find his evidence is strong or weak?

4. What is Seligman's point in arguing that people give money to charities mostly because it makes them feel good? Could you make a similar claim about *all* types of giving, say, like sending the kids through college, acting as a volunteer firefighter, or paying the babysitter extra money for a job well done?

5. a. What is the *function* of feeling good with respect to the act of giving? Can you imagine a world where people give to other people or organizations they care about, but then they feel *bad* about having given, or *indifferent*?

b. Professor K helps his kids get through college; Professor K gives money to the local homeless shelter; Professor K gives money to West Point; Professor K stays extra hours in his office to help students and doesn't get paid for it; Professor K gives money to Greenpeace; Professor K gives money to the NRA. He feels good. Next day, some cosmic event has changed the world. Nobody feels good when they give to their kids, the homeless shelter, the NRA. No matter what they give, no matter who it goes to, they don't feel good. Will Professor K continue to give? Can you imagine a world where the act of giving is dissociated from the experience of feeling good? Explain.

6. a. If I spread out my annual $700 of giving to several organizations instead of just a few, Seligman claims this is "irrational." Why? Because the money would be more effective if it was focused on fewer charities. Is Seligman realistic in his assessment? Explain. Can you think of any other areas of your life where you might spend your money more effectively, more rationally?

    b. Suppose you play in the local symphony—they have an annual fund drive for instruments. You also attend a church—they have a building fund. You are active in a literacy program at the local library—a few extra books for the kids. You maintain a professional membership in a philosophy organization that gives scholarships in philosophy for outstanding and needy students. You contribute to the NRA. There goes the $700. Better to have given it *all* to the church? *All* to the NRA? Must we always be so *rational?* How do you think Seligman would respond?

7. Seligman asks why people should donate money to charities when the government is already taking taxes from our paychecks and giving it to charitable causes. What is Seligman's point in claiming people already give to charity through their taxes? Does his position differ from "I already gave at the office"?

8. Someone might respond to Seligman that even though the government gives to charitable causes, personal charitable giving is still needed because there are still many ills in society that are not adequately addressed. The homeless need shelter and food, poor kids need vaccinations, public libraries need books, money is needed for literacy programs, local efforts need to be funded to save cultural artifacts and landmarks, many people need medical care but have no money. How do you think Seligman would respond to this claim?

9. Why does Seligman think it may be better to put your spare $10,000 in the stock market than an average charity? How strong is his argument for putting it in the market? Does he claim (or imply) that money in the stock market will eventually fund the same types of programs you might donate to? Do you find his position realistic?

10. Imagine everyone in your town who contributes to the symphony, the local animal shelter, the homeless shelter, the literacy program—imagine that everyone stopped giving to charities and put it all in the stock market. Would you lose the symphony, the new books in the library, the local food bank that gives food to the poor and elderly, the dental tools volunteers use at the local museum to scrape their fossils clean? Does Seligman imply such things will somehow be paid for by government or by an expanding stock market? Does he explain how?

11. What if the stock market goes down?

12. Is part of Seligman's argument based on unspoken assumptions of what he believes an "average charity" is? Does he give any examples of the types of charities that are worthy or not worthy of your money?

13. Make two lists of charities. List the ones you think Seligman would support, and list the ones you would support. What do you think?

Concluding Questions and Observations

1. Imagine we all pay our taxes, and all the companies making profits pay their taxes too, but there is still a need in many communities for adequate shelter and clothing, books in school libraries, lunch programs for hungry kids, meals-on-wheels for shut-ins, day care for moms who want to find employment during the day, and so on. Even West Point can use a few extra dollars for uniforms. Do you think it's acceptable to say the payment of taxes is enough?

2. Has business *any* obligation other than making money? Would it be desirable for more companies to integrate values and corporate giving into their daily operations like Ben & Jerry's? What do you think would happen if more companies tried?

3. If you agree with Seligman that it's better to put your money in the stock market than give it to charity, should you avoid purchasing shares in companies like Ben and Jerry's?

Chapter 5

School Uniforms

Background

IN 1996 PRESIDENT CLINTON, declaring a need to restore discipline in schools, signed an Executive order instructing the Department of Education to issue a special manual on school uniforms to all 16,000 school districts in the United States. The manual acts as a guide for districts that want to initiate voluntary or mandatory school uniform policies. With the encouragement of the president and other vocal advocates, many school districts across the United States have created voluntary or mandatory policies. A few examples include Long Beach, Phoenix, Memphis, Baltimore, Kansas City, Seattle, and Richmond. In 1998 the largest school system in the United States, the New York City schools, adopted a mandatory school uniform policy covering kindergarten through grade 6, and in some cases through grade 8. The policy affects over half a million students.

School district uniform policies vary in their details. Some cover only elementary schools, some cover elementary and middle schools, and some apply to high schools as well, though these are not near as plentiful as those in the lower grades. Most district policies, such as that in New York City, allow kids to "opt-out" if they so choose, with parental approval. Some of these provisions require the student to move to another school where uniforms are not required. Type of dress required varies; some policies are rigorous, some lenient. In many communities local businesses have helped disadvantaged kids who cannot afford to buy uniforms.

The following five articles touch on numerous issues concerning school uniforms, from freedom of expression, peer pressure, and reducing violence in schools to the psychological need for adolescents to function within boundaries set by adults.

Readings

Article 5.1 Our first reading is *The President's Radio Address–February 24, 1996,* where President Clinton discusses restoring order to the schools. Clinton believes wearing a school uniform can go a long way toward restoring discipline in schools and cutting down on violence associated with disparities in clothing kids wear to school.

Article 5.2 Our second reading is President Clinton's *Memorandum on the School Uniforms Manual,* dated the same day as his radio address in article 5.1. It is in this memorandum that Clinton directs the Secretary of Education to distribute the *Manual on School Uniforms* to each of the 16,000 school districts in the United States. The *Manual,* developed by the Department of Education (with input from the Justice Department), offers guidance to school districts that want to initiate school uniform policies.

Article 5.3 William F. Buckley, Jr. is the founder of the conservative magazine the *National Review* and was its editor-in-chief until 1990. A prolific writer on politics and culture, Buckley has authored many books, and was awarded the American Book Award for Best Mystery (paperback) in 1980. In his 1996 State of the Union speech, President Clinton declared his support for school uniforms, and Buckley thought the idea a sound one. Buckley declared his support for Clinton's proposal in the *National Review* in an article entitled *School Uniforms?!*

Article 5.4 In *Adolescent Immaturity and Trench Coat Uniform,* Leonia K. Kurgan, a psychoanalyst, addresses the issue of school uniforms from the perspective of adolescent health and the unconscious. Kids need to express themselves, even rebel, as part of a normal process of growth. But they need responsible, well-defined parameters for behavior as well. Kurgan claims a school uniform can act as a valuable psychological limit for students, especially during adolescence when the growth process is, by nature, testing its limits. She uses the shootings at Columbine High School as an example of behavior that got out of control, and wonders if uniforms might have made enough of a difference to avert the tragedy.

Article 5.5 The case against school uniforms falls to Dennis Evans, former high school principal, and now professor of education at the University of California at Irvine. In *School Uniforms: An "Unfashionable" Dissent,* Evans takes his thoughts previously published in *Phi Delta Kappan* (vol. 78, No. 2, Oct. 19, 1996, p. 139) and expands on them especially for *The Thinking Reader.* In the course of his argument Evans rejects practically every claim or promise offered by proponents of school uniforms. He argues we should be giving kids responsibilities commensurate with their age and maturity, which would include letting them dress the way they please. Kids, especially those approaching adolescence, need to learn to respect diversity and the expression of others, as well as learn how to express themselves. This encourages respect for our government and political system, and helps to develop responsible citizens as well.

5.1 The President's Radio Address—February 24, 1996

WILLIAM J. CLINTON

GOOD MORNING. This morning I want to talk with you about what we can do to break the hold of gangs and violence in our schools and what we can do to create an atmosphere in our schools that promotes discipline and order and learning.

Today I'm visiting Long Beach, California, a community that has helped to restore order to its schools by requiring elementary and middle school students to wear uniforms. I believe that if parents and school officials decide to take this step, the rest of us should support them.

Let me tell you why. As I said in my State of the Union Address, our Nation is in a moment of great possibility, a time when more of our people will be able to live out their dreams than ever before, a time of fabulous opportunity. But we all know it's also a time of uncertainty, a time when we face economic challenges, educational challenges, challenges to our family, to our environment, to the safety of our streets.

We will master this moment only if we meet those challenges together. When we are divided we defeat ourselves, but when Americans are together we are never defeated. That's how we have to meet all the major challenges facing our Nation: strengthening our families; building economic security for every working family; fighting crime and drugs and gangs; protecting our environment; maintaining our leadership for peace and freedom in the world; continuing to reform and reinvent our Government so that it is smaller and less bureaucratic, but still strong enough to serve the American people better.

And none of these goals can be achieved unless we meet our seventh challenge: to give our children—all our children—a good, world-class education. And we know that our children cannot learn in schools where weapons, gang violence, and drugs threaten their safety or where plain unruliness and disorder and lack of discipline make learning impossible. Most of our schools are safe, but no parent who walks a child to the bus stop and waves goodbye in the morning should ever have to

wonder if that child will return home safely when the last bell rings.

Our administration has worked hard to make our schools safer: getting parents more involved in schools, keeping guns out, teaching that drugs are wrong, supporting random drug testing of student-athletes, letting communities know that schools need not be religion-free zones. I have challenged our schools to teach values and citizenship through character education. And if a juvenile kills or maims as an adult, he should be prosecuted as an adult.

But we must do more, and local communities must lead the way. I believe we should give strong support to school districts that decide to require young students to wear school uniforms. We've all seen the tragic headlines screaming of the death of a teenager who was killed for a pair of sneakers or jewelry or a designer jacket. In Detroit, a 15-year-old boy was shot for his $86 basketball shoes. In Fort Lauderdale, a 15-year-old student was robbed of his jewelry. Just this past December in Oxon Hill, Maryland, a 17-year-old honor student was killed at a bus stop, caught in the cross-fire during the robbery of another student's designer jacket.

School uniforms are one step that may be able to help break this cycle of violence, truancy, and disorder by helping young students to understand that what really counts is what kind of people they are, what's on the inside, to remember that what they're doing at school is working, not showing off their own clothes or envying another student's clothes.

Two years ago Long Beach, California, was the first school district in our Nation to require elementary and middle school students to wear uniforms to class. So far, the results have been encouraging. In the first year of school uniforms, both fights between students and students bringing guns to school were cut in half. Overall crime in the schools was cut by more than a third. Just as encouraging was the way Long Beach pulled

From Weekly Compilation of Presidential Documents *32, no. 9 (1996): 366.*

together: the board of education voting, starting a uniform program; parents actively supporting it; businesses and churches and civic organizations helping to buy uniforms for the students who can't afford them; and students using their new freedom from fear and freedom from insecurity and freedom from envy to learn.

Aziza Walker, a fourth-grader from Long Beach, wrote me this letter. "It is easier to pick out what I want to wear. It's more convenient for my mom, so she won't have to wash so many colors. It also helps me when I walk home with my cousin or by myself. So I won't get shot, beaten, or robbed by a gang or just by some maniac on the street."

We have a basic, old-fashioned bottom line. We must get violence out of our schools, and we must put discipline and learning back in our schools. If it means teenagers will stop killing each other over designer jackets, then our public schools should be able to require their students to wear school uniforms. If it means that the schoolrooms will be more orderly, more disciplined, and that our young people will learn to evaluate themselves by what they are on the inside instead of what they're wearing on the outside, then our public schools should be able to require their students to wear school uniforms.

Let me be clear: Washington will not tell our schools what to do. We know the best teacher for a child is a loving parent, and the decision whether to require uniforms should be made by parents, by teachers, by local schools. But if they want to do it, we want to help them understand how it can be done. That's why today I signed a directive instructing the Secretary of Education to distribute a new manual on school uniforms to every school district in the Nation. Rather than telling schools what to do, we are providing a roadmap for setting up the school uniform policy for schools who choose to start one.

Every one of us has an obligation to work together, to give our children freedom from fear and the freedom to learn. If we act together, we can give them the chance to make the most of their young lives and to build better futures.

Thanks for listening.

5.2 Memorandum on the School Uniforms Manual

WILLIAM J. CLINTON

Memorandum for the Secretary of Education
FEBRUARY 24, 1996

SUBJECT: MANUAL ON SCHOOL UNIFORMS

QUALITY EDUCATION IS CRITICAL to America's future and the future of our children and families. We cannot educate our children, however, in schools where weapons, gang violence, and drugs threaten their safety. We must do everything possible to ensure that schools provide a safe and secure environment where the values of discipline, hard work and study, responsibility, and respect can thrive and be passed on to our children. Most schools are safe. But we must have zero tolerance for threats to safety in our schools. It is time to make every school the safest place in its community. Parents should be able to send their children to learn free of fear. All of our schools should be permitted to focus on their original purpose: education.

Many local school districts have made school uniforms an important part of an overall program to improve school safety and discipline. Too often, we learn that students resort to violence and theft simply to obtain designer clothes or fancy sneakers. Too often, we learn that clothing items worn at school, bearing special colors or insignias, are used to identify gang membership to instill fear among students and teachers alike.

If student uniforms can help deter school violence, promote discipline, and foster a better

From Weekly Compilation of Presidential Documents, *March 4, 1996, pp. 368–69.*

learning environment, then we should offer our strong support to the schools and parents that try them. We should applaud parents, teachers, and school leaders when they take courageous action to make our schools safe and free of gangs, drugs, and violence.

The Long Beach, California, school district recently found that after students started wearing uniforms, there was a substantial decrease in student drug cases, sex offenses, assault and battery cases, and fights. The learning environment improved as teachers could focus more on education and less on discipline. Many other schools—in Baltimore, Cincinnati, Dayton, Detroit, Los Angeles, Miami, Memphis, Milwaukee, Nashville, New Orleans, Phoenix, Seattle, and St. Louis—have also adopted mandatory or voluntary school uniform policies with promising results.

I thus asked you, in consultation with the Attorney General, to develop information about how local school districts have made uniforms part of their school safety and discipline programs. The Department of Education, with input from the Department of Justice, has now developed a new "Manual on School Uniforms," which sets forth the benefits of school uniforms; provides a road map for establishing a school uniform policy for schools interested in school uniforms; and describes various model uniform programs from a number of school districts across the Nation.

Because maintaining safe and disciplined schools is an urgent priority in every local community, I today direct you promptly to distribute the Manual on School Uniforms to each of the Nation's 16,000 public school districts. I also direct you to provide copies of the Manual to appropriate organizations representing parents, teachers, and school administrators, and to make it available to interested members of the public.

School uniform programs are just one of the many initiatives undertaken by local school officials and parents to improve school safety and discipline. Other steps—such as truancy reduction programs, student-athlete drug testing, drug and gang prevention initiatives, zero tolerance for weapons, assisting teachers in addressing discipline problems, conflict resolution programs, and character resolution initiatives—have also been used to improve the education of our children. The Department of Education, in consultation with the Department of Justice, should continue to develop guidance and information about these and other initiatives so that local organizations, families, and educators throughout the Nation have the tools available to make our schools safe, drug-free, and crime-free.

Discussion and Assignments

Note: This material applies to the two preceding articles.

1. Clinton cites incidents where students have been victims of violence from gang members because of the clothes or colors they were wearing, and incidents where students have been robbed or shot for their designer clothes. What relationship do you believe exists between the wearing of expensive or designer clothes and violence at elementary, middle, and high schools? Do you believe Clinton's assessment is accurate?

2. In many states, like California, school districts are given the legal authority to regulate clothing worn by students so the clothes will not become a distraction or a danger to other students; for example, clothes that are too revealing and gang attire can legally be prohibited. Do you think it's possible for a school district to accomplish the same ends by enforcing laws that allow the schools to restrict attire without requiring all schoolchildren to wear uniforms?

3. What grades or ages does Clinton focus on when discussing the compulsory wearing of school uniforms? Do you believe this aspect of his argument is important? Why or why not?

4. What is the official government position on school uniforms (articles 5.1 and 5.2)? Do you detect any inconsistency between the stated government position and Clinton's handling of the issue?

5. Does Clinton take into account objections to his proposal?

6. What are the two strongest pieces of evidence Clinton offers to support his conclusion that schoolchildren should wear uniforms? In a paragraph for each, explain why they are strong. What is the weakest piece of evidence he offers to support his argument? In a paragraph explain why it is weak.

7. In each of the two articles Clinton offers an argument in support of schoolchildren wearing uniforms. Reconstruct Clinton's argument in either of the two articles using the following argument form: Issue, Definitions, Premises, Conclusion. Be sure to use only clear, declarative statements. Work with only one of the articles; don't try combining the two. I've filled in a few pieces from article 5.1 to get you going.

Issue: Whether the wearing of school uniforms would be beneficial for our schoolchildren.

Definitions: (You might want to specify the grades Clinton has in mind when he refers to schoolchildren.)

Premises: 1. Weapons, gang violence, and drugs threaten some of our schoolchildren at the schools they attend.

2. Unruliness, disorder, and lack of discipline plague some of our schoolchildren at the schools they attend.

(Keep going!)

Conclusion:

5.3 School Uniforms?!

WILLIAM F. BUCKLEY, JR.

ONE COMMENTATOR DEALT BRAVELY with the seven general categories of national problems addressed by President Clinton and finished his appraisal with the sentence, "Why on earth does the leader of the free world have to concern himself with school uniforms?"

Well now, there are those who found that the most novel and potentially the most resonant sentence in the President's address. Flash ahead ten years, close your eyes, answer the question: "What was the highlight of President Clinton's State of the Union speech in 1996?" Right, the answer will be: Oh, that's the speech in which he came out for school uniforms. . . . To say that was the "highlight" of the speech is of course to take lib-

erties, consigning all else he said to generic political thought. The President declared in favor of health care, law and order, unity, growth, and husbandry. So does every candidate running for President. It was the school-uniform bit that caught the attention of the unwary, who asked first, What does Mr. Clinton know about school uniforms? and asked second, How is it that he intuits their importance?

Not long ago a public-school teacher in New York City wrote to *The Wall Street Journal* a letter bristling with authenticity, relating that the foremost problem in the city's schools was: discipline. In the absence of it, she complained, practically nothing else is possible. What has been

From National Review *48, no. 3 (1996): 71. Reprinted with permission.*

called the "hijacker's leverage" is operative here. Just as one terrorist can dictate the movements of a super-jet carrying five hundred passengers, so one unruly student can, for as long as he is able to keep it up, affect the climate of a schoolroom. In the late Sixties, one senior at Harvard appeared at the office of the president hours before the Commencement ceremony demanding that he be scheduled as a speaker during the ceremony. If not, he informed the stunned president, the ceremony would not proceed. A half-dozen noisy protestors, even in an assembly of two thousand, can make solemn processions impossible; as also, studious classrooms.

The head of Cardinal Hayes High School in New York made a point of it some years ago. That school—formally a diocesan school although many of its students are of other faiths, 85 percent of them minorities—has arresting academic attainments; 85 percent of its graduates go on to college, compared with less than 15 percent in comparable public schools made up of identically endowed students. It is very important, the principal told his visitor, to insist on a school uniform. Why? one naturally wondered. Because, he said, the symbol irradiates several things. The first is that the student is a member of a regulated community.

When you are in uniform, your dress bespeaks hierarchy. The symbol is very important. At Cardinal Hayes the students are simply not expected to be late in arriving at school, and punctuality is accepted as a part of the system: related, in a way, to the requirement that the students wear their simple grey jackets and pants, a shirt and a tie. On the question of disorder in the classrooms it is as simple as that there is no disorder in the classrooms. Defenders of the antinomian behavior of so many public-school students confide to you that the reason for the success of the private schools is that they simply expel anyone who is in any way nonconformist. But such chaos-defenders run into statistics: 2 percent of the students at Cardinal Hayes are expelled.

The maintenance of order, the minor conformity that issues from the wearing of identical uniforms, is always a latent problem because the schools deal with boys and girls who are going through their unruly period in life. The sociologist who some time ago remarked that a single broken and unrepaired window is an invitation to corollary shambles gave us all an epiphany. Of course it is true! we realize. Student unruliness is met in different seasons in different ways. At Eton in the 1830s the students outnumbered faculty by about 100 to 1, and the notorious Doctor Keate attempted to solve his problem by flogging a dozen students every day. We shrink from such measures, but ought to welcome civilized substitutes, and the school uniform is the beginning of wisdom in this field, and we say hurrah to the President for coming upon that insight.

Discussion and Assignments

1. Buckley supports Cardinal Hayes's statement that a school uniform "irradiates several things." According to Hayes and Buckley, what things does a uniform irradiate, and to what end does it perform this function?

2. Does Buckley imply that compulsory school uniforms have something to do with the number of high school students entering college from Cardinal Hayes High School? Do you see a connection?

3. "The maintenance of order, the minor conformity that issues from the wearing of identical uniforms, is always a latent problem because the schools deal with boys and girls who are going through their unruly period in life." Does Buckley define what he means by "going through their unruly period in life"? What do you think he means by this? Do you think he betrays any feelings or opinions with this reference?

4. What is the "hijacker's leverage"? What specific examples or analogies does Buckley use to illustrate this concept, and how does he claim it is related to school uniforms? Do you think his use of analogies to illustrate this point are strong or weak? Buckley also employs an example of a broken window. Why does he use this example in the way he does, and how effective an example do you think it is in making his point? Can you think of any other examples that would have worked better to make the point he is making?

5.4 Adolescent Immaturity and Trench Coat Uniform

LEONIA K. KURGAN

ADOLESCENCE IS TRADITIONALLY a time of trying on different roles. When I was a teenager I had two images for my grown up self. Either I would become a scientist like Marie Curie who discovered radium, or I would be another Cleopatra. As these fantasies became clearer, I realized I saw Cleopatra as a courtesan who was beautiful and fascinating; "Age would not wither her nor custom stale her infinite variety." The realities were I was not beautiful enough, nor did I want to be a courtesan, and I did not want to be a scientist and work in a dark laboratory. I did not stay with either role. I went on to do other things. I married, I had children, I became a psychoanalyst.

In the recent Littleton tragedy, Eric Harris and Dylan Kiebold also played a particular role. They were not required to wear prescribed school uniforms. Instead, they wore long black trench coats to school—the uniform of a gang called the Trench Coat Mafia. Harris and Klebold played out a particular role where they identified themselves with Adolf Hitler's values. The uniforms they wore were reminiscent of the Nazi regime. The killings they carefully planned took place on April 20th which was Adolph Hitler's birthday.

Traditionally, American schoolchildren have not been required to wear uniforms, with the exception of parochial and a few private schools. Is it because it hinders the ability to freely express their personalities? Is this goal more reachable because children do not wear school uniforms? I think most teenagers are terrified to be different. They desperately try to conform to social mores, whether it be behavior or dress code. I remember how traumatized my friend's fifteen-year-old son was when he immigrated to Los Angeles from South Africa. He was not quite sure what was "cool" to wear every day to school. In South Africa he had a prescribed compulsory school uniform he could rebel against. Here there was nothing to push against and nothing was clear. The boy suffered acute anxiety. Of course there were other contributory factors, but the lack of a prescribed uniform did contribute to the boy's unhappiness.

Many families in America suffer the trauma of feeling like outsiders based on differences in wealth, ethnicity, race, and origin. Where there are no prescribed school uniforms, the social barriers of the haves and the have nots may be accentuated. It may become painfully clear which parents cannot afford expensive clothes for their children. Not wearing a school uniform, which may have started off as an effort to be democratic, can end in a painful situation for an already vulnerable teenager. Perhaps we should rethink whether our children should wear clearly defined uniforms to school every day. Without adequate parental or school restrictions, matters can and do get out of control. Wearing a school uniform will protect children from gang attacks where wearing a particular colour may be associated with a set, for example bloods wear red.

Perhaps more basic than all of the above is to recognize the (unconscious) murderous feelings of being a teenager. Donald Winnicott, noted psychiatrist and a leading authority on adolescent and child psychology, said that in the unconscious fantasy life, growth at puberty and in adolescence is inherently an aggressive act. This gets played out in the unconscious fantasy as a struggle between the generations, a struggle of life and death where one wins and one loses. If the adults hand over the responsibility of playing this life-game too soon and abdicate at the moment the adolescent comes close to "killing" them, all the imaginative activity and striving of immaturity is lost. The adolescent is then no longer able to rebel and has his or her triumph too early.

At Columbine High School, Harris and Klebold wore long black trench coats to school every day. They were loners, taunted and badly treated by their jock peers, not accepted by the so-called "in" crowd. They resented this but contributed to it by their dress and behavior. We do not know how deeply disturbed they were. Harris was being treated with Luvox, a mood altering drug. Maybe they would have done what they did no matter what, but I wonder how the daily wearing of the trench coat uniform helped maintain Harris and Kobold's cruel and evil intent. The two boys had been preparing arsenals in the garages of their parents' home for over a year. Were the parents so disconnected from their children's lives that they had not noticed? Had they abdicated from the (unconscious) life and death struggle with their adolescent children? Whatever the reason, the two youths, instead of "killing" their parents in unconscious fantasy and when grown up, later continuing the battle with their own children, took the battle into the arena of siblings, killed twelve peers and injured twenty-five others.

Winnicott believed that to be immature is a healthy quality of being an adolescent and that only time can cure that. Maturity comes with age. Yet there cannot be the challenge of the immature growing girl or boy without the presence of a responsible parent-figure. It is important to provide children with a safer world to live in—a place with more adult controls—a place where unconscious murderous feelings can stay in the realm of fantasy and not become a hideous reality. I know that to talk with the general public of unconscious fantasies is not very popular. Yet, unless we as a culture acknowledge the presence of unconscious motivation we will constantly be faced with behavior that is violent, cruel, greedy and difficult to understand.

In the light of the foregoing discussion, the issue of school uniforms, a seemingly small thing, is not so small at all. It attempts to raise consciousness, to explain the importance of the need for responsible adults to set limits. What happened at Littleton is but one example of a spate of teenage violence and killings. At Columbine High School (which is representative of many schools in America) there was no dress code that expressed the values of the community, the school and the parents. If there had been one, it might have served as a psychological limit providing the students with security and a sense of belonging. Maybe their rebellion would not have taken such an anti-social turn. Maybe the compulsory wearing of a school uniform may have made a difference to what did happen.

Discussion and Assignments

1. In paragraph 4 Kurgan offers two specific reasons for having a school uniform policy, namely, that by not having uniforms the distinction between the haves and the have nots "may be accentuated," and that by wearing a school uniform children may be protected from gang attacks. Select one of these two reasons and in a 200 word essay support the claim as a conclusion, offering whatever additional evidence you think relevant.

2. Kurgan offers a theory of the unconscious to support her view that kids should wear school uniforms. In a 300 word essay explain this theory and how it is

related to adolescent maturity. See if you can offer examples from everyday life, outside of school, to illustrate how the theory sheds light on the developmental process of youth.

3. A critic might respond to Kurgan that there are many struggles adolescents go through while growing up, the messages clothes send being just one of them. And while diversity and value of clothes may heighten anxiety among some youth, diversity in clothes can also act as a catalyst for growth, get kids to accept differences and similarities, and familiarize them with the inevitable disparities present in our economic and social lives. Do you believe this would be a reasonable response to Kurgan's position? How do you think Kurgan would respond to such claims?

4. Harris and Klebold murdered their classmates for real, instead of killing their parents in fantasy. According to Kurgan, what connection do these acts have to the setting of parameters by (a) Harris and Klebold's parents and (b) the school and community?

5. Kurgan states that Harris and Klebold contributed to their unhappy situation by wearing their trench coats and engaging in other self-destructive behavior. She claims the situation may have been ameliorated if the students at Columbine wore school uniforms. A critic might respond that Harris and Klebold were bent on striking back for the way they felt they were treated, and that wearing trench coats was just one of many ways their unconscious minds drove them to respond. From this perspective wearing trench coats was more of a *symptom* of the problems at Columbine than a cause that contributed to the tragedy. In other words, considering how strongly they felt about their treatment, even if they were not allowed to wear trench coats, it's likely they would have chosen other forms of behavior that would have contributed to a tragedy. How do you think Kurgan would respond to such a criticism? How do you respond to such a criticism?

6. What role do you believe the trench coats played in the tragedy at Columbine? Why do you think Harris and Klebold wore them? Do you think if there was a school uniform policy at Columbine there might have been a better chance to avoid the tragedy? Do you believe uniforms can help resolve behavior/attitudinal problems of youths that run as deep as those at Columbine?

7. Kurgan states that kids need to wear uniforms to express the values of the community and parents. But this raises a disturbing question: Didn't the community, parents, and administration of the school have plenty of time to express their values *before* the tragedy?

8. What are the two strongest pieces of evidence Kurgan employs to support her conclusion that schoolchildren should wear school uniforms? In a paragraph on each, explain why they are strong. What is the weakest piece of evidence Kurgan employs to support her case that schoolchildren should wear uniforms? In a paragraph explain why the evidence is weak.

9. Reconstruct Kurgan's argument using the following argument form: Issue, Definitions, Premises, Conclusion. Be sure to use only clear, declarative statements. I've added a few pieces to get you going.

Issue: There is a need for schoolchildren to wear school uniforms in order to express the values of their community and parents, and to serve as a psychological limit, especially for adolescents.

Definitions: (Define here any terms that need clarification.)

Premises: (List your premises in their most logical order.)
1. It is psychologically healthy for children and adolescents to grow up within clearly defined behavioral limits.
2. Wearing a school uniform will protect children from gang attacks.

Conclusion:

5.5 School Uniforms: An "Unfashionable" Dissent

DENNIS L. EVANS

IN RESPONSE TO PARENTAL and political pressure and bolstered by the "bully pulpit" endorsement of the President, a number of school districts across the nation have already adopted or are contemplating the adoption of mandatory school uniform policies. Admittedly, the idea of requiring uniforms for public school students does offer some beguiling promises. Advocates promote such policies as a way to reduce gang attire and its attendant problems; they also view uniforms as a way to blur the economic distinctions among students, and even as a way to create a more serious learning environment in the schools. What possibly could be the down-side of such promises?

To begin with, the programs in public schools which have gained parental support, media attention and thus political advocacy (such as the highly publicized one in Long Beach, California) are, with rare exception, operant only in elementary and middle schools. In such settings the age of the children dictates that the problems which school uniforms allegedly solve don't really exist to any significant degree in the first place. Concomitantly, elementary and middle school age children are not as yet strongly impacted by developmental issues such as individual decision-making, personal rights, and concern with justice and thus, unlike high schoolers, they do not see required school uniforms as being intrusive, unfair and objectionable.

In California, the State education code has for years allowed any school district wherein the style and/or color of clothing can affect the safety of students and/or disrupt the learning environment, to establish a dress code specifically prohibiting the wearing of gang attire and regalia, clothing which is too revealing, or articles of clothing embellished with inappropriate language or logos. Such necessary and reasonable restrictions have been consistently upheld by the courts. If such dress restrictions are in place and if they are being consistently enforced then the adoption of a mandatory school uniform policy, while it might make a school administrator's life a bit easier, is redundant and unnecessary. (It will be interesting to see how the courts handle the inevitable challenges to mandated school uniforms since there is a significant difference between a public school (the government) reasonably prohibiting an individual from wearing specific attire because of legitimate issues related to student safety or the learning environment versus the much more draconian policy of requiring all students to dress uniformly. To avoid such sticky legal issues most public school districts such as Long Beach have to this point opted for "voluntary or opt-out policies," but besides being oxymoronic, voluntary policies simply won't work when tried at the high school level.)

Where gang members are concerned, the wearing of school uniforms will be cosmetic only, and certainly will not alter gang mentality nor reduce antisocial, gang-related behavior on or off the campus. Ironically, mandating school uniforms might even make it easier to be a gang member since school administrators and law enforcement officials will not be able to observe which pupils wear gang trappings. While a mandatory school uniform policy will do nothing to reduce the attraction that gang membership holds for some adolescents, on a broader scale it might well cause others who now use their mode of attire as a benign form of rebellion to find other more serious means of expression. Adolescence is a time when resistance to adult authority is not only predictable but developmentally necessary as teens break away from childhood dependencies and grow toward self-hood; concomitantly it is also a time when issues of fairness, justice, and making one's own decisions become very important. A mandatory school uniform policy, by taking away a realm of individual choice from youngsters who have done nothing wrong, unwisely runs counter to the developmental imperatives of adolescence.

That school uniforms will blur the economic distinctions among students is a specious argument. Unlike adults, most children and adolescents don't care much about such distinctions anyway (at least as exemplified by what they wear to school; rich kids are often sloppily attired while their less affluent classmates are often very well-dressed). Those who are impressed by economic distinctions won't have their attitudes changed by simply putting on a uniform. Do those who see this cosmetic leveling as a positive feature of school uniforms also propose to ban high school students from driving cars to school, from wearing jewelry, and from carrying money? Do they also propose to eliminate or make free all of the various activities wherein school costs truly do create an economic hardship for certain youngsters and their families, e.g., participation in school activities, going to the school prom, or buying school rings and yearbooks? Economic distinctions are part of the fabric of our society and they will not be unraveled by simply covering them with a uniform.

Finally, the notion that school uniforms will somehow create a more academic school environment and thus improve achievement has no evidence to support it. To the contrary, in my 21 years of experience as a high school principal some of the most outlandish students, from the perspective of my personal biases regarding their clothing and/or hair styles, were also some of the most out-standing scholars, leaders, and school citizens. The key word in that last sentence is *some*, because kids are not "uniform" and they are impossible to categorize by their attire. Past cheating scandals at West Point and Annapolis, sadly point out that uniforms have little to do with creating an environment conducive to true scholarship and academic achievement.

But beyond all of the above and even if, for the sake of argument, we were to concede that a mandatory school uniform policy could accomplish what its advocates promise, there would still remain compelling reasons for opposition to such a practice particularly at the high school level. Those reasons have to do with the fundamental purposes of schooling and concomitantly with the role of the public school as an extension of government. One basic reason for school is the training of future citizens. In a democratic society citizenship means maintaining the tension between individual rights and responsibilities. We should be developing attitudes in our students which will cause them to honor diversity and differences while at the same time recognizing personal and collective responsibilities to the common good. We should not be sending them a message that equates sartorial sameness with civic virtue. We should be providing our students, consistent with their maturity, ever-increasing opportunities for decision-making while at the same time causing them to reflect on the consequences of that decision-making. We should not be structuring school policies to deny students the citizenship experience of making personal decisions within a framework of necessary regulations. In my experience as a high school principal those policies which had their origin in teacher and/or administrator expediency as opposed to an ethical contemplation of what was best for students generally turned out to be ineffective or even worse, counterproductive to the basic purposes of the school. Mandatory school uniforms represent such a policy.

We need to remember that our public schools exist as creations of government. Through the reserved powers provisions of the 10th Amendment to the U.S. Constitution each state government has the sovereign power to establish and govern the public schools of that state. Local school boards exist at the pleasure of state government and must support and be consistent with state law. When a local school board decides to tell students what must be worn to school, in reality it is the government giving that order. Do we want the government/school telling us what our children must wear to school? Currently there are only two government sponsored institutions in our country that can tell people what to wear: one is the military and the other is prison. Let's not allow our public schools to become the third.

Discussion and Assignments

1. Evans states that most of the school districts in the United States that have embraced school uniforms are elementary and middle schools, not high schools. Why is this important for Evans, and what implication does he draw from this fact?

2. In reference to question 1, Kurgan believes some of the greatest benefits from mandatory uniforms would be gained in the high schools. Yet most districts have restricted mandatory school uniforms to elementary and middle schools. Why do you think school districts are reluctant to impose schools uniform policies in the high schools? Do you think excluding high schools from such policies is advisable?

3. Evans offers an interesting twist on the familiar argument that uniforms would prevent gang members from wearing gang attire to school. He claims uniforms might actually make it more difficult to identify gang members. This raises a perplexing question: what would Evans prefer, gang members wearing gang attire, or uniforms that allow them to blend in? Or is there another alternative?

4. What is the relationship of choice and adolescence for Evans, and why is this so important with respect to school uniforms? How does Evans's position on this point differ from Kurgan's position. How is it that both Evans and Kurgan recognize the importance of adolescent responsibility and choice, yet come to different conclusions about wearing uniforms?

5. President Clinton speaks of kids being shot for their designer clothes; Leonia Kurgan states, "It may become painfully clear which parents cannot afford expensive clothes for their children"; but Dennis Evans believes most kids don't care much for economic distinctions, pointing out that many well-to-do kids dress sloppily. Is this only an apparent difference of opinion, or do they have a genuine disagreement about similar states of affairs?

6. In paragraph 7 Evans states, "We should be developing attitudes in our students which will cause them to honor diversity and differences while at the same time recognizing personal and collective responsibilities to the common good." According to Evans, how would school uniforms detract from these goals?

7. What are the two strongest pieces of evidence Evans offers to support his case against kids wearing school uniforms? In a paragraph on each explain why you believe they are strong. What is the weakest piece of evidence Evans offers to support his case against kids wearing uniforms? In a paragraph explain why you believe it's weak.

8. Leonia Kurgan believes students need psychological limits that provide security and a sense of belonging, that too much freedom without responsible parameters can be hurtful to kids, possibly even dangerous. Does Evans fully

appreciate the negative emotional, and possibly physical, dimension Kurgan speaks of?

9. Reconstruct Evans's argument using the following argument form: Issue, Definitions, Premises, Conclusion. Remember to use clear, declarative statements throughout your presentation.

Issue:
Definitions:
Premises:
Conclusion:

Chapter 6

Channel One

Background

BEGUN IN 1989, Channel One is a commercially produced television news program by the Primedia Corporation for distribution in middle schools and high schools. Over 12,000 schools subscribe to Channel One with a viewership of over 8.1 million students, more than five times the (teen) viewing audience of ABC, CBS, NBC, and CNN combined. All told, over 40 percent of teenagers in the United States watch Channel One. The program has won dozens of broadcasting awards with its youthful reporters, including the prestigious George Foster Peabody Award. The program is routinely lauded by its supporters for its handling of sensitive issues. Still, with all its success, the meteoric rise of Channel One belies the controversial nature of the news channel from the start.

Channel One claims to "teach" the news to students by sending them, via satellite, a daily 12-minute news program focusing on current issues of the day. When schools sign a three-year contract with Channel One, they agree to show the program to their students on 90 percent of their school days. Each 12-minute broadcast includes four 30-second commercials from sponsors such as Nike, McDonald's, Doublemint Gum, Pepsi, Taco Bell, Oxy-10, Head & Shoulders, and Skittles—products aimed at a teenage audience. The ads go for a reported $200,000 for a half-minute. A daily 12-minute diet of Channel One adds up to roughly six days of school by the end of the year. In return for their commitment to show the program, each school subscribing to Channel One receives a satellite dish, a television for each classroom, two VCRs, and a continuous satellite feed that can be used for other educational purposes (all estimated at about $25,000). Channel One claims a 99 percent renewal rate, with additional schools on a waiting list for equipment and service. Channel One is shown in 47 states and the District of Columbia. With 40 percent of the teenage population as an audience, an advertiser on Channel One can reach the largest group of teenagers in the United States ever.

There has been considerable opposition to Channel One focusing largely on the daily two minutes of advertising it integrates into the newscast. Opponents argue that Channel One is nothing more than a for-profit commercial enterprise, its principal aim to turn kids into consumers. Schoolchildren should be learning how to reason critically about commercials while in school, not be subjected to them. Moreover, critics claim Channel One presents the news in a one-size-fits-all manner, much like ABC or NBC News, leaving local teachers with little opportunity to tailor the teaching of important local, national, and international issues to the needs and abilities of their students. They argue that schools are more inclined to sign up for Channel One just to get the free technology the subscription brings. If schools were not so strapped for funds, they wouldn't welcome the likes of Nike and McDonald's into the classroom to sell their wares. On May 20, 1999, the U.S. Senate Committee on Health, Education, Labor and Pensions held a hearing on Channel One. One of the articles in this study section, Mark Crispin Miller's *How to Be Stupid* (article 6.3) was presented at the Senate hearings.

Channel One on the Web

The 12-minute Channel One News, created for middle schools and high schools, is the central component in a constellation of services sponsored by Primedia called the Channel One Network. Primedia offers additional services—Web sites—meant to assist parents, teachers, and students in their studies associated with Channel One News. The Web sites also address other concerns related specifically to teenagers. The Web sites are ChannelOne.com, Teach1.com, Teachworld.com, and ChannelOneParents.com. You should examine these sites to gain an appreciation for Channel One's broad scope, and how it has become an integral part of everyday teaching in so many schools across the United States.

For a critical appraisal of commercials as they relate to children, plus material specifically on Channel One, check the Commercial Alert Web site at essential.org/alert/channel_one. Congressional testimony from the May 20, 1999, hearing on Channel One can be found there. Especially important is William Hoynes's critical appraisal of Channel One's news, *News for a Captive Audience,* which can be found at this site. Hoynes's article makes an excellent companion piece to Mark Crispin Miller's *How to Be Stupid: The Lessons of Channel One* (article 6.3) in this study section.

You can also find Ralph Nader's *Commercial Education: How Channel One Wastes School Time and Pushes Products on Schoolkids* at the *San Francisco Bay Guardian*'s (SFBG) Web site at sfbg.com. This op-ed piece, from Nader's column in the SFBG newspaper, is the one referred to by Casey Lartigue (article 6.5) in this study section.

Readings

Article 6.1 Our first article is a collection of brief comments/interviews from 12 individuals on Channel One gathered by Susan Mueller for the *Business Journal Serving San Jose & Silicon Valley*. The impressions gathered represent a broad spectrum of positions on Channel One in the classroom.

Article 6.2 Michael J. Sandel's *Ad Nauseam,* from *The New Republic,* offers a plethora of examples to illustrate how commercials have found their way into schools, from free science experiments to free book covers. An opponent of commercialization in schools, Sandel reserves special criticism for Channel One which he views as the most egregious example of crossing the line in the effort to sell products to schoolkids.

Article 6.3 Mark Crispin Miller is a professor of Media Ecology at NYU and is the director of the Project of Media Ownership (PROMO). In *How to Be Stupid: The Lessons of Channel One* Miller claims the news on Channel One is just "filler" to get from one ad to the next—the ads cleverly produced to get kids hooked on unhealthy products like hamburgers, soda pop, and candy bars, as well as products like skin cleansers that appeal to the inadequacies kids feel in the teenage years. Critics like Sandel and Miller claim ads have no place in public schools, and that the introduction of advertising into the school system by Channel One violates the tradition of keeping kids from being bombarded by special interest groups seeking profit. Both see the increasing commercialization of schools as a threat to the autonomy schools have traditionally relied on to teach kids to think for themselves.

Article 6.4 In *Hot News in Class,* Samuel Gwynne examines how effectively Channel One covers the news—which stories are covered, reporting style, presentation, and so on—and he comes up with high marks. He concludes Channel One News ranks favorably with major network news organizations in reporting news and in knowing how to address their audience, in this case teenagers.

Article 6.5 Our last article is by Casey Lartigue, Jr., from the Cato Institute, entitled *Anti-Channel One Crusade Is Failing.* Lartigue argues it should be left up to individual schools if they want to subscribe to Channel One. He points out that 12,000 schools have signed on for Channel One's services, the news program has won numerous awards, and they have a 99 percent renewal rate. He suggests Channel One has already carved out a favorable niche for itself with educators and students, and that opponents of Channel One are not facing reality—millions of teenagers and educators like the news program, commercials and all. To move the criticisms of Channel One from the public to Congress is, for Lartigue, an admission of defeat. When the critics couldn't convince the educators and students to reject Channel One, they went to Congress in hopes they might have better luck there.

6.1 Twelve Interviews

COMPILED BY SUSAN MUELLER

In Return for Providing School Funding and Other Resources, Should Channel One, or Any Advertising, Be Allowed at Schools?

Rafael Diaz, Manager, Printer's Ink Bookstore, Mountain View I object to commercials being shown in the classroom on this basis. When I grew up in the '50s, we were taught the most important role was that of being a citizen. Today,

From the Business Journal Serving San Jose & Silicon Valley *13, no. 53 (April 1, 1996): 8. Reprinted with permission.*

the emphasis seems to be on the role of being a consumer.

Let's also discuss the use of any television in schools as opposed to reading for information. Just by default, TV and other forms of technically produced information cost money because it is in real time and it is edited by minutes.

With reading, you learn to think for yourself. Radio and TV give an impression and so much information is missing due to efficiency. Therefore, the focus is often on the sensational rather than on content. For example, if you remember the television coverage of the Mississippi River flood last year, it seemed as if the entire Midwest was under water, and cameras honed in on the moment of suffering by the farmers.

But in print, we read that most of those farmers lost a whole year because they could not plant for about six months after the waters receded. The perspective changes considerably when you know the greater scope. We must read many sources for this, not what we get on a 30-second sound bite.

A student's imagination can be more exciting—as movies in their heads—than any TV program could ever create. Reading exercises the mind and TV is not aerobics for the mind. It is passive.

It is true that some books are like mind candy. Every book I sell here means something to somebody. Reading begets reading and also makes you a better writer. If you want to talk high-tech, you must read to use the Internet. It is the modern technology and our most common skill is reading.

In addition, we share our common cultural values in written form, including music. A book is a keeper, you will still have it tomorrow. Channels change. Reading is the basic skill of the literate person.

Tony Brazeau, instructional television coordinator, Santa Clara County Office of Education   There are a number of issues here. Schools like free offers. Look at Netday '96. Industry has been generous to schools, but Channel One has too many strings attached. The saying goes, "There is no free lunch." Is Channel One worth it? I don't think it is worth losing funding over.

[Schools apparently could face the possibility of losing some government funding.]

Some of the other gifts schools receive could bring up similar issues. For example, Apple Computer gives equipment and software and, no doubt, assumes the students will buy their products in the future.

In fact, any equipment with a nameplate on it is advertising. The schools are loaded with these corporate logos. When you watch TV there is a logo such as CNN or NBC. But those stations are not requiring students to watch for a certain number of minutes.

Art Darin, director, K–12 Partnership Alum Rock–East Side Joint Venture, former associate principal, Overfelt High School, San Jose   We have gone to Sacramento and talked to the Senate Education Committee and we have gone to court and won the right to use Channel One's programming. We went through a controversial process with the school board. It was an unfortunate amount of time to have to put in. It was energy taken away from school work.

The majority of the students and the teaching staff support the use of Channel One and its value. There is a small group who opposed the use of Channel One, but I think they have a personal agenda and are not looking at what the majority wants.

The county office stopped sending audiovisual resources. So we created our own. We can download noncommercial educational programs, and have done so with over 400 videos.

Channel One produces a magazine telling about what is available. The news channel is where the commercials are shown and they are very restricted in terms of length and appropriateness. We show the news channel four days.

With Channel One we can criticize, and when we do, we get an immediate response from them. The kids can vote on programs and send that vote in. As any tool used in the classroom, our teachers have the choice of making this a dynamic learning situation for our students. Those teachers certainly up its value.

Jim Cunneen, state assemblyman, Campbell   I'm not opposed to injecting a little capitalism into the classroom. We need our partnerships with business. With oversight and some restrictions, why not use Channel One programming?

With the ability to decide for themselves, the local school districts can use commonsense restrictions. Kids are already bombarded with commercials and we can live with a couple of minutes of commercials. They only get two minutes of commercials for 12 minutes of news [on Channel One].

I would be willing to experiment and try a new approach. It might help restore the people's confidence in public education. We need to develop strategic partnerships with business and educational entrepreneurs.

Reuben Dano, store manager, Stacey's Bookstore, Cupertino   My first thought is that I would not want my child in a school that used Channel One advertising and programming. But if it had to be, I would want my child to be interactive with a teacher. If the teacher stopped the program, gave out some reading material, held a discussion and then went back to the TV program, there might be some merit to it.

I have noticed, even with all the high-tech games available to kids and videos, an upswing in the number of books we are selling to the child market. When children are in the store, we overhear their conversations and a couple of things take place. When a child shows an interest in a particular book topic, they will often say that a parent or grandparent was the source of that interest. The student has been pushed, in a good way, toward reading more.

Again, I am advocating adult interaction. When I was a student, TV and videos or public school classes did not teach me that much. But in high school, I read two or three extra books a week and learned that so much is out there beyond my surroundings. Learning all about Beijing was an eye-opener.

Sometimes I yearn for the days when I had time to read so many books. I think I used up the high school library, went to other libraries and then to bookstores. This bookstore caters to professionals of all types, plumbers, businesspeople and engineers. Their children often run up to the parent with a book, sort of begging. The parent often balks a little, reconsiders and then says, "Put it up here on the counter." These are the same children whose conversations in the store include discussions of on-line games and videos.

Linda Murray, superintendent, San Jose Unified School District   This district chose not to subscribe to Channel One programming because we object to the commercials. The children are a captive audience and this takes advantage of them. It is just not appropriate to let a company do that for profit. The children should not be used; it is a form of exploitation, since the children are seen as possible purchasers of the advertisers' products.

In the extreme, public education could be a very large and profitable market. So we are very conservative about our students being used for someone's gain.

In addition, TV is passive. For example, if you are teaching about current events, having the students read periodicals is a superior method over television. The reading is active on the part of the student and they are practicing their reading skills, encountering new vocabulary.

In both situations, the lessons should be followed up by discussion, of course. But with the periodical, the discussion can refer back to the piece at hand. Once the channel has broadcast, we can only refer back to what was remembered.

Ronald Lind, director of organizing, United Food and Commercial Workers, Local 428 AFL-CIO, San Jose   As long as the Republicans dominate in Sacramento, the education system will be in crisis, because there will be no funding. We need to develop partnerships between education, business, government and labor, to make the system work.

I have no objection to Channel One. If there is a potential conflict over advertising, a partnership up-front can monitor the advertising as to content and quantity.

Steve Tedesco, president and CEO, San Jose Metropolitan Chamber of Commerce   Opponents of Channel One contend its brief advertising segments are somehow warping the minds of our children. The implication is that business, as it conducts commerce through advertising, is bad. That is propaganda we must counter at every turn.

Fortunately, young people can and do make informed decisions about responding to advertising messages. They do it every day, as do all consumers.

It seems tragic that misdirected concerns about Channel One's advertising may result in the loss of an outstanding educational program. Cash-strapped public schools should be free to accept high-quality resources like Channel One to help enrich our children's learning experiences.

Angelo Lygizos, owner, Arena Cafe & Grill Sports Bar, San Jose   Absolutely, yes, we should use

Channel One. Let us give the children quality educational viewing, as opposed to the violent and pornographic movies many of them can see at night. They will see the difference.

There is nothing wrong with seeing a little advertising. They could even learn from it. Some of them might want to grow up and be in that field.

They will also learn some consumer skills. The teacher can teach analytical thinking with regard to the commercials.

Of course, I expect the teachers to definitely assist in the process of using Channel One.

John Vasconcellos, state assemblyman, Santa Clara Public schools are mandatory; children are a captive audience. It seems inappropriate to subject them to commercial advertising.

Who assesses the healthfulness of what is advertised? A larger issue is that of bias. Each of us humans sees through our bias. So you have programming designed and chosen by somebody other than our educators, somebody not accountable to the school board, with that person's bias.

My father was a public school administrator. He taught me how precious is the relationship a teacher has, how he or she must teach as objectively as possible.

If this came up for a vote today, I would be against using Channel One programs.

Kenneth Fong, president and CEO, Clontech Laboratories, Palo Alto If outstanding educational programs cannot be produced without support from corporations, I believe proper recognition of the corporations as sponsors is appropriate.

This could be similar to what PBS has done to recognize the sponsors of some of their excellent programs. It was done with such good taste that this commercial-tie thing did not even enter the minds of the viewers.

Ann Wells, principal, Ann Wells Personnel Services Inc., Sunnyvale Let's use it [Channel One]. The schools need all the help they can get. I read about teachers spending their salary money for supplies. I did it myself when I taught. The schools need more resources. When this first came out, I thought it was a wonderful idea. With regard to any argument about bias, remember that teachers have bias too. It is everywhere.

And children are accustomed to commercials. The teachers have an opportunity to react to the commercials whenever that is appropriate.

Discussion and Assignments

1. Rafael Diaz is critical of the use of television in the classroom and favors reading as an instrument of learning. What is the strongest piece of evidence he offers in criticizing the use of television in the classroom? In a paragraph explain why you believe it's strong. What is the weakest piece of evidence he offers to support his claim that reading is preferential as an instrument of learning? In a paragraph explain why you think it's weak.

2. State Assemblyman Jim Cunneen states: "Kids are already bombarded with commercials and we can live with a couple of minutes of commercials. They only get two minutes of commercials for 12 minutes of news." Do you think Cunneen has offered sufficient justification to let Channel One advertise in classrooms?

3. What are the two types of objections Linda Murray has to using Channel One? Does she offer clearly defined reasons for her views? Compare how she establishes her case with Jim Cunneen's reasoning. Which is the clearer?

4. What is *propaganda* according to Steve Tedesco? Do you agree with the way Tedesco characterizes opponents to Channel One as spreading propaganda? Does he characterize the opponents of Channel One fairly?

5. Angelo Lygizos suggests the advertisements on Channel One may be used by teachers to instruct students in critical thinking. Do you think this is a reasonable suggestion? Why or why not? If teachers focused their attention on analyzing the

ads for the purpose of teaching kids critical thinking—if the ads became instructional material as well as the news—do you think the schools might endanger their contracts with Channel One? (If kids are encouraged to discuss the news, why shouldn't they analyze or discuss the ads?)

6.2 Ad Nauseam

MICHAEL J. SANDEL

WHEN THE BOSTON RED SOX installed a display of giant Coke bottles above the left field wall this season, local sportswriters protested that such tacky commercialism tainted the sanctity of Fenway Park. But ballparks have long been littered with billboards and ads. Today, teams even sell corporations the right to name the stadium: the Colorado Rockies, for example, play in Coors Field. However distasteful, such commercialism does not seem to corrupt the game or diminish the play.

The same cannot be said of the newest commercial frontier—the public schools. The corporate invasion of the classroom threatens to turn schools into havens for hucksterism. Eager to cash in on a captive audience of consumers-in-training, companies have flooded teachers with free videos, posters and "learning kits" designed to sanitize corporate images and emblazon brand names in the minds of children. Students can now learn about nutrition from curricular materials supplied by Hershey's Chocolate or McDonald's, or study the effects of the Alaska oil spill in a video made by Exxon. According to *Giving Kids the Business,* by Alex Molnar, a Monsanto video teaches the merits of bovine growth hormone in milk production, while Proctor & Gamble's environmental curriculum teaches that disposable diapers are good for the earth.

Not all corporate-sponsored educational freebies promote ideological agendas; some simply plug the brand name. A few years ago, the Campbell Soup Company offered a science kit that showed students how to prove that Campbell's Prego spaghetti sauce is thicker than Ragu. General Mills distributed science kits containing free samples of its Gusher fruit snacks, with soft centers that "gush" when bitten. The teacher's guide suggested that students bite into the Gushers and compare the effect to geothermal eruptions. A Tootsie Roll kit on counting and writing recommends that, for homework, children interview family members about their memories of Tootsie Rolls.

While some marketers seek to insinuate brand names into the curriculum, others take a more direct approach: buying advertisements in schools. When the Seattle School Board faced a budget crisis last fall, it voted to solicit corporate advertising. School officials hoped to raise $1 million a year with sponsorships like "the cheerleaders, brought to you by Reebok" and "the McDonald's gym." Protests from parents and teachers forced the Seattle schools to suspend the policy this year, but such marketing is a growing presence in schools across the country.

Corporate logos now clamor for student attention from school buses to book covers. In Colorado Springs, advertisements for Mountain Dew adorn school hallways, and ads for Burger King decorate the sides of school buses. A Massachusetts firm distributes free book covers hawking Nike, Gatorade and Calvin Klein to almost 25 million students nationwide. A Minnesota broadcasting company pipes music into school corridors and cafeterias in fifteen states, with twelve minutes of commercials every hour. Forty percent of the ad revenue goes to the schools.

The most egregious example of the commercialization in schools is Channel One, a twelve-minute television news program seen by 8 million students in 12,000 schools. Introduced in 1990 by

From The New Republic *217, no. 9 (1997): 23. Reprinted with permission.*

Whittle Communications, Channel One offers schools a television set for each classroom, two VCRs and a satellite link in exchange for an agreement to show the program every day, including the two minutes of commercials it contains. Since Channel One reaches over 40 percent of the nation's teenagers, it is able to charge advertisers a hefty $200,000 per thirty-second spot. In its pitch to advertisers, the company promises access to the largest teen audience in history in a setting free of "the usual distractions of telephones, stereos, remote controls, etc." The Whittle program shattered the taboo against outright advertising in the classroom. Despite controversy in many states, only New York has banned Channel One from its schools.

Unlike the case of baseball, the rampant commercialization of schools is corrupting in two ways. First, most corporate-sponsored learning supplements are ridden with bias, distortion and superficial fare. A recent study by Consumers Union found that nearly 80 percent of classroom freebies are slanted toward the sponsor's product. An independent study of Channel One released earlier this year found that its news programs contributed little to students' grasp of public affairs. Only 20 percent of its airtime covers current political, economic or cultural events. The rest is devoted to advertising, sports, weather and natural disasters.

But, even if corporate sponsors supplied objective teaching tools of impeccable quality, commercial advertising would still be a pernicious presence in the classroom because it undermines the purposes for which schools exist. Advertising encourages people to want things and to satisfy their desires: education encourages people to reflect on their desires, to restrain or to elevate them. The purpose of advertising is to recruit consumers; the purpose of public schools is to cultivate citizens.

It is not easy to teach students to be citizens, capable of thinking critically about the world around them, when so much of childhood consists of basic training for a commercial society. At a time when children come to school as walking billboards of logos and labels and licensed apparel, it is all the more difficult—and all the more important—for schools to create some distance from a popular culture drenched in the ethos of consumerism.

But advertising abhors distance. It blurs the boundaries between places, and makes every setting a site for selling. "Discover your own river of revenue at the schoolhouse gates!" proclaims the brochure for the 4th Annual Kid Power Marketing Conference, held last May in New Orleans. "Whether it's first-graders learning to read or teenagers shopping for their first car, we can guarantee an introduction of your product and your company to these students in the traditional setting of the classroom!" Marketers are storming the schoolhouse gates for the same reason that Willie Sutton robbed banks—because that's where the money is. Counting the amount they spend and the amount they influence their parents to spend, 6- to 19-year-old consumers now account for $485 billion in spending per year.

The growing financial clout of kids is itself a lamentable symptom of parents abdicating their role as mediators between children and the market. Meanwhile, faced with property tax caps, budget cuts and rising enrollments, cash-strapped schools are more vulnerable to the siren song of corporate sponsors. Rather than raise the public funds we need to pay the full cost of educating our schoolchildren, we choose instead to sell their time and rent their minds to Burger King and Mountain Dew.

Discussion and Assignments

1. Sandel employs the use of numerous examples to make his point that there is too much commercialism in the schools. How effective is he in employing his examples? Which example do you find the most convincing? Why? Which example do you find the least convincing? Why?

2. Sandel states that some companies aim to sell an ideological agenda, while others aim to plug their brand name. Is the distinction between the two

always clear? Should we be more concerned with one than with the other?

3. What is the purpose of a school according to Sandel? How does advertising in schools violate this purpose? Do you agree with Sandel on this point? Is it possible to agree with Sandel on this point, but still allow advertising in the schools?

4. Sandel reserves his most critical comments for Channel One, claiming it is the "most egregious example of commercialization in schools." What specific reasons does Sandel offer to support his case against Channel One? List the reasons, in clear declarative statements, in their most logical order.

5. Reconstruct Sandel's argument against the advertising of commercial products in public schools using the following argument form: Issue, Definitions, Premises, Conclusion. Remember to use clear, declarative statements throughout your presentation. I've filled in the Issue and the Conclusion for you.

Issue: Whether it is advisable to allow the advertising of commercial products in public schools.

Definitions:

Premises:

Conclusion: We should not allow the advertising of commercial products in public schools.

6.3 How to Be Stupid: The Lessons of Channel One

MARK CRISPIN MILLER

NEWS, OF COURSE, is not the point of Channel One—any more than it's the point of those commercial TV newscasts that many of us watch at home night after night. If the basic aim of all such TV shows were really journalistic, it might be possible to glean from them some simple daily understanding of the world; but what we get these days from TV news is loud, speedy filler, which—with minimal background, and no context—leaves the mind with nothing but some evanescent numbers, a helpless sense of general disaster, a heavy mental echo of official reassurance and (not too surprisingly) an overwhelming vague anxiety.

The news on Channel One leaves this impression—for it looks and sounds a lot like what we get on regular TV, only more so. Genially presented by its very young and pretty (and meticulously multiracial) team of anchors, the "news" is even more compressed and superficial than the stuff the networks give us: big accidents and major snowstorms, nonstories about the Super Bowl, horse-race coverage of domestic politics, bloody images of foreign terrorism, the occasional nerve-wracking and

largely unenlightening visit to some scary place like Haiti or Tibet, and features—either grim or inspirational—on teens suffering from various high-profile torments (cancer, AIDS, addiction).

Of course, it being TV news, much of it is starkly painful—gory corpses in the streets of Tel Aviv, stretchers hefted from a midnight train wreck in suburban Maryland, survivors weeping after Oklahoma City, etc. When, on the other hand, it isn't horrible or sad, the news on Channel One is just confusing: a blast of isolated factoids about very distant and extremely complicated fights (e.g., Bosnia) and the equally complex—and, for that matter, distant—wrangles in the federal limelight (e.g., Clinton's budget vs. the Republicans'), all of it dressed up with the usual brilliant, zippy graphics, but none of it made clear or relevant enough to bear in mind. A student with a photographic memory might be able to retain those random facts and figures, but most kids wouldn't be, nor is there any reason why they should.

As inane as it may seem, however, the news on Channel One, by turns horrific and confusing, does

EXTRA! *(May 1997). Reprinted by permission of the author.*

serve an important purpose—just like the news on regular TV. In either case, the news is, to repeat, no more than filler. Its real function is not journalistic but commercial, for it is meant primarily to get us ready for the ads. What this means is that the news must, on the one hand, keep us sitting there and watching, as an M.C. has to keep his audience mildly entertained between the acts; but it must also constantly efface itself, must keep itself from saying anything too powerful or even interesting, must never cut too deep or raise any really troubling questions, because it can never be permitted to detract in any way from the commercials. Its aim must be, in short, to keep our eyes wide open and our minds asleep, so that the commercial will look good to us, sound true to us, and thereby work on us.

The Ads in Context

If the news on Channel One often seems perplexingly abstract, offering no clear impression from those many sudden, pointless names and numbers, that perplexity enhances the effect of the commercials. So brightly focused and so dazzlingly insistent, each stands out luminous and sharp in the bewildering murk of factoids like a high-tech lighthouse in a blinding fog. The routine horror of the news on Channel One also indirectly bolsters the commercials, which proffer their young viewers a fantastic antidote to all those tragic woes and bloody dangers.

Skeletal and nearly bald, a real teenager with leukemia suffers through the agonies of chemotherapy—just after a fictitious teenaged girl (full-bodied, and with all her hair) finds happiness by using Clearasil. Buildings explode and people mourn in Bosnia (with its "brutal and complex story of ethnic hatreds and violent nationalism")—and then we see the Buffalo Bills, locked up and deprived of lunch by their demanding coach, chomp with furtive relish on their Snickers bars ("Hungry? Why wait?"). And so on.

Surely all the mass advertising on the TV news thus benefits from such delicious contrast with the uglier images of telejournalism (as long as those other images are not too ugly). The ads on Channel One would seem to be especially powerful, however, because they thrive by contrast not just with the news before and after them, but with the whole boring, regimented context of the school itself.

Imagine, or remember, what it's like to have to sit there at your desk, listening to your teacher droning on, with hours to go until you can get out of there, your mind rebelling and your hormones raging. It must be a relief when Channel One takes over, so you can lose yourself in its really cool graphics and its tantalizing bursts of rock music—and in the advertisers' mind-blowing little fantasies of power: power through Pepsi, Taco Bell, McDonald's, Fruit-A-Burst and/or Gatorade ("Life Is a Sport. Drink It Up!"), power through Head 'n' Shoulders, Oxy-10 and/or Pantene Pro-V Mousse (". . . a stronger sense of style!"), power through Donkey Kong and/or Killer Instinct ("PLAY IT LOUD!") and/or power through Reebok ("This is my planet!").

Buy the Power!

Of all the promises that advertising makes us, this promise of a certain rude empowerment—personal, immediate and absolute—is now the one that comes at us most often. Although it comes at all of us countless times each day, we see the promise used most often in those ads that are directed at the weakest of us: the poor, women generally—and kids, as Channel One makes clear. Over and over, the product flashes into view as something that you ought to pay for not because you might enjoy it but because it promises to make you indestructible, as tough as nails, as hard as steel: a Superman or Superwoman.

"I'm a guided missile," grunts the famous football player—so big and strong because of Reebok, evidently, so if you buy those shoes you'll be that big and strong (and famous). A hot babe beams at us and pops a stick of Doublemint—and then she's happily kissing this buff guy, whose hands are out of sight while she has her arms wrapped around his neck, so that it's obvious—just from a glance—who's in control. (Then there's a different babe, and the same thing happens.) Such fantasies appear to answer—and, of course, also exacerbate—the ferocious longing of their captive audience for freedom, independence, confidence and strength, which adolescents generally lack, and know they lack.

It isn't necessary to pay close attention to those loaded images in order for their message to get through to you. Indeed, mass advertising tends to be devised on the correct assumption that its audience will not be studying it carefully, but merely flipping through the magazines, driving right on past the billboards, and only half-watching—or even fast-forwarding—the TV spots. Thus the kids required to sit through Channel One, although they might appear to zone out during the commercials, are still likely to get the point, which is conveyed explosively enough to register through their peripheral vision, and which thus comes at them repeatedly—as all successful propaganda must.

And that point, again, is very simple (which is, of course, another requisite of winning propaganda). That point is: "Buy the power." As simple as it sounds, however, there is much more to the ads than that—for advertising never merely makes its most apparent pitch, but at the same time always offers up a vision of how you should live, and of how the world around you ought to be. It's one thing to say that the ads idealize power and identify the products with that power. But what exactly is that "power"? And what precisely is it that the advertising asks its teenaged audience to do, and think, in order to attain that "power"? These are crucial questions, since Channel One is, after all, by now required in thousands of our nation's schools, as a daily part of the curriculum. What, then, are its lessons?

Lesson #1: "Watch."

This is in fact the fundamental teaching of each ad, expertly hammered home by every virtuoso shot, every pointless, jarring cut, every stupefying jangle of computer graphics. It's also the most basic teaching of the ads en masse: for everybody in those ads is always staring at something (either at the product or at us), and is also himself or herself spectacular: as icy-cool and drop-dead gorgeous as the product. Now and then we see a kid contentedly waiting in line, but no kid depicted in the ads is ever reading, ever thinking, nor ever even unselfconsciously conversing with some other kid(s). Sometimes—briefly, just before their rescue by the product—they might look anxious, lonely, doubtful. Otherwise, they are all alike continuously rapt in a Spielbergian state of blithe, wide-eyed wonderment, watching it all, and loving every minute of it—just as the student audience is meant to do.

(Of course, Channel One includes many a loud ad for movies and TV from Fox, Time Warner, Universal and other such educators.)

The ads sometimes baldly celebrate that posture of euphoric gaping—as in an amazing spot for Skittles, a 30-second masterpiece that might be taken as an accurate dream-vision of what Channel One itself is all about. On the slate-gray face of a dead planet, under a luminous night sky, a bevy of cartoonish reptiles (each a different Skittle-color) slowly poke their cute, round, bleary dino-faces out of their respective hidey-holes, like prairie dogs just waking up. "Yum?" each one says groggily: "Yum?" Suddenly a shimmering wave of multicolored light hits the horizon and then flares across the sky—and all the little dinos perk right up and follow its swift course in pop-eyed wonder, together swaying from left to right in perfect unison.

In the wake of that celestial surge there is a shower of—meteors? No: Skittles, which drop and bounce amid the rooted crowd like day-glo-colored balls of manna, and the critters noisily gulp them down. "Yum," they now say, getting sleepy: "Yum." They sink back down into their holes. Finally, there's a long shot of the ruined planet and its many-hued Saturnian ring, which—we now see—constantly revolves around the sphere, so that that same exhilarating surge of colored light must dazzle those hole-dwellers regularly every day. We then hear this command, uttered in a childish whisper (and also printed on the screen): "Skittles. Taste the rainbow!"

The groggy little ones, their empty world, the daily light-show and its putatively yummy vision of the product: In its grotesque way the vision functions as a tidy allegory of Channel One itself, whose viewers are likewise always being promised an immediate reward for their continued watching.

Lesson #2: "Don't Think."

The sort of watching that is urged on teenagers by Channel One (and also urged on all of us by advertising generally) involves no reflection, no interpretation: on the contrary. First of all, the spectacle is much too fast and noisy to permit, much less encourage, any thoughtfulness; and yet the ads discourage thinking not just automatically, because of their distracting visuals and manic pace, but also, it would seem, deliberately, by taking every opportunity to celebrate stupidity. While forever hyping its commitment to the endless sharpening of the teenaged mind ("Imagine knowing everything," etc.), Channel One continually assures its audience, through the commercials, that it's really cool to be an idiot.

This is partly a result of the great corporate interest—prevalent throughout the entertainment industries—in exploiting the inevitable rebelliousness of adolescent boys. Whether on Channel One or regular TV, the ads aimed at that uneasy group appeal to a defiant boorishness that, in the real world, routinely lands a lot of young men in jail, and that the movie studios and video-game manufacturers endlessly glamorize in works like Happy Gilmore, Ace Ventura 2: When Nature Calls and Down Periscope ("See It and Win!"), Virtual Boy, Donkey Kong 2 and Killer Instinct ("PLAY IT LOUD!"), among many others advertised on Channel One. Since that loutish posture is as anti-intellectual as it is antisocial, the celebration of stupidity in Channel One's commercials owes a lot to that particularly noxious form of target marketing.

And yet it isn't only Channel One's male-oriented ads that say it's cool to be an idiot: All the advertising makes that point repeatedly, and makes it to the viewers of both sexes—for advertising (which is, of course, a form of propaganda) must forever tell its audience not to think.

Those cuddly reptiles gulping Skittles are just one species of the many simple, hungry organisms that Channel One's commercials represent as excellent consumers. Such beings know all you need to know: Any higher inquiry—or any inquiry at all—is laughable, the ads imply. "Woah!" breathes a frenetic youngster, having just wolfed down a very crunchy spoonful of the cereal in the bowl he's gripping: "How do they cram all that graham into Golden Grahams?" A halo of bright multicolored question marks pulsates and jiggles all around his head as he engages in moronic speculation—rendered for us in high-speed cartoons—about exactly how they cram all that graham. ("But how?" he finally asks again, then shrugs and takes another mouthful.)

Although portrayed as godlike, the big celebrities who do the ads on Channel One are likewise hailed for having heads of near-perfect emptiness. "Some people say I've got too much on my mind," Shaquille O'Neal murmurs at us, sitting tall in an expensive leather lounger (slick hip-hop bopping in the background). "Movies, music, toys. Correction: There's only one thing in my head: the championship." (Quick shots of Shaq looking like a winner.) "That's what's in my head," he says, then adds, "This is my planet." (And that's the Reebok logo on his chest.)

Over and over, the ads idealize ignorance: like the kid who wonders about nothing but how "they" make that cereal so sugary, and like the famous athlete in whose mind (he says) there's nothing but the fact that he's a famous athlete, the ads' countless momentary heroes each know only what the advertisers want their audience to know. The beauties talking earnestly about their faces and Noxema, or about their hair and Pantene Pro-V Mousse, and the dog who drinks a Pepsi (in a happy dream he's having about drinking Pepsi), and the animated M&M's who would do anything to get into that ad for M&M's ("I wanna be in that commercial!"): All those empty-headed figures speeding through the ads on Channel One are nothing but role models for the spread of Channel One's commercial propaganda, which wants its youthful audience to be just as thoughtless, easily distracted and obsessed. Those speedy figures are, in fact, the opposite of proper students (and therefore don't belong in schools).

Lesson #3: "Let Us Fix It."

The ads on Channel One also promote stupidity by representing all of life as nothing but a series of extremely simple problems, each soluble through the immediate application of some very smart commodity or other. To all your problems, Channel One keeps telling its young audience, we have the solutions. This myth promotes stupidity, first of all, by ruling out all problems any higher, deeper, more complex or general than, say, your boredom or your dandruff. Such trivialization must make students blind not only to the daunting truths and major questions of philosophy and history, but also to the harder, richer pleasures still available beyond the screaming little world of Channel One (where, for example, "nothin's more intense than slammin' a Dew!").

While grossly oversimplifying everything, moreover, that myth of the advertisers' total competence, of their ability to solve, at once, your every "problem," also promotes stupidity by suggesting that there is no worthwhile knowledge other than the knowledge of elite technicians (who are, of course, all working for Nintendo, Reebok, Mars, AT&T and the other major corporate advertisers, while you're just sitting there in front of that TV). Channel One's commercials are all, finally, celebrations of technology: not only are the ads themselves mind-bending feats of digital f/x, but they all tout the video games and pimple creams and running shoes as masterworks of technical design. Even tasty treats like Golden Grahams ("But how?"), and that "scorching new four-alarm, double-decker taco from Taco Bell," are sold primarily as the efficient and ingenious products of those corporations' labs.

It is their mystique of high technology that finally makes those ads and goods alike appear so very powerful—and that is meant to make the rest of us feel helpless, needy, stupid. (The news on Channel One continually reconfirms that view, through numerous awe-struck reports on seeming scientific breakthroughs.) If you have any power at all, you can thank us for it, the ads tell their young viewers: "All that stuff your parents never dreamed of . . . AT&T is bringing it all within your reach!" proclaims a commercial for AT&T ("Your true choice"), which ends by asking for submissions to an essay contest on the theme "How Technology Has Benefited My Education."

Just as ads have done for well over a century, the ads on Channel One routinely try to wow their audience with brisk bits of pseudoscientific hooey, along with many clever mock-explanatory visuals. "The exclusive pro-vitamin formula penetrates, improving your hair," we're assured by a sweet, breathy female voice, as we watch a fleet of gently tumbling golden pellets disappear into the auburn scalp of an expensive-looking redhead. In another ad, an exuberant "science teacher," posed before his bunsen burners and reports, tells how he managed to teach "Chad" (whom we see repeatedly in handsome close-up) that "science is a beautiful thing," because "science is the key to clear skin." ("The medicine in Oxy-10 penetrates, it helps eliminate pimples fast," the "teacher" says by way of explanation.) He concludes: "Scientific equation: Oxy-10 equals great skin!"

Again, these are devices—the fake "authority," the vaguely scientific-sounding mumbo-jumbo—that advertising has been using on the public since the 19th century. Their patent falseness makes them grossly inappropriate for use inside our schools—where children ought to learn to think, not to be taken in.

Lesson #4: "Eat Now."

While you need almost nothing in your head, you must put this—and lots of this—into your mouth. Of all the lessons taught day after day on Channel One, this one may have the most immediate effect, because that visual stimulus—watching someone chewing, sipping, gulping, licking his/her lips—is irresistible, especially when you're hungry and/or thirsty.

The same tantalizing tactic is routine on Channel One. Because teens tend almost always to be hungry, and because they're not allowed to eat in school, the many spots for candy, pizza, chewing gum, tacos, cereal and burgers, for Pepsi, Gatorade and Mountain Dew, are probably the most successful ads on Channel One, which shows—by far—more ads for drink and munchies than for any other category of product. Stuck there with their stomachs growling, the viewers of Channel One must feel downright tormented by the last shot in those ads for Snickers (with its dark nougat, chunks of peanut, gooey caramel, rippling chocolate): "Hungry? Why wait?"

Thus those sleepy critters gulp their Skittles, that curious kid scarfs down his Golden Grahams, those happy diners at McDonald's chow down on their Big Macs, and so on. And yet there's evidently more to the appetite(s) aroused by Channel One than the mere biological need for carbohydrates. The teenagers are hungry not for bread alone but for autonomy, security, control; and so the ads don't simply make the munchies look delicious, but represent them as a tasty means to personal "empowerment." "How does Shaquille O'Neal get fired up for a game? With a scorching new four-alarm double-decker taco from Taco Bell!"—and, after tearing into one of those hot, gloppy, crunchy little beauties, Shaq goes tearing down the court—in flames! (And he scores!)

And yet it is the girls more than the boys who are endlessly assured that eating makes you powerful. "Well duh, of course it's delicious!" snaps a pretty adolescent blonde about her Frosted

Cheerios, and then a pert (and light-skinned) African-American preteen confides, "It's way too good for adults!" (Each girl hefts a spoon and holds a giant bowlful of the stuff.) And it's the girls who are enticed by Channel One's commercials for such cheap treats as Doublemint and Winterfresh, which taste so good that they'll make you taste good, and therefore make you overpoweringly delectable, just like the product (a promise made through countless careful images of slender, lovely chewers variously "in control").

Lesson #5: "You're Ugly."

Although it hypes itself as a brave new instrument of teenage "mind expansion," Channel One—that is, its owners and its sponsors—would certainly prefer that its young audience not become acute enough to grasp certain glaring contradictions in each broadcast.

For example, there's a huge—and highly profitable—contradiction within many of the ads themselves: between the likely physical effects of all that grease and sugar advertised so festively, and the tiptop physical condition of those great-looking hunks and babes and famous athletes doing all the eating and the drinking in the ads. In fact, the diet advertised on Channel One would—and actually does—make kids obese: fatter nowadays than ever, the statistics tell us. But such reports cannot compete with those deliciously misleading images of, say, the Buffalo Bills all eating Snickers, or Shaquille O'Neal getting "fired up for a game" by eating stuff from Taco Bell.

Such images insist, obliquely, that all that fattening food won't make you fat at all but (magically!) exceptionally fit—just as the images aimed at the girls imply that a diet of M&M's and fries and Pepsi won't inevitably make you tubby, give you zits and cavities and dull your hair, but will somehow help to make you just as slender, buxom, bright-eyed, radiant and peppy as those primping, winking models, who seem to have those buff boys under control.

Although they certainly don't want their viewers to be unattractive, the advertisers do want all of us to feel as fat, zitty, flaky, haggard, flabby, pale and smelly as it takes to get us buying what we're told we need so as to come across like winners. As old as advertising itself, this subversive tactic too has no place in the classroom, whose adolescent inmates generally feel bad enough about themselves already—as Channel One reminds them often. "NERVOUS about going back to school?" demands an ad for Clearasil in one September broadcast. "No wonder. With those ZITS." The numerous teen-oriented spots for skin creams, dandruff shampoos, mousse, breath-sweeteners and conditioners (the second biggest product category on Channel One) make clear exactly how the students are advised to see themselves: as horrors, in dire need of the assurances, advice and goods pitched "free" in each day's broadcast.

Lesson #6: "Just Say Yes."

Aside from the upbeat commercial spots for edibles, cosmetics, sportswear and entertainment, Channel One's broadcasts also include a number of solemn public service ads (PSAs) made mostly by the Ad Council on behalf of various pro bono enterprises. Such sound directives—telling kids to use their seat belts, work for charitable outfits, wear their helmets when they go skateboarding, stay away from crack, recycle—might appear to justify those daily broadcasts in our nation's schools, by making Channel One appear morally impeccable and socially progressive. (There can be little doubt that Channel One includes those PSAs for that very purpose, as a way to disarm resistance and muffle criticism.)

For all their apparent civic-mindedness, however, the PSAs actually make Channel One a more effective means of selling teenagers on all that dubious merchandise—for those kinder, gentler spots actually enhance the crass commercial pitch by masking its true character. Thanks to them, the students can more readily half-believe that all of this is "educational"—that this relentless daily come-on has some "higher purpose." Channel One can't really be telling us to think about nothing but ourselves (can it?), if it includes that moving voluntarist promo for the Points of Light Foundation: "Do Something Good. Feel Something Real." Nor could the program really be requiring us to sit here gaping at TV commercials, just like at home—because Channel One is also urging us to try some jazz, check out some modern art: "Arts and Humanities. There's Something In It for You," concludes a spot for the National Cultural Alliance.

And of course there are all those scary messages from the Partnership for a Drug-Free America, played every week on Channel One: crafty teenaged pushers lurking in the schoolyard, or even in the hallways, offering their wares—and all the younger kids, so tough and self-possessed, just tell those predators to beat it! Channel One must really want us to have independent minds if it keeps on warning us like that.

And yet the contradiction here is total, for the only moral difference between the individual drug-dealers and the corporate advertisers in our nation's schools is one of scale: The advertisers are immeasurably richer, and have done a lot more harm. Both work full-time to lure the children into absolute and permanent dependency, and both do so exclusively for profit's sake. Both, therefore, would prefer that their young targets be ill-educated on the subject of addiction. Thus the advertisers help put out that cautionary propaganda, which demonizes the individual (black) pusher—and thereby helps obscure the advertisers' own addictive mission.

Addiction 101

For it is addiction that the advertisers sell on Channel One (and everywhere else): They want to hook the kids forever, to have them needing all that junk forever, to have them all forever paying for it. While the stuff they sell does not, of course, induce a catastrophic physical dependency like heroin or crack, the way they sell it powerfully glamorizes the destructive spiritual condition of all addicts, whatever they may crave: the desperate neediness (you need it now!) and ever-more-acute insatiability (now you need more!). Thus, despite their many stern denunciations of the illegal market in the streets, the advertisers only make such drug use all the likelier and more widespread, by urging children—daily, hourly—into just the sort of appetite that, in many people, must be fed, in one way or another.

First of all, the ads teach that you can and should surrender to your craving right away: "Hungry? Why Wait?" The jokey tone of the solicitation (which is the usual tone of advertising to the young) cannot quite hide the deadly earnestness of that appeal, which the commercials make incessantly, both verbally and visually. You may be told to "Do the Dew" or "Bite the Burst" or "Taste the Rainbow," but the imperative is quite the same in every case, and reconfirmed in image after image: Eat it, drink it, wear it, play it now. With their extreme compression and extraordinary vividness, the ads present a world in which there isn't any saving, any planning toward the buying of the product, nor any pleasurable anticipation of the buying of the product—nor even any savoring of that product in itself (which once gone is forgotten, and you want another one). In that fantastic world, the only things are you and it; and since it's yours—and even if it isn't yours—you take it, and you take it now ("Why wait?").

While thus continuously urging your immediate self-indulgence, the ads on Channel One also promote the addict's attitude through the usual psychotic overestimation of the modest items that they sell. It isn't just a candy bar, it isn't just a pair of pants—it's a delirium, an orgasm, an apocalypse of fun. The admakers use every visual and aural means available to make the everyday experience of tasting this or wearing that seem like a sort of psychedelic wet dream, in which you feel like you've never felt before: ecstatic and all-powerful.

Thus the products are routinely advertised as working just like drugs: You swallow them, and go delightfully insane. Kids gulp candy or chomp into burgers or take crunchy bites of cereal—and their eyes light up, they beam and laugh and dance like lunatics. A ballerina pops a stick of Winterfresh, and breaks into exuberant motion (and a line of little girls in tutus imitates her buoyant steps). A quartet of hip-looking guys take slugs of Mountain Dew ("nothin's more intense!")—and lift off, wearing rocket belts, each one embracing an exotic-looking babe.

A blase youngster sitting on his bed, and bored out of his skull by his Dad's earnest lecture on the birds and bees, discreetly pops a Starburst—and then obviously comes. While Dad obliviously natters on, the kid imagines a tremendous wave, then sits bolt upright with a look of wired euphoria, and then he's suddenly a joyous swimmer in deep bright blue waters, amid giant floating chunks and slices of fresh fruit. ("The juice is loose!" screams out the all-male chorus as the boy settles back looking slyly satiated and that big fool leaves the room.)

Such images can only lead to a widespread sense of disappointment (and have no doubt contributed to cases of emotional disorder among teenagers). The problem here is not that kids will actually believe that munching Skittles is like dropping acid.

Rather, it's the likelihood that all that wild music and intoxicating imagery, inappropriately linked with mere consumer goods, has established an impossible standard of enjoyment. Every pleasure, the commercials say, must be a major kick such as you've never felt in all your life (and such, of course, as you can only get from PepsiCo or Mars or Reebok or Nintendo). Thus that propaganda makes it ever harder to recall what actual pleasures should be like; and so it's only natural that the kids bombarded by those ads would come to feel ever more jaded, ever more blase—numb enough, perhaps, to need those still more dangerous stimulants that Channel One so piously deplores.

To recognize the falseness of that propaganda, to learn to read its images, and also to read widely and discerningly enough to start to understand the all-important differences between a good life and a bad one: such are the proper aims of school. Which is why Channel One should not be there.

Discussion and Assignments

Introduction and The Ads in Context

1. Miller states the news on Channel One is nothing more than "filler" for getting the audience ready for the ads. What specifically does Miller mean by "filler"? According to Miller what relationship does the *quality* of news programming on Channel One have to do with the ads?

Buy the Power!

2. According to Miller, how are the ads on Channel One made to appeal to the general psychological dispositions of teenagers? What is the relationship between the feeling of power and control the ads convey, and the products they sell?

Lesson #1: "Watch."

3. Miller closes this section with the comment that the advertisement for Skittles is like an allegory of Channel One itself. How are the reptiles in the ad like the kids in class watching Channel One? Why, according to Miller, is this type of *watching* objectionable? Do you agree or disagree with Miller on this point?

Lesson #2: "Don't Think."

4. Miller claims the ads on Channel One glamorize ignorance. Do you agree with Miller on this point?

Lesson #3: "Let Us Fix It."

5. How does Channel One's ads misrepresent the complexity of life, according to Miller? What role does technology play in this misrepresentation? Do you agree or disagree with Miller on this point?

Lesson #4: "Eat Now."

6. Why target a teenage audience with food ads? Miller claims the food ads on Channel One are intentionally associated with being powerful or in control. How is this especially so with girls, according to Miller? Do you agree or disagree with Miller on this point? If Miller has a point here, can you offer any other evidence to help him prove his case?

Lesson #5: "You're Ugly."

7. What is the contradiction Miller speaks of between how foods are sold on Channel One and the actual effects of the foods themselves? Do you think Miller

has a strong objection here? Or is he making too much of the issue? Do you believe such ads affect how teenagers view themselves?

Lesson #6: "Just Say Yes." and Addiction 101

8. In the last two sections Miller introduces the notion of addiction by comparing the advertisers on Channel One to drug dealers. But a careful reading from the beginning of Miller's paper will yield several specific reasons why he believes the analogy of comparing advertisers to drug dealers is a strong one.

   a. What are the similarities between drug dealers selling drugs to kids and the way in which products on Channel One are sold to kids, according to Miller? List the specific characteristics Miller claims both have in common.

   b. How fair a characterization is it when Miller compares the dependence drug dealers cultivate in kids with the dependence advertisers cultivate in their viewers?

Concluding Questions

9. In his closing paragraphs Miller suggests a darker relation may exist between the standards portrayed in the ads on Channel One and the use of illicit drugs—that the ads establish an impossible standard of enjoyment, making it easier for kids to use drugs in search of more powerful stimulants. Do you agree or disagree with Miller on this point? In a 300 word essay take a position, pro or con, on Miller's claim that the ads on Channel One encourage standards that make it easier for kids to try drugs.

10. What is the proper aim of a school, according to Miller? What is the proper aim of a school according to *you?* Do you believe Channel One can occupy a meaningful place in a school, according to the aims you believe a school should have?

11. If you were defending Channel One from Miller's criticisms, how would you respond? Create an argument using the following argument form: Issue, Definitions, Premises, Conclusion. Remember to use clear, declarative statements throughout your presentation.

   Issue: Whether Channel One should be allowed to broadcast its news program, including commercials, in public schools.
   Definitions:
   Premises:
   Conclusion:

6.4 Hot News in Class

Samuel C. Gwynne

Compared with most of her classmates at the University of Southern California, Lisa Ling had an exciting vacation last summer. While others were waiting tables or sunning at the beach, the 22-year-old senior was interviewing the Dalai Lama in his palace of exile in Dharmsala, India. She also spent time in Tibet, where she was arrested for posing as a tourist, but not before

From Time, *December 18, 1995, p. 79. Reprinted with permission.*

smuggling out four hours of contraband video. In Algeria she traveled with an armed escort, and in Iran she was threatened with detention. And she still got back in time for the start of classes in September.

Though few adult TV watchers know her, Ling is a celebrity to millions of American teenagers. In between classes at U.S.C., she works as a correspondent for Channel One News, which sends a daily 12-minute newscast to 12,000 American secondary schools. Since its debut in 1990, Channel One has been a controversial operation, mainly because inside each program it packages two minutes of commercials for products like Pepsi and Reebok shoes. Created by media entrepreneur Christopher Whittle (who sold it last year to K-III Communications), Channel One still raises hackles in some quarters: officials in New York State, for instance, have thus far refused to allow the newscast into schools.

Yet after five years on the air, Channel One News has filled an important niche. The program now reaches 8 million students, or 40% of all teenagers in the country. That is roughly five times the number of teens who watch newscasts on ABC, CBS, NBC and CNN combined. And though the mix of MTV-style graphics, rock music and on-air pop quizzes is more sprightly than anything Peter Jennings or Tom Brokaw delivers, the newscast is hardly dumbed down.

In contrast to the sports-and-celebrity-heavy format of its early days, the newscast now stresses social issues of interest to young people, with enterprising stories on the homeless, teens in prison and endangered wolves. It has featured interviews with Janet Reno, Benazir Bhutto and Mikhail Gorbachev—who dropped by Channel One's Hollywood studio for the chat. The news program won a prestigious Peabody Award for its coverage of AIDS, and in 1994 beat out such network competition as *Prime Time Live* for an award at the Chicago Film Festival.

Perhaps most impressive is its coverage of world affairs. At a time when the broadcast networks are cutting back on their overseas coverage, Channel One has sent its squad of nine correspondents, ranging in age from 18 to 28, to Haiti, Rwanda, Bosnia and other global hot spots. Their stories frequently run three or four minutes—enormous by network-news standards—and have an immediacy that the young audience can relate to. Reporting from Rwanda, correspondent Anderson Cooper took viewers along on a trip through the country in which his car got stuck in the mud and ran out of gas, before reaching scenes of slaughter so grisly he at one point gagged on camera. Cooper was also in Haiti in the days before the downfall of the Cédras regime. His reports had an appealing casualness and intimacy: "I was just listening to some Bob Marley. I was listening to the line, 'I don't want to wait in vain for your love,' and shots went off."

Most of Channel One's staff of 200 have little professional experience, and about half are still in school. "We look for people who can connect to our audience," says David Neuman, a former NBC programming vice president who took over Channel One's news operation in 1992. "We don't want jackets and ties. No pretensions, no poses. That arrogance that you usually see in the news business doesn't work here. If you start acting that way, some 14-year-old out there will see right through it and say, 'You make me sick.'"

Apparently, the strategy is working. Two independent studies have shown that more than 90% of teachers in Channel One schools approve of the show and find it useful; the program has a 99% renewal rate. In one of the studies, the University of Michigan's Jerome Johnston found a 6%-to-8% increase in awareness of current events among students who watch Channel One regularly.

More established news organizations are starting to take notice. Channel One has been involved in a joint reporting project with *U.S. News & World Report* and *60 Minutes* and has an ongoing relationship with ABC News. "We are very impressed by their product," says ABC News vice president Bill Abrams. "They do serious stories that are credible, well produced and as good or better than most TV stations." Indeed, the network earlier this year paid Channel One perhaps the ultimate compliment: it hired away Cooper, Channel One's man in Rwanda and Haiti, to become ABC's youngest correspondent.

Discussion and Assignments

1. What standards or model does Gwynne employ to evaluate the quality of Channel One's news broadcast? Do you think the standards or model is reasonable for Channel One's audience? Why or why not?

2. Why, according to Gwynne, is Channel One so effective at connecting with its teenage audience? Does Gwynne leave out any important evaluative considerations in his appraisal of Channel One? What would you include in evaluating Channel One's performance that Gwynne left out?

3. Critics like Mark Crispin Miller (article 6.3) claim that most network news is no more than a continuous stream of calibrated sound bites, superficial coverage of complex affairs, and that it is this wasteland Channel One mimics in the morning hours for captive school kids. How do you think Gwynne would respond to such a criticism? How does such a criticism speak to Gwynne's standards, and to those who support Channel One?

4. Gwynne notes that some of Channel One's stories run as long as three to four minutes in length, "enormous" by network news standards. Does a three- to four-minute news story strike you as "enormous"? Does this claim imply anything about Gwynne's and Channel One's expectations of school kids? If kids can watch natural history, social science, or humanities documentaries that run from one-half hour to one hour long (e.g., the Discovery Channel and Cousteau documentaries), do you think it's possible kids could focus their interest on news stories for a longer period as well? If so, does this speak in any way to Channel One's effectiveness as a news channel, and to the educational standards it sets for teenagers?

6.5 Anti–Channel One Crusade Is Failing

CASEY LARTIGUE, JR.

CALLING COMMERCIALIZED EDUCATIONAL programming "parental neglect," consumer advocate Ralph Nader led the charge against Channel One during a Senate Labor and Human Resources Committee panel that convened on Thursday. Rather than recognizing that more than 12,000 schools freely chose to subscribe to Channel One's award-winning programming, Nader called it "a taxpayer rip-off" for its inclusion of two minutes of commercials to the ten minutes of news it shows daily in schools. He also criticized it for giving the schools estimated grants of $25,000 each in electronic hardware.

Nader made the case for a Senate investigation of Channel One in a May 12th op-ed in the *San Francisco Bay Guardian*. Nader's various spin-off organizations have been criticizing Channel One for years. But since the nation's schools have ignored Nader's petitions, he has decided that brute force is needed after all. In 1998 a coalition led by Commercial Alert, a Nader-affiliated group, convinced Sen. Richard Shelby (R-Ala.) to call for Senate hearings on Channel One.

Channel One's critics are fighting a losing battle and turning to Congress in desperation because they have failed to get support from the very people who could legitimize their crusade: teachers, students, administrators and parents. Even the education organizations that passed resolutions against Channel One in 1989 and 1990 seem to

From The Cato Institute, *Today's Commentary, May 24, 1999. Printed with permission of the author.*

have realized that the battle has been lost. None of them signed the letter the anti–Channel One coalition sent to CEOs of companies that advertise on Channel One asking them to pull their ads, and none of them will be testifying at the hearings. The education establishment hasn't reversed its early opposition to Channel One, but it seems to have realized something that Nader and his crowd refuse to admit: the people who watch Channel One want the program, even with commercials.

Schools eagerly sign up for Channel One despite the hostility from groups like Nader's anti-business Commercial Alert. The estimated 8 million students watching every morning and 400,000 educators, who prescreen it, like what they're seeing according to a three-year study of 156 U.S. public schools by the University of Michigan's Institute for Social Research.

Two-thirds of the teachers using Channel One said they would "strongly" or "very strongly" recommend the program. Another quarter of the teachers said they would recommend it, but "with reservations." Only 7 percent said that they would not recommend it. Sixty-one percent of principals in the same schools felt that their schools' current events materials were better because of Channel One's programming. Only one principal felt that the curriculum was weaker with Channel One.

The anti–Channel One coalition first tried to shame advertisers into not advertising on Channel One when it was founded a decade ago. When that failed, they threatened boycotts. Some states even sued (and threatened to withhold funding from) schools in their states that accepted Channel

One. Despite the criticism, the dire warnings, the hysterical attacks, school after school signed up for Channel One's free equipment, news, and commercials.

The anti–Channel One coalition can't even convince people in their own states to reject the network. Sen. Shelby, who called for the Senate hearings, and Channel One critic Jim Metrock are both based in Alabama, where 438 schools (70 percent) subscribe to Channel One. Before turning to the Senate for a national ban, Metrock and Shelby should convince their fellow Alabamans.

The anti–Channel One crowd has lost in the courts, in the marketplace of ideas, and, most important, in the schools. Despite knowing that administrators at 12,000 schools prescreen Channel One every morning, that 99 percent of schools renew the three-year contract, that at least one independent study has found that students are more knowledgeable about current events after watching Channel One, and that numerous parents have also seen Channel One for themselves and support it, Channel One's critics refuse to admit defeat.

Although it is questionable that the Senate should investigate Channel One at all, as long as the senators are involved, they should watch Channel One for themselves and attest to its educational value for teenagers. As for Nader, his only lesson for the students is: If you find that you are losing the battle in the marketplace of ideas, and that your opponents continue to excel despite your insults and threats, take it to the hallowed halls of Congress.

Discussion and Assignments

1. Lartigue cites several statistics (e.g., Channel One has a 99 percent renewal rate) to support his case that schools should be allowed to subscribe to Channel One if they want to. What are the two strongest statistics he employs to support his argument? In a paragraph on each explain why are they so helpful in supporting his argument? Are there any statistics he employs that incline you to ask for clarification or more details? Which ones are they, and what is it you would like clarified?

2. From what perspective does Lartigue address the issue of commercials on Channel One?

3. Lartigue criticizes Ralph Nader for being critical of Channel One's policy of giving $25,000 of hardware to schools that subscribe to Channel One. Critics like Nader

claim schools find it hard to turn down Channel One because they do not have the money to purchase the technology on their own. Lartigue argues that subscribing to Channel One is essentially an issue of freedom of choice. Indeed, in his first paragraph he states that "12,000 schools freely chose to subscribe to Channel One's award-winning programming." If in fact many schools do not have the money to buy $25,000 of hardware, plus a continuous cable line feed, how are we to assess Lartigue's claim that all 12,000 schools *freely choose* to subscribe to Channel One?

4. What standards does Lartigue employ to assess the quality of Channel One's programming? Do you agree or disagree with the standards?

5. Does Lartigue meet the objections of his critics? If he left out something important, what specifically is it, and how might he have best met the objection?

Concluding Questions and Observations

1. Defenders of Channel One have claimed the commercials in the Channel One broadcasts are not much different from the ads schoolchildren see in the newspapers they read at school for their school assignments, or the ads they see on the Internet when they search for information for their school assignments. In a 300 word essay assess the strength or weakness of this analogy by comparing newspaper ads and Internet ads to Channel One ads. Should the ads on Channel One be acceptable in public schools because we already approve of kids reading newspapers in schools that have ads, and we also permit them to search the Internet where there are ads? How similar or dissimilar are the situations?

Chapter 7

The Tabloids and Checkbook Journalism

Background

CHECKBOOK JOURNALISM refers to the practice of paying money to a nontraditional news source for a news story. Examples of checkbook journalism are as easy to find as the checkout counter at your local supermarket. Many of the familiar tabloids like *The National Enquirer,* the *Globe,* and the *Star* routinely pay for stories and pictures that fill their pages. For example, about half of the 25 to 30 stories in each issue of the *Star* are paid for.

In addition to their permanent staffs, the tabloids rely on a network of tipsters and freelance photographers to gather their stories. Informants from the inside, a hairdresser or a chauffeur, are typical sources. So is the young man delivering flowers to a movie star. A short gossip piece may go for as little as $100, while a cover story at the *Star* goes for about $5,000. The really big stories go for much more. Tony Frost, editor of the *Globe,* was reported to have paid over $210,000 for pictures of Princess Diana with Dodi Fayed on a yacht in the Mediterranean. The *Star* is said to have paid $500,000 for exclusive photo rights to O. J. Simpson's homecoming party after his acquittal at his criminal trial. The *Star* paid $35,000 for a picture of Bill Cosby, the entertainer, with Autumn Jackson, the woman who claimed she was his illigitimate daughter (article 7.3).

Of the three top-selling tabloids noted above, the *Globe* has been most willing to test the boundaries of journalistic acceptability. The *Globe* published murder pictures of JonBenet Ramsey, and autopsy photos of Ron Goldman and Nicole Brown Simpson, the murder victims O. J. Simpson was acquitted of killing in his criminal trial. And it was the *Globe* that published the story on sportscaster Frank Gifford's encounters with Suzen Johnson. The *Globe* has acknowledged paying Johnson in the "five-figures" for her story, and is widely believed to have videotaped the encounters between her and Gifford as well (articles 7.5 to 7.7). In his effort to flush out adulterous hypocrites in government during the impeachment hearings of President Clinton, Larry Flint, publisher of *Hustler* magazine, offered up to $1 million to anyone who could prove a congressman or high ranking government official had had an adulterous affair. When the dust settled House Speaker-Designate Bob Livingston's political career was over. When he resigned, Livingston was next in line to officiate over Clinton's impeachment hearings.

The persistence and ingenuity of the tabloids has often left the mainstream press in a catch-up mode. Though the mainstream press roundly criticizes the tabloids for their methods of news gathering, they often find themselves reporting on stories the tabloids broke. In 1992 the *Star* was the first newspaper to report on President Clinton's affair with Gennifer Flowers (for a reported $150,000). The *Star* scored big again with their story on Dick Morris, a political consultant to President Clinton, when they caught wind of Morris's trysts with Sherry Rowlands, a prostitute (for a reported "low five-figures" sum). As it turned out, Morris was letting Rowlands listen in on telephone conversations with the president. It was *The National Enquirer* that got a photo of Donna Rice on Senator Gary Hart's lap on the boat "Monkey Business." The picture all but ended Hart's presidential aspirations. In what is easily one of their greatest prizes, the *Enquirer* got a picture of O. J. Simpson in Bruno Magli shoes. The picture likely played a role in securing a conviction in Simpson's civil trial. A reward offered by the *Enquirer* brought a tip that helped capture Mikhail Markhasev, the man who murdered Ennis Cosby, Bill Cosby's son.

As a group, the mainstream media voice strong disapproval of paying for news, though it's not always clear if the distinction between paying for a story and reporting stories for free is as obvious as they claim. For example, former President Gerald Ford and former Secretary of State Henry Kissinger signed million dollar contracts with NBC News as "advisor consultants" soon after they left office. Former White House Chief-of-Staff H. R. Haldeman, a principal figure in the Watergate scandal, signed a deal with CBS News to tell his story. More recently ABC News paid $16,000 for a video from Nathan Dykeman, a close friend of Dylan Klebold, one of the alleged shooters at Columbine High School. ABC claimed the accompanying interview Dykeman gave ABC News was for *free*. When the network was criticized for the payment, a spokeswoman for ABC News stated in the future they will disclose when they engage in financial arrangements to secure a story from "an unusual, non–news-gathering source" (articles 7.1 and 7.2).

With notable exceptions, such as the Dykeman video and interview just mentioned, traditional news organizations claim they don't pay for news, and regard the prohibition on such payments as sacred. Money for the news, they claim, is the lifeblood of the tabloids, not the legitimate media. They claim when news is traded for money you can never be sure whether the individual is giving an accurate account or exaggerating the story. News organizations need to report unbiased facts. Payment for a story runs the risk the story will be made more attractive by shading the details or by outright falsification. Another issue is credibility. Journalists, reporters, and news organizations need to closely guard their credibility; they claim that if they're paying for news, encouraging the sale of news to the highest bidder, their credibility will suffer.

For their part, the tabloids see no reason to be critical of paying for stories. The standards are clear for responsible journalism, with or without cash changing hands. Check out the story to see if it's accurate and truthful. If it adds up, it's news. Paying for a story doesn't necessarily mean the journalist or news organization has been irresponsible, or that the story is inaccurate.

Encompassing the narrow parameters of paying for the news are broader issues concerning the relation of tabloids to the mainstream media. The pay-for-news tabloids are popular, and they're supported by a more literate, discerning population than the mainstream media would like to admit. (Indeed, *Time* magazine named Steve Coz, editor of *The National Enquirer,* one of the 100 most influential people of 1997.) This can be so only if they strike a responsive cord in their readers. What do the tabloids do, what is it they offer, that readers find so appealing? This study section will address the issue of paying for news, and the popularity and function of the tabloids in American culture.

Readings

Articles 7.1 and 7.2 Our first two readings are from the magazine *Editor & Publisher;* the first is an unsigned editorial by the magazine, and the second an essay by Mark Fitzgerald. Both articles focus on ABC News's payment of $16,000 for a video from Nathan Dykeman, a friend of one of the suspected shooters (Dylan Klebold) at Columbine High School. ABC News claimed it paid for the rights to the video only, and that the interview it conducted with Dykeman was for free. Many critics disagreed, claiming the network engaged in checkbook journalism.

Article 7.3 Also from *Editor & Publisher,* John Sullivan's *Defending Play for Pay* chronicles reporter Christopher Doherty's efforts to secure Autumn Jackson's story for the tabloid the *Globe.* Entertainer Bill Cosby had a brief affair with Jackson's mother, and Autumn Jackson claimed Cosby was her father. The initial offer to Jackson for the story reportedly rose from $3,000 to $25,000, but no contract was ever signed. Doherty claims the main reason the deal didn't go through was that Jackson refused to take a polygraph test. Jackson was eventually convicted of trying to extort money from Cosby. Doherty testified at the trial. The article gives us a glimpse into the inner workings of how tabloids get their stories, and their justifications for securing them with cash payments.

Article 7.4 In his article *In Defense of Checkbook Journalism,* Nicholas von Hoffman points out that ABC charged Super Bowl prices for advertising when Barbara Walters interviewed Monica Lewinsky, and they got the interview for free. Von Hoffman sees no reason why Lewinsky should not have been paid for her appearance. He's critical of those who claim paying for stories encourages individuals to exaggerate or fabricate events for money, arguing there are plenty of other motives for individuals to exaggerate or make up stories for the consumption of the media.

Article 7.5 Steve Coz, editor of the popular tabloid *The National Enquirer,* published *When Tabloids Cross the Line* in *The New York Times* soon after the *Globe* published its stories on sportscaster Frank Gifford's two secret rendezvous with Suzen Johnson in a $400 per night hotel room. The article is as much about checkbook journalism as it is about the ethical parameters the *Globe* tested when it reported its story. The *Globe* was believed to have paid the hotel expense, secretly filmed Gifford and Johnson's two encounters, and paid Johnson several thousand dollars for the story. Coz claims the *Globe* entrapped Gifford, thereby creating news rather than reporting the news. The editorial director of the *Globe,* Dan Schwartz, insists it's Frank Gifford's behavior that's at issue, not the *Globe*'s, claiming police departments act in a similar fashion every day.

Article 7.6 *Gifford Tumbles into Tabloid Trap,* by Howard Kurtz from *The Washington Post,* is of particular interest because of the way Kurtz covers both the Gifford story and the *Globe* at the same time. Mainstream media like *The Washington Post* claim they don't cover stories like the Gifford story, preferring to leave such fare to the tabloids. But in this case Kurtz manages to report on the Gifford story by way of reporting on the *Globe.* His comments on the *Globe's* participation in securing the story constitute a fair portion of what he has to say.

Article 7.7 In *Getting Kathie Lee,* William Powers examines Kurtz's treatment (article 7.6) of the Gifford story and the *Globe.* The Kurtz article, Powers claims, is an example of how the mainstream press slips in coverage of stories they say are not worth reporting, by covering them as ethical issues related to the tabloids. This way they slip in coverage of the scandal, all the while appearing to be above it all— and, unlike the tabloids, they get the stories for free. His critical remarks place the tabloids within a specific ethical framework in American society, their morality targeted to a broad middle-class consensus, focused most prominently on the "sins" of hypocrisy and pride. Though the tabloids may be cruel, their honesty does speak to specific moral norms held in common by much of the American populace, even more so than the mainstream press.

7.1 Put Away the Checkbook

ABC'S THIN EXPLANATION is a good reminder for all, journalism is not a science, but a matter of trial and error. And, as in our personal lives, journalism often learns best from its errors rather than its lucky streaks. In that spirit, we in the press should be grateful . . . sort of . . . to ABC News for reminding us all once more how insidious are the temptations of checkbook journalism.

ABC News stoutly denies that it engaged in anything so loathsome as checkbook journalism. Let's look at the facts. Everybody covering the Columbine High School shootings has been trying to talk at length with Nathan Dykeman, an 18-year-old who apparently was the best friend of one of the presumed gunmen. So far, only two news organizations have: *The National Enquirer,* which paid Dykeman a reported $10,000, and ABC News, which acknowledges paying $16,000.

Both paid Dykeman for access to video games, a high-school yearbook, and other materials. ABC aired a home video showing presumed gun-man Dylan Klebold as well as a music video in which Klebold acts out a violent fantasy at the high school. ABC says it bought this material only to bring context to the Dykeman interview, which it claims it did not pay for. In other words, it paid the subject of a news story—but it did not pay the subject of a news story for an interview.

That's their story, anyway, and we're not surprised that few people are buying it. As we report elsewhere in this issue, ABC News' subtle parsing didn't pass the smell test among many of the journalists gathering last weekend at the Investigative Reporters and Editors national conference in Kansas City, Mo. Nor is that reaction confined to reporters hard-wired for skepticism.

The furor ABC News kicked up may, in fact, be the best thing about the whole episode. It is prompting an examination of conscience about a practice that is, as we see with ABC, all too easily rationalized away. The uproar reminds us that checkbook journalism encourages its recipients to tell reporters what they want to hear. Checkbook

From Editor & Publisher *132, no. 24 (1999): 50. Reprinted with permission.*

journalism manages to impugn the integrity of both giver and receiver—a point that is not lost on readers and viewers.

The flak ABC News is getting reminds us, too, that even a very good news organization can slip. The most heartening thing of all, though, was that when other responsible journalists saw what ABC had done, they erupted in disdain—instead of deciding that the ground rules of good journalism had changed and that it was time to reach for their own checkbooks.

ABC News says that in the future it will make on-air disclosures of any financial arrangements when it purchases things from a nontraditional news source such as Dykeman. Full disclosure from news organizations is something always to be desired. We can't help thinking, though, that the disclosure that will best serve to keep ABC News away from any further dabbling in checkbook journalism was when the payment to Dykeman was first reported on the front page of *The New York Times* business section.

7.2 For ABC News . . . "The Price Is Right"

MARK FITZGERALD

WHEN ABC NEWS paid $16,000 to a friend of one of the presumed Columbine High School killers in Littleton, Colo., many in the press wondered what it was buying: the homemade music video and other footage of alleged gunman Dylan Klebold— or the exclusive interview with the 18-year-old it identified as Klebold's best friend?

The payment, revealed in *The New York Times* May 31, had many at the Investigative Reporters and Editors (IRE) national conference June 3–6 wondering if journalism is now at another critical juncture. To many, the payment represented the entrance of a big-name, mainstream news organization into the murky waters of checkbook journalism.

"It's checkbook journalism. If you're paying for the tape to get the interview—it's checkbook journalism," says Bob Greene, the retired assistant managing editor of Long Island, N.Y.–based *Newsday* who is often considered the "Father of IRE."

ABC News says that's not the case at all. In its first response to the payment revelation, it said there was no connection between the payment for the videos and the interview with Klebold's friend, Nathan Dykeman. In the report airing on "Good Morning America" May 24, an ABC reporter said the network had "obtained the rights to his [Dykeman's] home video."

Even as IRE was meeting in Kansas City, Mo., ABC was changing its policy to require reporters to make an on-air disclosure of any financial arrangement from "an unusual, non–news-gathering source," as a spokeswoman put it.

It is the practice itself that is wrong, says James Neff, a former columnist for *The [Cleveland] Plain Dealer* who has written several investigative books, including *Mobbed Up*, a biography of former International Brotherhood of Teamsters president Jackie Presser. "When money transfers to the subject of an interview, that is wrong. I would never do that, and in the classes I teach, I say that is wrong," says Neff. "I've sold exclusive video footage I have gathered on a project," he notes, "and I have no problem with that. But it is a very different story when you are [selling] and you are the subject of the interview."

Greene, who now teaches journalism at Hofstra University in Hempstead, N.Y., says he is somewhat optimistic that the practice will not spread. "I don't think so because everybody is screaming and shouting about it," he says. The reaction to the incident, Greene says, reminds him of the furor when *The New York Times* and NBC News used the name of the woman who accused William Kennedy Smith of rape in a widely reported case in Florida, arguing it was justified because her name had been disclosed by the *Globe*, a supermarket tabloid. "Everybody shouted and screamed then. The *Times* and NBC did it once, and then nobody did it again. This can

From Editor & Publisher *132, no. 24 (1999): 10. Reprinted with permission.*

go either way—it will go backwards or it will go forward because everybody says everybody does it. I'm inclined to think that sanity will prevail," Greene says. One big reason: "They don't have the budget anymore! ABC, CBS—they're all cutting back. I can't imagine anyone in the networks wanting to go into checkbook journalism."

Mainstream newspapers are not likely to be the targets for those with stories to sell, Greene and other IRE members say. "Most of the people who go around hustling this stuff are going to go to the *Globe* or *The [National] Enquirer,* where they can get the real money for it," Greene says.

Print reporters are likely to be spared the pressure for two other reasons, says Neff, now director of Ohio State University's Kiplinger Fellows program. "I would say there is almost no problem in print, because that is such a taboo. I don't see them coming to newspapers because we don't need this kind of thing. I feel sorry for TV because they do need compelling pictures," Neff says.

Public repulsion can eliminate certain TV practices, some broadcasters at the conference noted. The best evidence of that is the virtual disappearance of the "ambush interview," in which camera crews chase after news subjects who clearly do not want to talk. "We started to feel there was a real backlash to it," says Julie Kramer, senior producer for WCCO-TV in Minneapolis. "People began to feel sympathetic towards the people being chased."

"I think they're sort of passe now," adds Eric Engberg, CBS News correspondent in the network's Washington, D.C., bureau. A reporter a couple of decades ago, he says, "could do a lot of things expecting the public to applaud him because he was fighting against evil. We are not the heroes anymore," Engberg says. "The public views us as bullies and know-it-alls, people who throw their weight around unfairly—and in certain instances we have behaved that way."

For investigative journalists writing for newspapers and other print media, the pressure to whip out the checkbook rarely comes from people like the presumed Littleton shooter's friend, says author Neff. "Where we are being held up and asked to pay for information is from the state and federal government agencies who are privatizing all these data. Those are the real pirates," says Neff.

Discussion and Assignments

Note: This material applies to the two preceding articles.

1. Why do the editors of *Editor & Publisher* and Mark Fitzgerald accuse ABC News of checkbook journalism? What is it about the payment of $16,000 to Nathan Dykeman that disturbs the editors and Fitzgerald so much?

2. Suppose someone were to argue the following:

   The National Enquirer paid Nathan Dykeman $10,000, and ABC News paid him $16,000, not much by today's standards. News is really just another commodity, and Dykeman just happened to have some of the commodity the news organizations wanted. Why should news organizations get his story for free, make money from it, and leave him with nothing more than a sense of civic duty? If you want to turn a profit from reporting and selling the news, like *The National Enquirer* and ABC do, why shouldn't you pay for it like any other business? Considering the stories they got, I'd say that at $26,000 they got a pretty good deal.

   Respond with a 300 word essay, either pro or con.

3. Construct an argument, either pro or con, regarding ABC News paying Nathan Dykeman $16,000 for his video (and free interview) using the following form:

   Issue: Whether it was appropriate for ABC News to pay Nathan Dykeman $16,000 for a video of Dylan Klebold and an interview.
   Definitions:
   Premises:
   Conclusion:

7.3 Defending Play for Pay

JOHN SULLIVAN

CHRISTOPHER DOHERTY BELIEVES he is like any other reporter whose job it is to cover a controversial story—even if it means serving as a "middle man" to negotiate a contract to pay for a story he wants to publish. The freelance reporter for the national supermarket tabloid, the *Globe*, recently testified how he negotiated a $25,000 contract for Autumn Jackson's exclusive story about her claim that she is entertainer Bill Cosby's illegitimate daughter.

Jackson and her two accomplices were convicted on July 25 for attempting to extort approximately $40 million from Cosby. They now face a possible prison term of 12 years and fines of $750,000. Doherty told the court that Jackson—who had been supported over the years by Cosby after he had a brief affair with her mother (although Cosby denies Jackson is his daughter)—told him she needed the money because she was broke and living out of her car.

But few reporters, especially those in the mainstream press, are authorized to offer large sums of money in order to get an exclusive, high-profile story. In the case of Autumn Jackson, Doherty said, matter-of-factly, "I acted very much as a go-between."

Although *Globe* Los Angeles bureau chief Mary Ann Norbom is Doherty's immediate supervisor—who he was in constant contact with during the negotiations with Jackson's people—"the ultimate decision was with [*Globe* editor] Tony Frost, especially with this kind of money involved," Doherty said. The reporter, who has been working for the weekly tabloid on a day-rate basis for almost four years, said on the stand that he was working with Jackson's representative on the same day that Cosby's son Ennis was murdered. At that point, Doherty was told by his editors to get the story "at all costs."

Doherty testified that the initial offer of $3,000 went to $25,000, but no one was able to sign the contract. When the amount reportedly rose to $50,000, Doherty said Jackson would not be paid until the story was checked out and published. Two days after Ennis Cosby's murder, the now-convicted extortionists were arrested in New York City.

Doherty believes that despite their "pay for play" reputation, the national "supermarket" tabloids work very hard to find the truth to the sometimes sensational stories they publish. "We do pay for stories, but only for when they're truthful and that we can satisfy ourselves that they are truthful. It's a fallacy to think that we throw money at people for stories that they've dreamt up."

But Doherty's view of what journalism and the *Globe* is all about is certainly not a prevalent view among most journalists. "I think it's abominable," said Sig Gissler, a professor in the Graduate School of Journalism at Columbia and former editor of the *Milwaukee Journal,* commenting on the checkbook journalism methods the tabloids employ. "It harms the credibility of news organizations, and credibility is vital. I regard it [credibility] as the crown jewel of journalism. And when you pay for stories, you tarnish that credibility."

Gissler said that the journalism the tabloids practice not only induces people to exaggerate and fabricate because they know they can get money for their stories, but encourages people to embrace an extortion mentality—"either you pay me money or I'll take it to a supermarket tabloid."

Although Doherty says he has no idea what Jackson's motive was, the main reason the deal the *Globe* had with her did not go through was because she refused to take a polygraph test. "For someone who we are about to consider paying a large amount of money to, if she isn't confident enough to take a polygraph, then alarm bells are going to start ringing," said Doherty.

The reporter said he believes any mainstream newspaper or magazine would have pursued the Autumn Jackson claims, whether they eventually acceded to her monetary demands or not. "If a reporter from *Time* magazine or *The New York Times* received a phone call from Autumn Jackson, he or she would have been equally excited about the prospects of the story and would have pursued it just as aggressively as I did," said Doherty.

From Editor & Publisher *130, no. 31 (1997): 14. Reprinted with permission.*

Walter Jacobsen, managing editor of *Time* magazine, disagrees with Doherty. "I think a reporter from *Time* would have probably pursued it, but we would not have been as aggressive and probably would have felt it was a violation of family privacy and not proceeded with the story."

Although *The New York Times* did publish a story on checkbook journalism related to Doherty's testimony, a spokesperson said the newspaper would not comment on hypothetical or speculative scenarios.

Doherty, who has subsequently written a detailed, first-person story on himself for the *Globe* about his role in the case, strongly believes that his presence in the courtroom served a purpose. "My testimony proves that we as reporters and journalists, although we pay for accurate stories, doesn't mean we don't act in a responsible manner."

But Gissler thinks that as a journalistic principle, it's a bad practice to buy stories. "The net result, of course, from our side, is that it makes us [the newspapers] less credible. And we need to be enhancing our credibility. Sometimes the tabloids do unearth important stories. But as they say, even a blind pig can find an acorn."

Discussion and Assignments

1. Christopher Doherty claims he acted responsibly when he acted as a go-between in the Autumn Jackson negotiations. What evidence does he offer to convince you that a reporter can both pay for news and act responsibly? What is the strongest piece of evidence he offers? In a paragraph explain why you think it's strong. What's the weakest piece of evidence he offers to support his claim? In a paragraph explain why you think it's weak.

2. Why does Sig Gissler disagree with Doherty about paying for news? What's the strongest piece of evidence he offers to support his claim that reporters should not pay for stories? In a paragraph explain why you think it's so strong. What's the weakest piece of evidence he offers to support his claim that reporters should not pay for stories? In a paragraph explain why you think it's weak.

3. Of the two opposing views, Doherty and Gissler (questions 1 and 2), who has the stronger argument? Why?

4. Gissler claims that paying for stories "encourages people to embrace an extortion mentality—either you pay me or I'll take it to a supermarket tabloid." Look up the word *extortion* in your dictionary. Do you think it's appropriate when Gissler uses the term *extortion* in this context? Can you think of examples of how we use this word in other situations? How do those situations compare to paying for news?

7.4 In Defense of Checkbook Journalism

Nicholas von Hoffman

Monica S. Lewinsky may not fully take the place of a blockbuster movie hit, the likes of which have been in short supply at Disney of late, but she has done her bit to brighten up the ledger. Whether Ms. Monica's recent visit with Barbara Walters will long be remembered by most of us is doubtful, but the accounting department at ABC should cherish those golden moments the former Beverly Hills teenager brought to the company. Reports have it that the network was charging as much as $800,000 for a half minute commercial—near Super Bowl prices.

From The Wall Street Journal *March 8, 1998, p. A18. Reprinted with permission.*

What made the program so super delicious for ABC is that, thanks to the network's super high standards of journalistic ethics, it was not necessary to pay Super Bowl costs for Super Bowl profits. The estimated $35 million dollars in profits were garnered at no cost save ordinary overhead, thanks to the star performer appearing gratis. Ms. Monica wasn't paid a centime according to the proud disclaimer at the start of the program.

Assuming that ABC wasn't joshing us, Ms. Monica has more reason to complain of her treatment at the hands of the network than anything alleged of Ken Starr or Bill Clinton. Imagine, taking a pertly innocent 25-year-old ex-intern and making that kind of money off her without so much as a dollar in cash compensation. Talk about damsel abuse! You may be sure that Disney doesn't treat Donald Duck in so shabby a fashion.

But what else could they do? Had ABC rewarded Ms. Monica for her labors, ABC News would have been guilty of the crime of checkbook journalism. This is a felony not known to other areas of endeavor where it is assumed that people will be compensated for providing goods and services. (In Ms. Monica's case, it's hard to know what category to assign her: Is she a piece of goods or a highly specialized service?) But, however defined, she was the sine qua non, the raw material, without which ABC could have gotten its 35 mil.

Paper mills pay for the logs from which they manufacture the giant rolls of newsprint which are then bought and paid for by newspapers so that they will have something upon which to print the truth. No money, no logs, but the other raw material necessary to the news business, to wit, information, may not, according to the canon of newsbiz ethics, be bought and paid for. It would have been a sin and an ethical lapse for ABC to pay Monica either for her information or her performance or her not entirely displeasing image.

For a journalistic enterprise to practice checkbook journalism, that is to pay for the use of other people's intellectual property, is to relegate itself to the baser regions where the tabloids dwell. Mainline, mainstream respectables don't pay for stories because people who are paid to provide information may embellish the facts or even make them up. Never mind that news organizations daily circulate an incalculable number of embellished or fabricated stories supplied to them by people with motives other than money. Never mind that news organizations themselves will embellish or fabricate, the most recent glaring example of which was the Time/CNN confection of the Operation Tailwind story, a far-fetched yarn about the U.S. using poison gas years ago in Laos.

We may assume that Time-Warner's people made up this nonsense to kick up viewership and circulation, presumably in order to make more money. Hence, by the reasoning of those who deplore checkbook journalism, Time-Warner ought to abjure salaries and profits, since it was love of lucre which enticed it into broadcasting untruth. The only conclusion is that everybody in the newsbiz ought to fold up shop except National Public Radio, but then, again, the NPR staff is compensated. So, there you have it, money is ruining everything, just as mother said.

It is a tribute to the oral prestidigitation of the media managers that they have conned so many people into going along with these itty-bitty-ain't-we-pretty ethics. How they have gulled their raw material providers into free-of-charge cooperation surpasses understanding. They have done so even though adoption of checkbook journalism on a grand scale would surely improve the quality of what presently appears in our newspapers and on our television screens.

By and large, the news we value most is the news the media buys for cash, namely financial and sports information. Monica is the exception, a free lunch. She is a rare pigeon who brought in 70 million viewers pro bono, so to speak.

Ordinarily consumers get what the media pay for, which isn't much. If news were bought for what it's worth, news outlets would be more selective in what they offered their public, and politicians, knowing the better the interview, the higher the fee, might make an effort to say something somebody might think worth listening to. Under this arrangement, the right to cover Congress or the White House might be auctioned off, as the Olympics are. Over time the men and women of Washington could conceivably promote their sport as the National Football League has done, thereby fetching billions in fees.

Whether this new source of income would be sufficient to save Social Security time alone would tell, but in the meantime the arrangement might save our collective sanity.

The strictures against checkbook journalism are not the only idiosyncratic prohibition of this sort. Ticket scalping is another such. No laws prohibit antique scalping, or financial instrument scalping or real estate scalping, but when it comes to wrestling matches or Broadway musicals buying low and selling high can land a person in jail.

Another object of inexplicable though strenuous disapproval is loan sharking, which is defined as charging too much interest, and how much is too much? Finely calibrated instruments called shark-o-meters can answer the question, but if you ask the stock market it will tell you any interest above zero is too much. The bond market may give you a different reply. Ask a bad risk, and he'll tell you 125% interest per diem is better than two smashed knee caps.

If approached by a reporter to give your opinion of such ethical obiter dicta, before you reply, you might want to ask, "How much you payin', buddy?"

Discussion and Assignments

1. Von Hoffman states, "It would have been a sin and an ethical lapse for ABC to pay Monica either for her information or her performance or her not entirely displeasing image." Why does von Hoffman disagree with ABC's not paying Lewinsky for her interview?

2. What's the strongest piece of evidence von Hoffman offers to convince you news organizations should be willing to pay for stories? In a paragraph explain why you think it's strong. What's the weakest piece of evidence he offers? In a paragraph explain why you think it's weak.

3. Von Hoffman claims news organizations circulate embellished and fabricated stories every day, supplied by people with motives other than money. Does he illustrate what he means by this with examples? Is von Hoffman's claim a reasonable one? Can you illustrate what he means with a few examples? Let me offer a short list of (relatively) *noncash motives* that might qualify for what von Hoffman speaks of: love, hate, envy, dismay, admiration; the desire to appear courageous, brave, or to be a hero; politics, religion; the desire to appear you are doing your job at the local museum, elementary school, mayor's office, National Guard armory, or toxic dump.

   Does broadening the scope of motives make von Hoffman's argument more plausible? If so, just how far-reaching might the scope of fabricated stories extend in the "legitimate" media?

4. Von Hoffman ends his article by employing several analogies to support his argument. Which analogies strike you as most supportive of his case, and which do not?

5. a. Construct an argument opposed to von Hoffman's argument that mainstream news organizations should be able to pay for news. Use the following form: Issue, Definitions, Premises, Conclusion. You might want to study articles 7.1 to 7.3 to gather additional ideas to combine with yours. Remember to list your premises in clear, declarative statements, in the order they make the most sense.

   Issue: Whether the mainstream media should consider purchasing news stories.
   Definitions: (You may want to define *mainstream media*.)
   Premises:
   Conclusion: The mainstream media should not consider purchasing news stories.

   b. Now write a 300 word essay employing the argument you constructed.

7.5 When Tabloids Cross the Line

STEVE COZ

LANTANA, FLA.—Dogged reporters. Perspiring publicists. Anonymous tipsters. Long-lens cameras. High-speed chases. Secret sources. Flowing cash. Tedious stakeouts. Sleepless nights. Welcome to the world of tabloid journalism.

Such tried and true tabloid practices got *The National Enquirer* the photo of Donna Rice sitting on Gary Hart's lap. And *Star* magazine used typical tabloid techniques to get the story of Dick Morris, the President's adviser, sharing political secrets with Sherry Rowlands during their trysts at the Jefferson Hotel in Washington.

But the cat and mouse game between tabloids and public figures took an ugly turn earlier this month. It has been reported that the Florida-based *Globe* tabloid paid Suzen Johnson, a former flight attendant, to fly to New York City and entice Frank Gifford, the sports broadcaster, into meeting her in a hotel room. And if that doesn't sound outrageous enough, the reports also say the *Globe* arranged to secretly videotape the rendezvous. (The *Globe*'s editor would not say how the videotape was obtained.)

Mr. Gifford's wife, the TV personality Kathie Lee Gifford, set the table for tabloid scrutiny of her home life by publicly rhapsodizing about her happy marriage. She and Mr. Gifford certainly profited from this image. But without the *Globe*'s purported entrapment, Mr. Gifford would not have been in that hotel room. The *Globe* in effect created a story that humiliated the Giffords.

Don't get me wrong. *The Enquirer*, just like any other tabloid, would love to break a real story on the Giffords' marriage. Inquiring minds want to know, and that is why tabloids cover the private lives of celebrities. But the critical word here is "cover." We've chased down the cheating spouse, we've tried to get the telling pictures, we've reported the news. But we've never created the lover.

Examine *Star*'s coverage of Mr. Morris's affair with Ms. Rowlands, a prostitute. Star paid Ms. Rowlands thousands of dollars to dish the dirt, and she knew photographers were taking pictures of her with Mr. Morris on the balcony of their hotel room. But there is a very important difference between the Morris story and what has been reported about the Gifford story: Ms. Rowlands was actually having an affair with the married Mr. Morris for a year, and she claimed to know about his views, morals and actions. *Star*'s challenge was to confirm her story.

Although Ms. Johnson claimed that she and Mr. Gifford had flirtatious phone talks after meeting four years ago on a plane, she herself has said they did not rendezvous before meeting in the hotel. The *Globe* said its news gathering was fair. It wasn't.

What's next? Is someone going to buy a case of vodka and deliver it to a celebrity who is a recovering alcoholic and then report to readers that the star went on a binge?

When you create the news, you aren't reporting. There are enough real stories to cover without creating them. Tabloids don't need to orchestrate events. Those that report news that they've manufactured are lying to their readers.

From The New York Times, *Late Edition, East Coast, May 29, 1997, p. 21. Reprinted with permission.*

Discussion and Assignments

1. According to Coz, what's the distinction between creating rather than reporting the news? Can you think of any real-life or imagined situations where the distinction between the two is not as clear as Coz claims? Do you believe it applies to the *Globe* and the Frank Gifford situation as Coz claims?

2. Coz claims that "without the *Globe*'s purported entrapment, Mr. Gifford would not have been in that hotel room." Do you believe this is a reasonable claim? Do you

agree with Coz that the *Globe* entrapped Gifford? Why does Coz believe this one issue is so important? What do you believe constitutes entrapment?

3. More on entrapment and analogy. *Globe* Editorial Director Dan Schwartz is reported to have said the following: "The issue is not what we did, the issue is what Frank Gifford did. . . . If we did something that someone would consider close to entrapment, I'd say so do the police every day in catching criminals. We caught a moral criminal" (article 7.6).

   a. How strong is Schwartz's analogy of police catching criminals and the *Globe* catching a moral criminal? Does Schwartz's analogy convince you that the *Globe* didn't entrap Frank Gifford? From Schwartz's comment, is it possible to arrive at a definition of entrapment?

   b. Locate the analogies and examples Coz uses to make his case that the *Globe* entrapped Gifford, for example, buying a case of vodka and having it delivered to a recovering alcoholic, and comparing the Gifford affair to the Dick Morris affair. How strong or effective are these analogies and examples in making his case?

4. From Coz's perspective, did checkbook journalism have anything to do with the *Globe*'s handling of the Gifford affair?

5. Imagine it's your job as managing editor of the *Globe* to construct an argument in response to Coz's claim that you crossed the line and entrapped Frank Gifford. With the integrity of your tabloid being questioned, not to mention the heat you're taking from the mainstream press, the *Globe* can use a strong argument to defend its actions. So give it your best shot (and see if you can sell a few more copies in the process).

   a. Create an argument defending the *Globe*'s actions using the following argument form: Issue, Definitions, Premises, Conclusion. Remember to use only clear, declarative statements as premises, and list them in the order they make the most sense. I've included a few pieces to get you going.

   Issue: Whether the *Globe* entrapped Frank Gifford in a hotel room with Suzen Johnson, and then reported the rendezvous in the *Globe,* or whether they reported a legitimate news story.

   Definitions: (You knew it was coming: At the very least, you'll have to define *entrapment.*)

   Premises: Frank Gifford initiated contact with Suzen Johnson and carried on a flirtatious phone relationship with her for four years.
   Frank Gifford twice went to the hotel room of his own free will.

   Conclusion:

   b. Now write a 300 word essay arguing your case by employing the argument you constructed.

6. I've outlined Coz's argument below. Discuss my breakdown with your classmates. Would you make any changes?

When Tabloids Cross the Line, by Steve Coz

   Issue: When tabloids create news, they aren't reporting news; they are creating lies.

   Definitions: 1. *Create news* means to pay money to a person to engage in actions for the purpose of creating a story that can then be reported.

   2. *Tried and true reporting practices* means specific activities used to cover stories that have been widely used in the past and are known and accepted by the readers.

Premises:
1. Tabloids should cover and report news to confirm stories.
2. Tabloids use tried and true reporting practices such as using long-lens cameras, anonymous tipsters, and secret sources to confirm their stories.
3. The *Enquirer* used tried and true reporting practices to get a picture of Donna Rice on Gary Hart's lap.
4. The *Star* used traditional tabloid reporting practices to confirm that Dick Morris, the president's adviser, was having a tryst with Sherry Rowlands, a prostitute.
5. Reports say that the *Globe* paid Suzen Johnson to fly to New York and entice Frank Gifford into meeting her in a hotel room.
6. Reports say that the *Globe* paid to have the sexual encounter between Gifford and Johnson videotaped.
7. Suzen Johnson said she had flirtatious phone calls but never a rendezvous with Gifford before meeting in the hotel room.
8. Without the *Globe*'s entrapment of Frank Gifford, he would not have been in the hotel room.

Conclusion: The *Globe* broke the rules of tabloid journalism by creating a story by entrapping Frank Gifford into a sexual encounter with Suzen Johnson, thereby creating rather than reporting the news.

7.6 Gifford Tumbles into Tabloid Trap: *Globe*'s Tactics in Liaison Cause a Stir

HOWARD KURTZ

IT LOOKS LIKE A TYPICAL TABLOID EXPOSÉ: Intimate photos of former football star Frank Gifford embracing a blonde who is very definitely not Kathie Lee Gifford.

But the *Globe* did more than just publish the pictures: The supermarket tabloid paid the former flight attendant to entice Gifford into a Manhattan hotel room where a video camera was hidden, say sources familiar with the story. In other words, the *Globe* helped orchestrate the liaison between Gifford and a woman he had not previously slept with.

Even some veteran tabloid warriors were stunned. "There's a difference between reporting the news and creating the news," said Steve Coz, editor of the rival *National Enquirer*. "It's one thing to catch a celebrity cheating and another to induce or entrap them. Without the *Globe*, there would be no story here. I'm in the tabloid industry, and this is way over the top. It's downright cruel."

Globe Editorial Director Dan Schwartz dismissed such criticism, saying: "The issue is not what we did, the issue is what Frank Gifford did. . . . If we did something that someone would consider close to entrapment, I'd say so do the police every day in catching criminals. We caught a moral criminal."

Globe Editor Tony Frost would not confirm what one source described as a minimum $75,000 payment to the woman, Suzen Johnson. But, he said. "it's reasonable to expect that on stories like this the *Globe* does pay for accurate information."

That the apparent triangle involves morning talk show host Kathie Lee Gifford—whom Schwartz called "a symbol of wholesomeness in American marriages"—seemed certain to magnify the tawdry tale. Indeed, as the *Globe* gleefully noted, Kathie Lee Gifford boasted in her autobiography that for her husband, a "Monday Night Football" sportscaster, "cheating is out of the question."

From The Washington Post, *Saturday, Final Edition, May 17, 1997, p. H01. Reprinted with permission.*

But the *Globe*'s role is also drawing scrutiny. Bill O'Reilly, the former host of "Inside Edition," called the story "an outrage" and said "the reporting should be centered on how this woman set up this guy. I don't think the story is adultery, because that's not a news story unless a public figure is putting himself up as a family-values guy."

After this week's *Globe* alleged that Frank Gifford, 66, was romancing Johnson, 46, the Gifford family called the story fabricated garbage. The cohost of "Live With Regis and Kathie Lee" complained about a "cash-for-trash society" and said that the *Globe* might next report that she and Regis Philbin were having an alien baby. That was too much for the Florida-based tabloid.

"Initially we had no intention of using that video," Frost said. "Our hands were forced . . . after the Giffords and their lawyer attacked us and ridiculed our initial story and threatened to sue us. In the face of such strenuous denials and attempts to discredit our information, we had to prove we were telling the truth."

The Giffords have now changed their tune. They said in a statement that "this experience has been as painful for us as it would be for any other couple" and asked "that our privacy be respected at this difficult time."

Next week's issue of the *Globe*—"CHEATING FRANK CAUGHT ON CAMERA!"—will include 10 "sizzling photos" from the videotape, taken on April 30 and May 1 in a $400-a-night suite at the Regency Hotel. One *Globe* picture was published in yesterday's *New York Post*.

The *Globe* article makes clear that Gifford had not previously had an affair with Johnson, although it says he had flirted with her for four years. The piece quotes Gifford as telling her: "I've wanted to do this from the day I met you. You are beautiful."

A source close to the Giffords confirmed that the family is extremely upset over what it sees as the *Globe*'s entrapment techniques.

O'Reilly, who now hosts a Fox News Channel talk show, said that "Inside Edition" prohibited such hidden-camera video on private property. "If I were Gifford I'd do two things," he said. "I'd shut up the wife immediately, and I'd have my attorneys look into . . . charges against the woman and anyone who entered into a business deal with the woman."

This is not the first time the *Globe* has bedeviled the Gifford family in recent weeks. The *Globe* was the only supermarket tabloid to run an unobscured picture of the teenage babysitter who allegedly had an affair with Michael Kennedy, the brother of Massachusetts Rep. Joseph Kennedy. Frank Gifford's daughter, Victoria, is divorcing Michael Kennedy in the wake of the scandal.

The *Globe* says Johnson met Gifford on a 1993 flight and that he slipped her his private phone number. They maintained a telephone relationship and once tried to arrange a meeting, the paper says, but it never came off until the Regency rendezvous. "We didn't invite Frank Gifford to that hotel room," Frost said. "He didn't just go once, he went twice."

Globe editors declined to discuss their arrangement with Johnson. Schwartz said the tabloid is still holding back some "X-rated evidence." "We don't feel we have to explain every detail of how we got the story, just as *The Washington Post* didn't explain every detail of how it got the Watergate story," he said. "We were extremely close to participants in the story, which you can read any way you want."

7.7 Getting Kathie Lee

WILLIAM POWERS

WHENEVER THE SUPERMARKET TABLOIDS break another journalistic rule, the white-shirt media culture reacts in a fashion so familiar and routinized that it has become a kind of ceremony. One of the tabloids publishes a story that is outrageous not merely for its substance, which is usually sexual, but for the methods by which it was obtained: a hidden camera or tape recorder, a cash payment to

From The New Republic, *June 9, 1997, p. 11. Reprinted with permission.*

a source. Almost immediately, a story appears in *The Washington Post* under the byline of media reporter Howard Kurtz, who plays two distinct but equally essential roles in this ritual. First, by delivering the scandal as a media story, Kurtz launders the news itself for mainstream resale. Generally, the *Post* and its peers consider stories about the trysting habits of politicians and entertainers far too downmarket for their news columns. But when one of these stories arrives in the frame of a chin-scratcher about media ethics, it's perfectly respectable. Second, by reporting that the tabloids have committed (again) a hideous transgression against journalistic ethics, Kurtz keeps the media gentry for whom he speaks at a comfortable distance from their guttersnipe cousins.

Thus, on May 17, the *Post* published Kurtz's report on the story of Frank Gifford's extramarital dalliance. "It looks like a typical tabloid exposé: Intimate photos of former football star Frank Gifford embracing a blonde who is very definitely not Kathie Lee Gifford," Kurtz wrote. "But the *Globe* did more than just publish the pictures: The supermarket tabloid paid the former flight attendant to entice Gifford into a Manhattan hotel room where a video camera was hidden, say sources familiar with the story. In other words, the *Globe* helped orchestrate the liaison between Gifford and a woman he had not previously slept with. Even some veteran tabloid warriors were stunned."

And so another juicy story paid for by the tabs passes into the mainstream press—for free. This process is fairly transparent, but the elite media get away with it by building their coverage of tabloid journalism upon two potent falsehoods: (1) that the tabloids are an alternative universe which is certainly amoral, and possibly immoral; and (2) that the stories which come from this place amount to "trash," information which plays to our basest instincts while telling us nothing worthwhile about ourselves. In fact, as the Frank Gifford story demonstrates, the supermarket weeklies are the unlikely tribunes of an exacting moral code, a set of rules that reflects how most Americans think about the world much more faithfully than does the minimalist moral system that informs the coverage of the big media outlets. By refusing to see this, we deny ourselves a true understanding of why tabloid journalism is so popular, profitable and influential, and why the prestige press will never sate its hunger for tabloid stories.

To understand the way the tabloids are misrepresented in the mainstream, one has to draw a distinction between journalistic methods and messages. It goes without saying that the tabloids have little regard for the principles taught in journalism school. Though some of them, most notably *The National Enquirer,* have become increasingly accurate in recent years, they still practice a fast-and-loose brand of reportage in which there are basically no rules except one: avoid libel suits.

But saying that the tabloids flout the journalistic code of ethics, bowing to no god except sales, is not to say that the stories they publish carry a similarly nihilistic message. On the contrary, undergirding all tabloid journalism is a rigid code of right and wrong, in which people are held to very particular standards of behavior. In this system, which may be the closest thing we have today to a universal populist ethos, all the ancient social norms are honored: thou shalt not kill, rape, steal, lie and so forth. But in the tabloids' reckoning of the world, which is calculated to mirror that of the supermarket masses, two sins in particular—pride and hypocrisy—have special importance. This is why the JonBenet Ramsey case, which in the tabloid storyline is really about two parents who exploited their daughter's beauty to feed their own pride, is the premier tabloid story of the day. Many children are murdered each year, but this is not just a murder story, it's a morality play about a "tiny beauty" and her wicked stage parents. "Away from the bright lights," the *Star* reported, "she just wanted to be a normal kid." This is probably pretty much the way most Americans see the story, too.

And to the tabloids, the O.J. Simpson story, which preceded JonBenet in the number-one spot, was not a parable about race, as the mainstream media suggested. It was about a celebrity who thought he was above the law. (And this is certainly the way a lot of people saw the O.J. case.) Nothing raises tabloid fury more than the spectacle of a celebrity getting away with something, or getting above himself. In the pages of *The National Enquirer,* drug abuse, infidelity and myriad other wrongs are often forgiven, but if you are caught pretending to be something you're not—*caught being too big for your britches*—they'll flay you. Far from mindlessly adoring celebrities in the way the

New York glossies and many newspapers do, the tabloids cover movie stars and other famous people with one eye narrowed, ever-vigilant for phoniness, grossness or some species of immoral behavior. Violators are swiftly, gleefully cut down. It is ruthless and ugly and cruel, but it is arguably more honest than the way the proper press covers these things. Who do you think has a truer sense of Roseanne—the average tabloid reader or the reader of John Lahr's *New Yorker* valentine? When Magic Johnson was revealed to be infected with the HIV virus, who did a more brutally honest job of covering the story of his promiscuous lifestyle—the tabs or the *Times*?

Which brings us back to Frank Gifford and, more importantly, to his wife, Kathie Lee. There is something about Kathie Lee Gifford that seems to drive a lot of people crazy, a chirpy perkiness suspect for its degree and its ubiquity ("In the morning/ In the evening/Ain't we got fun?") that violates the tabloids' cardinal rule: no phoniness. Gifford herself has referred to the problem, observing, in a *TV Guide* article, that half of America "want[s] to throw up every time they see me." Howard Stern, whose stock-in-trade is outing phonies, regularly savages Mrs. Gifford. *The Washington Post*'s TV critic Tom Shales has tapped the same vein, upbraiding Gifford for "mercilessly" exploiting her children, for "flaunting her affluence," and for her "self-delusional megalomania."

That the Frank Gifford story is really about Kathie Lee is obvious from the cover of the May 27 issue of the *Globe,* which bears the headline "CHEATING FRANK CAUGHT ON CAMERA!" Notably, the cover's photo of Kathie Lee is larger than that of Gifford, and, at the top left corner of the page, there is a black circle in which this phrase is printed in yellow block letters: "POOR KATHIE LEE." The tone here is the one we reserve for misfortunes that befall evil neighbors: the unmistakable sound of back-fence schadenfreude. Inside, the *Globe* explains why it published the damning photos. When it reported in the previous issue (without photos) that Gifford had been unfaithful, "a teary-eyed Kathie Lee blasted" the story in a commencement address at Marymount University, where she said "we live in a cash for trash age. . . ." The *Globe* notes: "Ironically, the Catholic school, which campaigns against sweatshop abuses, honored Kathie Lee even though she was lambasted because her clothing line was made by Honduran kids working 20-hour days." So, the *Globe* said, it was "forced to print these revealing photos to prove to the 43-year-old Live [With Regis & Kathie Lee] hostess that her cheating husband is the one not telling the truth."

In short, the people demanded the head of Kathie Lee Gifford, and the *Globe* delivered. There's a cultural animus driving this story, and many others like it. It's easy to view them as just tabloid trash, remarkable only for the ethical lapses committed along the way. The elite media would have us view the situation like this, and no wonder: they've got a pretty good racket going on, pickpocketing the tabs' expensive stories with one hand and tsk-tsking them with the other. The real story, of course, is a tabloid classic. It's all about the hypocrisy and pride of a high-class set: the broadsheet press. Better hope the *Globe* doesn't get ahold of this one.

Discussion and Assignments

Note: This material applies to the two preceding articles.

1. Powers opens his third paragraph with the following line: "And so another juicy story paid for by the tabs passes into the mainstream press—for free." Why is Powers critical of Kurtz's article? According to Powers, how do Kurtz and the mainstream media misrepresent the tabloids? Do you agree with Powers that the tabloids are misrepresented in the way he claims?

2. Powers claims the tabloids subscribe to a particular ethical code. What is the code Powers is speaking of, and how is the code related to the mainstream press?

3. What are the two "sins" of particular importance Powers claims the tabloids focus on that appeal to their readers? Do you think Powers is accurate in his appraisal?

How does Powers contrast this feature of the tabloids with the mainstream press? Last, which of the two media—the tabloids or mainstream press—would you judge more responsible in reporting on these two personal character traits of public figures?

4. What is Powers's message in *Getting Kathy Lee?* Does it change your view of the tabloids?

5. Do either Kurtz or Powers discuss the role of offering money for a story in their articles? Are there any implied meanings to be gathered from the two on the subject of checkbook journalism?

Chapter 8

The Bell Curve

Background

IN 1994 RICHARD J. HERRNSTEIN and Charles Murray published *The Bell Curve: Intelligence and Class Structure in American Life.* The book immediately became the object of fierce debate. Much of the controversy has centered around the authors' analysis of race, genes, and IQ, as well as the social policy recommendations they make in light of their analysis that intelligence is largely determined by a person's genes.

Murray and Herrnstein claim that cognitive ability, or "a general factor of mental ability," can be measured through numerous standardized tests—we sometimes call them IQ tests—such as the National Longitudinal Survey of Youth (NLSY), Wechsler Intelligence Scale for Children, Stanford-Binet, Ravens Standard Progressive Matrices, and the ACT and SAT college entrance exams. The authors call the *general factor of mental ability* the "*g*" factor for short. They claim the disparities in cognitive abilities between races, as identified through IQ tests, can't be attributed to cultural bias or environmental factors alone. They conclude that intelligence is to a large degree genetically based and hereditary. Races reside at their respective levels or ranges of cognitive abilities. There are exceptions, of course, individuals who score out of the mean IQ range for their race, but as a whole, race and genes act as effective barometers for estimating a dominant range of IQ for individuals as a whole. Just as there are anatomical and biological differences among the races that are genetically based, so there may be genetically based differences in intelligence as well.

The Bell Curve concentrates on three major racial groups: whites, East Asians, and blacks. Murray and Herrnstein estimate that intelligence is roughly 60 percent genetically based (selected from a broader range they set at 40 to 80 percent). East Asians, including Japanese, Chinese, and "probably" Koreans, are at an IQ group mean higher than the group mean for non-Hispanic whites. The difference is about three IQ points (one-fifth of a standard deviation). East Asians score higher on nonverbal intelligence than whites, while being equal or slightly lower on verbal intelligence. The divide is greater, however, when comparing European or white Americans and African Americans, which the authors peg at 15 IQ points (one standard deviation).

Just as the authors claim cognitive stratification is largely based on race and genes, they make a similar claim that an individual's socioeconomic status can be largely traced to cognitive ability as well. The higher the IQ, the more likely an individual's socioeconomic level will be higher. And since East Asians and European white Americans generally have higher IQS than blacks, it's no surprise, Murray and Herrnstein contend, that they also have higher socioeconomic levels. They succeed at the more challenging jobs, and reap the financial and social rewards that come with the work. For Murray and Herrnstein IQ is the single most accurate indicator of potential productivity for an employer. It's preferable for an employer to know the IQ of a prospective employee than it is to know his or her grades in college, to conduct an interview, or to examine letters of recommendation.

Murray and Herrnstein attribute many of America's societal ills to misplaced social policy based, at least in part, on incorrect assumptions of peoples' abilities. Though they do not explicitly carve out specific positions on the social issues uppermost in the readers' minds, the implications of their approach are clear. Responsible social policy should take into account the realities of natural cognitive stratification and instill a greater sense of self-reliance in individuals and families. It is unlikely many aspects of the welfare state would survive their scrutiny, especially those that aim to artificially equalize the work and socioeconomic status of individuals whose natural abilities would restrict them to levels of modest or nominal achievement.

The social policy recommendations the authors draw from their study of race and IQ have drawn heavy criticism. Critics argue it is dangerous to advance social policy based on a problematic theory of the heritability of IQ; in effect, they accuse the authors of employing dubious science to serve their politics. Moreover, many have questioned whether an IQ exists in the way Murray and Herrnstein claim it does. For these critics, most notably Stephen Jay Gould (article 8.3), there is no such thing as a *g* or general factor of mental ability, an intelligence quotient that is static, undifferentiated, and subject to quantification. According to Gould, *g* is a convenient fiction created by a particular group of psychometricians who mistakenly believe intelligence is a sort of linear, objective, isolatable entity in the head.

Alternatives to Murray and Herrnstein's theory of *g* include the theories of those (like Gould) who believe humans actually possess several or *multiple intelligences,* as opposed to the two types of abilities that Murray and Herrnstein discuss. Murray and Herrnstein speak exclusively of the verbal and logico-mathematical abilities, but the theory of multiple intelligences expands the number of intelligences to at least nine: verbal/linguistic, musical, logical/mathematical, visual/spatial, bodily/kinesthetic, intrapersonal, interpersonal, naturalist, and existential. Proponents of this theory claim it better accounts for the overall complex nature of ability and achievement in human beings, that it offers a more holistic understanding of how humans interact with other humans, their environment, and themselves. In contrast to multiple intelligences, Robert J. Sternberg (article 8.7) has argued for a more cultural or *process*-oriented conception of intelligence. What it means to be intelligent will change according to the culture you live in. If you hunt or sing, or paint well, and if these things are highly valued in the culture you live in, you will be regarded as "intelligent." In a society that values hunting above all other skills, a rocket scientist won't place particularly high on the intelligence scale.

At the end of Murray and Herrnstein's *Race, Genes and IQ–An Apologia* (article 8.2), they say, "This difficult topic calls up an unending sequence of questions." This is an understatement. However one may feel about the arguments advanced in *The Bell Curve,* it remains a challenging work on a difficult and fascinating subject of importance. Soon after you wander into *The Bell Curve*'s labyrinth of psychometrics and scientific data mixed with social policy, you appreciate how wide a scope of specialists the debate encompasses, how far-reaching the implications it holds for politics, social policy, and human relations, and how important it is to openly subject its views to critical scrutiny. Murray himself has said the subject matter of *The Bell Curve* should be afforded the opportunity of debate "in polite society." The following selection of diverse articles is an attempt to do just that.

Readings

Article 8.1 *As the Bell Curves* is a conversation between Dan Seligman and Charles Murray, coauthor of *The Bell Curve.* The conversation offers insights into Murray's views on the efficacy of IQ testing and its ability to objectively assess intelligence. Additionally he offers views on social issues such as affirmative action, welfare recipients with low IQs, and the low numbers of minorities accepted into law schools. Since Murray and Herrnstein's *Race, Genes and IQ–An Apologia* (article 8.2) does not discuss social policy, this brief conversation is valuable for understanding Murray's views on the relation between IQ and the creation of social policy.

Article 8.2 At the time of his death in 1994, coauthor Richard Herrnstein was a professor of psychology at Harvard University. Charles Murray is a Bradley Fellow at the American Enterprise Institute in Washington, D.C. His many publications include the books *The Bell Curve; The Underclass Revisited; Income Inequality and IQ; What It Means to Be a Libertarian: A Personal Interpretation;* and *Losing Ground: American Social Policy 1950-1980.* Our selection, *Race, Genes, and IQ–An Apologia,* parts III and IV of which were adapted from *The Bell Curve,* is taken from a special issue on the book from the journal *The New Republic.* In this piece Murray and Herrnstein argue some of the more controversial points made in *The Bell Curve,* in particular, their views on the connection between IQ, race, and genes. Though Murray has often remarked that IQ and race is not the only subject of *The Bell Curve,* and that he believes much of the book's value is lost on the reader when the issue of IQ and race is stressed to the exclusion of the book's other concerns, IQ and race has nevertheless remained the flashpoint of debate since *The Bell Curve*'s publication. *Race, Genes, and IQ–An Apologia* serves as an accessible summary of Murray and Herrnstein's views.

Article 8.3 *Curveball* is a review of *The Bell Curve* by Stephen Jay Gould, professor of paleontology at Harvard University, and author of the classic work on intelligence *The Mismeasure of Man.* Gould focuses much of his criticism on the integrity of the *g* factor, or *general factor of intelligence,* that Murray and Herrnstein rely on for much of their theory on race, genes, and the heritability of IQ. According to Murray and Herrnstein, "The broadest conception of intelligence is embodied in *g*" (article 8.2, part IV, paragraph 44). But Gould claims Murray and Herrnstein offer no rationale to justify the use of *g* or to persuade us it even exists. In building his case against the *g* factor, Gould opens his paper by identifying four "shaky premises" *The Bell Curve* is based on, most of which he claims are false. Gould argues intelligence is not something that lends itself to static, isolated appraisal, a fundamental presupposition of *The Bell Curve*. According to Gould, since the authors' theory of the heritability of IQ is built on a series of shaky premises, such as the isolatability of IQ, their overall enterprise is doomed to failure from the outset.

Article 8.4 In *The Case Against* The Bell Curve, Gregg Easterbrook argues for a more "commonsense" approach to the issue of IQ and race. He claims many black kids play basketball for many more hours than white kids, so it's no surprise that they play better than white kids. And the same applies to school. If black kids had as many opportunities to study as white kids, they would match their white classmates on tests as well as on the court.

Article 8.5 *The Assault on the Human Spirit:* The Bell Curve, by Randolph Quaye, is taken from the journal *The Black Scholar,* which published a special symposium issue on *The Bell Curve*. Quaye argues that environmental factors, not race and genes, are responsible for low IQ scores. Poor education and racial discrimination are the prime culprits here. Disparity in IQ scores, then, is a result of racial segregation and prejudice, and cannot be attributable to the inevitability of genetics.

Article 8.6 In *Dumb Students? Or Dumb Textbooks?* education historian Diane Ravitch argues that school textbooks before WWII made greater demands on students than textbooks after the war. She argues the drop-off in test scores coincides with a decrease in the level of difficulty in textbooks used in schools. Ravitch suggests the weakened status of the books and instruction might account for low IQ test scores.

Article 8.7 Robert J. Sternberg is a professor of psychology and education at Yale University. In *For Whom Does* The Bell Curve Toll? Sternberg rejects the notion that intelligence is an innate immutable entity within the individual that can be quantified. Instead, he argues that intelligence is located in the interaction between the attributes of the individual and his or her environment. Thus, conceptions of intelligence will change according to the values of a society. In one society a rocket scientist will be regarded as intelligent, in another a hunter might be. If you happen to be a good writer as Sternberg is, and if that is what society values, then your status will be much improved over those people with other, less valued skills.

Article 8.8 Max Weiner is dean emeritus of the Graduate School of Education at Fordham University, and Bruce Cooper is a professor of education at the Graduate School of Education, Administration Policy and Urban Education, at Fordham University. In a short commentary from the journal *Education Week* Weiner and Cooper propose that disparities in IQ between blacks and whites may be attributed to environmental factors related to poverty and lack of adequate medical care. In particular, when the birth weight of black American babies is compared to babies of other countries, they rank 71st in the world. Since prenatal care, nutrition, and rearing of the very young can have a direct effect on development of IQ and learning, the authors argue poverty may play a significant role in explaining low test scores of black children.

Article 8.9 *Statement:* The Bell Curve was authored by the National Institutes of Health—Department of Energy (NIH-DOE) Joint Working Group on the Ethical,

Legal, and Social Implications of Human Genome Research, and endorsed by the National Society of Genetic Counselors. The authors state that the discipline of genetics is complex and that its mysteries appear greater as more knowledge of the field is gained. They are clearly uncomfortable with claims made about the heritability of intelligence, especially by Murray and Herrnstein, both of whom are not geneticists. In addition they state that they "deplore" the efforts of Murray and Herrnstein to use genetics to inform social policy.

Article 8.10   Our last article is a biting, satiric piece by Art Levine, entitled *Why Are Jews So Rich?* Levine applies his literary skills to highlight the dangers of racial prejudice and discrimination by way of a fictional review. The review is of an imaginary follow-up book to *The Bell Curve* by Charles Murray entitled *The Jew Curve.*

8.1 As the Bell Curves

Dan Seligman and Charles Murray

Is The Bell Curve *the Stealth Public-Policy Book of the 1990s?*

DS: Three years after publication of *The Bell Curve,* I find myself endlessly reading news stories about great national controversies in which all the participants do their best to ignore the data you and Dick Herrnstein laid on the table. Three recent examples:

1. the row over school vouchers, whose advocates (e.g., Bill Bennett in *The Wall Street Journal*) endlessly take it for granted that poor performance by students reflects only inadequacies by the teaching profession—inadequacies among the learners being a huge unmentionable;
2. the President's astounding proposal (never characterized as such) that all American youngsters, including those with IQs at the left tail, should have at least two years of college;
3. the expressions of surprise and rage when it turned out that, in the absence of affirmative action, prestigious law schools would be admitting hardly any black students. The participants in these controversies were in no sense talking back to *The Bell Curve.* They were pretending its data do not exist. What's your perspective?

   CM: I read the same stories you do and ask the same question: Do these guys know but pretend not to? Or are they still truly oblivious? In the case

of education vouchers, there is a sensible reason to ignore *The Bell Curve:* inner-city schools are overwhelmingly lousy. Bill Bennett has read the book, understands it, and (rare indeed) has defended it on national television. But his battle cry is, and should be, "These kids are getting a raw deal"—not a lot of qualifications about the difficulties in raising IQ.

Bill Clinton and his pandering on college education is another story altogether. Vouchers for elementary school can be a good policy idea, no matter what our book says about IQ. But universal college education cannot be. Most people are not smart enough to profit from an authentic college education. But who among Republicans has had the courage to call Clinton on this one? A lot of silence about *The Bell Curve* can be put down to political cowardice.

Affirmative action was still politically sacrosanct when *The Bell Curve* came out in October 1994. Within a year, the tide had swung decisively. Did the book play any role? Damned if I know. Dick and I were the first to publish a comprehensive account of the huge gaps in SAT scores at elite colleges, but I have found not a single citation of the book during the affirmative-action debate.

My best guess—and the broad answer to your question—is that *The Bell Curve* is the stealth public-policy book of the 1990s. It has created a subtext

From National Review *49, no. 23 (1997): 43. Reprinted with permission.*

on a range of issues. Everybody knows what the subtext is. Nobody says it out loud.

DS: I am reading with fascination your "afterword" in the paperback edition, and I have an argumentative question about the passage where you speculate on long-term responses to the book. You postulate a three-stage process. In stage one, the book and its authors take endless rounds of invective from critics who simply want to suppress the message that human beings differ in mental ability. These critics turn to thought control because they look at your findings and conclude, in Michael Novak's words, that "they destroy hope"—a hope which Novak sees as a this-worldly eschatological phenomenon. In stage two, the invective attracts the interest of scholars not previously involved in these disputes. They look over the empirical record, deciding in the end that your case is supportable and may indeed have been understated in some areas. In stage three, these scholars build on your work, and in the end do more than *The Bell Curve* itself to demolish those eschatological hopes. In the long run, the thought control shoots itself in the foot.

This process seems entirely plausible. But I wonder: Will the truth ever break out of the academic world? Remember, the basic message (including even a genetic factor in the black-white gap) was already pretty well accepted by scholars in the mid Eighties as the Snyderman-Rothman book documented. What I never see is acceptance of any part of this message in the public-policy world, where the term "IQ" is seldom uttered without the speaker's sensing a need to dissociate himself from it.

Among many horror stories is the current row over Lino Graglia, the University of Texas law professor now in trouble for having stated an obvious truth: that black and Mexican-American students are "not academically competitive" with white students. Graglia gave the most benign possible explanation for this educational gap: minority students were not genetically or intellectually inferior but were suffering from a cultural background in which scholarship was not exalted. But that explanation got him nowhere. He has been attacked by every editorial page in Nexis that has weighed in on the matter. (He did better in the letters columns.)

Now, I can see the process you envision going forward—with some scholars and maybe even

some journalists looking at actual academic performance at Texas and other universities. What I cannot imagine is defenders of Graglia surfacing in any institutional setting—at least not in the realms of politics and education, nor in major media. Meanwhile, what with Texas campus demonstrations and Jesse Jackson's call for Graglia to be made a social pariah (cheered at the demonstrations), scholars have got the crucial message: Stay under cover if you hold beliefs challenging to those eschatological hopes.

CM: Graglia said "culture." What everybody heard was "genes." As soon as anyone argues that racial differences in intelligence are authentic, not an artifact of biased tests, everyone decodes that as saying the differences are grounded in genes. It is a nonsequitur, but an invariable one in my experience. America's intellectual elites are hysterical about the possibility of black-white genetic differences in IQ.

As you know, *The Bell Curve* actually took a mild, agnostic stand on the subject. Dick Herrnstein and I said that nobody yet knows what the mix between environmental and genetic causes might be, and it makes no practical difference anyway. The only policy implication of the black-white difference, whatever its sources, is that the U.S. should return forthwith to its old ideal of treating people as individuals.

But how many people know this? No one who hasn't read the book. Everyone went nuts about genes, so much so that most people now believe that race and genes is the main topic of our book.

Why? The topic of race and genes is like the topic of sex in Victorian England. The intellectual elites are horrified if anyone talks about it, but behind the scenes they are fascinated. I will say it more baldly than Dick and I did in the book: In their heart of hearts, intellectual elites, especially liberal ones, have two nasty secrets regarding IQ. First, they really believe that IQ is the be-all and end-all of human excellence and that someone with a low IQ is inferior. Second, they are already sure that the black-white IQ difference is predominantly genetic and that this is a calamity—such a calamity indeed that it must not be spoken about, even to oneself. To raise these issues holds a mirror up to the elites' most desperately denied inner thoughts. The result is the kind of reaction we saw to Lino Graglia.

But when people say one thing and believe another, as intellectual elites have been doing about race, sooner or later the cognitive dissonance must be resolved. It usually happens with a bang. When the wall of denial gives way, not only will the received wisdom on race and IQ change, the change will happen very rapidly and probably go much too far. The fervor of the newly converted is going to be a problem. I fully expect, if I live another twenty years, to be in a situation where I am standing on the ramparts shouting: "Genetic differences weren't a big deal when we wrote *The Bell Curve* and they still aren't a big deal."

DS: Watching Clinton perform in Little Rock the other day, and picking up especially on his lament about the extent and persistence of discrimination (including employment discrimination) in American life, I went back for one more look at that table on page 324 of *The Bell Curve*—the one showing that job discrimination is essentially nonexistent in the United States today. At least it is nonexistent among the younger workers in that huge sample from the National Longitudinal Survey of Youth.

Your argument begins by noting that when you control for age, education, and socioeconomic status (SES), black earnings are still only 84 percent of white earnings, which implies continuing discrimination. As the table shows, however, when you bring IQ into the picture, everything changes. Even if you forget about education and SES and control only for age and IQ, the black-white earnings gap essentially disappears. To be precise: when you average the results for many different occupational categories, blacks of similar age and IQ make 98 percent as much as whites. When you control for gender as well, the figure goes to 101 percent.

These findings seem stunning to me, on several counts. First, they show that employers are astonishingly good at seeing through the imperfect credentials represented by educational levels and family background, and at figuring out which job prospects have the most ability. Second, the findings are surely big news—and good news. They imply that much, or most, or essentially all (depending on the extent to which NLSY data can be generalized to the labor force as a whole) of what is routinely identified as invidious discrimination is nothing of the sort. It is rational behavior by employers and it shows them to be amazingly color-blind. So why is this news not on the front pages?

CM: Think about how that front-page story would have to be headlined. It would have to convey the thought, BLACKS WITH EQUAL IQS GET EQUAL PAY. You see the problem. No matter how reasonable the explanation, it is not intellectually permissible at this moment in history for blacks or women to have different outcomes from white males. If you really want egregious examples of that attitude, don't bother with IQ and blacks. Look at the military performance of women. A military officer came into my office some months ago, almost with tears in his eyes. "We're killing people," he said, referring to the degradation of entrance requirements and training standards for combat pilots—a degradation carried out so that enough women could get through. How many journalists in major U.S. papers have been willing to write that story straightforwardly? When the problem of female combat performance is mentioned at all, it is with an "on the one hand, on the other hand" presentation, even though one side has all the data and the other side is only an attitude.

DS: Let me ask you to weigh in more heavily on an issue we touched on earlier—the "average child" fallacy. This is the notion that any normal child can learn anything if only he gets the right teaching. Your data make plain that this view is nonsense. Indeed, you add: "Critics of American education must come to terms with the reality that in a universal education system many students will not reach the level of education that most people view as basic."

That thought was so important that you put it in italics. In our current debate on national standards and educational reform, however, no one is paying attention to it—certainly not Bill Clinton, but also not many conservatives. I recently caught Jeanne Allen of the provoucher Center for Educational Reform in a debate on CNN. She was complaining about education bureaucrats "that don't believe, or don't necessarily think, all children are capable of learning to the highest level. I think that's scary."

Isn't it about time to scold conservative fans of education reform for persistently dodging reality when they're out there selling vouchers?

CM: I propose a new term: "suspension of belief," defined as "basing a public-policy stance on an assumption about human beings that one knows to be untrue of oneself." Do you suppose Jeanne Allen believes herself capable of learning to the highest level if we're talking, say, about quantum mechanics? Of course not. Only a few silly people who have never tested themselves are under the illusion that they have no educational limits.

Putting that last sentence on the screen, however, makes me pause. Many bright liberal-arts graduates have not tested themselves. In the liberal arts and some of the soft sciences it is possible to get a PhD without having to confront that awful moment: "My God, studying hard won't be enough. It is beyond the power of my intellect to understand this." With me, it came halfway through a graduate course on the theory of matrices, and it was an invaluable lesson. Isaac Asimov once gave a rule of thumb for knowing when you've hit the wall: when you hear yourself saying to the professor, "I think I understand."

Another factor may also be operating here: the isolation of the cognitive elite. If you have never had a close acquaintance with an IQ below 100, then you have no idea what "dumb" really means.

Should we scold our conservative allies for this kind of naivete? Chide, I guess. But I am uncomfortably aware of a sentence in a well-known conservative tome that reads, "I suggest that when we give such parents [who are actively engaged in their child's education] vouchers, we will observe substantial convergence of black and white test scores in a single generation." The book is *Losing Ground,* page 224. So I have a first-stone problem here.

DS: One last question: Have you had second thoughts about formulations in *The Bell Curve?*

CM: If Dick and I were writing it again, I suppose we would go over the section on race and put in a few more italics, and otherwise try to grab readers by the shoulders and shake them out of their hysteria. But it probably wouldn't do any good. We would certainly incorporate an analysis of siblings into the chapters of Part II that deal with IQ and social problems—the kind of analysis I did in that Public Interest article you mentioned earlier. And there's a highly technical error we

made that had the effect of understating the statistical power of our results; I would like to fix that. But that's about all. The book's main themes will endure just fine.

The reality of a cognitive elite is becoming so obvious that I wonder if even critics of the book really doubt it. The relationship of low IQ to the underclass? Ditto. Welfare reform is helping the argument along, by the way, as journalistic accounts reveal how many welfare mothers are not just uneducated, but of conspicuously low intelligence. The intractability of IQ? Dick and I said that IQ was 40 to 80 percent heritable. The identical-twin studies continue to suggest that the ultimate figure will turn out to be in the upper half of that range. More importantly, the literature on "nonshared environment" has developed dramatically since Dick and I were researching *The Bell Curve.* Its core finding is that, whatever the role of environment may be in determining IQ, only a small portion of that role consists of influences that can be manipulated (through better child-rearing, better schools, etc.). For practical purposes, the ability of public policy to affect IQ is probably smaller than Dick and I concluded.

With regard to race differences, nothing has happened to change our conclusions about the cultural fairness of the tests, the equal predictive validity of the tests, or the persistence of the 15-point gap. Recent data from the NLSY indicate that in the next generation not only is the black-white gap failing to shrink, but it may be growing.

So I do not expect any major finding in *The Bell Curve* to be overturned. I realize that attacking the book has become a cottage industry. *The New York Times* recently used one such attack to announce that our "noxious" conclusions have been definitively refuted. But in the same month that this most recent definitive refutation was published, the journal *Intelligence* had a special issue devoted to IQ and social policy. The articles in it are not written as defenses of *The Bell Curve;* they just happen to make our case on a wide variety of points. And that's the way the debate will eventually be resolved—not as a judgment about a book that has been almost buried by controversy, but by continuing research on the same issues. As that happens, it is not just that Dick and I will be proved right. We will be proved to have been—if you will pardon the expression—conservative.

Discussion and Assignments

1. Charles Murray states *The Bell Curve* may be the "stealth public policy book of the 1990s." What does he mean by this? How does he think *The Bell Curve* has affected the creation of public policy so far? If he is correct, what might this say about public policy in the future? What might this say about public officials who create public policy?

2. *"BLACKS WITH EQUAL IQS GET EQUAL PAY."* What do Seligman and Murray mean by this statement? To what degree does IQ determine Murray's opinion that there is no discrimination against blacks in the workplace? Do you believe comparing IQ scores is an appropriate way to determine if there is discrimination? What IQ evidence would be needed to prove there is discrimination?

3. What is the "average child fallacy"? What implications do Seligman and Murray draw from the fallacy? How does the fallacy shed light on their views on the heritability of IQ? Do you draw the same implications from the fallacy that Seligman and Murray do? Do you think as many people subscribe to the fallacy as they imply?

4. Is it as apparent to you as it is to Murray that there is a cognitive elite in the United States? What is the obvious relation between IQ and the "underclass" according to Murray? Is this relationship apparent to you?

5. Murray claims the topic of race, genes, and IQ in the United States is like the topic of sex in Victorian England. Do you agree or disagree with him on this point?

8.2 Race, Genes and I.Q.—An Apologia

CHARLES MURRAY AND RICHARD J. HERRNSTEIN

I.

THE PRIVATE DIALOGUE ABOUT RACE in America is far different from the public one, and we are not referring just to discussions among white rednecks. Our impression is that the private attitudes of white elites toward blacks is strained far beyond any public acknowledgment, that hostility is not uncommon and that a key part of the strain is a growing suspicion that fundamental racial differences are implicated, in the social and economic gap that continues to separate blacks and whites, especially alleged genetic differences in intelligence.

We say "our impression" because we have been in a unique position to gather impressions. Since the beginning of 1990, we have been writing a book about differences in intellectual capacity among people and groups and what those differ- ences mean for America's future. As authors do, we have gotten into numberless conversations that begin, "What are you working on now?" Our interlocutors have included scholars at the top- ranked universities and think tanks, journalists, high public officials, lawyers, financiers and corpo- rate executives. In the aggregate, they have split about evenly between left and right of the political center.

With rare exceptions, these people have shared one thing besides their success. As soon as the sub- ject turned to the question of I.Q., they focused on whether there was any genetic race differences in intelligence. And they tended to be scared stiff about the answer. This experience has led us to be scared as well, about the consequences of igno- rance. We have been asked whether the question of racial genetic differences in intelligence should

From The New Republic, *October 31, 1994, pp. 27–37. Reprinted by permission of tyhe author.*

even be raised in polite society. We believe there's no alternative. A taboo issue, filled with potential for hurt and anger, lurks just beneath the surface of American life. It is essential that people begin to talk about this in the open. Because raising this question at all provokes a host of fears, it is worth stating at the outset a clear conclusion of our research: the fascination with race, I.Q. and genes is misbegotten. There are all sorts of things to be worried about regarding intelligence and American life, and even regarding intelligence and ethnicity. But genetics isn't one of them.

II.

First, the evidence, beginning with this furiously denied fact: intelligence is a useful construct. Among the experts, it is by now beyond much technical dispute that there is such a thing as a general factor of cognitive ability on which human beings differ and that this general factor is measured reasonably well by a variety of standardized tests, best of all by I.Q. tests designed for that purpose. These points are no longer the topic of much new work in the technical journals because most of the questions about them have been answered.

Intelligence as measured by I.Q. tests is predictive of many educational, economic and social outcomes. In America today, you are much better off knowing a child's I.Q. score than her parents' income or education if you want to predict whether she will drop out of high school, for example. If you are an employer trying to predict an applicant's job productivity and are given a choice of just one item of information, you are usually better off asking for an I.Q. score than a résumé, college transcript, letter of recommendation or even a job interview. These statements hold true for whites, blacks, Asians and Latinos alike.

This is not to say that I.Q. is destiny—in each of these instances, I.Q. is merely a better predictor than the alternatives, not even close to a perfect one. But it should be stated that the pariah status of intelligence as a construct and I.Q. as its measure for the past three decades has been a function of political fashion, not science.

Ethnic differences in measured cognitive ability have been found since intelligence tests were invented. The battle over the meaning of these differences is largely responsible for today's controversy over intelligence testing itself. The first thing to remember is that the differences among individuals are far greater than the differences among groups. If all the ethnic differences in intelligence evaporated overnight, most of the intellectual variation in America would endure. The remaining inequality would still strain the political process, because differences in cognitive ability are problematic even in ethnically homogeneous societies.

Even using the word "race" is problematic, which is why we use the word ethnicity as well as race in this article. What does it mean to be "black" in America, in racial terms, when the word black (or African American) can be used for people whose ancestry is more European than African? How are we to classify a person whose parents hail from Panama but whose ancestry is predominantly African? Is he Latino? Black? The rule we follow here is a simple one: to classify people according to the way they classify themselves.

III.

We might start with a common question in America these days: Do Asians have higher I.Q.s than whites? The answer is probably yes, if Asian refers to the Japanese and Chinese (and perhaps also Koreans), whom we will refer to here as East Asians. How much higher is still unclear. The best tests of this have involved identical I.Q. tests given to populations that are comparable except for race. In one test, samples of American, British and Japanese students aged 13 to 15 were given a test of abstract reasoning and spatial relations. The U.S. and U.K. samples had scores within a point of the standardized mean of 100 on both the abstract and spatial relations parts of the test; the Japanese scored 104.5 on the test for abstract reasoning and 114 on the test for spatial relations—a large difference, amounting to a gap similar to the one found by another leading researcher for Asians in America. In a second set of studies, 9-year-olds in Japan, Hong Kong and Britain, drawn from comparable socioeconomic populations, were administered the Ravens Standard Progressive Matrices. The children from Hong Kong averaged 113; from Japan, 110; and from Britain, 100.

Not everyone accepts that the East Asian–white difference exists. Another set of studies gave a battery of mental tests to elementary school children in Japan, Taiwan and Minneapolis, Minnesota. The key difference between this study and the other two was that the children were matched carefully on many socioeconomic and demographic variables. No significant difference in overall I.Q. was found, and the authors concluded that "this study offers no support for the argument that there are differences in the general cognitive functioning of Chinese, Japanese and American children."

Where does this leave us? The parties in the debate are often confident, and present in their articles are many flat statements that an overall East Asian–white I.Q. difference does, or does not, exist. In our judgment, the balance of the evidence supports the notion that the overall East Asian mean is higher than the white mean. Three I.Q. points most resembles a consensus, tentative though it still is. East Asians have a greater advantage in a particular kind of nonverbal intelligence.

The issues become far more fraught, however, in determining the answer to the question: Do African Americans score differently from whites on standardized tests of cognitive ability? If the samples are chosen to be representative of the American population, the answer has been yes for every known test of cognitive ability that meets basic psychometric standards. The answer is also yes for almost all studies in which the black and white samples are matched on some special characteristics—juvenile delinquents, for example, or graduate students—but there are exceptions.

How large is the black-white difference? The usual answer is what statisticians call one standard deviation. In discussing I.Q. tests, for example, the black mean is commonly given as 85, the white mean as 100 and the standard deviation as fifteen points. But the differences observed in any given study seldom conform exactly to one standard deviation. In 156 American studies conducted during this century that have reported the I.Q. means of a black sample and a white sample, and that meet basic requirements of interpretability, the mean black-white difference is 1.1 standard deviations, or about sixteen I.Q. points.

More rigorous selection criteria do not diminish the size of the gap. For example, with tests given outside the South only after 1960, when people were increasingly sensitized to racial issues, the

number of studies is reduced to twenty-four, but the mean difference is still 1.1 standard deviations. The National Longitudinal Survey of Youth (NLSY) administered an I.Q. test in 1980 to by far the largest and most carefully selected national sample (6,502 whites, 3,022 blacks) and found a difference of 1.2 standard deviations.

Evidence from the SAT, the ACT and the National Assessment of Educational Progress gives reason to think that the black-white I.Q. difference has shrunk by perhaps three I.Q. points in the last twenty years. Almost all the improvement came in the low end, however, progress has stalled for several years and the most direct evidence, from I.Q. tests of the next generation in the NLSY, points to a widening black-white gap rather than a shrinking one.

It is important to understand that even a difference of 1.2 standard deviations means considerable overlap in the cognitive ability distribution for blacks and whites, as shown for the NLSY population in [Figure 1]. For any equal number of blacks and whites, a large proportion have I.Q.s that can be matched up. For that matter, millions of blacks have higher I.Q.s than the average white. Tens of thousands have I.Q.s that put them in the top few percentiles of the white distribution. It should be no surprise to see (as everyone does every day)

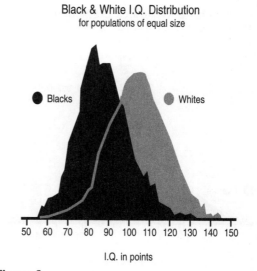

Figure 1

Source: Illustration by Jim Holloway for *The New Republic.*

African Americans functioning at high levels in every intellectually challenging field. This is the distribution to keep in mind whenever thinking about individuals.

But an additional complication must be taken into account: in the United States, there are about six whites for every black. This means that the I.Q. overlap of the two populations as they actually exist in the United States looks very different from the overlap in [Figure 1]. [Figure 2] presents the same data from the NLSY when the distributions are shown in proportion to the actual population of young people in the NLSY. This figure shows why a black-white difference can be problematic to society as a whole. At the lower end of the I.Q. range, there are about equal numbers of blacks and whites. But throughout the upper half of the range, the disproportions between the number of whites and blacks at any given I.Q. level are huge. To the extent that the difference represents an authentic difference in cognitive functioning, the social consequences are huge as well. But is the difference authentic? Is it, for example, attributable to cultural bias or other artifacts of the test? There are several ways of assessing this. We'll go through them one by one.

Black & White I.Q. Distribution
Proportional to the ethnic composition of the U.S.

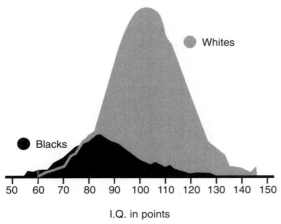

Figure 2

Source: Illustration by Jim Holloway for *The New Republic.*

External evidence of bias. Tests are used to predict things—most commonly, to predict performance in school or on the job. The ability of a test to predict is known as its validity. A test with high validity predicts accurately; a test with poor validity makes many mistakes. Now suppose that a test's validity differs for the members of two groups. To use a concrete example: the SAT is used as a tool in college admissions because it has a certain validity in predicting college performance. If the SAT is biased against blacks, it will underpredict their college performance. If tests were biased in this way, blacks as a group would do better in college than the admissions office expected based just on their SATs. It would be as if the test underestimated the "true" SAT score of the blacks, so the natural remedy for this would be to compensate the black applicants by, for example, adding the appropriate number of points to their scores.

Predictive bias can work in another way, as when the test is simply less reliable—that is, less accurate—for blacks than for whites. Suppose a test used to select police sergeants is more accurate in predicting the performance of white candidates who become sergeants than in predicting the performance of black sergeants. It doesn't underpredict for blacks, but rather fails to predict at all (or predicts less accurately). In these cases, the natural remedy would be to give less weight to the test scores of blacks than to those of whites.

The key concept for both types of bias is the same: a test biased against blacks does not predict black performance in the real world in the same way that it predicts white performance in the real world. The evidence of bias is external in the sense that it shows up in differing validities for blacks and whites. External evidence of bias has been sought in hundreds of studies. It has been evaluated relative to performance in elementary school, in the university, in the military, in unskilled and skilled jobs, in the professions. Overwhelmingly, the evidence is that the standardized tests used to help make school and job decisions do not underpredict black performance. Nor does the expert community find any other systematic difference in the predictive accuracy of tests for blacks and whites.

Internal evidence of bias. The most common charges of cultural bias involve the putative cultural loading of items in a test. Here is an SAT analogy item that has become famous as an example of cultural bias:

RUNNER: MARATHON (A) envoy: embassy
(B) martyr: massacre (C) oarsman: regatta
(D) referee: tournament (E) horse: stable

The answer is "oarsman: regatta"—fairly easy if you know what both a marathon and a regatta are, a matter of guesswork otherwise. How would a black youngster from the inner city ever have heard of a regatta? Many view such items as proof that the tests must be biased against people from disadvantaged backgrounds. "Clearly," writes a critic of testing, citing this example, "this item does not measure students' 'aptitude' or logical reasoning ability, but knowledge of upper-middle-class recreational activity." In the language of psychometrics, this is called internal evidence of bias.

The hypothesis of bias again lends itself to direct examination. In effect, the SAT critic is saying that culturally loaded items are producing at least some of the black-white difference. Get rid of such items, and the gap will narrow. Is he correct? When we look at the results for items that have answers such as "oarsman: regatta" and the results for items that seem to be empty of any cultural information (repeating a sequence of numbers, for example), are there any differences?

The technical literature is again clear. In study after study of the leading tests, the idea that the black-white difference is caused by questions with cultural content has been contradicted by the facts. Items that the average white test-taker finds easy relative to other items, the average black test-taker does, too; the same is true for items that the average white and black find difficult. Inasmuch as whites and blacks have different overall scores on the average, it follows that a smaller proportion of blacks get right answers for either easy or hard items, but the order of difficulty is virtually the same in each racial group. How can this be? The explanation is complicated and goes deep into the reasons why a test item is "good" or "bad" in measuring intelligence. Here, we restrict ourselves to the conclusion: *The black-white difference is generally wider on items that appear to be culturally neutral than on items that appear to be culturally loaded.* We italicize this point because it is so well established empirically yet comes as such a surprise to most people who are new to this topic.

Motivation to try. Suppose the nature of cultural bias does not lie in predictive validity or in the content of the items but in what might be called "test willingness." A typical black youngster, it is hypothesized, comes to such tests with a mindset different from the white subject's. He is less attuned to testing situations (from one point of view), or less inclined to put up with such nonsense (from another). Perhaps he just doesn't give a damn, since he has no hopes of going to college or otherwise benefiting from a good test score. Perhaps he figures that the test is biased against him anyway, so what's the point. Perhaps he consciously refuses to put forth his best effort because of the peer pressure against "acting white" in some inner-city schools.

The studies that have attempted to measure motivation in such situations generally have found that blacks are at least as motivated as whites. But these are not wholly convincing, for why shouldn't the measures of motivation be just as inaccurate as the measures of cognitive ability are alleged to be? Analysis of internal characteristics of the tests once again offers the best leverage in examining this broad hypothesis. Here, we will offer just one example involving the "digit span" subtest, part of the widely used Wechsler intelligence tests. It has two forms: forward digit span, in which the subject tries to repeat a sequence of numbers in the order read to him, and backward digit span, in which the subject tries to repeat the sequence of numbers backward. The test is simple, uses numbers familiar to everyone and calls on no cultural information besides numbers. The digit span is informative regarding test motivation not just because of the low cultural loading of the items but because the backward form is a far better measure of "g," the psychometrician's shorthand for the general intelligence factor that I.Q. tests try to measure. The reason that the backward form is a better measure of g is that reversing the numbers is mentally more demanding than repeating them in the heard order, as you can determine for yourself by a little self-testing.

The two parts of the subtest have identical content. They occur at the same time during the test. Each subject does both. But in most studies the black-white difference is about twice as great on backward digits as on forward digits. The question then arises: How can lack of motivation (or test willingness) explain the difference in performance on the two parts of the same subtest?

This still leaves another obvious question: Are the differences in overall black and white test scores attributable to differences in socioeconomic status? This question has two different answers depending on how the question is understood, and confusion is rampant. There are two essential answers and two associated rationales.

First version: If you extract the effects of socioeconomic class, what happens to the magnitude of the black-white difference? Blacks are disproportionately in the lower socioeconomic classes, and class is known to be associated with I.Q. Therefore, many people suggest, part of what appears to be an ethnic difference in I.Q. scores is actually a socioeconomic difference. The answer to this version of the question is that the size of the gap shrinks when socioeconomic status is statistically extracted. The NLSY gives a result typical of such analyses. The black-white difference in the NLSY is 1.2. In a regression equation in which both race and socioeconomic background are entered, the difference between whites and blacks shrinks to less than .8 standard deviation. Socioeconomic status explains 37 percent of the original black-white difference. This relationship is in line with the results from many other studies.

The difficulty comes in interpreting what it means to "control" for socioeconomic status. Matching the status of the groups is usually justified on the grounds that the scores people earn are caused to some extent by their socioeconomic status, so if we want to see the "real" or "authentic" difference between them, the contribution of status must be excluded. The trouble is that socioeconomic status is also a result of intelligence, as people of high and low cognitive ability move to high and low places in the class structure. The reason parents have high or low socioeconomic status is in part a function of their intelligence, and their intelligence also affects the I.Q. of the children via both genes and environment.

Because of these relationships, "controlling" for socioeconomic status in racial comparisons is guaranteed to reduce I.Q. differences in the same way that choosing black and white samples from a school for the intellectually gifted is guaranteed to reduce I.Q. differences (assuming race-blind admissions standards). These complications aside,

a reasonable rule of thumb is that controlling for socioeconomic status reduces the overall black-white difference by about one-third.

Second version: As blacks move up the socioeconomic ladder, do the differences with whites of similar socioeconomic status diminish? The first version of the SES/I.Q. question referred to the overall score of a population of blacks and whites. The second version concentrates on the black-white difference within socioeconomic classes. The rationale goes like this: blacks score lower on average because they are socioeconomically at a disadvantage. This disadvantage should most seriously handicap children in the lower socioeconomic classes, who suffer from greater barriers to education and job advancement than do children in the middle and upper classes. As blacks advance up the socioeconomic ladder, their children, less exposed to these barriers, will do better and, by extension, close the gap with white children of their class.

This expectation is not borne out by the data. A good way to illustrate this is to use an index of parental SES based on their education, income and occupation and to match it against the mean I.Q. score, as shown in [Figure 3]. I.Q. scores increase with economic status for both races. But as the figure shows, the magnitude of the black-white

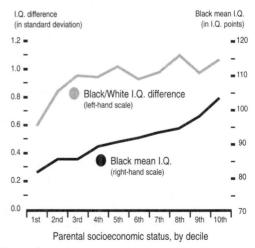

Black I.Q. scores rise with socioeconomic status, but the Black/White difference remains.

Figure 3

Source: Illustration by Jim Holloway for *The New Republic.*

difference in standard deviations does not decrease. Indeed, it gets larger as people move up from the very bottom of the socioeconomic ladder. The pattern shown in the figure is consistent with many other major studies, except that the gap flattens out. In other studies, the gap has continued to increase throughout the range of socioeconomic status.

IV.

This brings us to the flashpoint of intelligence as a public topic: the question of genetic differences between the races. Expert opinion, when it is expressed at all, diverges widely. In the 1980s Mark Snyderman, a psychologist, and Stanley Rothman, a political scientist, sent a questionnaire to a broad sample of 1,020 scholars, mostly academicians, whose specialties give them reason to be knowledgeable about I.Q. Among other questions, they asked, "Which of the following best characterizes your opinion of the heritability of the black-white difference in I.Q.?" The answers were divided as follows: The difference is entirely due to environmental variation: 15 percent. The difference is entirely due to genetic variation: 1 percent. The difference is a product of both genetic and environmental variation: 45 percent. The data are insufficient to support any reasonable opinion: 24 percent. No response: 14 percent.

This pretty well sums up the professional judgment on the matter. But it doesn't explain anything about the environment/genetic debate as it has played out in the profession and in the general public. And the question, of course, is fascinating. So what could help us understand the connection between heritability and group differences? A good place to start is by correcting a common confusion about the role of genes in individuals and in groups.

Most scholars accept that I.Q. in the human species as a whole is substantially heritable, somewhere between 40 percent and 80 percent, meaning that much of the observed variation in I.Q. is genetic. And yet this information tells us nothing for sure about the origin of the differences between groups of humans in measured intelligence. This point is so basic, and so misunderstood, that it deserves emphasis: that a trait is genetically transmitted in a population does not

mean that group differences in that trait are also genetic in origin. Anyone who doubts this assertion may take two handfuls of genetically identical seed corn and plant one handful in Iowa, the other in the Mojave Desert, and let nature (i.e., the environment) take its course. The seeds will grow in Iowa, not in the Mojave, and the result will have nothing to do with genetic differences.

The environment for American blacks has been closer to the Mojave and the environment for American whites has been closer to Iowa. We may apply this general observation to the available data and see where the results lead. Suppose that all the observed ethnic differences in tested intelligence originate in some mysterious environmental differences—mysterious, because we know from material already presented that socioeconomic factors cannot be much of the explanation. We further stipulate that one standard deviation (fifteen I.Q. points) separates American blacks and whites and that one-fifth of a standard deviation (three I.Q. points) separates East Asians and whites. Finally, we assume that I.Q. is 60 percent heritable (a middle-ground estimate). Given these parameters, how different would the environments for the three groups have to be in order to explain the observed difference in these scores?

The observed ethnic differences in I.Q. could be explained solely by the environment if the mean environment of whites is 1.58 standard deviations better than the mean environment of blacks and .32 standard deviation worse than the mean environment for East Asians, when environments are measured along the continuum of their capacity to nurture intelligence. Let's state these conclusions in percentile terms: the average environment of blacks would have to be at the sixth percentile of the distribution of environments among whites and the average environment of East Asians would have to be at the sixty-third percentile of environments among whites for the racial differences to be entirely environmental.

Environmental differences of this magnitude and pattern are wildly out of line with all objective measures of the differences in black, Asian and white environments. Recall further that the black-white difference is smallest at the lowest socioeconomic levels. Why, if the black-white difference is entirely environmental, should the advantage of the "white" environment compared to the "black" be greater among the better-off and better-educated blacks and whites? We have not been able to think of a plausible reason. Can you? An appeal to the effects of racism to explain ethnic differences also requires explaining why environments poisoned by discrimination and racism for some other groups—against the Chinese or the Jews in some regions of America for example—have left them with higher scores than the national average.

However discomfiting it may be to consider it, there are reasons to suspect genetic considerations are involved. The evidence is circumstantial, but provocative. For example, ethnicities differ not just in average scores but in the profile of intellectual capacities. A full-scale I.Q. score is the aggregate of many subtests. There are thirteen of them in the Wechsler Intelligence Scale for Children, for example. The most basic division of the subtests is into a verbal I.Q. and a performance I.Q. In white samples the verbal and performance I.Q. subscores tend to have about the same mean, because I.Q. tests have been standardized on predominantly white populations. But individuals can have imbalances between these two I.Q.s. People with high verbal abilities are likely to do well with words and logic. In school they excel in history and literature; in choosing a career to draw on those talents, they tend to choose law or journalism or advertising or politics. In contrast, people with high performance I.Q.s—or, using a more descriptive phrase, "visuospatial abilities"—are likely to do well in the physical and biological sciences, mathematics, engineering or other subjects that demand mental manipulation in the three physical dimensions or the more numerous dimensions of mathematics.

East Asians living overseas score about the same or slightly lower than whites on verbal I.Q. and substantially higher on visuospatial I.Q. Even in the rare studies that have found overall Japanese or Chinese I.Q.s no higher than white I.Q.s, the discrepancy between verbal and visuospatial I.Q. persists. For Japanese living in Asia, a 1987 review of the literature demonstrated without much question that the verbal-visuospatial difference persists even in examinations that have been thoroughly adapted to the Japanese language and, indeed, in tests developed by the Japanese themselves. A study of a small sample of Korean infants adopted into white families in Belgium found the familiar elevated visuospatial scores.

This finding has an echo in the United States, where Asian American students abound in science subjects, in engineering and in medical schools, but are scarce in law schools and graduate programs in the humanities and social sciences. Is this just a matter of parental pressures or of Asian immigrants uncomfortable with English? The same pattern of subtest scores is found in Inuits and American Indians (both of Asian origin) and in fully assimilated second- and third-generation Asian Americans. Any simple socioeconomic, cultural or linguistic explanation is out of the question, given the diversity of living conditions, native languages, educational systems and cultural practices experienced by these groups and by East Asians living in Asia. Their common genetic history cannot plausibly be dismissed as irrelevant.

Turning now to blacks and whites (using these terms to refer exclusively to Americans), ability profiles also have been important in understanding the nature, and possible genetic component, of group differences. The argument has been developing around what is known as Spearman's hypothesis. This hypothesis says that if the black-white difference on test scores reflects a real underlying difference in general mental ability (g), then the size of the black-white difference will be related to the degree to which the test is saturated with g. In other words, the better a test measures g, the larger the black-white difference will be.

By now, Spearman's hypothesis has been borne out in fourteen major studies, and no appropriate data set has yet been found that contradicts Spearman's hypothesis. It should be noted that not all group differences behave similarly. For example, deaf children often get lower test scores than hearing children, but the size of the difference is not correlated positively with the test's loading on g. The phenomenon seems peculiarly concentrated in comparisons of ethnic groups. How does this bear on the genetic explanation of ethnic differences? In plain though somewhat imprecise language: the broadest conception of intelligence is embodied in g. At the same time, g typically has the highest heritability (higher than the other factors measured by I.Q. tests). As mental measurement focuses most specifically and reliably on g, the observed black-white mean difference in cognitive ability gets larger. This does not in itself demand a genetic explanation of the ethnic difference but, by asserting that "the better the test, the greater the ethnic difference," Spearman's hypothesis undercuts many of the environmental explanations of the difference that rely on the proposition (again, simplifying) that the apparent black-white difference is the result of bad tests, not good ones.

There are, of course, many arguments against such a genetic explanation. Many studies have shown that the disadvantaged environment of some blacks has depressed their test scores. In one study, in black families in rural Georgia, the elder sibling typically had a lower I.Q. than the younger. The larger the age difference is between the siblings, the larger is the difference in I.Q. The implication is that something in the rural Georgia environment was depressing the scores of black children as they grew older. In neither the white families of Georgia, nor white or black families in Berkeley, California, were there comparable signs of a depressive effect of the environment.

Another approach is to say that tests are artifacts of a culture, and a culture may not diffuse equally into every household and community. In a heterogeneous society, subcultures vary in ways that inevitably affect scores on I.Q. tests. Fewer books in the home mean less exposure to the material that a vocabulary subtest measures; the varying ways of socializing children may influence whether a child acquires the skills, or a desire for the skills, that tests test; the "common knowledge" that tests supposedly draw on may not be common in certain households and neighborhoods.

So far, this sounds like a standard argument about cultural bias, and yet it accepts the generalizations that we discussed earlier about internal evidence of bias. The supporters of this argument are not claiming that less exposure to books means that blacks score lower on vocabulary questions but do as well as whites on culture-free items. Rather, the effects of culture are more diffuse.

Furthermore, strong correlations between home or community life and I.Q. scores are readily found. In a study of 180 Latino and 180 non-Latino white elementary school children in Riverside, California, the researcher examined eight sociocultural variables: (1) mother's participation in formal organizations, (2) living in a segregated neighborhood, (3) home language level, (4) socioeconomic status based on occupation and education of head of household, (5) urbanization, (6) mother's achieve-ment values, (7) home ownership, and (8) intact biological family. She then showed that once these sociocultural variables were taken into account, the remaining group and I.Q. differences among the children fell to near zero.

The problem with this procedure lies in determining what, in fact, these eight variables control for: cultural diffusion, or genetic sources of variation in intelligence as ordinarily understood? By so drastically extending the usual match for socioeconomic status, the possibility is that such studies demonstrate only that parents matched on I.Q. will produce children with similar I.Q.s—not a startling finding. Also, the data used for such studies continue to show the distinctive racial patterns in the subtests. Why should cultural diffusion manifest itself by differences in backward and forward digit span or in completely nonverbal items? If the role of European white cultural diffusion is so important in affecting black I.Q. scores, why is it so unimportant in affecting Asian I.Q. scores?

There are other arguments related to cultural bias. In the American context, Wade Boykin is one of the most prominent academic advocates of a distinctive black culture, arguing that nine interrelated dimensions put blacks at odds with the prevailing Eurocentric model. Among them are spirituality (blacks approach life as "essentially vitalistic rather than mechanistic, with the conviction that nonmaterial forces influence people's everyday lives"); a belief in the harmony between humankind and nature; an emphasis on the importance of movement, rhythm, music and dance, "which are taken as central to psychological health"; personal styles that he characterizes as "verve" (high levels of stimulation and energy) and "affect" (emphasis on emotions and expressiveness); and "social time perspective," which he defines as "an orientation in which time is treated as passing through a social space rather than a material one." Such analyses purport to explain how large black-white differences in test scores could coexist with equal predictive validity of the test for such things as academic and job performance and yet still not be based on differences in "intelligence," broadly defined, let alone genetic differences.

John Ogbu, a Berkeley anthropologist, has proposed a more specific version of this argument. He suggests that we look at the history of various minority groups to understand the sources of differing levels of intellectual attainment in America. He distinguishes three types of minorities: "autonomous minorities" such as the Amish, Jews and Mormons, who, while they may be victims of discrimination, are still within the cultural mainstream; immigrant minorities," such as the Chinese, Filipinos, Japanese and Koreans within the United States, who moved voluntarily to their new societies and, while they may begin in menial jobs, compare themselves favorably with their peers back in the home country; and, finally, "castelike minorities," such as black Americans, who were involuntary immigrants or otherwise are consigned from birth to a distinctively lower place on the social ladder. Ogbu argues that the differences in test scores are an outcome of this historical distinction, pointing to a number of castes around the world—the untouchables in India, the Buraku in Japan and Oriental Jews in Israel—that have exhibited comparable problems in educational achievement despite being of the same racial group as the majority.

Indirect support for the proposition that the observed black-white difference could be the result of environmental factors is provided by the worldwide phenomenon of rising test scores. We call it "the Flynn effect" because of psychologist James Flynn's pivotal role in focusing attention on it, but the phenomenon itself was identified in the 1930s when testers began to notice that I.Q. scores often rose with every successive year after a test was first standardized. For example, when the Stanford-Binet I.Q. was restandardized in the mid-1930s, it was observed that individuals earned lower I.Q.s on the new tests than they got on the Stanford-Binet that had been standardized in the mid-1910s; in other words, getting a score of 100 (the population average) was harder to do on the later test. This meant that the average person could answer more items on the old test than on the new test. Most of the change has been concentrated in the nonverbal portions of the tests.

The tendency for I.Q. scores to drift upward as a function of years since standardization has now been substantiated in many countries and on many I.Q. tests besides the Stanford-Binet. In some countries, the upward drift since World War II has been as much as a point per year for some spans of years. The national averages have in fact changed by amounts that are comparable to the fifteen or so I.Q. points separating whites and blacks in America. To put it another way, on the average, whites today may differ in I.Q. from whites, say, two generations ago as much as whites today differ from blacks today. Given their size and speed, the shifts in time necessarily have been due more to changes in the environment than to changes in the genes. The question then arises: Couldn't the mean of blacks move fifteen points as well through environmental changes? There seems no reason why not—but also no reason to believe that white and Asian means can be made to stand still while the Flynn effect works its magic.

V.

As of 1994, then, we can say nothing for certain about the relative roles that genetics and environment play in the formation of the black-white difference in I.Q. All the evidence remains indirect. The heritability of individual differences in I.Q. does not necessarily mean that ethnic differences are also heritable. But those who think that ethnic differences are readily explained by environmental differences haven't been tough-minded enough about their own argument. At this complex intersection of complex factors, the easy answers are unsatisfactory ones.

Given the weight of the many circumstantial patterns, it seems improbable to us—though possible—that genes have no role whatsoever. What might the mix of genetic and environmental influences be? We are resolutely agnostic on that.

Here is what we hope will be our contribution to the discussion. We put it in italics; if we could, we would put it in neon lights: *The answer doesn't much matter.* Whether the black-white difference in test scores is produced by genes or the environment has no bearing on any of the reasons why the black-white difference is worth worrying about. If tomorrow we knew beyond a shadow of a doubt what role, if any, were played by genes, the news would be neither good if ethnic differences were predominantly environmental, nor awful if they were predominantly genetic.

The first reason for this assertion is that what matters is not whether differences are environmental or genetic, but how hard they are to change. Many people have a fuzzy impression that if cognitive ability has been depressed by a disadvantaged environment, it is easily remedied. Give the small child a more stimulating environment, give the older child a better education, it is thought, and the environmental deficit can be made up. This impression is wrong. The environment unquestionably has an impact on cognitive ability, but a record of interventions going back more than fifty years has demonstrated how difficult it is to manipulate the environment so that cognitive functioning is improved. The billions of dollars spent annually on compensatory education under Title I of the Elementary and Secondary Education Act have had such a dismal evaluation record that improving general cognitive functioning is no longer even a goal. Preschool education fares little better. Despite extravagant claims that periodically get their fifteen minutes of fame, preschool education, including not just ordinary Head Start but much more intensive programs such as Perry Preschool, raises I.Q. scores by a few points on the exit test, and even those small gains quickly fade. Preschool programs may be good for children in other ways, but they do not have important effects on intelligence. If larger effects are possible, it is only through truly heroic efforts, putting children into full-time, year-round, highly enriched day care from within a few months of birth and keeping them there for the first five years of life—and even those effects, claimed by the Milwaukee Program and the Abecedarian Project, are subject to widespread skepticism among scholars.

In short: If it were proved tomorrow that ethnic differences in test scores were entirely environmental, there would be no reason to celebrate. That knowledge would not suggest a single educational, preschool, day care or prenatal program that is not already being tried, and would give no reason to believe that tomorrow's effects from such programs will be any more encouraging than those observed to date. Radically improved knowledge about child development and intelligence is required, not just better implementation of what is already known. No breakthroughs are in sight.

The second reason that the concern about genes is overblown is the mistaken idea that genes mean there is nothing to be done. On the contrary, the distributions of genetic traits in a population can change over time, because people who die are not replaced one-for-one by babies with matched DNA. Just because there might be a genetic difference among groups in this generation does not mean that it cannot shrink. Nor, for that matter, does genetic equality in this generation mean that genetic differences might not arise within a matter of decades. It depends on which women in which group have how many babies at what ages. More broadly, genetic causes do not leave us helpless. Myops see fine with glasses and many bald men look as if they have hair, however closely myopia and baldness are tied to genes. Check out visual aids and gimmicks on any Macintosh computer to see how technology can compensate for innumeracy and illiteracy.

Now comes the third reason that the concern about genes needs rethinking. It is to us the most compelling: there is no *rational* reason why any encounter between individuals should be affected in any way by the knowledge that a group difference is genetic instead of environmental. Suppose that the news tomorrow morning is that the black-white difference in cognitive test scores is rooted in genetic differences. Suppose further that tomorrow afternoon, you—let us say you are white—encounter a random African American. Try to think of any way in which anything has changed that should affect your evaluation of or response to that individual and you will soon arrive at a truth that ought to be assimilated by everyone: nothing has changed. That an individual is a member of a group with a certain genetically based mean and distribution in any characteristic, whether it be height, intelligence, predisposition to schizophrenia or eye color has no effect on that reality of that individual. A five-foot man with six-foot parents is still five feet tall, no matter how much height is determined by genes. An African American with an I.Q. of 130 still has an I.Q. of 130, no matter what the black mean may be or to what extent I.Q. is determined by genes. Maybe for some whites, behavior toward black individuals would change if it were known that certain ethnic differences were genetic—but not for any good reason.

We have been too idealistic, one may respond. In the real world, people treat individuals according to their membership in a group. Consider the young black male trying to catch a taxi. It makes no difference how honest he is; many taxi drivers will refuse to pick him up because young black males disproportionately account for taxi robberies.

Similarly, some people fear that talking about group differences in I.Q. will encourage employers to use ethnicity as an inexpensive screen if they can get away with it, not bothering to consider black candidates.

These are authentic problems that need to be dealt with. But it puzzles us to hear them raised as a response to the question, "What difference does it make if genes are involved?" Two separate issues are being conflated: the reality of a difference versus its source. An employer has no more incentive to discriminate by ethnicity if he knows that a difference in ability is genetic than if he knows it is "only" environmental. To return to an earlier point, the key issue is how intractable the difference is. By the time someone is applying for a job, his cognitive functioning can be tweaked only at the margins, if at all, regardless of the original comparative roles of genes and environment in producing that level of cognitive functioning. The existence of a group difference may make a difference in the behavior of individuals toward other individuals, with implications that may well spill over into policy, but the source of the difference is irrelevant to the behavior.

VI.

In *The Bell Curve,* we make all of the above points, document them fully and are prepared to defend them against all comers. We argue that the best and indeed only answer to the problem of group differences is an energetic and uncompromising recommitment to individualism. To judge someone except on his or her own merits was historically thought to be un-American, and we urge that it become so again.

But as we worked on the discussion in the book, we also became aware that ratiocination is not a sufficient response. Many people instinctively believe that genetically caused group differences in intelligence must be psychologically destructive in a way that environmentally caused differences are not. In a way, our informal survey of elites during the writing of the book confirmed this. No matter what we said, we found that people walked away muttering that it *does* make a difference if genes are involved. But we nonetheless are not persuaded. It seems to us that, on the contrary, human beings have it in them to live

comfortably with all kinds of differences, group and individual alike.

We did not put those thoughts into the book. Early on, we decided that the passages on ethnic differences in intelligence had to be inflexibly pinned to data. Speculations were out, and even provocative turns of phrase had to be guarded against. The thoughts we are about to express are decidedly speculative, and hence did not become part of our book. But if you will treat them accordingly, we think they form the basis of a conversation worth beginning, and we will open it here.

As one looks around the world at the huge variety of ethnic groups that have high opinions of themselves, for example, one is struck by how easy it is for each of these clans, as we will call them, to conclude that it has the best combination of genes and culture in the world. In each clan's eyes, its members are blessed to have been born who they are—Arab, Chinese, Jew, Welsh, Russian, Spanish, Zulu, Scots, Hungarian. The list could go on indefinitely, breaking into ever smaller groups (highland Scots, Glaswegians, Scotch-Irish). The members of each clan do not necessarily think their people have gotten the best break regarding their political or economic place in the world, but they do not doubt the intrinsic, unique merits of their particular clan.

How does this clannish self-esteem come about? Any one dimension, including intelligence, clearly plays only a small part. The self-esteem is based on a mix of qualities. These packages of qualities are incomparable across clans. The mixes are too complex, the metrics are too different, the qualities are too numerous to lend themselves to a weighting scheme that everyone could agree upon. The Irish have a way with words; the Irish also give high marks to having a way with words in the pantheon of human abilities. The Russians see themselves as soulful; they give high marks to soulfulness. The Scotch-Irish who moved to America tended to be cantankerous, restless and violent. Well, say the American Scotch-Irish proudly, these qualities made for terrific pioneers.

We offer this hypothesis: Clans tend to order the world, putting themselves on top, not because each clan has an inflated idea of its own virtues, but because each is using a weighting algorithm that genuinely works out that way. One of us had a conversation with a Thai many years ago about the Thai attitude toward Americans. Americans have technology and capabilities that the Thais do not have, he said, just as the elephant is stronger than a human. "But," he said with a shrug, "who wants to be an elephant?" We do not consider his view quaint. There is an internally consistent logic that legitimately might lead a Thai to conclude that being born Thai gives one a better chance of becoming a complete human being than being born American. He may not be right, but he is not necessarily wrong.

If these observations have merit, why is it that one human clan occasionally develops a deep-seated sense of ethnic inferiority vis-à-vis another clan? History suggests that the reasons tend to be independent of any particular qualities of the two groups, but instead are commonly rooted in historical confrontations. When one clan has been physically subjugated by another, the psychological reactions are complex and long-lasting. The academic literature on political development is filled with studies of the reactions of colonized peoples that prove this case. These self-denigrating reactions are not limited to the common people; if anything, they are most profound among the local elites. Consider, for example, the deeply ambivalent attitudes of Indian elites toward the British. The Indian cultural heritage is glittering, but that heritage was not enough to protect Indian elites from the psychological ravages of being subjugated.

Applying these observations to the American case and to relations between blacks and whites suggests a new way of conceptualizing the familiar "legacy of slavery" arguments. It is not just that slavery surely had lasting effects on black culture, nor even that slavery had any broad negative effect on black self-confidence and self-esteem, but more specifically that the experience of slavery perverted and stunted the evolution of the ethnocentric algorithm that American blacks would have developed in the normal course of events. Whites did everything in their power to explain away or belittle every sign of talent, virtue or superiority among blacks. They had to—if the slaves were superior in qualities the whites themselves valued, where was the moral justification for keeping them enslaved? And so everything that African Americans did well had to be cast in terms that belittled the quality in question. Even to try to document this point leaves one open to charges of condescension, so successfully did whites manage to coopt the value

judgments. Most obviously, it is impossible to speak straightforwardly about the dominance of many black athletes without being subject to accusations that one is being backhandedly anti-black.

The nervous concern about racial inferiority in the United States is best seen as a variation on the colonial experience. It is in the process of diminishing that African Americans define for themselves that mix of qualities that makes the American black clan unique and (appropriately in the eyes of the clan) superior. It emerges in fiction by black authors and in a growing body of work by black scholars. It is also happening in the streets. The process is not only normal and healthy, it is essential.

In making these points, there are several things we are not saying that need to be spelled out. We are not giving up on the melting pot. Italians all over America who live in neighborhoods without a single other Italian, and who may technically have more non-Italian than Italian blood, continue to take pride in their Italian heritage in the ways we have described. The same may be said of other ethnic clans. For that matter, we could as easily have used the examples of Texans and Minnesotans as of Thais and Scotch-Irish in describing the ways in which people naturally take pride in their group. Americans often see themselves as members of several clans at the same time—and think of themselves as 100 percent American as well. It is one of America's most glorious qualities.

We are also not trying to tell African Americans or anyone else what qualities should be weighted in their algorithm. Our point is precisely the opposite: no one needs to tell any clan how to come up with a way of seeing itself that is satisfactory; it is one of those things that human communities know how to do quite well when left alone to do it. Still less are we saying that the children from any clan should not, say, study calculus because studying calculus is not part of the clan's heritage. Individuals strike out on their own, making their way in the Great World according to what they bring to their endeavors as individuals—and can still take comfort and pride in their group affiliations. Of course there are complications and tensions in this process. The tighter the clan, the more likely it is to look suspiciously on their children who depart for the Great World—and yet also, the more proudly it is likely to boast of their successes once they have made it, and the more likely that the children will one day restore some of their ties with the clan they left behind. This is one of the classic American dramas.

We are not preaching multiculturalism. Our point is not that everything is relative and the accomplishments of each culture and ethnic group are just as good as those of every other culture and ethnic group. Instead, we are saying a good word for a certain kind of ethnocentrism. Given a chance, each clan will add up its accomplishments using its own weighting system, will encounter the world with confidence in its own worth and, most importantly, will be unconcerned about comparing its accomplishments line-by-line with those of any other clan. This is wise ethnocentrism.

In the context of intelligence and I.Q. scores, we are urging that it is foolish ethnocentrism on the part of European Americans to assume that mean differences in I.Q. among ethnic groups must mean that those who rank lower on that particular dimension are required to be miserable about it—all the more foolish because the group I.Q. of the prototypical American clan, white Protestants, is some rungs from the top.

It is a difficult point to make persuasively, because the undoubted reality of our era is that group differences in intelligence are intensely threatening and feared. One may reasonably ask what point there is in speculating about some better arrangement in which it wouldn't matter. And yet there remain stubborn counterfactuals that give reason for thinking that inequalities in intelligence need not be feared—not just theoretically, but practically.

We put it as a hypothesis that lends itself to empirical test: hardly anyone feels inferior to people who have higher I.Q.s. If you doubt this, put it to yourself. You surely have known many people who are conspicuously smarter than you are, in terms of sheer intellectual horsepower. Certainly we have. There have been occasions when we thought it would be nice to be as smart as these other people. But. like the Thai who asked, "Who wants to be an elephant?" we have not felt inferior to our brilliant friends, nor have we wanted to trade places with them. We have felt a little sorry for some of them, thinking that despite their high intelligence they lacked other qualities that we possessed and that we valued more highly than their extra I.Q. points.

When we have remarked upon this to friends, their reaction has often been, "That's fine for you to say, because you're smart enough already." But we are making a more ambitious argument: it is not just people with high I.Q.s who don't feel inferior to people with even higher I.Q.s. The rule holds true all along the I.Q. continuum.

It is hard to get intellectuals to accept this, because of another phenomenon that we present as a hypothesis, but are fairly confident can be verified: people with high I.Q.s tend to condescend to people with lower I.Q.s. Once again, put yourself to the test. Suppose we point to a person with an I.Q. thirty points lower than yours. Would you be willing to trade places with him? Do you instinctively feel a little sorry for him? Here, we have found the answers from friends to be more reluctant, and usually a little embarrassed, but generally they have been "no" and "yes," respectively. Isn't it remarkable: just about everyone seems to think that his level of intelligence is enough, that any less than his isn't as good, but that any more than his isn't such a big deal.

In other words, we propose that the same thing goes on within individuals as within clans. In practice, not just idealistically, people do not judge themselves as human beings by the size of their I.Q.s. Instead, they bring to bear a multidimensional judgment of themselves that lets them take satisfaction in who they are. Surely a person with an I.Q. of 90 sometimes wishes he had an I.Q. of 120, just as a person with an I.Q. of 120 sometimes wishes he had an I.Q. of 150. But it is presumptuous, though a curiously common presumption among intellectuals, to think that someone with an I.Q. of 90 must feel inferior to those who are smarter, just as it is presumptuous to think a white person must feel threatened by a group difference that probably exists between whites and Japanese, a gentile must feel threatened by a group difference that certainly exists between gentiles and Jews or a black person must feel threatened by a group difference between blacks and whites. It is possible to look ahead to a world in which the glorious hodgepodge of inequalities of ethnic groups—genetic and environmental, permanent and temporary—can be not only accepted but celebrated.

This difficult topic calls up an unending sequence of questions. How can intelligence be treated as just one of many qualities when the marketplace puts such a large monetary premium on it? How can one hope that people who are on the lower end of the I.Q. range find places of dignity in the world when the niches they used to hold in society are being devalued? Since the world tends to be run by people who are winners in the I.Q. lottery, how can one hope that societies will be structured so that the lucky ones do not continually run society for their own benefit?

These are all large questions, exceedingly complex questions—but they are no longer about ethnic variations in intelligence. They are about *human* variation in intelligence. They, not ethnic differences, are worth writing a book about—and that's what we did. Ethnic differences must be dreaded only to the extent that people insist on dreading them. People certainly are doing so—that much is not in dispute. What we have tried to do here, in a preliminary and no doubt clumsy way, is to begin to talk about the reasons why they need not.

Discussion and Assignments

Part I

1. What is it that Murray and Herrnstein say they have noticed about the private attitudes of the white elite toward blacks? *Who* are the white elite, and does this view correspond with your knowledge of the white elite, or any other educated white people you know, toward blacks?

2. Why is it essential that people begin to talk about the relationship of race, genes, and intelligence in the open, according to Murray and Herrnstein? Do you share this same sense of necessity?

Part II

3. Murray and Herrnstein claim if you are an employer, you are usually better off knowing the IQ of a job applicant than having any other single piece of information about that individual, including a resume, an interview, or a written recommendation. How plausible does this claim sound to you? Imagine you are filling out a job application and part of the document reads like this:

JOB APPLICATION—PIGGY BANK CONSTRUCTION COMPANY
Name (Last, MI, First) _____
Address _____
Work Experience (Last Position First) _____
Education (Last Degree First) _____
IQ (List All Tests and Dates) _____
Recommendations (Attach letters at end of application)

Should an employer be permitted to ask for your IQ text scores on a job application? How do you believe the information would be used by prospective employers? Can you imagine a situation where such a question might be to your advantage or disadvantage if you were an applicant? How would a job application asking you for your IQ test scores differ from a college application requiring SAT or ACT scores?

4. How do Murray and Herrnstein use the terms *race* and *ethnicity* in their paper? How do they go about classifying an individual as being a member of a particular race?

Part III

5. Study Figures 1 and 2. Why do Murray and Herrnstein claim the second graph illustrates why cognitive differences between blacks and whites can be "problematic

to society as a whole." What do you think the authors mean by this? Do you agree or disagree with the authors?

6. What is *external evidence of bias*? Do Murray and Herrnstein believe there is any external evidence of bias present in the IQ tests used in their research? Do you believe their analysis of external evidence of bias is adequate?

7. What is *internal evidence of bias* (cultural bias)? Do Murray and Herrnstein believe there is any internal evidence of bias present in the IQ tests used in their research? What is their surprising answer to this question for the newcomer to this subject? Do you think their discussion of internal evidence of bias is adequate?

8. What do Murray and Herrnstein say about bias associated with the *motivation to try?* Do they believe there is any motivation-to-try bias present in the IQ tests used in their research? Explain the example they offer to refute claims of motivation-to-try bias. Does the example offer sufficient reason to believe there is no motivation-to-try bias in IQ tests?

9. According to Murray and Herrnstein, can the black-white IQ gap be attributed to socioeconomic status? What is the most convincing piece of evidence they cite on this issue? What is the most unconvincing? Can you think of something important they left out?

Part IV

10. According to Murray and Herrnstein, can the black-white IQ gap be attributed to environmental factors? What is the most convincing piece of evidence they cite to support their case on this issue? What is the least unconvincing? Can you think of something important they left out?

11. Murray and Herrnstein discuss Wade Boykin's theory which attributes the black-white gap in IQ to cultural factors. What is Boykin's position, and do you think it's a reasonable response to Murray and Herrnstein's position?

12. Murray and Herrnstein discuss John Ogbu's theory which also attributes the black-white IQ gap to cultural factors. What is Ogbu's position, and do you think it's a reasonable response to Murray and Herrnstein's position?

13. The *Flynn effect* is often cited as a possible explanation for how the black-white IQ gap might close due to environmental factors. What is the Flynn effect? Do Murray and Herrnstein give an adequate argument for its existence? Do they offer good reasons why they believe the Flynn effect will not close the IQ gap? If the Flynn effect actually exists, could this raise any questions about the validity of Murray and Herrnstein's overall theory? What do you make of the Flynn effect?

Part V

14. In the beginning of Part V, the authors state: "Here is what we hope will be our contribution to the discussion. We put it in italics; if we could, we would put it in neon lights: *The answer doesn't much matter.* Whether the black-white difference in test scores is produced by genes or the environment has no bearing on any of the reasons why the black-white difference is worth worrying about."

At first this appears to be a perplexing claim, but then the authors go on to offer three reasons to explain the statement. Briefly, what are they? Are they clear and well argued? Do you find the reasons convincing?

15, Are the authors convincing when they place the IQ disparities within a context of other genetic predispositions, such as eye color, the tendency to develop schizophrenia, or the tendency to be tall?

Part VI

16. Murray and Herrnstein close their paper with a discussion of clans—how clans develop a sense of community, identity, and worth, and how they relate themselves to other individuals and their clans or groups. Each clan assesses and celebrates its own accomplishments according to its own weighting system. The authors celebrate this cultural diversity as "wise ethnocentrism." Individuals are multidimensional, and this is how they should be understood and appreciated.

Why this change of emphasis by the authors after they spent so much time establishing that East Asians are genetically predisposed to have higher IQs than whites and blacks, and whites higher IQs than blacks?

8.3 Curveball

STEPHEN JAY GOULD

1   THE BELL CURVE, by Richard J. Herrnstein and Charles Murray (Free Press; $30), subtitled *Intelligence and Class Structure in American Life*, provides a superb and unusual opportunity to gain insight into the meaning of experiment as a method in science. The primary desideratum in all experiments is reduction of confusing variables: we bring all the buzzing and blooming confusion of the external world into our laboratories and, holding all else constant in our artificial simplicity, try to vary just one potential factor at a time. But many subjects defy the use of such an experimental method—particularly most social phenomena—because importation into the laboratory destroys the subject of the investigation, and then we must yearn for simplifying guides in nature. If the external world occasionally obliges by holding some crucial factors constant for us, we can only offer thanks for this natural boost to understanding.

2   So, when a book garners as much attention as *The Bell Curve*, we wish to know the causes. One might suspect the content itself—a startlingly new idea, or an old suspicion newly verified by persuasive data—but the reason might also be social acceptability, or even just plain hype. *The Bell Curve*, with its claims and supposed documentation that race and class differences are largely caused by genetic factors and are therefore essentially immutable, contains no new arguments and presents no compelling data to support its anachronistic social Darwinism, so I can only con-

clude that its success in winning attention must reflect the depressing temper of our time—a historical moment of unprecedented ungenerosity, when a mood for slashing social programs can be powerfully abetted by an argument that beneficiaries cannot be helped, owing to inborn cognitive limits expressed as low I.Q. scores.

3   *The Bell Curve* rests on two distinctly different but sequential arguments, which together encompass the classic corpus of biological determinism as a social philosophy. The first argument rehashes the tenets of social Darwinism as it was originally constituted. "Social Darwinism" has often been used as a general term for any evolutionary argument about the biological basis of human differences, but the initial nineteenth-century meaning referred to a specific theory of class stratification within industrial societies, and particularly to the idea that there was a permanently poor underclass consisting of genetically inferior people who had precipitated down into their inevitable fate. The theory arose from a paradox of egalitarianism: as long as people remain on top of the social heap by accident of a noble name or parental wealth, and as long as members of despised castes cannot rise no matter what their talents, social stratification will not reflect intellectual merit, and brilliance will be distributed across all classes; but when true equality of opportunity is attained smart people rise and the lower classes become rigid, retaining only the intellectually incompetent.

From The New Yorker, *November 28, 1994, pp. 139–149. Reprinted with permission.*

4   This argument has attracted a variety of twentieth-century champions, including the Stanford psychologist Lewis M. Terman, who imported Alfred Binet's original test from France, developed the Stanford-Binet I.Q. test, and gave a hereditarian interpretation to the results (one that Binet had vigorously rejected in developing this style of test); Prime Minister Lee Kuan Yew of Singapore, who tried to institute a eugenics program of rewarding well-educated women for higher birth rates; and Richard Herrnstein, a coauthor of *The Bell Curve* and also the author of a 1971 *Atlantic Monthly* article that presented the same argument without the documentation. The general claim is neither uninteresting nor illogical, but it does require the validity of four shaky premises, all asserted (but hardly discussed or defended) by Herrnstein and Murray. Intelligence, in their formulation, must be depictable as a single number, capable of ranking people in linear order, genetically based, and effectively immutable. If any of these premises are false, their entire argument collapses. For example, if all are true except immutability, then programs for early intervention in education might work to boost I.Q. permanently, just as a pair of eyeglasses may correct a genetic defect in vision. The central argument of *The Bell Curve* fails because most of the premises are false.

5   Herrnstein and Murray's second claim, the lightning rod for most commentary, extends the argument for innate cognitive stratification to a claim that racial differences in I.Q. are mostly determined by genetic causes—small differences for Asian superiority over Caucasian, but large for Caucasians over people of African descent. This argument is as old as the study of race, and is almost surely fallacious. The last generation's discussion centered on Arthur Jensen's 1980 book *Bias in Mental Testing* (far more elaborate and varied than anything presented in *The Bell Curve,* and therefore still a better source for grasping the argument and its problems), and on the cranky advocacy of William Shockley, a Nobel Prize-winning physicist. The central fallacy in using the substantial heritability of within-group I.Q. (among whites, for example) as an explanation of average differences between groups (whites versus blacks, for example) is now well known and acknowledged by all, including Herrnstein and Murray, but deserves a restatement by example. Take a trait that

is far more heritable than anyone has ever claimed I.Q. to be but is politically uncontroversial—body height. Suppose that I measure the heights of adult males in a poor Indian village beset with nutritional deprivation, and suppose the average height of adult males is five feet six inches. Heritability within the village is high, which is to say that tall fathers (they may average five feet eight inches) tend to have tall sons, while short fathers (five feet four inches on average) tend to have short sons. But this high heritability within the village does not mean that better nutrition might not raise average height to five feet ten inches in a few generations. Similarly, the well-documented fifteen-point average difference in I.Q. between blacks and whites in America, with substantial heritability of I.Q. in family lines within each group, permits no automatic conclusion that truly equal opportunity might not raise the black average enough to equal or surpass the white mean.

6   Disturbing as I find the anachronism of *The Bell Curve,* I am even more distressed by its pervasive disingenuousness. The authors omit facts, misuse statistical methods, and seem unwilling to admit the consequences of their own words.

7   The ocean of publicity that has engulfed *The Bell Curve* has a basis in what Murray and Herrnstein, in an article in *The New Republic* last month, call "the flashpoint of intelligence as a public topic: the question of genetic differences between the races." And yet, since the day of the book's publication, Murray (Herrnstein died a month before the book appeared) has been temporizing, and denying that race is an important subject in the book at all; he blames the press for unfairly fanning these particular flames. In *The New Republic* he and Herrnstein wrote, "Here is what we hope will be our contribution to the discussion. We put it in italics; if we could, we would put it in neon lights: *The answer doesn't much matter.*"

8   Fair enough, in the narrow sense that any individual may be a rarely brilliant member of an averagely dumb group (and therefore not subject to judgment by the group mean), but Murray cannot deny that *The Bell Curve* treats race as one of two major topics, with each given about equal space; nor can he pretend that strongly stated claims about group differences have no political impact in a society obsessed with the meanings and

consequences of ethnicity. The very first sentence of *The Bell Curve*'s preface acknowledges that the book treats the two subjects equally: "This book is about differences in intellectual capacity among people and groups and what those differences mean for America's future." And Murray and Herrnstein's *New Republic* article begins by identifying racial differences as the key subject of interest: "The private dialogue about race in America is far different from the public one."

9   Furthermore, Herrnstein and Murray know and acknowledge the critique of extending the substantial heritability of within-group I.Q. to explain differences between groups, so they must construct an admittedly circumstantial case for attributing most of the black-white mean difference to irrevocable genetics—while properly stressing that the average difference doesn't help in judging any particular person, because so many individual blacks score above the white mean in I.Q. Quite apart from the rhetorical dubiety of this old ploy in a shopworn genre—"Some of my best friends are Group X"—Herrnstein and Murray violate fairness by converting a complex case that can yield only agnosticism into a biased brief for permanent and heritable difference. They impose this spin by turning every straw on their side into an oak, while mentioning but downplaying the strong circumstantial case for substantial malleability and little average genetic difference. This case includes such evidence as impressive I.Q. scores for poor black children adopted into affluent and intellectual homes; average I.Q. increases in some nations since the Second World War equal to the entire fifteen-point difference now separating blacks and whites in America; and failure to find any cognitive differences between two cohorts of children born out of wedlock to German women, reared in Germany as Germans, but fathered by black and white American soldiers.

10   *The Bell Curve* is even more disingenuous in its argument than in its obfuscation about race. The book is a rhetorical masterpiece of scientism, and it benefits from the particular kind of fear that numbers impose on nonprofessional commentators. It runs to eight hundred and forty-five pages, including more than a hundred pages of appendixes filled with figures. So the text looks complicated, and reviewers shy away with a knee-jerk claim that, while they suspect fallacies of

argument, they really cannot judge. In the same issue of *The New Republic* as Murray and Herrnstein's article, Mickey Kaus writes, "As a lay reader of *The Bell Curve,* I'm unable to judge fairly," and Leon Wieseltier adds, "Murray, too, is hiding the hardness of his politics behind the hardness of his science. And his science, for all I know, is soft. . . . Or so I imagine. I am not a scientist. I know nothing about psychometrics." And Peter Passell, in the *Times:* "But this reviewer is not a biologist, and will leave the argument to experts."

11   The book is in fact extraordinarily one-dimensional. It makes no attempt to survey the range of available data, and pays astonishingly little attention to the rich and informative history of its contentious subject. (One can only recall Santayana's dictum, now a cliché of intellectual life: "Those who cannot remember the past are condemned to repeat it.") Virtually all the analysis rests on a single technique applied to a single set of data—probably done in one computer run. (I do agree that the authors have used the most appropriate technique and the best source of information. Still, claims as broad as those advanced in *The Bell Curve* simply cannot be properly defended—that is, either supported or denied—by such a restricted approach.) The blatant errors and inadequacies of *The Bell Curve* could be picked up by lay reviewers if only they would not let themselves be frightened by numbers—for Herrnstein and Murray do write clearly, and their mistakes are both patent and accessible.

12   While disclaiming his own ability to judge, Mickey Kaus, in *The New Republic,* does correctly identify the authors' first two claims that are absolutely essential "to make the pessimistic 'ethnic difference' argument work": "(1) that there is a single, general measure of mental ability; (2) that the I.Q. tests that purport to measure this ability . . . aren't culturally biased."

13   Nothing in *The Bell Curve* angered me more than the authors' failure to supply any justification for their central claim, the sine qua non of their entire argument that the number known as *g,* the celebrated "general factor" of intelligence, first identified by the British psychologist Charles Spearman, in 1904, captures a real property in the head. Murray and Herrnstein simply declare that the issue has been decided, as in this passage from

their *New Republic* article: "Among the experts, it is by now beyond much technical dispute that there is such a thing as a general factor of cognitive ability on which human beings differ and that this general factor is measured reasonably well by a variety of standardized tests, best of all by I.Q. tests designed for that purpose." Such a statement represents extraordinary obfuscation, achievable only if one takes "expert" to mean "that group of psychometricians working in the tradition of *g* and its avatar I.Q." The authors even admit that there are three major schools of psychometric interpretation and that only one supports their view of *g* and I.Q.

14   But this issue cannot be decided, or even understood, without discussing the key and only rationale that has maintained *g* since Spearman invented it: factor analysis. The fact that Herrnstein and Murray barely mention the factor-analytic argument forms a central indictment of *The Bell Curve* and is an illustration of its vacuousness. How can the authors base an eight-hundred-page book on a claim for the reality of I.Q. as measuring a genuine, and largely genetic, general cognitive ability—and then hardly discuss, either pro or con, the theoretical basis for their certainty?

15   Admittedly, factor analysis is a difficult mathematical subject, but it can be explained to lay readers with a geometrical formulation developed by L. L. Thurstone, an American psychologist, in the nineteen-thirties and used by me in a full chapter on factor analysis in my 1981 book *The Mismeasure of Man*. A few paragraphs cannot suffice for adequate explanation, so, although I offer some sketchy hints below, readers should not question their own I.Q.s if the topic still seems arcane.

16   In brief, a person's performance on various mental tests tends to be positively correlated—that is, if you do well on one kind of test, you tend to do well on the other kinds. This is scarcely surprising, and is subject to interpretation that is either purely genetic (that an innate thing in the head boosts all performances) or purely environmental (that good books and good childhood nutrition boost all performances); the positive correlations in themselves say nothing about causes. The results of these tests can be plotted on a multidimensional graph with an axis for each test. Spearman used factor analysis to find a single dimension—which

he called *g*—that best identifies the common factor behind positive correlations among the tests. But Thurstone later showed that *g* could be made to disappear by simply rotating the dimensions to different positions. In one rotation Thurstone placed the dimensions near the most widely separated attributes among the tests, thus giving rise to the theory of multiple intelligence (verbal, mathematical, spatial, etc., with no overarching *g*). This theory (which I support) has been advocated by many prominent psychometricians, including J. P. Guilford, in the nineteen-fifties, and Howard Gardner today. In this perspective, *g* cannot have inherent reality, for it emerges in one form of mathematical representation for correlations among tests and disappears (or greatly attenuates) in other forms, which are entirely equivalent in amount of information explained. In any case, you can't grasp the issue at all without a clear exposition of factor analysis—and *The Bell Curve* cops out on this central concept.

17   As for Kaus's second issue, cultural bias, the presentation of it in *The Bell Curve* matches Arthur Jensen's and that of other hereditarians, in confusing a technical (and proper) meaning of "bias" (I call it "S-bias," for "statistical") with the entirely different vernacular concept (I call it "V-bias") that provokes popular debate. All these authors swear up and down (and I agree with them completely) that the tests are not biased—in the statistician's definition. Lack of S-bias means that the same score, when it is achieved by members of different groups, predicts the same thing; that is, a black person and a white person with identical scores will have the same probabilities for doing anything that I.Q. is supposed to predict.

18   But V-bias, the source of public concern, embodies an entirely different issue, which, unfortunately, uses the same word. The public wants to know whether blacks average 85 and whites 100 because society treats blacks unfairly—that is, whether lower black scores record biases in this social sense. And this crucial question (to which we do not know the answer) cannot be addressed by a demonstration that S-bias doesn't exist, which is the only issue analyzed, however correctly, in *The Bell Curve*.

19   The book is also suspect in its use of statistics. As I mentioned, virtually all its data derive from one analysis—a plotting, by a technique called multiple regression, of the social behaviors that agitate us, such as crime, unemployment, and births out of wedlock (known as dependent variables), against both I.Q. and parental socioeconomic status (known as independent variables). The authors first hold I.Q. constant and consider the relationship of social behaviors to parental socioeconomic status. They then hold socioeconomic status constant and consider the relationship of the same social behaviors to I.Q. In general, they find a higher correlation with I.Q. than with socioeconomic status; for example, people with low I.Q. are more likely to drop out of high school than people whose parents have low socioeconomic status.

20 But such analyses must engage two issues—the form and the strength of the relationship—and Herrnstein and Murray discuss only the issue that seems to support their viewpoint, while virtually ignoring (and in one key passage almost willfully hiding) the other. Their numerous graphs present only the form of the relationships; that is, they draw the regression curves of their variables against I.Q. and parental socioeconomic status. But, in violation of all statistical norms that I've ever learned, they plot *only* the regression curve and do not show the scatter of variation around the curve, so their graphs do not show anything about the strength of the relationships—that is, the amount of variation in social factors explained by I.Q. and socioeconomic status. Indeed, almost all their relationships are weak; very little of the variation in social factors is explained by either independent variable (though the form of this small amount of explanation does lie in their favored direction). In short, their own data indicate that I.Q. is not a major factor in determining variation in nearly all the social behaviors they study—and so their conclusions collapse, or at least become so greatly attenuated that their pessimism and conservative social agenda gain no significant support.

21 Herrnstein and Murray actually admit as much in one crucial passage, but then they hide the pattern. They write, "It [cognitive ability] almost always explains less than 20 percent of the variance, to use the statistician's term, usually less than 10 percent and often less than 5 percent. What this means in English is that you cannot predict what a given person will do from his I.Q.

score. . . . On the other hand, despite the low association at the individual level, large differences in social behavior separate groups of people when the groups differ intellectually on the average." Despite this disclaimer, their remarkable next sentence makes a strong causal claim. "We will argue that intelligence itself, not just its correlation with socioeconomic status, is responsible for these group differences." But a few percent of statistical determination is not causal explanation. And the case is even worse for their key genetic argument, since they claim a heritability of about sixty percent for I.Q., so to isolate the strength of genetic determination by Herrnstein and Murray's own criteria you must nearly halve even the few percent they claim to explain.

22 My charge of disingenuousness receives its strongest affirmation in a sentence tucked away on the first page of Appendix 4, page 593: the authors state, "In the text, we do not refer to the usual measure of goodness of fit for multiple regressions, R^2, but they are presented here for the cross-sectional analyses." Now, why would they exclude from the text, and relegate to an appendix that very few people will read, or even consult, a number that, by their own admission, is "the usual measure of goodness of fit"? I can only conclude that they did not choose to admit in the main text the extreme weakness of their vaunted relationships.

23 Herrnstein and Murray's correlation coefficients are generally low enough by themselves to inspire lack of confidence. (Correlation coefficients measure the strength of linear relationships between variables; the positive values run from 0.0 for no relationship to 1.0 for perfect linear relationship.) Although low figures are not atypical for large social-science surveys involving many variables, most of Herrnstein and Murray's correlations are very weak—often in the 0.2 to 0.4 range. Now, 0.4 may sound respectably strong, but—this is the key point—R^2 is the square of the correlation coefficient, and the square of a number between zero and one is less than the number itself, so a 0.4 correlation yields an r-squared of only .16. In Appendix 4, then, one discovers that the vast majority of the conventional measures of R^2, excluded from the main body of the text, are less than 0.1. These very low values of R^2 expose the true weakness, in any meaningful vernacular sense,

of nearly all the relationships that form the meat of *The Bell Curve*.

24   Like so many conservative ideologues who rail against the largely bogus ogre of suffocating political correctness, Herrnstein and Murray claim that they only want a hearing for unpopular views so that truth will out. And here, for once, I agree entirely. As a card-carrying First Amendment (near) absolutist, I applaud the publication of unpopular views that some people consider dangerous. I am delighted that *The Bell Curve* was written—so that its errors could be exposed, for Herrnstein and Murray are right to point out the difference between public and private agendas on race, and we must struggle to make an impact on the private agendas as well. But *The Bell Curve* is scarcely an academic treatise in social theory and population genetics. It is a manifesto of conservative ideology, the book's inadequate and biased treatment of data displays its primary purpose— advocacy. The text evokes the dreary and scary drumbeat of claims associated with conservative think tanks: reduction or elimination of welfare, ending or sharply curtailing affirmative action in schools and workplaces, cutting back Head Start and other forms of preschool education, trimming programs for the slowest learners and applying those finds to the gifted. (I would love to see more attention paid to talented students, but not at this cruel price.)

25   The penultimate chapter presents an apocalyptic vision of a society with a growing underclass permanently mired in the inevitable sloth of their low I.Q.s. They will take over our city centers, keep having illegitimate babies (for many are too stupid to practice birth control), and ultimately require a kind of custodial state, more to keep them in check—and out of high-I.Q. neighborhoods—than to realize any hope of an amelioration, which low I.Q. makes impossible in any case. Herrnstein and Murray actually write, "In short, by *custodial state,* we have in mind a high-tech and more lavish version of the Indian reservation for some substantial minority of the nation's population, while the rest of America tries to go about its business."

26   The final chapter tries to suggest an alternative, but I have never read anything more almost grotesquely inadequate. Herrnstein and Murray yearn romantically for the good old days of towns and neighborhoods where all people could be given tasks of value, and self-esteem could be found for people on all steps of the I.Q. hierarchy (so Forrest Gump might collect clothing for the church raffle, while Mr. Murray and the other bright ones do the planning and keep the accounts—they have forgotten about the town Jew and the dwellers on the other side of the tracks in many of these idyllic villages). I do believe in this concept of neighborhood, and I will fight for its return. I grew up in such a place in Queens. But can anyone seriously find solutions for (rather than important palliatives of) our social ills therein?

27   However, if Herrnstein and Murray are wrong, and I.Q. represents not an immutable thing in the head, grading human beings on a single scale of general capacity with large numbers of custodial incompetents at the bottom, then the model that generates their gloomy vision collapses, and the wonderful variousness of human abilities, properly nurtured, reemerges. We must fight the doctrine of *The Bell Curve* both because it is wrong and because it will, if activated, cut off all possibility of proper nurturance for everyone's intelligence. Of course, we cannot all be rocket scientists or brain surgeons, but those who can't might be rock musicians or professional athletes (and gain far more social prestige and salary thereby), while others will indeed serve by standing and waiting.

28   I closed my chapter in *The Mismeasure of Man* on the unreality of *g* and the fallacy of regarding intelligence as a single-scaled, innate thing in the head with a marvelous quotation from John Stuart Mill, well worth repeating:

> The tendency has always been strong to believe that whatever received a name must be an entity or being, having an independent existence of its own. And if no real entity answering to the name could be found, men did not for that reason suppose that none existed, but imagined that it was something particularly abstruse and mysterious.

29   How strange that we would let a single and false number divide us, when evolution has united all people in the recency of our common ancestry—thus undergirding with a shared humanity that infinite variety which custom can never stale. E pluribus unum.

Discussion and Assignments

1. Gould claims *The Bell Curve* is predicated on four basic assumptions, all of which are shaky, most of which are false. What are these assumptions and how effective is he in characterizing them? Do you agree that they serve the function Gould claims?

2. In paragraph 9 Gould cites three important pieces of evidence he claims Murray and Herrnstein chose to ignore in their book. Examine these three pieces of evidence. Which do you regard as the most convincing? Which as the least convincing? Do you think these issues are so compelling that Murray and Herrnstein should have included them in their book? Why or why not?

3. In paragraph 13 Gould opens his discussion of Murray and Herrnstein's treatment of the *g* factor, or general factor of intelligence. In a paragraph, outline Gould's criticism of the *g* factor and how he applies this criticism to Murray and Herrnstein's use of the *g* factor in *The Bell Curve*.

4. Go back and locate those four assumptions Gould discusses at the beginning of his paper, the four "shaky premises" Gould claims Murray and Herrnstein's book is built on. How do these "shaky" assumptions relate to Gould's criticism of the *g* factor? In light of these assumptions, how effective is Gould in summing up and criticizing the existence of the *g* factor?

5. In paragraphs 17 and 18 Gould discusses two types of bias, statistical bias (S-bias) and cultural bias (V-bias). What is the distinction between the two? Does Gould imply that V-bias could be responsible for the black-white IQ gap? Does he offer any evidence to support his suspicions?

6. In his closing paragraphs, Gould states, "We must fight the doctrine of *The Bell Curve* both because it is wrong and because it will, if activated, cut off all possibility of proper nurturance for everyone's intelligence." Do you agree with Gould that the doctrine of *The Bell Curve* would cut off the proper nurturance of everyone's intelligence? Why or why not?

7. Toward the end of his review Gould speaks to possible changes in social policy associated with *The Bell Curve*: cutting back welfare, cutting back Head Start, curtailing affirmative action, trimming programs for slower learners in schools and shifting moneys to the brightest kids. Do you agree with Gould that such changes are a logical outcome of *The Bell Curve?* Do you share his feelings that the changes would be for the worse? What social policy implications do you see coming from *The Bell Curve?*

8. Gould's review is a superb example of both questioning the roots of an argument and then adding additional criticism, through examples, to convince you the foundational criticisms he just offered are justified.

   a. He opens his paper by listing the four "shaky premises" he claims *The Bell Curve* is based on. These are *foundational* criticisms striking at the heart of *The Bell Curve*. The "shaky" assumptions endanger the integrity of the *g* factor—the claim by Murray and Herrnstein that intelligence is quantifiable via specific kinds of tests. Gould reasons if he can shake this foundation, the house *The Bell Curve* is built on will fall.

   b. Additionally he devotes much of his critical paper to related issues to prove that Murray and Herrnstein are mistaken in their theory of quantifying IQ and that they are employing an inconsistent methodology. The possibility of test bias, the authors' questionable use of statistics, ignoring instances of adopted black children with high IQs, the authors' rejection of fruitful work of the past in the area in which they seek to make a contribution—these are a few of the issues Gould raises, intending to cast doubt on the theory of *The Bell Curve* and to show that, as a whole, the theory suffers from a fatal inconsistency in its methodology.

c. Does Gould treat his subjects fairly? Does he characterize their views accurately?

d. What would you like to have seen Gould discuss that he didn't? Why?

8.4 The Case Against *The Bell Curve*

GREGG EASTERBROOK

COMMON SENSE AND SOUND SCIENCE show that the IQ debate is far from black and white.

Years ago, hoping to persuade this publication to hire me, I quit a decent job in Chicago and moved to Washington. Unemployed and low on money, I lived in a seedy neighborhood behind the Navy Yard in Southeast D.C. Because the editor of this magazine unaccountably took his time in acknowledging my merit as an applicant, to blow off steam I played basketball on the local court several hours each day. I was the only white player in the game, accepted at first as a charity case. After a few weeks on the blacktop, however, I was startled to discover other players wanting me on their team. After two months of daily basketball, I found myself able to hold my own in one-on-one matches against the hot players from nearby Eastern High School. I was squaring my shoulders for accurate jump shots, ducking under other players for layups—the sorts of coordinated, classy-looking moves I had never been able to do before and have not been able to do since.

It would hardly be a wild guess that practice had improved my game, and that lack of practice has since eroded it. Charles Murray and the late Richard Herrnstein would say, however, I had suddenly acquired basketball genes. Then just as suddenly, I lost them!

Page after page of obstruent data and marching columns of Pearson correlations in the new book *The Bell Curve* by Murray and Herrnstein, which holds that success in life is mainly determined by inherited IQ and that statistically significant differences in inherited intellect exist among the races, imply that the issues at play in the IQ dispute are so sophisticated only readers of high intelligence can grasp them. This isn't so. Most commonsense aspects of the IQ debate are more significant than the statistical motes and jots—and being much better understood, are a sounder basis for social policy. The complex statistical claims of *The Bell Curve* have received extensive notice in initial reactions to the work. In the end the book's commonsense faults are more telling. Blacktop basketball offers an entry point for understanding why.

The reverse of the notion that blacks are born with less intelligence than whites is that blacks are born with more athletic potential. Well-meaning people who believe that whites are smarter than blacks often quickly add, "But look at how gifted blacks are physically," citing the undeniable black dominance of basketball. Yet if blacks have superior innate athletic ability, why are hockey, tennis, and many other lucrative sports largely dominated by whites? As the writer Farai Chideya will show in a forthcoming book, of the approximately 71,000 Americans who earn livings from sports (broadly defined to include golfers, skaters, and so on), only 10 percent are black.

A likely explanation for black success in basketball is not some mystically powerful jumping gene—natural selection may have favored strength and size in people, but what are the odds it ever favored jumping?—but that many blacks practice the sport intensely. For good or ill, thousands of black kids spend several hours per day through their youth playing basketball. By the time age 18 is reached, it shows: In general, blacks are really good at basketball. Meanwhile, hockey and tennis are usually practiced in youth by whites, who in turn dominate these sports.

From Washington Monthly *26, no. 12 (1994): 17. Reprinted with permission.*

In all the complex arguments about inheritability and environment in IQ, the mundane, commonsense question of practice time is often overlooked. Other things being equal, what you practice is what you're good at. As Charles Darwin once wrote to his cousin Francis Galton, founder of the eugenics movement: "I have always maintained that, excepting fools, men [do] not differ much in intellect, only in zeal and hard work."

As a longtime basketball-league participant and a mediocre small-college football player, I have spent a notable portion of my life being knocked down, run past, and otherwise outperformed by black athletes. None ever struck me as possessing any mystical genetic athletic ability, though it may be that as a group they hold some small edge over whites. What often does strike me as a black basketball player in a pickup game hits his shot and I miss mine is the thought: "He's taken that shot maybe five million times in his life, and I've taken it maybe five thousand." It's safe to say that if there had been no color barrier to college basketball in the 1940s and 1950s, blacks would not have dominated in those years, because at that time few blacks practiced basketball as much as the best white players of the period. By coincidence, the week before *The Bell Curve* was published, the "Science Times" section of *The New York Times* ran a prominent article on new research showing that the most accomplished violinists and other artistic performers spend significantly more time practicing than the less accomplished—though presumably they enjoy the advantage of genetic gifts. There seemed to me a pellucid connection between this research and the Herrnstein-Murray thesis.

Another missed connection concerns a 1990 flap at the University of California at Berkeley. There, a tenured anthropologist, Vincent Sarich, began to say that black success in basketball proved the inherited basis of talent, which in turn supported the view that whites could inherit superior mental faculties. Sarich's argument is revealingly faulty: He would tell classes that "There is no white Michael Jordan . . . nor has there ever been one." Actually there was a white Michael Jordan— the late Pete Maravich. Maravich scored much more than Jordan in college and had the same league-leading scoring average in the NBA, 31 points per game. Maravich had the same ability as Jordan to throw the no-look pass, to dunk in ways that appeared to defy certain laws of physics, and so on. Jordan became a sports legend because his college and pro teams were champions; this happened because Jordan was a highly disciplined defensive performer and an astute judge of the court situation. Maravich, in contrast, became something of a standing joke, even to sportswriters eager for white stars, because his teams always lost. Maravich was a hopelessly selfish performer, inert on defense and he never passed up a shot. The comparison between Jordan and Maravich both defies the stereotype of the white player as disciplined and the black player as the gunner, and undermines the notion of black genetic dominance generally.

So if white kids as a group spend more time practicing schoolwork, should we then be surprised that they score better on school-related tests? Herrnstein and Murray acknowledge that 150 hours of extra study will raise the typical student's SAT score by 40 points—a commonsense confirmation that scholastic practice makes for scholastic success. True, the score-boosting effects of extra study on SAT tests reach a plateau beyond which further practice adds little. Yet seeing that behavior (study time) alters brain-test outcome, and then concluding as *The Bell Curve* does that brain performance is mainly genetic, is an inverted form of the logic that Stalin's favorite scientist, Trofim Lysenko, employed to contend that genetic characteristics are acquired during a person's life. That many white kids may spend more hours studying than many black kids may well be an argument that some minority parents are negligent in compelling their children to hit the books. But this is an argument about environment, not inheritance.

It is not racist for Herrnstein and Murray to study whether there are differences in inherited IQ. Some commentators have attempted to reject *The Bell Curve* out of hand on grounds of racism, and thereby avoid dealing with its discomfiting contentions. Yet obviously people talk about the mental abilities of various groups, usually in whispers; better to talk about this in the open. For this reason, in my affiliation with *The Atlantic Monthly*, I favored that magazine's publication of some of Herrnstein's earlier work. I agreed with the decision of *The New Republic* to put an excerpt from *The Bell Curve* on its cover. And I am glad Herrnstein and Murray (the principal author) wrote *The Bell Curve,* which is not a racist work, though it is fantastically wrong-headed. Bringing the arguments about race, inheritance, and IQ out into the open in Murray's straightforward writing style is a useful service—especially because the more you know about this line of thought, the less persuasive it becomes. . . .

Discussion and Assignments

1. Easterbrook states that *The Bell Curve*'s commonsense faults are the most telling. What is Easterbrook speaking of, and why does he use blacktop basketball to make his point?
2. Easterbrook, who is white, loves to play basketball. But apparently the black athletes, and even black kids from high school, are better than he is. Does Easterbrook ever consider their superiority may come from *both* natural factors (their genes may give them a slight physical advantage) and environmental factors (frequent practice)? Does this sound like a reasonable possibility to you? Why or why not?
3. How are Easterbrook's comments on the percentage of blacks who earn a living from sports, and his comments on hockey and tennis, intended to support his case? Is he persuasive on this account? Could it be that certain genetic characteristics might enable one to excel at some sports, like basketball and sprinting, but not others? How might Easterbrook respond to this suggestion?
4. What assumptions can you identify in Easterbrook's argument? How well does Easterbrook consider objections to his theory of blacktop basketball?

8.5 The Assault on the Human Spirit: *The Bell Curve*

RANDOLPH QUAYE

THE BELL CURVE by Richard Herrnstein and Charles Murray provides its supporters a pseudo-scientific explanation for justifying racism, sexism and classism in American society and beyond. It feeds on ignorance, fear and incites and invigorates those who for a long time have tried and succeeded in blaming blacks for the social ills of society. It provides, as most ideological psuedoscientific theories that have done in the past, the "spark" for self blame and rationalizes the social injustice and discrimination prevalent in our society. The book is nothing more than a revisionist eugenic idea, a social Darwinism that comprises still another polemic against the dignity and worth of black people. It represents for the 21st century and beyond what the Eugenics movements stood for in the early part of the 20th century. The movement represents the enticing possibility of social control through biological efficiency, heavily weighted with notions of racism and elitism.

The Bell Curve's message about the inevitability of existing patterns of inequality rests on a series of claims concerning intelligence. In particular, that: (1) human intelligence is reducible to a unitary core trait; (2) IQ increasingly determines or strongly influences socioeconomic status and behavior; (3) IQ is distributed unevenly throughout the population in general and by race in particular; and (4) cognitive ability is given and substantially determined by genetic inheritance (Reed 1994). These claims are untenable, but not

From The Black Scholar *25, No. 1 (1995): 41–43. Reprinted with permission.*

surprising. After all, William Shockley, a recipient of the Nobel Prize in physics argued in 1969 that "the major deficit in negro intellectual performance must be primarily of hereditary origin and thus relatively irremediable by practical improvements in the environment" (Schiller 1989). That Shockley is not alone in his beliefs is seen in a recent statement made by the president of Rutgers University when he stated that, "the average SAT score for African Americans is 750 . . . Do we set a standard in the future so that we don't admit anybody? Or do we deal with a disadvantaged population that does not have the genetic hereditary background to have a higher average?" While Dr. Lawrence's statement may have been unintended, such statements only fuel an already explosive situation with the publication of *The Bell Curve*.

As Stephen J. Gould recounts in *The Mismeasure of Man,* science, like all aspects of culture, reflects attitudes and prejudices that are present within society. Throughout history, science (especially) pseudoscientific inquiry has been used to perpetuate social stratification and justify racism and sexism. To think that in this age of the technological super highway we would be debating the merit of biological determinism is not only absurd but reflects the moral decay within academia, where people like Murray and Herrnstein will go to any lengths to project a viewpoint which for decades has been refuted and rejected. (See Howard Gardner, *The Frames of Mind*.)

After all, IQ scores and economic status are influenced by environmental factors (Schiller 1989). Thus, the discussion on genetics is not only misplaced, and misguided, but also downright racist. What accounts for black educational deficiencies is not genetics, but the structural and racial barriers inherent in American society. Racial discrimination in our school system is alive and well. Segregation exists still. Inequality of educational opportunities across income classes tends to be reinforced by the way schools are financed, where over half of all elementary and secondary school expenditures are supported by local property taxes (Schiller 1989). The implication is clear: Children in poorer states and in poorer school districts are denied adequate educational resources. Such schools are more likely to attract poorly pre-

pared teachers and to have poor library facilities and lack instructional technology. This is why study upon study has consistently shown that students in suburban America have done better than their counterparts in poorer areas.

Another important barrier to education is family income. Table 1 demonstrates that 55 percent of all high income ($50,000 plus) families have at least one child in college, while among the lowest-income families (under $10,000) only 14 percent have a child in college. Thus, the socioeconomic status of one's family has a significant impact on a child's chances for a college education (Schiller 1989). Table 2 displays the important connection between socioeconomic status and access to education. With the poverty rate among blacks (33 percent) three times higher than whites (11 percent), which thus influences education for their children, blacks face a far greater likelihood of being poor (Schiller 1989).

There are underlying reasons accounting for the greater percentage of blacks in poverty. For example, trends in the labor market create and maintain a certain proportion of low-paying unstable jobs (Gilbert and Kahl 1993).

In the labor market segmentation theory, Piore (1979) provides that those who enter the labor market at the secondary level are more likely to be paid lower wages, work under poor conditions and experience little opportunity for advancement. To explain why the working poor fall on the wrong side of the divide, Gilbert and Kahl (1993) offered two explanations. First, the structure of job opportunities offered by the economy and second, the relative standing of workers, attitudes of employers and the effect of social networking have major implications for wage earnings for African Americans. In a similar study conducted by Wachtel and Betsey (1972), they discovered that economic structure has a substantial impact on wages, independent of personal characteristics.

While education supposedly predicts income and by implication, social standing, education yields greater economic returns to white males than either women or African Americans (Schiller 1989). In 1990, the average yearly earnings of college-educated African American men were 73 percent of the earnings of their white counterparts

(Gilbert and Kahl, 1993). Thus while college education might explain some of the disparity, it is only an equalizer if people have good access [to] education.

These are just some of the structural barriers that need further attention and scrutiny. The wider implications of *The Bell Curve* is the social and political changes that it addresses. Issues elaborated by segment of the population that, "welfare as we know it should be abolished, because it subsidizes birth among poor women who are disproportionately of the low end of the intelligence distribution." In his earlier writings, Murray had

vehemently maintained that any attempt to correct centuries of social and economic injustices would fail, simply because the causes are not structural and environmental, but the result of weak cognitive ability. As Fanon, the Martiniquan psychoanalyst, writer and revolutionary stated, "to tell the truth, the proof of success lies in a whole social structure being changed" and this more than anything else is how the story should be told. To do less is to introduce a stale debate which does not enrich but impoverishes the intellectual discourse on race relations in America and in the diaspora.

Table 1
Percent of Families with Children*
in College Full-Time, by Family
Income and Race (1985)

| | Total | Family Income | | | | | |
		Under $10,000	$10,000–$19,999	$20,000–$29,999	$30,000–$39,999	$40,000–$49,999	$50,000–and over
All	35.1	13.6	23.5	33.7	41.8	51.4	55.3
White	37.4	14.1	22.9	34.4	41.7	51.7	55.3
Black	21.9	11.8	23.0	27.5	41.0	45.6	–
Hispanic	23.5	13.7	22.8	20.9	43.4	38.8	–

*Children aged 18–24.

Source: U.S. Department of Education.

Table 2
College Graduation Rates,
by Socioeconomic Status and IQ

| Socioeconomic Status | IQ Score | | |
	Low	Middle	High
Low	1.8	5.4	19.6
Middle	2.1	9.5	27.4
High	2.9	17.9	46.7

Source: Bruce Eckland and Louis Henderson, *College Attainment—Four Years after High School.* Raleigh-Durham, NC: Research Triangle Institute, June 1981.

References

Eckland, Bruce and Henderson, L. 1981. *College Attainment—Four Years after High School,* Raleigh-Durham, NC: Research Triangle Institute.

Gardner, Howard. *Frames of Mind: The Theory of Multiple Intelligences,* and *Multiple Intelligences: The Theory in Practice.*

Gilbert, D. and Joseph Kahl. 1993. *The American Class Structure: A New Synthesis.* Wadsworth Publishing Company, 1993.

Gould, Stephen 1981. *The Mismeasure of Man.* New York: W. W. Norton.

Herrnstein, Richard and Murray Charles 1994. *The Bell Curve: Intelligence and Class Structure in American Life.* New York: The Free Press.

Piore, Michael, J. 1977. The Dual Labor Market and Its Implications. In *Problems in Political Economy: An Urban Perspective.* D.C. Heath.

Reed, Adolph 1994. Looking Backward, *The Nation,* November 28.

Schiller, Bradley 1989. *The Economics of Poverty and Discrimination.* New Jersey: Simon and Schuster.

Wachtel, Howard and Charles Betsey. Employment at Low Wages. *Review of Economics and Statistics,* 44, 1972.

Discussion and Assignments

1. In his first paragraph Quaye states *The Bell Curve* is "nothing more than a revisionist eugenic idea, a social Darwinism that comprises still another polemic against the dignity and worth of black people." What does Quaye mean by "a revisionist eugenic idea"? Do you find him clear on this claim?

2. Does Quaye dispute Murray and Herrnstein's findings that blacks score lower on IQ tests than whites and East Asians? Does he question the legitimacy of the tests Murray and Herrnstein employ in evaluating intelligence? Does he accept the results of the tests as accurate?

3. What are the reasons for low test scores according to Quaye? What are the structural and racial barriers Quaye speaks of, and how are these barriers related to test scores? What do socioeconomic status and low test scores have to do with black people in particular?

4. In his second paragraph Quaye states the message of *The Bell Curve* rests on four fundamental claims, all of which are untenable. Does Quaye anywhere in his paper take issue with the claims themselves?

5. Quaye does offer an alternative or response to Murray and Herrnstein's theory that IQ is approximately 60 percent heritable and that blacks, as a group, have lower IQs than whites and East Asians.
   a. List the two strongest pieces of evidence he offers in criticizing Murray and Herrnstein's theory. In a paragraph for each, explain why you believe each piece of evidence is persuasive.
   b. Now list the weakest piece of evidence Quaye employs in his argument, and in a paragraph explain why you think the evidence is weak.

6. In his fourth paragraph Quaye states, "After all, IQ scores and economic status are influenced by environmental factors (Schiller 1989). Thus the discussion on genetics is not only misplaced, and misguided, but also downright racist." In light of this passage, and any others in his article:
   a. Does Quaye indicate to what degree he believes IQ is influenced by environmental factors? By emphasizing environmental factors does he imply there is no significant genetic factor in determining intelligence? Where does he stand on the issue of intelligence as a genetic trait?
   b. Quaye states the discussion on genetics in *The Bell Curve* is racist. Check your dictionary. Is he justified in making this claim? Do you believe he is justified in making such a claim in any sense of the word?

8.6 Dumb Students? Or Dumb Textbooks?

DIANE RAVITCH

IN 1994 THE MOST CONTROVERSIAL BOOK of the year was *The Bell Curve* by Charles Murray and Richard Herrnstein. Educators were outraged by its arguments for the heritability of intelligence and the substantial IQ differences among racial groups.

My reaction at the time was that the concept of group IQ is useless to teachers, because they must teach individual children, not group representatives with average IQs. Furthermore, as one of eight children, I know that even those who share the same heredity and environment can turn out very differently.

Despite all the protestations that greeted its publication, *The Bell Curve* seems to be the prevailing ideology in much of the educational world. Today educators and public officials across the nation, even those who condemn the book, set lower standards for college admission for specified minority groups, tacitly accepting the arguments of *The Bell Curve.*

The same logic was used by the College Board to explain that SAT scores were "recentered" to "reflect the composition" of the test-takers. The College Board explained the recentering—lowering the definition of what is average—on grounds that students who take the SAT today—30% from minority groups and 53% women—cannot be expected to achieve the same test scores as the original reference group of 1941, which was overwhelmingly white and 62% male. This seems to suggest that women and minorities aren't as smart as white males.

But it turns out that today's diverse crop of students is earning SAT math scores that nearly equal those of the largely elite group of 1941. By contrast, SAT verbal scores have been pitifully low for 20 years.

Instead of accepting poor verbal performance as the new norm, it would have been far better to find out why today's diverse students lack the vocabulary and verbal skills of earlier generations of students. My own hunch is that poor verbal scores are the result not of the students' racial, ethnic or gender composition, but of the schools' de-emphasis on careful reading and writing, the near abandon-

ment of basic literacy skills like grammar, syntax and spelling and the saturation of popular culture by television.

A recent study in the *American Educational Research Journal* supports the idea that schools have contributed to the lower verbal scores and that they can also reverse the trend. Professor Donald P. Hayes of Cornell University and two colleagues conclude that the biggest decline in the test scores, which occurred from 1963 to 1979, was due not to a change in the composition of the test-takers but to a progressive simplification of the language in schoolbooks.

The authors reviewed 800 textbooks used in elementary schools, middle schools and high schools between 1919 and 1991. They discovered that the vocabulary of the schoolbooks became easier and easier after World War II. They concluded that daily use of simplified textbooks across 11 years of schooling produces "a cumulating deficit in students' knowledge base and advanced verbal skill."

Even now, they find, the textbooks used in grades four through eight are "at their lowest level in American history" in terms of their language. In high school, only science books are written with any degree of verbal difficulty. According to their study, the average literature textbook used in the twelfth grade is even simpler than the seventh- or eighth-grade reader used before World War II.

SAT verbal scores began to fall when the students who entered first grade in 1952 became high school seniors. And the scores fell even further in the years afterward.

If Professor Hayes is right, schools can reverse the decline in verbal skills by introducing students to challenging materials starting in the first grade. This makes more sense than the claim that today's low verbal scores are the best that can be expected from test-takers who include large proportions of racial and ethnic minorities and women.

Success in school is, and always has been, the result of good teaching, individual student effort and a rigorous curriculum. That remains true, whether the students are male or female, black or white, Asian or Hispanic.

Discussion and Assignments

1. Why have SAT tests been "recentered" according to Ravitch?
2. If the original tests Ravitch refers to in 1941 were predominately of white males, and current tests indicate verbal scores are lower for *all* people—minorities, women, *and* white males—what makes Ravitch think racial and ethnic minorities and women can raise their scores through studying more difficult textbooks? Put another way, past experience (pre-WWII) indicates higher scores mostly for *white males,* not women and minorities. Do you think it's reasonable to assume the test scores of women and minorities will rise to the level white males had before WWII, since the test scores did not include them in the first place?
3. What do you believe is the strongest piece of evidence Ravitch offers to support her case? What do you believe is the weakest? Do you believe her argument is an adequate response to Murray and Herrnstein's theory? Why or why not?
4. Reconstruct Ravitch's argument using the following argument form: Issue, Definitions, Premises, Conclusion. Use your answers from questions 1 and 2.

Issue: Whether the dumbing down of textbooks may account for the dumbing down of verbal SAT scores for women and minorities.
Definitions: (Fill this in if you think the meaning of a term needs clarification.)
Premises:
Conclusion:

8.7 For Whom Does *The Bell Curve* Toll?

ROBERT J. STERNBERG

[This article was excerpted from a lecture sponsored by the Educational Press Association of America.]

JUST WHAT IS INTELLIGENCE? Richard Herrnstein and Charles Murray [authors of the controversial book *The Bell Curve*] would have us believe that, except for a few oddballs, psychologists are in fundamental agreement on this question and on the data they present in their book; only the lay public remains sadly uninformed. In fact, nothing could be further from the truth.

Psychologists today debate the meaning of intelligence every bit as much as they did in the day of (IQ test deviser) Alfred Binet, and almost all the interpretations in the Herrnstein/Murray book have been and will be actively debated among psychologists and other behavioral scientists.

Intelligence is the ability to perform in culturally valued ways and to produce culturally valued products. Note that it is an ability: A person could have ability, but not utilize it. IQ tests measure performances (e.g., knowing the meanings of words) and products (e.g., pencil lines on an electronically scannable answer sheet) that our culture happens to value.

Personally, I'm lucky. Our culture values writing, and I'm a decent writer. Not every culture even has analogous written forms of expression, however. Put me in a culture that highly values hunting skills, navigational finesse under the stars, or, for that matter, physical prowess, and I would look stupid pretty fast. On a test of general hunting ability, I will come out poorly, and my performance in a society of hunters will reflect my performance on the test. There have been and continue to be cultures that value these and other things. There is nothing special about IQ over the range of space and time just because we choose to make it special in our current culture.

From Vocational Education Journal, *May 1996, p. 62. Reprinted by permission of the publisher.*

We cannot assess intelligence in a vacuum. As the great Russian psychologist Lev Vygotsky pointed out, we cannot really know someone's underlying capacity but only his or her abilities as expressed through some form of measurement. The skills we value in our testing, such as speed of performance . . . ., may not be tested or even valued in other cultures. Some cultures might even have the "good sense" to realize that important problems and decisions in life are not made in the few seconds we are allowed to solve individual problems on IQ tests. We are always confounding a person's true level of underlying intelligence with the means we use to assess it.

I believe that what really matters in the world is not intelligence, *per se,* but actualized intelligence. The world is full of people who have the ability to accomplish great things, but who do next to nothing, either because they don't want to accomplish much or because they are not allowed to do so.

Really, no one is good at everything. If you look at super achievers, there are always plenty of things they don't do well. What they have in common is finding what they do well and making the most of it. I'm better verbally (I can write) than spatially (I can't get the suitcases to fit in the trunk of the car), so I have found a profession that enables me to capitalize on my verbal skills but makes no demands of my inferior spatial skills. Pablo Picasso certainly found his strength, and Albert Einstein, his.

I, like they, had a chance. I will not reach their heights, but the opportunities were certainly there. As a child of middle-class America, I was given the opportunity to be more or less what I wanted to be, given what I could be. Do children of the ghetto have the same opportunity? If such children really had the potential to be great scientists, artists, musicians or poets, how often would they even find it out? It's hard to become a great pianist if your parents can't pay for piano lessons, or a great scientist if you are not encouraged even to go to college. Are we really to believe that it is just IQ that holds people back from doing what our society values, or should we not just as well believe that it is society that holds them back from accomplishing what they otherwise might have, had the circumstances of their birth and early years been more favorable?

The bottom line is that intelligence is not just some innate or even internal function of the individual. Intelligence resides in the interaction between attributes of the individual and the nature of the environment in which the individual lives.

In education, there is increasing emphasis on performance testing (writing essays, doing projects) to the extent that it may eventually replace conventional assessment. Soon, it may be the good essay writer rather than the multiple-choice whiz whom we label as intelligent. However, many times people who excel in one assessment format will not do well in the other. So when such changes take place, what is viewed as an "improvement" in testing will really be merely the substitution of one set of cultural artifacts for another. We will change whom we value, but not the fact that culturally we value certain things over others and then label the people who do these things well as "intelligent."

Discussion and Assignments

1. Robert J. Sternberg is a fine writer, but a poor hunter. What do these differing abilities have to do with his theory of intelligence and cultural values?

2. According to Sternberg's theory, would a first-rate hunter from a hunting society be as "smart" as a first-rate poet or painter or scientist, from societies that value other abilities? According to his theory, would it be possible to take five individuals from dramatically different cultures, administer the same or similar IQ tests, and objectively compare their cognitive abilities? Could you do so with Murray and Herrnstein's theory?

3. Sternberg states "Intelligence resides in the interaction between attributes of the individual and the nature of the environment in which the individual lives." What does he mean by this? What implications can you draw from this position?

4. In a 300 page paper, contrast Sternberg's theory with Murray and Herrnstein's theory of intelligence. Which theory do you think more closely captures what you would call intelligence?

8.8 Commentary on *The Bell Curve*

MAX WEINER AND BRUCE COOPER

THE CONCLUSION REACHED BY Richard J. Herrnstein and Charles Murray—that blacks are intellectually inferior—is, to be kind, misdirected. The argument should not be that African-Americans are born inferior. Rather, the conditions under which many poor urban black infants are brought into this world are so destructive that the disadvantaged newborn never has a real life chance.

The research findings are scattered but convincing. First, black infants are more likely to be born to very young; unwed mothers than are their white counterparts. Second, black pregnant teenagers are one-fifth as likely to get good medical care. Third, very young mothers, according to UNICEF, are six times more likely to have premature births, to deliver seriously underweight babies, and to witness the deaths of their infants at birth or during the first year. In 1993, UNICEF found that the United States was shamefully ranked 17th in the world for low birthweight—with about 7 percent of infants being born clinically underweight. This puts us behind Europe, Japan, much of the Middle East, Czechoslovakia, and Costa Rica.

But when *black* Americans' births alone are considered, the U.S. ranking for low birthweight drops shockingly to 71st in the world—worse, for example, than Senegal, Cameroon, Madagascar, Egypt, Panama, Iran, and Zambia. Thus, the birth demographics—the intolerably high percentage of black young people having children—are both a cause of later problems and the result of earlier ones.

Mr. Herrnstein and Mr. Murray proffer hereditary explanations for poor intellectual performance when social and medical ones are right under their noses. Imagine thousands of babies of very young, unwed mothers, born clinically underweight (less than 5.5 pounds or 2,500 grams), being reared by teenagers in conditions of poverty and instability. How can an infant born into these conditions hope to prepare for school?

Sadly, the "bell curve" arguments will continue to rage, only to distract us from attacking the real problems in a creative, meaningful way. We owe it to our children, our communities, and ourselves to put in the forefront the birth of healthy children, born to mature, caring, and able mothers and fathers. Girls and boys (future mothers and fathers) of all races and colors need homes, love, and support. They need responsible adults to look up to. They should learn to delay having babies until they themselves are no longer children.

From Education Week, *January 11, 1995, p. 2. Reprinted by permission of the author.*

Discussion and Assignments

1. What are the comparative birth weight statistics for blacks in the United States and other countries, and what sources do Weiner and Cooper cite as authorities?

2. Why are the birth weight statistics important in making Weiner and Cooper's argument? What does birth weight have to do with ability or achievement? Do Weiner and Cooper explain this adequately? Do they cite any literature or data as evidence to convince you of their position?

3. How might Murray and Herrnstein respond to Weiner and Cooper? Do Weiner and Cooper convince you that environmental factors, especially the low birth weight and other attending medical issues in early life, might be the reason for low test scores on IQ tests by black children?

4. Scientists are currently studying to see if there is a correlation between low birth weight and IQ. Weiner and Cooper imply there may be a strong correlation between the two once enough evidence is in. (Some researchers also believe a number of *learning disabilities* may be attributed to low birth weight as well,

though Weiner and Cooper do not explicitly state this.) With the evidence Weiner and Cooper offer, can you think of other conditions that may be present for black low birth weight kids soon after birth that may impair their cognitive development (e.g., lack of proper nutrition)?

Afterthought: Murray and Herrnstein do briefly discuss the relation of low birth weight and IQ in *The Bell Curve,* and conclude there appears to be no apparent correlation. They point out, too, that there have been few studies in the area in order to caution the reader there is not much to go on for drawing definitive conclusions. Interestingly, they make the additional claim that white women of low IQ are more likely to give birth to low birth weight babies than women of higher IQ and, further, that socioeconomic status *does not* affect the results of the statistics in a significant way. That is, a woman who is *not poor* and has a low IQ is almost as likely to have a low birth weight baby as a woman who has a low IQ and *is poor.* The authors state on these latter points that the data is anything but abundant. What do you think Murray and Herrnstein are implying by offering such observations?

Since Weiner and Cooper published their short piece, there has been more research on the relation of low birth weight to cognitive ability, so the literature is now beginning to accumulate. For example, in an article published in the medical journal *The Lancet* on July 31, 1999, David Skuse discusses research "that concludes that babies born after gestation of less than 32 weeks are at a substantial risk of global cognitive processing deficiencies." On appearance, this preliminary work would lend support to Weiner and Cooper's argument. But how much?

Ask yourself, has there been enough evidence presented to convince you that low birth weight can be a significant factor in accounting for the difference in black and white IQ scores? Yes? No? Is the jury still out?

8.9 Statement: *The Bell Curve*

NATIONAL INSTITUTES OF HEALTH

THIS STATEMENT WAS DEVELOPED by the National Institutes of Health—Department of Energy (NIH-DOE) Joint Working Group on the Ethical, Legal, and Social Implications of Human Genome Research (ELSI Working Group). This statement is endorsed by the National Society of Genetic Counsellors.

In 1994, a highly publicised book, Richard Herrnstein and Charles Murray's *The Bell Curve,* claimed that IQ is largely genetically determined and that the differences in IQ between ethnic groups are substantially explained by genetic factors. We are especially concerned about the impact of *The Bell Curve,* and books developing similar themes, because we believe that the legitimate successes of the Human Genome Project in identify-

ing genes associated with human diseases should not be used to foster an environment in which mistaken claims for genetic determination of other human traits gain undeserved credibility.

Herrnstein and Murray suggest that IQ explains social problems such as crime, welfare dependence, and single parenting. They state that sociocultural barriers to personal advancement have largely been removed and, consequently, social success and high IQ are highly correlated. They assert that, to the extent that IQ is genetically determined, programmes to eliminate inequalities are thus doomed to failure. Herrnstein and Murray are especially concerned that high birth rates among the poor and the "dysgenic" behaviour of women with high IQs, who are not bearing enough children, are

From Journal of Medical Ethics *22 (1996): 190.*

threatening the population with genetic decline. According to them, these trends are "exerting downward pressure on the distribution of cognitive ability in the United States."

The authors follow this analysis with policy recommendations. They propose eliminating welfare, which they believe subsidises birth among poor women, thus lowering the average intelligence of the population. They suggest ending remedial education programmes because the results are not worth the cost, given the claimed significant genetic determination of IQ differences. They urge the development of programmes of social support that would encourage women from the higher socioeconomic classes to have more children.

Neither Herrnstein nor Murray are geneticists, nor have they carried out studies themselves on the genetic basis of behaviour. Their lack of training and experience in genetics does not disqualify them from evaluating genetic research nor from drawing their own conclusions. However, as geneticists and ethicists associated with the Human Genome Project, we deplore *The Bell Curve*'s misrepresentation of the state of genetic knowledge in this area and the misuse of genetics to inform social policy.

We urge consideration of the following three points: First, Herrnstein and Murray invoke the authority of genetics to argue that "it is beyond significant technical dispute that cognitive ability is substantially heritable." Research in this field is still evolving, studies cited by Herrnstein and Murray face significant methodological difficulties, and the validity of results quoted are disputed. Many geneticists have pointed out the enormous scientific and methodological problems in attempting to separate genetic components from environmental contributors, particularly given the intricate interplay between genes and the environment that may affect such a complex human trait as intelligence.

Second, even if there was consensus on the heritability of cognitive ability, lessons from genetics are misrepresented. The authors argue that because cognitive ability is substantially heritable, it is not possible to change it and that remedial education is not worth the effort or cost. This is neither an accurate message from genetics nor a necessary lesson from efforts at remedial education. Heritability estimates are relevant only for the specific environment in which they are measured. Change the environment and the heritability of traits can change remarkably. Saying a trait has high heritability has never implied that the trait is fated to be. Height is both genetically determined and dependent on nutrition. Common conditions in which genetics play a role, such as diabetes or heart disease, can be corrected with insulin or cholesterol-lowering drugs and diet. The disabilities associated with single-gene conditions, such as phenylketonuria or Wilson disease, can also be prevented or significantly ameliorated by medical or nutritional therapy.

Third, the more scientists learn about human genes the more complexity is revealed. This complexity has become apparent as more genes correlated with human genetic diseases are discovered. We are only beginning to explore the intricate relationship between genes and environment and between individual genes and the rest of the human genome. If anything, the lack of predictability from genetic information has become the rule rather than the exception. Simplistic claims about the inheritance of such a complex trait as cognitive ability are unjustifiable; moreover, as the history of eugenics shows, they are dangerous.

Genetic arguments cannot and should not be used to determine or inform social policy in the areas cited by Herrnstein and Murray. Since the lessons of genetics are not deterministic, they do not provide useful information on deciding whether or not to pursue various programmes to enhance the capabilities of different members of society. Those decisions are moral, social, and political ones.

Discussion and Assignments

1. The authors of the NIH-DOE statement note that neither Murray nor Herrnstein are geneticists. What is their chief objection on this issue? Do the authors believe Murray and Herrnstein's lack of formal training in this area should prevent them from making critical observations in the area? Do you agree or disagree with the authors on this point?

2. The authors of the NIH-DOE statement emphasize three points. State each of these points clearly, summarize each one of them, and discuss specifically why you think each is important from the perspective of the authors.
3. What is the relation between genetics and social policy for the authors of the statement? What differences do they have with Murray and Herrnstein over this issue? Do you agree with the authors on this point? Why or why not?

8.10 Why Are Jews So Rich?

ART LEVINE

A SCANT TWO YEARS AFTER Charles Murray's incendiary *The Bell Curve* provoked a furor among liberal opinion-makers with its views on race and intelligence, Mr. Murray has returned with an even more controversial work on yet another taboo subject: Jewish wealth. As he did in the earlier work, Mr. Murray marshals an impressive body of evidence that will surely send liberals into paroxysms of outrage. But whether one agrees or disagrees with the findings in Mr. Murray's book, the government or society that persists in ignoring the vital issues raised by his research does so at its peril.

"At a time of widening class divisions and shrinking opportunities for well-paying jobs," he argues, "a hidden source of resentment—the role of Jews in the economy—lurks beneath the surface of American life and clouds our ability to solve our economic dilemmas. It is vital that people begin to talk about this publicly. Failure to do so could only heighten the anti-Semitism that arises during periods of economic dislocation." In Mr. Murray's grim view, the lingering resentment towards Jews—as many as a fifth of Americans hold some anti-Semitic views, surveys show—could lead to an upsurge in discrimination and even hate crimes. The author posits a disturbing future in which Jews, increasingly isolated from other Americans, wall themselves off in high-priced ghettos and find themselves attacked by an impoverished Gentile underclass. Only by exploring in an honest, tough-minded way Jewish economic power—and the significant role of what he argues is the largely inherited trait of greed—can we hope to avoid such a tragic fate, he says.

Jews are the most economically successful group in American society, or, as Mr. Murray dubs them, "the overclass." Jewish family income is 72 percent more than the national average and even when minority groups are removed from the analysis, Jewish income is 34 percent more than that of Gentile white ethnic groups. (The author notes that Jewish families earn 50 percent more than "God-fearing, hard-working Irish-Americans.") Although Jews make up only three percent of the population, they account for approximately a fifth of the very rich, i.e. millionaires and above.

The book effectively uses graphics and charts to underscore these points. In one striking chart, the income curve for "Jews" and "Regular Americans" is compared, with a disproportionate Jewish clustering at the higher end of the $50,000 scale or above.

What accounts for these differentials in group achievement? Aware of the storm of criticism this book may arouse, Mr. Murray offers extensive evidence that shows that educational background or even IQ are not the primary factors that account for Jews' higher income. "Even when educational attainment is the same, Jewish families headed by males with four or more years of college still earn 75 percent higher incomes than those of other ethnic groups," he notes. The slight advantage in IQ test scores reported by Jews is not large enough to explain why they in general are richer than everyone else. "Something more than brains is at work," he says.

That something, he argues in the book's most controversial chapter, is greed. Here, Mr. Murray's

From Washington Monthly *26, no. 12 (1994): 26. Reprinted with permission.*

provocative analytic insights and policy prescriptions go beyond those of earlier American students of ethnicity and income. The author uses a veritable controversial of research [sic] both current and historical, to underscore the picture of Jews driven by what Mr. Murray, a free-market advocate, concedes is "the basic engine of capitalism: greed." As academics have pointed out since the early 1900s, greed is the "g-factor" that motivates anyone—Jew and non-Jew alike—to strive to earn more money for themselves and their families. Pointing to the overwhelming evidence of Jewish economic superiority, Mr. Murray contends, "Everyone has the 'g-factor,' but Jews have more of it."

In making his case, he explores everything from medieval writings about Jewish money lenders to the role of Jewish-dominated investment banking firms, such as Goldman Sachs, in the spate of corporate raids in the 1980s. He pays special attention to Michael Milken and Ivan Boesky, whose "Greed is Good" credo serves, the book contends, as the "secret text" of Jewish life.

Most striking is Mr. Murray's contention that the g-factor is genetically passed down from generation to generation. Drawing on the work of distinguished sociobiologists, Mr. Murray says that the g-factor, reflecting the evolutionary impulse toward self-preservation, has a significant hereditary component, somewhere between 40 percent and 80 percent. Jews—regardless of their upbringing—simply pass along more of it to their offspring.

It's an interesting point, but one open to alternative explanations that he tends to overlook. The wealth and greed that have been so widely observed among Jews over the centuries could be due to a cultural heritage that emphasizes achievement and money hoarding rather than a genetic predisposition. One regrets that Mr. Murray did not explore these possibilities more fully.

Still, he is no rabid anti-Semite, but a serious scholar whose work has long been influential in shaping a conservative agenda. A fellow at the American Enterprise Institute, his book *Losing Ground* highlighted how the welfare system fosters a destructive dependence; his last book, *The Bell Curve,* which argued for the immutability of apparent racial differences in intelligence, has been cited by the Republican president-elect in proposals to abolish Head Start and spend the money

instead on courses in advanced computer science for prep-school students. But Mr. Murray notes that none of his findings about Jews in general should affect how we treat Jews as individuals. "Not all Jews are greedy, and not all Jews are rich," he observes. "Everyone deserves to be treated fairly on his or her own merits, even if they are, as a group, plutocratic Christ-killers."

Mr. Murray's reasoned perspective on this matter should go a long way toward ameliorating concerns that he is some kind of bigot. Even so, he doubtless will continue to arouse the ire of the political correctness mandarins, in large measure because of his use of cutting-edge research that flouts the conventional wisdom. In *The Bell Curve,* he respectfully cited the research of J. Philipe Rushton, a psychologist at the University of Western Ontario, who contends that "Negroids" are on the lowest rung of the human race, having developed a warm weather "reproductive strategy" that emphasizes promiscuous sex, high fertility rates, and relatively little nurturing of each child. Accordingly, Rushton contends, they have evolved smaller brains and larger penises than "Caucasoids" or "Mongoloids" [Asians]. In this new work, Mr. Murray has similarly broadened the scope of the debate on the Jewish question by highlighting the research of noted scholar Hans Lincoln Rockwell. Mr. Rockwell has stuffed controversy with his quantitative analyses of the correlation between certain oft-cited Jewish activities and traits, and larger social problems. For instance, he has linked data from the FBI's *Uniform Crime Report* with a sophisticated regression analysis of Jewish religious observances—and it demonstrates an apparent upswing in the kidnapping and murder of children 12-and-under during the month of April, when Jews celebrate Passover. Mr. Rockwell contends that this statistical trend is due to the use by Jews of the blood of Christian children to make matzoth, the unleavened bread that plays a central role in the Passover tradition.

Despite the anger such theories often provoke, Mr. Rockwell is recognized by many colleagues as a serious scholar. One of his most striking statistics, for instance, notes that of the 52 reported slayings of children in April 1994, a disproportionate number of them occurred in Los Angeles and New York City, cities with large Jewish populations. Rockwell has carefully analyzed the various factors that might account for this anomaly, and concluded that only the ritual slaying theory makes sense. "I have not been able to think of a plausible alternative explanation," the author quotes Mr. Rockwell as saying. "Can you?" Mr. Rockwell has also commissioned extensive laboratory studies that show that a key molecule found in blood—carbon—is also an ingredient in matzoth. "Case closed," Mr. Rockwell asserts.

In the face of heated criticisms of this research on both moral and scientific grounds, Mr. Murray defends Rockwell as "not . . . a crackpot" and notes that "Rockwell has responded to his critics with increasingly detailed and convincing empirical evidence." As for himself, Murray says "I remain resolutely agnostic on the validity of Rockwell's research. Only time will tell whether his work will ultimately be proven right or wrong, but that it is legitimate science there can be no doubt."

In his own way, Mr. Murray has also fearlessly explored new territory. In *The Jew Curve*, he makes a strong case for the role of a Jewish elite in distorting economic outcomes in American society. His solutions to the resulting income inequality will also draw fire, although they're just sketched in at the end. He notes with regret that "there can be no genuine free market as long as Jews are free of all restraints." Mr. Murray has proposed—in the form of "theoretical thought-experiments"—a number of remedial steps that could be taken: state seizures of excess profits of Jewish millionaires "to promote productive investment rather than hoarding by a selfish few"; abolishing onerous antidiscrimination statutes that discourage members of the Gentile "clans" from hiring their own kind; and so on. But he draws the line at extremist measures: No one should be forced to wear a yellow star.

Mr. Murray has done a valuable service by ending the shroud of censorship that has made Jewish wealth and other burning ethnic issues "pariahs in the world of ideas for the last 50 years," as he puts it. A democratic society clearly deserves a rational discourse on these critical subjects. It is for that reason we eagerly await Mr. Murray's next work in the series, a look at the cognitive stumbling blocks thwarting Polish-American advancement. It is tentatively entitled *How Many Polacks Does It Take to Screw in a Light Bulb? A Quantitative Analysis.*

Discussion and Assignments

1. What are some functions of satire?
2. Levine uses the Jews and their history as the literary vehicle to express his views on *The Bell Curve*. What is the relationship between the Jews, their history, and blacks in Levine's satire?
3. What is Levine saying about the relationship between the lessons of history, misguided social policy, prejudice, and Murray and Herrnstein's work?
4. What appears to be the driving force behind the social policies Levine outlines in his article (e.g., misguided science, fear of other racial groups, prejudice)?
5. Is Levine going too far, or does he have a legitimate point? If the former, what has he said or implied that you find objectionable? If the latter, what specifically is the point worth making?
6. If Levine has whetted your appetite for satire, get a copy of Voltaire's *Candide*. Few pieces compare to this little gem.

Concluding Questions and Observations

1. In what sense could *The Bell Curve* be a positive or negative social or political force? What relation might *The Bell Curve* have to public policy? What kinds of changes can you imagine coming from a social policy based on *The Bell Curve*? For example, how would policy in schools be affected?

Chapter 9

Duty of Care

Background

WHAT LEGAL OBLIGATIONS, if any, does a woman have to her fetus before her child is born? Should a fetus have rights? If so, what rights should it have, and how would we relate its rights to those of the mother carrying the fetus? The extension of rights to fetuses has most often taken the form of arguing for protection from potentially dangerous behaviors by the mother. Alcohol consumption and drug abuse while pregnant can have significant damaging effects on the unborn. Physical abnormalities and impaired cognitive development are characteristic of the clinical definition of fetal alcohol syndrome (FAS). Children who suffer from FAS also frequently exhibit characteristic facial anomalies, are small for their age, and exhibit certain deficits in central nervous system development. The effects of illicit drug use are similarly damaging, though the range of abnormalities differs from that caused by alcohol. The chronicle of consequences brought on by alcohol and drug abuse while pregnant, together with increasing incidents of such cases, has persuaded some to argue that a pregnant woman has a duty to care for her fetus, that pregnancy brings with it responsibilities for two persons, not one. Such arguments invariably yield conflicting views of rights, pitting the health concerns of the fetus against the rights and psychological and physical health of the mother.

Duty of care arguments attempt to establish requirements or behaviors that can be identified to assess injury to the fetus or baby after birth. If the pregnant mother engages in certain behaviors, like drinking excessive amounts of alcohol, then there is an increased risk of damage to the fetus and, by extension, an increased risk for long-term injury to the baby. Proponents of duty of care not only believe it's the moral duty of a pregnant woman to care for her fetus, but they insist on a legal duty as well. Legal duty implies the possibility of prosecution if the woman is believed to put her fetus in danger or if the fetus is injured and is born with compromised health. Various arguments have been devised by duty of care advocates, for example, prosecution of the mother under existing child neglect laws, but on the whole, prosecutions in both the United States and Canada have been unsuccessful; the courts have sided with the liberty of the mother as opposed to the interests of the fetus.

A focal point of the debate is that the fetus is not considered a person and, thus, is not considered to have rights. The pregnant mother is considered one individual, not two. But if the mother is indeed one person, how can she be allowed to engage in behavior that may result in injury to another person, though at the time of injury the life affected is a fetus? Legally the fetus does not assume the status of a person until it is born. But its health can be compromised for its entire life because of the behaviors of its mother during its earliest stages of life. Duty of care advocates insist fetuses should be accommodated in this dilemma with rights of protection. Freedom of behavior of the mother, it is reasoned, should stop at the point where the health of the fetus is at risk. If a pregnant woman uses illicit drugs, drinks heavily, or otherwise abuses her body and injures her fetus, she should be prosecuted for her actions.

The implementation of protective/punitive measures invariably requires restricting the freedom of the mother. George Annas (article 9.1) likens such restrictions to relegating pregnant women to the status of a "fetal container." To restrict the freedom of the mother under threat of prosecution is to tell the mother that the well-being of the fetus is more important than her own well-being or freedom. Her personal freedom now effectively supplanted by the health concerns of the fetus, the universe of her actions would be defined by the parameters of prescriptive health care dictated by her doctor. The advice of the doctor would no longer be advice, it would be a command. The pregnant woman, Annas reasons, would become a servant to her fetus.

Alan Dershowitz (article 9.2) argues that once a woman decides not to have an abortion, she then assumes additional responsibilities to her fetus to ensure its good health. Responsibility to the fetus comes with the decision to have a baby. The argument attempts both to advocate a woman's right to choose by acknowledging her right to have an abortion, and to protect the rights of the unborn so they may later live lives free from damage associated with substance abuse during pregnancy.

Last, there is a complex socioeconomic dimension to the duty of care argument. Some pregnant women who are alcoholics or drug addicts find it difficult to quit their substance abuse, even if they want to. From this perspective, the pregnant woman takes on the complexion of a victim, just like her fetus. Some argue that it is senseless to threaten a woman with prosecution for endangering her fetus when she is struggling with an addiction to drugs. From this perspective, treatment programs would be more effective than prosecution. With this strategy both the mother and fetus would benefit. The mother would not be alienated out of fear of prosecution, and the danger for the fetus would be minimized because the mother would be in treatment. But what if the mother does not seek treatment, refuses treatment, or does not follow through on her treatment program?

Readings

Article 9.1 George J. Annas is the Edward Utley professor and chair of the Health Law Department at the Boston University School of Public Health. In *Pregnant*

Women as Fetal Containers Annas argues that a doctor's advice to a patient is just that, advice, and it can in no way be interpreted as an order or directive with the weight of law. To treat the fetus as if it were a separate individual would be to place a higher priority on the fetus than the mother, thereby restricting the mother's freedom, turning her into a servant to her fetus. The mother would become a fetal container for the patient, the fetus.

Article 9.2 Alan Dershowitz is a professor of law at Harvard University. In *Drawing the Line on Prenatal Rights,* Dershowitz claims that once a woman has decided to have a baby, she is legally obligated to take care of her fetus so it will not suffer injury from substance abuse. Since substance abuse can result in serious, long-term damage to the child, some restriction of freedom on the part of the mother would be warranted. The fetus then is regarded as having rights, at least in the context of protecting it from its mother who might knowingly endanger it through her behavior.

Article 9.3 In *Some Words on Fetal Rights,* Kate Murphy argues the case for women as "autonomous beings," claiming that any acceptance of fetal rights would reduce women to the status of fetal carriers. She also broadens the scope of the argument to include forced cesareans and restrictions on women in the workplace.

9.1 Pregnant Women as Fetal Containers

GEORGE J. ANNAS

IN MARGARET ATWOOD'S *The Handmaid's Tail,* most women are sterile, and the few who retain the capacity to bear children have reproduction as their exclusive function. As one handmaid describes her station. "We are two-legged wombs, that's all; sacred vessels, ambulatory chalices." This future scenario strikes many as unlikely, but a recent criminal indictment directly raises the issue of when it is legally acceptable to treat a pregnant woman as a container, while treating the welfare of the fetus she contains as more significant than hers.

Mrs. Pamela Monson is the subject of what may be the first criminal charge ever brought against a woman for acts and omissions during pregnancy. Criminal charges were filed against her in California in October 1986. The available reports suggest that sometime very late in her pregnancy Mrs. Monson was advised by her physician not to take amphetamines, to stay off her feet, to avoid sexual intercourse, and, because of a placenta previa, to seek immediate medical treatment if she began to hemorrhage.

According to the police, Mrs. Monson noticed some bleeding the morning of November 23, 1985. Nevertheless, she remained at home, took some amphetamines, and had intercourse with her husband. She began bleeding more heavily, and contractions began sometime during the afternoon. It was only later, perhaps, "many hours" later, that she went to the hospital. Her son was born that evening. He had massive brain damage, and died about six weeks thereafter.

Police lieutenant Randy Narramore has said, "We contend that she willfully disobeyed instructions (of the doctor) and as a direct result the child was born brain dead [sic] and later died" (*Washington Post,* October 2, 1986). District

Reprinted with author's permission. Originally published in Hastings Center Report, *December 1986, pp. 13–14.*

Attorney Harry Elias says simply that she "did not follow through on the medical advice she was given" (*New York Times,* October 9, 1986). Police officials wanted Mrs. Monson prosecuted for murder, but the District Attorney has decided to proceed with a prosecution under a California child support statute.

The support statute itself has been amended many times since it was first passed in 1872, and during much of the subsequent time applied only to fathers. The relevant part of the current version reads:

> If a parent of a minor child *willfully omits,* without lawful excuse, *to furnish* necessary clothing, food, shelter or *medical attendance, or other remedial care* for his or her child, he or she is guilty of a misdemeanor punishable by a fine not exceeding two thousand dollars, or by imprisonment [for one year] (emphasis added) (Cal. Penal Code, Sec. 270 [West, 1986]).

A later provision decrees that "a child conceived but not yet born is to be deemed an existing person insofar as this section is concerned."

Use of this statute, instead of a homicide charge, avoids the issue of causation, since violation of the duty itself violates the statute regardless of the consequences to the fetus or child. Thus, for example, a father's failure to provide food for his children would violate the statute, even if the mother was also to provide her children with food from another source. Why the father hasn't been charged in this case is puzzling.

Very few cases have attempted to define the scope of the statute, and the only cases that deal with its application to fetuses were decided during the Depression. These cases hold that a father can fail to provide food, clothing, and shelter to the "unborn child" and that because these needs are "common to all mankind," proof of their "necessity" is not required. In regard to "medical attendance and other remedial care," however, "in a prosecution based on failure to furnish them, it would be incumbent on the prosecution to make affirmative proof of their necessity" (*People v. Yates,* 298 p. 961, 962 [(LA. Sup. 1931]). Such proof would, of course, require medical testimony. Mrs. Monson did provide "medical attendance" by seeking prenatal care and by seeking assistance in childbirth at a hospital.

Fetal Neglect

The District Attorney's use of this provision is an attempt to extend child support statutes to create a crime of "fetal neglect." Does it mean that the pregnant woman must, in effect, live for her fetus? That she must legally "stay off her feet" if walking or working might induce contractions? That she commits a crime if she does not eat only healthy foods; smokes or drinks alcohol; takes any drugs (legal or illegal); has intercourse with her husband?

And how does such a criminal law change the nature of the doctor-patient relationship? It seems evident that, to the police, the doctor's patient was not Mrs. Monson at all, but her fetus. It also seems evident that although the police spoke of "advice" and "instructions," they believed that the physician was giving the fetal container, Mrs. Monson, orders—orders that she *must* follow or face criminal penalties, including jail.

In this case, for example, the doctor had instructed Mrs. Monson not to have intercourse with her husband during the remainder of her pregnancy, because it might induce contractions and a premature delivery. She nonetheless engaged in intercourse. The prosecution alleges that such "disobeying instructions" or "failure to follow through on medical advice" is grounds for criminal action. This strikes me as both silly and dangerous. Silly because medical *advice* should remain *advice:* physicians are neither law makers nor seers.

After the fact prosecutions would not help individual fetuses. Dangerous because medical advice is a vague term that can cover almost anything. Effectively monitoring compliance would require confining pregnant women to an environment in which eating, exercise, drug use, and sexual intercourse could be controlled. This could, of course, be a maximum security country club, but such massive invasions of privacy can only be justified by treating pregnant women during their pregnancy as nonpersons. Like Margaret Atwood's handmaids, they have only one function: to have the healthiest children we can make them have.

Other quandaries arise if we apply child neglect statutes to fetuses. Unlike a child, the fetus is absolutely dependent upon its mother and cannot itself be "treated" without in some way invading the mother. The "fetal protection" policy enunciated by the prosecution seems to assume that like mother and child, mother and fetus are two separate individuals, with separate rights. But treating them separately before birth can only be done by favoring one over the other in disputes. Favoring the fetus radically devalues the pregnant woman and treats her like an inert incubator, or a culture medium for the fetus.

This view makes women unequal citizens, since only they can have children, and relegates them to performing one main function: childbearing. It is one thing for the state to view the fetus as a patient; it is another to assume that the fetus's interests are in opposition to its mother, and to require the mother to be the fetus's servant.

Child neglect covers a wide variety of activities, but generally involves failure to provide necessities like clothing, food, housing, or medical attention to the child. Such laws *do not,* however, require parents to provide optimal clothing, food, housing, or medical attention to their children; and do not even forbid taking risks with children (such as permitting them to engage in dangerous sports) or affirmatively injuring children (corporal punishment to teach them a lesson). None forbid mothers to smoke, take dangerous drugs, or to consume excessive amounts of alcohol, even though these activities may have a negative effect on their children.

While it seems draconian to apply the child neglect standards to the mother's life style during pregnancy, the California statute could be interpreted to apply to fetuses in a way never envisioned by the legislature. Certainly the legislature never intended that women must provide any more "clothing, food or shelter" to their fetuses than they provide for themselves. But what about the terms "medical attendance" and "remedial care"? Historically, medical attendance for the fetus meant medical attendance for the mother. If fetal surgery becomes an accepted procedure sometime in the future, however, "remedial care" may be applicable. Suppose, for example, that instead of the instructions the doctor gave Mrs. Monson, he had diagnosed her fetus as suffering from blocked ureters, and "recommended" surgery on the fetus to attempt to correct the problem. Would her failure to agree to this surgery be tantamount to "fetal neglect" for failure to provide her fetus with "necessary remedial care"?

This carries us into even more problematic waters. If women *must* "consent" to such "care" of their fetuses, they are relegated to the role of containers. Moreover their own rights are made so subordinate that the container may be opened to gain access to the fetus, even when the container may be damaged. (G. J. Annas, "Forced Caesareans: The Most Unkindest Cut of All," *Hastings Center Report,* June 1982, 16–17).

Waiving One's Right to Abortion

Some have argued that it is nonetheless fair to subject pregnant women to fetal neglect statutes because after they waive their right to abortion and decide to have a child, they take on added obligations to the future child, including providing it with such things as "necessary medical attendance." This argument seems misplaced for at least two reasons. First, such a "waiver" never in fact takes place. Women do not appear before judges or even notaries to waive their rights at any time during the pregnancy. Indeed, the vast majority of pregnancies in marriage are planned and welcomed, and viewing all pregnant women as potential aborters seems bizarre. Moreover, insofar as the right to terminate one's pregnancy is constitutionally protected, it remains a woman's legal right to the time of birth, at least when her life or health is at stake.

Second, and more important, women have a constitutional right to bear children if they are physically able to do so. To have a legal rule that there are no restrictions on a woman's decision to have an abortion, but if she elects childbirth instead, then the state will require her to surrender her basic rights of bodily integrity and privacy, creates a state-erected penalty on her exercise of her right to bear a child (D. E. Johnsen, the "Creation of Fetal Rights: Conflicts with Women's Constitutional Rights to Liberty, Privacy and Equal Protection," 95 *Yale Law Journal* 599, 618 [1986]). Such a penalty would (or at least should) be unconstitutional.

Attempts to define fetal neglect and to establish a prenatal police force to protect fetuses from their mothers, are steps backwards in terms of both women's rights and fetal protection. Women's rights will only be fostered when we treat women equally. The best chance the state has to protect fetuses is through actions to enhance the status of all women by fostering reasonable pay for the work they do and equal employment opportunities, and providing a reasonable social safety net, quality prenatal services, and day care programs. It is probably not coincidental that government is try-ing to blame the pregnant victims of poverty for their problems at the same time it is cutting funds for maternal and child health care and nutrition. If the state really wants to protect fetuses it should do so by improving the welfare of pregnant women— not by oppressing them.

Discussion and Assignments

1. In paragraph 12 Annas claims "after the fact prosecutions would not help individual fetuses." Analyze Annas's claim concerning prosecutions after the fact by offering examples. Could you make a similar claim about other types of acts that cause injury? Do you believe his claim strengthens or weakens his argument? Are you aware of many situations where prosecutions occur *before* the fact?

2. Annas points out that Mrs. Monson sought out prenatal medical attendance and assistance in childbirth at a hospital. Do these facts strengthen or weaken his argument for not prosecuting her for fetal neglect? Put another way, if Mrs. Monson had *not* sought out prenatal care and assistance in childbirth, would Annas then *approve* of prosecuting her for fetal neglect? Does it matter one way or the other, would it affect Annas's position on prosecution, if she sought help or did not seek help? If it doesn't matter, why do you think he brings it up?

3. Can you imagine a situation where Annas would advocate prosecuting a woman for fetal neglect? For example, would it make a difference if a pregnant woman drinks alcohol and uses drugs because she *wants* to injure her fetus? (Would there be any way to distinguish such a person from Mrs. Monson?) Explain the situation if you can imagine one. Explain why *not,* if you cannot imagine one.

4. Annas claims that it is impossible to treat the fetus "without in some way invading the mother." Do you agree with his characterization of this relationship between mother and fetus? Annas further claims that to treat the fetus and mother separately before birth would be to favor one party over the other in disputes. Do you agree with Annas's characterization of such treatment as taking sides in a dispute? State and explain your reasons.

5. Do you believe, as Annas claims, it would take massive invasions of privacy to ensure that women carry out their doctors' orders in caring for their fetuses? Do you think this is a reasonable claim? Why or why not?

6. What is the distinction Annas makes between *advice* and *orders* of a physician? Why does he claim that medical advice is a vague term? What consequences does he draw from this distinction concerning vagueness? Are Annas's examples effective in making his point? Offer two or three examples of your own to strengthen or weaken his argument.

7. Annas rejects the view that once a woman decides to have a child—that is, she decides not to have an abortion—she is obligated to consider the rights of the child she will soon have. What is Annas's rationale for rejecting this argument? Do you agree or disagree with him? Explain your rationale. Be sure to study Alan Dershowitz's article to better argue your case.

8. Under Annas's view, a woman could drink and use drugs while pregnant, give birth to a child with severe birth defects that it will endure for life, and the mother not be subject to prosecution, either during pregnancy or after the birth of her child. Opponents of Annas's view claim this is like knowing a crime is occurring, but not being able to do anything about it. How would Annas reply to such an objection?

9. Can you think of a workable solution that would ensure an acceptable degree of liberty for the mother, yet protect her child from being damaged from alcohol or drugs?

10. Annas notes that Mrs. Monson sought out medical attendance during her pregnancy, but she chose to not follow her doctor's advice. Apparently Mrs. Monson *did* have some prenatal services available, but her child nevertheless died. In light of Mrs. Monson's situation, what do you think of Annas's claim that the availability of prenatal services offers the best chance for protecting fetuses?

9.2 Drawing the Line on Prenatal Rights

ALAN DERSHOWITZ

THERE IS A DANGEROUS IMPLICATION in some pro-choice arguments that may frighten the Supreme Court into restricting or even overruling *Roe vs. Wade,* the 1973 decision that established women's right to abortion. The implication is that the right to abortion also precludes the state from requiring women to take any degree of prenatal care after they make the decision not to abort.

Syndicated columnist Ellen Goodman recently suggested this in criticizing the Bush Administration's efforts to overrule *Roe vs. Wade.* She wrote: "There are suggestions among those who talk of fetal rights that the government could constrain a pregnant woman's diet and physical activities, stamp out her cigarettes, empty her wine glass . . . or else." Goodman also invoked the specter of mandatory testing and treatment for the fetus.

Now, I am not a "fetal-rights" advocate. I favor *Roe vs. Wade.* I believe that a pregnant woman should have the right to choose between giving birth or having an abortion. But I am a human-rights advocate, and I believe that no woman who has chosen to give birth should have the right to neglect or injure that child by abusing their collective body during pregnancy.

Once a woman has made the decision to bear a child, the rights of that child should be taken into consideration. What happens to the child in the womb may have significant impact on his or her entire life. One example is the woman who drank half a bottle of whiskey a day while pregnant and gave birth to a mentally retarded child. She is now suing the whiskey company for not warning her about the relationship between heavy drinking during pregnancy and birth defects. Anyone who has spoken to an inner-city obstetrician is aware of the near epidemic of birth defects among babies born to heavy drug users.

This is not to argue for intrusive governmental rules on occasional drinking or smoking. But at the extremes, there is a compelling argument in favor of some protection for the future child against maternal excesses that threaten to cause enduring damage. Once a woman decides to give birth, a balance must be struck between her rights during the nine months of pregnancy and the equally real rights of her child during its life span. I believe that the balance should generally be struck in favor of the woman's privacy and against the power of state compulsion. But a balance, nonetheless, must be struck.

My colleague, Prof. Laurence Tribe, agrees with Goodman and argues as follows: "There's no principled way to say that the government can use women's bodies against their will to nurture the unborn without accepting the other serious and totalitarian implications about privacy." With respect, I disagree.

There is a principled distinction between totalitarian intrusions into the way a woman treats her body, and civil-libertarian concerns for the way a woman treats the body of the child she has decided to bear. That principled distinction goes back to

From Los Angeles Times, *Sunday, Home Edition, May 14, 1989, pt. 5, p. 5, col. 2. Reprinted with permission.*

the philosophy of John Stuart Mill and is reflected in the creed that "your right to swing your fist ends at the tip of my nose." In the context of a pregnant woman's rights and responsibilities in relation to the child she has decided to bear, the expression might be: "Your right to abuse your own body stops at the border of your womb."

Of course, any recognition that a future child may have rights—even limited ones—in relation to its mother, may be grist for the "right to life" mill. Anti-abortionists will argue that if a future child has the right not to be damaged during pregnancy, then it follows that the fetus has the even more important right not to be killed—i.e., aborted.

But the second conclusion does not necessarily follow from the first. Under *Roe vs. Wade,* a fertilized egg, or even a biologically more advanced fetus, has no right to be born unless the mother chooses to give birth. But it does not follow, as a matter of constitutionality, principle or common sense, that a woman has the right to inflict a lifetime of suffering on her future child, simply in order to satisfy a momentary whim for a quick fix.

A principled person can fully support a woman's right to choose between abortion or birth, without supporting the very different view that the state should have no power to protect the health of a future child. The state should begin by making prenatal care available to every pregnant woman. But we need not be frightened, by the specter of totalitarianism, from considering reasonable regulations designed to reduce the serious long-term problems caused by pregnant women who abuse their future children.

Proponents of a woman's right to abortion should not weaken their powerful argument in favor of a woman's right to control her body.

And, in the eyes of many who support choice, they do weaken it when they link it to the far weaker argument denying the state the power to protect babies who are to be born.

Discussion and Assignments

1. Dershowitz supports a woman's right to have an abortion, and also believes the state should intervene to protect a fetus from the dangers of alcohol and drug abuse. First, explain his rationale behind taking these two positions, then discuss why you believe they are compatible or incompatible.

2. In paragraph 4 Dershowitz claims, "Once a woman has made the decision to bear a child, the rights of that child should be taken into consideration." *When* exactly does a woman decide to have a child, according to Dershowitz? Do you agree that there is a time at which such a decision is made? How does Dershowitz differ from Annas on this issue? Which of the two do you think has the stronger argument? Explain why.

3. Does Dershowitz explain how the authorities might intervene on behalf of a fetus that is in danger from alcohol or drug abuse? Does he discuss specifically what the authorities should do? How do you think Dershowitz might reply to Annas's claim that massive invasions of privacy would be required to monitor the behavior of pregnant women?

4. Select one of the following and write a short argumentative essay:

   a. Construct a 300 word argument outlining why it is not desirable to monitor a pregnant woman (who is a substance abuser) because it would require massive invasions of her privacy. Be sure to include examples of how authorities might intervene on behalf of a fetus to protect it from its mother, and why such situations would not be desirable.

   b. Or take the other position. Construct a 300 word argument outlining why some form of monitoring a pregnant woman's behavior would be justified to protect her fetus from substance abuse. Again, be sure to use examples in your presentation.

5. Medical evidence increasingly indicates that drinking alcohol in the early stages of pregnancy may endanger the fetus. Where do you think Dershowitz would stand in situations where the mother is a substance abuser in early pregnancy, then stops as soon as she finds out she is pregnant—but her child is still born with birth defects? Would he have to support prosecution of the mother to stay consistent in his argument?

6. Do you think some pregnant women might avoid seeking medical treatment if they feel they will be prosecuted for fetal neglect? Explain your reasons. How do you think Dershowitz might reply to this claim? How do you think Annas or Murphy might respond to this claim?

9.3 Some Words on Fetal Rights

KATE MURPHY

Those concerned about fetal exposure to drugs might better spend their efforts trying to ensure women's access to appropriate treatment.

THE NEWS MADE THE FRONT PAGE of the *Globe and Mail:* the Supreme Court of Canada ruled that courts cannot control a pregnant woman's conduct even if her behavior poses a risk to the fetus. The decision centered around a young Native woman whom a court in Winnipeg had ordered into drug treatment because she sniffed glue during her pregnancy. The court's order was eventually overturned, but the debate over the fetus's rights versus the woman's autonomy continued right up until the Supreme Court verdict.

Reaction to the verdict was mixed. Right-to-life groups, as expected, decried it. An editorial in the *Globe and Mail,* a paper that has taken the "family values" position on everything from day care to single motherhood, spoke of the need for a "law to protect the unborn" [i.e. from women who have to earn the right to legal abortion by embracing incubator status during pregnancies they carry to term]. On a more thoughtful and less punitive note, some Aboriginal groups, noted *Globe* columnist Margaret Wente, worried that the decision would lead to an increase in the number of children affected by fetal alcohol syndrome, a significant problem in many Native communities. Feminist and reproductive rights groups, on the other hand, hailed the Supreme Court's ruling as a

victory for women. Women would no longer be treated as fetal containers, they said.

While I share concerns about the effects of prenatal exposure to alcohol and drugs on children, I agree with women's and reproductive rights advocates that the Supreme Court made a good—and in my opinion long overdue—decision. First, the ruling affirms women's status as autonomous beings as opposed to fetal carriers and guarantees at least to some extent freedom from unwanted bodily intrusion during pregnancy. This second impact will hopefully prevent Canada from sliding down a slippery slope into the fetal rights scenario that has unfolded in the United States over the past two decades or so. Canadians who care about women's freedom must make sure that such a scenario never happens here.

The fetal rights debate in the United States, explains political scientist Cynthia Daniels in her informative book *At Women's Expense,* has covered three major areas: forced medical interventions (generally caesarean sections but cervical stitching done to prevent miscarriage and blood transfusions as well), exclusion of women of "childbearing age" from jobs deemed dangerous to fetuses because of exposure to toxins, and legal prosecution of women who drink alcohol or use illegal drugs while pregnant. A smattering of other fetal rights cases has also come up, such as that of a mother of two preschool-aged children who was charged in

From Off Our Backs *28, no. 7 (1998): 10–11. Reprinted with permission.*

the death of her brain-damaged baby because during her pregnancy she had among other things disobeyed her doctor's orders to stay off her feet (a nearly impossible mandate to fulfill while caring for young children, as anyone with a minimum of baby-sitting experience would know). At times the fetal rights movement has gone from the ludicrous to the tragic. In 1987, a woman in Washington DC died following a court-ordered cesarean section meant to "rescue" her extremely premature fetus (who, by the way, did not survive). A court later ruled that forcing the woman to undergo the procedure was wrong, but some commentators still advocate forcing women to have cesareans against their will. These two and many other cases present a picture of what the Canadian Supreme Court's decision will hopefully nip in the bud.

Fetal rights advocates claim to be concerned about children (a familiar by-line used by, among others, singer Anita Bryant in her "Save the Children" campaign against gay teachers in California). However, a number of commentators have suggested that concern for children is not the only or even the primary driving force behind the fetal rights mania. More plausible motives cited include courts' greater identification with fetuses than with their mainly non-White mothers (women of color are disproportionately targeted in fetal rights cases), an attempt to regain the "selfless motherhood" ideal that women have supposedly left by the wayside in their rush out of the home and into the workplace, and discomfort with modern women's ability to control their reproductive lives through contraception and abortion. While all three arguments have their merit, I agree most with the third. The fetal rights movement seems like a last-ditch attempt to wrest control of women's reproduction out of their hands. More broadly, the fetal rights crusade can be seen as an effort to control women's lives in general, not only reproductively and sexually but economically and socially as well.

The practice of excluding presumably fertile women from "dangerous" jobs is a case in point. A number of employers in the 1970's and '80's pushed for laws barring women of childbearing age from positions in which their fetuses might be exposed to toxins. For example, some companies forbade fertile women to assemble car batteries in case the lead from the batteries damaged any of the women's fetuses. Interestingly, however, women in "female" jobs, such as nursing, faced no such restrictions (nor did they receive any protection from toxins they might encounter in the workplace) even though these women too were exposed to chemicals that posed risks to their fetuses. Were the "unborn children" (the term used by many fetal rights advocates) of women in male-dominated professions such as battery assembly more valuable than those of women in traditionally female ones? It isn't hard to suspect that the real motive behind the exclusion of women from the former positions was more an attempt to keep women "in their place" than to protect children.

Even a glance at forced cesareans makes one wonder whether their proponents are really so concerned about the "unborn children" they seek to rescue from their recalcitrant mothers. For example, Patrick Murphy, a Chicago city official who sought to force a woman to undergo a cesarean after she refused to do so for religious reasons, said that the woman should be allowed to give birth vaginally but that she should be hauled into court afterwards. Punishing a woman for daring to exercise her reproductive freedom rather than saving a fetus appeared to be Murphy's primary motivation. He also indirectly maligned the abortion rights movement by accusing the woman's defenders of considering the fetus a "clump of cells." The fact that women cannot be relegated to fetal carrier status apparently enrages the fetal rights lobby.

As writer Ellen Willis notes in an essay about the anti-abortion movement, sex has a way of rearing its head in discussions about fetuses and their rights. Part of the furor over the refusal of some women to undergo cesarean sections stems from the fact that a significant portion of them (fifty percent according to one survey) are not married. One obstetrician who believes such women should be considered "felons" writes with great indignation that some patients who refuse abdominal delivery want to escape bearing a child conceived in a nonmarital relationship. In other words, he is upset that women are, as Lithuanian-American poet Chrystos cleverly puts it, "having sex and getting away with it." Like the anti-abortionists, this obstetrician views the fetus not as an individual but as a "punishment for sex." His outrage stems as much from women's sexual as from their reproductive freedom.

The issue of legally prosecuting women who use drugs or drink alcohol while pregnant causes me more ambivalence than those of forcing women to undergo cesarean sections or excluding them from workplaces. While I do not object to a woman earning her living as she sees fit or refusing an operation that fetal rights advocates dismiss as a minor inconvenience but that in reality has a mortality rate at least double that of vaginal delivery, it is harder for me (a nondrinker who's never even had the urge to try port) to defend a woman's "right" to use illegal drugs. Still, I would stop short of supporting the legal prosecution of drug-using women, for several reasons. First, punishing them for their behavior might lead to a slippery slope that would open the way for other forms of fetal rights legislation. Second, just as in the case of forced cesareans, most of the women prosecuted for exposing their fetuses to drugs are minority women, even though their rate of drug use does not differ from that of White women. My final argument is that, as American writer Katha Pollitt correctly notes, while fetal rights activists are eager to slam women for using drugs, they're less eager to fight for these women's access to treatment.

It was not until 1993 that the New York State Court of Appeals ruled that drug rehabilitation centers could not refuse pregnant women as clients, which many centers had done. Those concerned about fetal exposure to drugs might better spend their efforts trying to ensure women's access to appropriate treatment than hauling them into court after the fact.

While the Canadian Supreme Court's decision was a relief and a triumph, we shouldn't think that it will resolve once and for all the matter of fetal rights. First, the ruling may well be challenged. A case about to go before the Supreme Court regarding a women who during pregnancy supposedly "failed to avoid a car accident" that led to her son's disability could have serious negative implications for women's rights if the Court rules that the woman can be "sued" for prenatal injuries. Also, we can concur with fetal rights activists that drug abuse by pregnant women is a social problem. The means of dealing with this problem, however, should lie in facilitating women's access to drug treatment and working to end the causes of substance abuse rather than prosecuting pregnant addicts. Finally, we must always be vigilant and ensure that the reproductive rights of all women are respected.

Discussion and Assignments

1. Murphy refers to the Canadian Supreme Court decision as a victory for women, and expresses her hope that the decision will prevent Canada from sliding down the same slippery slope the United States has gone down for the past two decades. What is the slippery slope Murphy speaks of?

2. Murphy suggests that concern for children is not the primary concern of fetal rights advocates. What is it that fetal rights advocates are interested in, according to Murphy? What evidence does she offer to support her claims?

3. Much of Murphy's article focuses on her claim that the fetal rights movement is really aimed at controlling women's lives. She illustrates her view with examples such as forced cesareans and efforts by companies to exclude women from traditionally male-dominated jobs. How does Murphy feel about excluding women from assembling car batteries? What evidence does Murphy offer to persuade you of the danger or lack of danger in assembling car batteries? Do you believe her comparison to the nursing profession is a legitimate one?

4. In paragraph 8 Murphy claims "part of the furor over the refusal of some women to undergo cesarean sections stems from the fact that a significant portion of them (50 percent according to one survey) are not married." What is Murphy's point here? Do you agree with her? Why or why not?

5. What is Murphy's position on forced cesareans? How does she relate this subject to fetal rights? Do you believe she offers a strong or weak argument against forced cesareans? Can you imagine a situation where you would advocate a forced cesarean section? Explain why or why not.

6. Murphy's argument puts her in the curious position (as she notes in paragraph 9) of defending a mother's "right" to use illegal drugs, even if it puts her fetus at risk. Does this aspect of her argument weaken her overall argument in defending a women's right to not be restricted in behavior while she is pregnant? Does her position on the right to use illegal drugs while pregnant compromise the consistency of her argumentation? Do you think she would assert similar liberties for a woman who is a substance abuser if she were *not* pregnant?

7. Murphy thinks if women are prosecuted for endangering their fetuses with alcohol or drugs they may soon be subject to other types of prosecution or control as well. What other types of prosecution does she have in mind? Do you believe it's possible to draw the line at prosecuting women for substance abuse, and not go down the slippery slope? Why or why not?

8. Murphy points out that most pregnant women prosecuted for fetal neglect, and those singled out for forced cesareans, are minority women. Why does Murphy believe this is important when arguing against prosecuting women for fetal neglect? Explain why you agree or disagree with her on this point.

Chapter 10

The Great Ape Project

Background

THE GREAT APE PROJECT (TGAP) is an idea, an organization, and a book. The book, published in 1993, includes 31 essays by scholars from diverse fields, each making his or her case why the four great apes—gorillas, orangutans, chimpanzees, and bonobos (pygmy chimpanzees)—should be given the same basic rights and protections as those enjoyed by humans. The fundamental aim of TGAP is to move the great apes from the category of *property* into the category of *persons* where they would be included with humans among a "community of equals." The articles in the book cite numerous studies of great apes to illustrate their intelligence, complex emotional lives, social behaviors and cultural practices, ability to use sign language, and the closeness of their genetic structure to humans. *A Declaration on Great Apes* (article 10.1) sets out the legal, moral, and protective boundaries the authors advocate as the means to integrate the great apes into the moral community of humans as equals. The *Declaration* would ensure: (1) the right to life: great apes would be protected, and killed only under extraordinary circumstances, such as self-defense; (2) the protection of individual liberty: no member of the community of equals could be deprived of his or her liberty, except in special circumstances, such as to protect other members of the community of equals; and (3) the prohibition of torture: it is forbidden to cause severe pain on a member of the community of equals. A careful study of the *Declaration* will inform the reader that its adoption would have far-reaching effects for relations between humans and great apes and, by implication, possibly other animals in the future. TGAP's objective is to have the *Declaration* formally adopted by the United Nations. Adoption by the UN would formally universalize the broadening of the moral community to include the great apes, providing an official, international forum where their interests would be recognized, eventually being afforded legal standing. Advocates of TGAP often draw the analogy that the great apes are treated much like slaves were treated in the past. From this perspective, the *Declaration* would be the great apes' Emancipation Proclamation, their legal right to not be owned and treated as property.

In October 1999 New Zealand became the first country to pass legislation extending individual rights to great apes. Though largely symbolic since there are fewer than 50 great apes in New Zealand, and none are used in research, the country formally prohibited the use of all great apes in research, testing, or teaching "unless such use is in the best interests of the non-human hominid" or its species. There are over 3,000 great apes held in captivity around the world. There are approximately 1,500 chimpanzees in six research facilities in the United States, and about 1,000 in facilities funded by the federal government.

Most contributors to TGAP argue the similarities between humans and apes are so great, behaviorally and genetically, that we're *all* best understood as apes. Great apes have been known to learn rudimentary communication skills with sign language, can recognize themselves in a mirror, have complex social structures among themselves, and have complex emotional lives—for example, they experience happiness, suffer, and grieve at the loss of loved ones. They're also capable of acts of altruism. Moreover, the genetic structure of great apes is very close to that of humans, sharing an estimated range of 98.6 percent to just under 99 percent with humans. Many argue that an adult chimpanzee has the intelligence of a young child, or that a severely retarded human would be at the same IQ level of a mature chimp. If we afford rights and protections to children and profoundly retarded humans who cannot speak or protect themselves (we don't put them in cages and conduct experiments on them), then why shouldn't we grant great apes the same rights and protections? In effect, advocates of TGAP claim the universe of our moral actions, restricted among humans, is mistakenly based on membership in a species, turning a blind eye to similarities of experience that cross species boundaries. If other beings can feel severe pain and suffer, if they can have vital emotional and intellectual experiences akin to what humans experience, then we should include those beings in our overall moral community to accommodate their needs (as we do our own needs). To recognize the great apes as persons, and give them basic moral rights as we do humans, would broaden the "community of equals," making our actions consistent among all beings capable of similar experiences.

There is a sense of urgency to TGAP as well. At the beginning of the 20th century there were nearly two million chimpanzees on the African continent. Now there are somewhere between 130,000 and 150,000 chimpanzees in Africa, comprising 98 percent of the world's population, the rest being held in zoos and by private parties. Increasingly, natural habitats of the great apes are being destroyed by unrestrained logging and development on the African continent. Poachers are active, selling apes to wealthy private collectors and zoos.

However, the greatest threat to the great apes' existence is the active "bushmeat" trade. Gorilla and chimpanzee meat, considered a delicacy by some, can be found in markets in central Africa, along with meats of other animals such as elephants. Debbie Cox, an Australian wildlife expert in charge of a chimpanzee sanctuary in Uganda, has reported as many as 30 chimps are killed each day (about 1,000 pounds of meat) in Congo alone. Possibly as many as 4,000 chimps and 3,000 gorillas were killed in 2000. As many as 25 percent of the chimps living in the Kibaale Forest in Uganda limp from injuries inflicted by snares. Hunters use trails made by logging companies in remote areas where apes were once protected by the forest. Vulnerable to hunters armed with guns, with park officials lacking resources and training to stop the poachers, the numbers of apes have dropped dramatically in recent years. Richard Leakey of the Kenya Wildlife Service has said that if the killing continues, the gorillas and chimpanzees may be hunted to extinction. All four types of great apes are listed as endangered species under the Endangered Species Act and under Appendix I of the Convention on International Trade in Endangered Species of Wild Fauna and Flora (CITES).

Robert Wokler (article 10.4) argues that the language of rights should not be applied to the great apes. He points out that in their natural surroundings the great apes do not show any inclination to develop a natural language. The concept of rights, so entwined with the utilization of sophisticated language, is foreign to their nature. While sympathetic to the goal of their improved treatment, Wokler insists the great apes would be better off if we understand them on their own terms, as unique animals with unique needs, rather than forcing upon them membership in a community they have neither requested nor need. By drawing the great apes closer to us by conferring rights, we recast their nature in our image, distorting our view of their place in the greater community of animals. Moreover, we run the risk of compromising our understanding of ourselves, and our place in the greater community of animals.

Wokler states in the concluding passages of his review of TGAP, "There must be a better way to demonstrate our goodwill to animals." He acknowledges the necessity to develop a suitable method to assist the great apes, and to this end he proposes the discussion be focused on their *needs* instead of rights. When offering this last suggestion, that the *language of needs* is a more appropriate way to express goodwill, he seems to imply that our sensitivity to the needs of the great apes should not stop with them alone, and that such an approach would be beneficial to all other creatures as well.

Readings

Article 10.1 *A Declaration on Great Apes* was signed by both the editors, Paola Cavalieri and Peter Singer, and the 34 contributors to the book *The Great Ape Project*. The *Declaration* articulates the purpose, goals, and vision of The Great Ape Project. The *Declaration* argues for three basic rights for great apes: the right to life, the protection of individual liberty, and the prohibition of torture. It is this document that brings together the diverse body of authors who contribute articles and influence to The Great Ape Project as a whole.

Article 10.2 Jane Goodall is the world's best known primatologist. She has published many scholarly and popular works, including her classic *In the Shadow of Man,* about her field study of chimpanzees in Tanzania. In *Chimpanzees–Bridging the Gap,* Goodall cites numerous ways chimpanzees share common physical features and behaviors with humans. The DNA structure of chimps is remarkably similar to that of humans, and they use tools and solve simple problems through reasoning. They grieve at the loss of loved ones and are capable of acts of altruism. Chimps have distinctive personalities and, as groups, have distinctive histories. They even evolve different behaviors in different parts of Africa. For example, the chimps of East Africa use tools to open hard-shelled fruits, but groups of chimps in West Africa don't. Goodall argues that, as our closest living ancestors in the animal kingdom, the great apes should be treated as individuals and granted the basic moral rights and protections humans grant each other. The way to most effectively bring this about is to support the principles found in *A Declaration on Great Apes.*

Article 10.3 James Rachels is a professor of philosophy at the University of Alabama, Birmingham. His many publications include *The End of Life: Euthanasia and Morality* (1986), *Created from Animals: The Moral Implications of Darwinism* (1990), and *Can Ethics Provide Answers?* (1996). In *Why Darwinians Should Support Equal Treatment for Other Great Apes,* Rachels combines insights from Aristotle and Darwin to argue his case for including the great apes in our moral community as individuals. With Aristotle we find the fundamental moral principal that similar cases should be treated alike, with differences in treatment being justified only when there is some relevant difference in the situations. With Darwin we find humans and other animals form, together, a broad, inclusive community. Humans are not fundamentally different from other animals; rather, all animals share a common heritage. In the case of the great apes, their similarity to humans is especially pronounced. They are intelligent, social individuals with "emotional lives similar to our own." If we are to be consistent in applying our moral standards, Rachels argues, we should include the great apes in our moral community as equals.

Article 10.4 Robert Wokler is senior research fellow at the University of Exeter. He is the author, editor, or coeditor of numerous books, mainly on Rousseau and Enlightenment themes. His most recent publications are *Rousseau; Inventing Human Science;* and *Rousseau and Liberty. Keeping It in the Family* is Wokler's review of the book *The Great Ape Project.* Wokler questions whether the language of rights is the most appropriate avenue for gaining improved treatment for great apes. He argues that similarities in the DNA of great apes and humans are deceptive in that, behaviorally, the two groups are very different. At best great apes have shown only the most rudimentary ability in acquiring linguistic skills, mainly through American Sign Language, and possess the conceptual ability of a two-year-old child. Wokler argues The Great Ape Project actually diminishes the unique identity of the great apes by claiming a stronger likeness to humans than exists. The consequences of refashioning the great apes in the image of man threatens to compromise our appreciation of their unique identities and needs. They can be protected, Wokler insists, without recasting their unique natures. Moreover, such refashioning drives a wedge between the great apes and humans on one side, and other threatened species, like tigers and whales, on the other.

Article 10.5 John Bignall is the senior editor at *Lancet* magazine. Written from the perspective of a great ape, John Bignall's *Rights for Homo Sapiens* portrays The Great Ape Project as more a matter of assuaging a bad conscience over the treatment of the great apes than an issue of granting them rights. It's *Homo sapiens* who kill and mistreat great apes, ruin their environment, and invade their private lives. *Homo sapiens* shouldn't act like they are giving great apes anything when they talk of giving them rights. *Homo sapiens* need to give themselves the right to stop mistreating great apes. This is all the great apes need.

10.1 A Declaration on Great Apes

PAOLA CAVALIERI AND PETER SINGER (EDITORS) AND CONTRIBUTORS TO *THE GREAT APE PROJECT*

WE DEMAND THE EXTENSION of the community of equals to include all great apes: human beings, chimpanzees, gorillas and orangutans.

"The community of equals" the moral community within which we accept certain basic moral principles or rights as governing our relations with each other and enforceable at law. Among these principles or rights are the following:

1. **The Right to Life**
   The lives of members of the community of equals are to be protected. Members of the community of equals may not be killed except in very strictly defined circumstances, for example, self-defence.

2. **The Protection of Individual Liberty**
   Members of the community of equals are not to be arbitrarily deprived of their liberty; if they should be imprisoned without due legal process, they have the right to immediate release. The detention of those who have not been convicted of any crime, or of those who are not criminally liable, should be allowed only where it can be shown to be for their own good, or necessary to protect the public from a member of the community who would clearly be a danger to others if at liberty. In such cases, members of the community of equals must have the right to appeal, either directly or, if they lack the relevant capacity, through an advocate, to a judicial tribunal.

3. **The Prohibition of Torture**
   The deliberate infliction of severe pain on a member of the community of equals, either wantonly or for an alleged benefit to others, is regarded as torture, and is wrong.

At present, only members of the species *Homo sapiens* are regarded as members of the community of equals. The inclusion, for the first time, of non-human animals into this community, is an ambitious project. The chimpanzee (including in this term both *Pan troglodytes* and the pygmy chimpanzee, *Pan paniscus*), the gorilla, *Gorilla gorilla*, and the orangutan, *Pongo pygmaeus*, are the closest relatives of our species. They also have mental capacities and an emotional life sufficient to justify inclusion within the community of equals. To the objection that chimpanzees, gorillas and orangutans will be unable to defend their own claims within the community, we respond that human guardians should safeguard their interests and rights, in the same ways as the interests of young or intellectually disabled members of our own species are safeguarded.

Our request comes at a special moment in history. Never before has our dominion over other animals been so pervasive and systematic. Yet this is also the moment when, within that very Western civilisation that has so inexorably extended this dominion, a rational ethic has emerged challenging the moral significance of membership of our own species. This challenge seeks equal consideration for the interests of all animals, human and nonhuman. It has given rise to a political movement, still fluid but growing. The slow but steady widening of the scope of the golden rule—"treat others as you would have them treat you"—has now resumed its course. The notion of "us" as opposed to "the other," which, like a more and more abstract silhouette, assumed in the course of centuries the contours of the boundaries of the tribe, of the nation, of the race, of the human species, and which for a time the species barrier had congealed and stiffened, has again become something alive, ready for further change.

The Great Ape Project aims at taking just one step in this process of extending the community of equals. We shall provide ethical argument, based on scientific evidence about the capacities of chimpanzees, gorillas and orangutans, for taking this step. Whether this step should also be the first of many others is not for The Great Ape Project to say. No doubt some of us, speaking individually, would want to extend the community of equals to many other animals as well; others may consider that

Reprinted from Paola Cavalieri and Peter Singer [eds.], The Great Ape Project: Equality Beyond Humanity *(Fourth Estate, London, 1993) by permission of the authors. © 1993 Paola Cavalieri and Peter Singer.*

extending the community to include all great apes is as far as we should go at present. We leave the consideration of that question for another occasion.

We have not forgotten that we live in a world in which, for at least three-quarters of the human population, the idea of human rights is no more than rhetoric, and not a reality in everyday life. In such a world, the idea of equality for nonhuman animals, even for those disquieting doubles of ours, the other great apes, may not be received with much favour. We recognise, and deplore, the fact that all over the world human beings are living without basic rights or even the means for a decent subsistence. The denial of the basic rights of particular other species will not, however, assist the world's poor and oppressed to win their just struggles. Nor is it reasonable to ask that the members of these other species should wait until all humans have achieved their rights first. That suggestion itself assumes that beings belonging to other species are of lesser moral significance than human beings. Moreover, on present indications, the suggested delay might well be an extremely long one.

Another basis for opposition to our demand may arise from the fact that the great apes—especially chimpanzees—are considered to be extremely valuable laboratory tools. Of course, since the main object of research is to learn about human beings, the ideal subject of study would be the human being. Harmful research on nonconsenting human beings is, however, rightly regarded as unethical. Because harmful research on nonconsenting chimpanzees, gorillas or orangutans is not seen in the same light, researchers are permitted to do things to these great apes that would be considered utterly abhorrent if done to human beings. Indeed, the value of the great apes as research tools lies precisely in the combination of two conflicting factors: on the one hand, the fact that, both physically and psychologically, they very closely resemble our own species; and on the other, the fact that they are denied the ethical and legal protection that we give to our own species.

Those who wish to defend the present routine treatment of the nonhuman great apes in laboratories and in other circumstances—disturbing details of which we present in this book—must now bear the burden of proof in refuting the case we make in these pages for including all great apes within the community of equals. If our arguments cannot be refuted, the way in which great apes other than humans are now treated will be shown to be an arbitrary and unjustifiable form of discrimination. For this, there will no longer be any excuse.

The resolution of a moral dispute is often just the beginning, not the end, of a social question. We know that, even if we can prove our view to be sound, we will still be far away from the moment when the dispersed members of the chimpanzee, gorilla and orangutan species can be liberated and lead their different lives as equals in their own special territories in our countries, or free in the equatorial forests to which they once belonged. As normally happens when ethical progress runs its course, the obstacles will be many, and opposition from those whose interests are threatened will be strong. Is success possible? Unlike some oppressed groups that have achieved equality, chimpanzees, gorillas and orangutans are unable to fight for themselves. Will we find the social forces prepared to fight on their behalf to bring about their inclusion within the community of equals? We believe that success is possible. While some oppressed humans have achieved victory through their own struggles, others have been as powerless as chimpanzees, gorillas and orangutans are today. History shows us that there has always been, within our own species, that saving factor: a squad of determined people willing to overcome the selfishness of their own group in order to advance another's cause.

Discussion and Assignments

1. What is "the community of equals" according to the authors of TGAP? Do you find their definition of "the community of equals" adequate?

2. Provision 1 of the *Declaration* asserts the right to life for those included in the community of equals. How might the right to life apply to the great apes? How might this provision affect humans? Be sure to use examples to illustrate your answers.

3. Provision 2 of the *Declaration* provides for the protection of individual liberty for those included in the community of equals. How might this provision apply to the great apes? How might this provision affect humans? Be sure to use examples to illustrate your answers.

4. Provision 3 of the *Declaration* provides for the prohibition of torture for those included in the community of equals. How might this provision apply to the great apes? How might this provision affect humans? Be sure to use examples to illustrate your answers.

5. If the *Declaration* were passed by the UN and recognized by the United States, how might we address the issue of keeping great apes in zoos?

6. If the *Declaration* were passed by the UN and recognized by the United States, would it be possible to keep great apes in enclosures or cages and conduct medical tests on them, for example, to conduct research on chimps to find a cure for AIDS?

7. Many people believe dolphins and porpoises are (in their own way) at least as intelligent as great apes, though we do not have sufficient evidence to prove so. Whales too have been noted for their intelligence. What observations or criticisms might you have regarding marine mammals that show unusual signs of intelligence, yet are not accounted for in TGAP?

8. If the *Declaration* were passed in the UN and great apes were officially recognized as persons or individuals, do you think nations would take an active role in protecting and caring for them?

9. What will the consequences be if the UN adopts the *Declaration on Great Apes?*

10.2 Chimpanzees—Bridging the Gap

JANE GOODALL

SHE WAS TOO TIRED AFTER THEIR LONG, hot journey to set to on the delicious food, as her daughters did. She had one paralysed arm, the aftermath of a bout of polio nine years ago, and walking was something of an effort. And so, for the moment, she was content to rest and watch as her two daughters ate. One was adult now, the other still caught in the contrariness of adolescence—grown up one moment, childish the next. Minutes passed. And then her eldest, the first pangs of her hunger assuaged, glanced at the old lady, gathered food for both of them and took it to share with her mother.

The leader of the patrol, hearing the sudden sound, stopped and stared ahead. The three following froze in their tracks, alert to the danger that threatened ever more sinister as they penetrated further into neighbouring territory. Then they relaxed: it was only a large bird that had landed in a tree ahead. The leader looked back, as though seeking approval for moving on again. Without a word the patrol moved on. Ten minutes later they reached a look-out place offering a view across enemy territory. Sitting close together, silent still, they searched for sign or sound that might indicate the presence of strangers. But all was peaceful. For a whole hour the four sat there, uttering no sound. And then, still maintaining silence, the leader rose, glanced at the others and moved on. One by one they followed him. Only the youngest, a youth still in his teens, stayed on for a few minutes by himself, reluctant, it seemed, to tear himself away from the prospect of violence. He was at that age when border skirmishes seemed exhilarating as well as challenging and dangerous. He couldn't help being fascinated, hoping for, yet fearing, a glimpse of the enemy. But clearly there would be no fighting that day and so he too followed his leader back to familiar haunts and safety.

We knew her as "Auntie Gigi." She has no children of her own, but two years ago she had more or less adopted two youngsters who had lost their own mother in an epidemic—pneumonia, probably. They were lucky, those two. Not that Gigi was all sweet and motherly, not at all. She was a tough old bird, somewhat mannish in many ways. But she made a perfect guardian for she stood no nonsense, not from anyone, and had high standing in her society. If anyone picked a quarrel with either of these two kids, he or she had Auntie Gigi to reckon with. Before Gigi came into the picture, one of the orphans, little Mel, had been cared for by Sam, a teenage youth. It was quite extraordinary—it wasn't even as though Sam was related to the sickly orphan. He had not even been close with Mel's mother during her life. Yet after she passed away, Sam and Mel became really close, like a loving father and child. Sam often shared his food with Mel, usually carried him when they went on long trips together, and even let the child sleep with him at night. And he did his best to keep him out of harm's way. Maybe it was because Sam's mother had got sick and died in that same epidemic. Of course, he'd not been spending much time with her then—he'd been out and about with the boys mostly. Even so, it is always a comfort if you can sneak off to Mum for a while when the going gets tough, and the big guys start picking on you. And suddenly, for Sam, his old mother wasn't there. Perhaps his closeness with that dependent little child helped to fill an empty place in his heart. Whatever the reason, Mel would almost certainly have died if Sam hadn't cared for him as he did. After a year Sam and Mel began spending less time together. And that was when Auntie Gigi took over.

* * *

Those anecdotes were recorded during our thirty-one years of observation of the chimpanzees of Gombe, in Tanzania. Yet the characters could easily be mistaken for humans. This is partly because chimpanzees do behave so much like us, and partly because I deliberately wrote as though I were describing humans, and used words like "old lady," "youth," and "mannish." And "Sam" was really known as "Spindle."

One by one, over the years, many words once used to describe human behaviour have crept into scientific accounts of nonhuman animal behaviour. When, in the early 1960s, I brazenly used such words as "childhood," "adolescence," "motivation," "excitement," and "mood" I was much criticised. Even worse was my crime of suggesting that chimpanzees had "personalities." I was ascribing human characteristics to nonhuman animals and was thus guilty of that worst of ethological sins—anthropomorphism. Certainly anthropomorphism can be misleading, but it so happens that chimpanzees, our closest living relatives in the animal kingdom, do show many human characteristics. Which, in view of the fact that our DNA differs from theirs by only just over 1 percent, is hardly surprising.

Each chimpanzee has a unique personality and each has his or her own individual life history. We can speak of the history of a chimpanzee community, where major events—an epidemic, a kind of primitive "war," a "baby boom"—have marked the "reigns" of the five top-ranking or alpha males we have known. And we find that individual chimpanzees can make a difference to the course of chimpanzee history, as is the case with humans. I wish there was space to describe here some of these characters and events, but the information, for those interested, can be found in my most recent book, *Through a Window*.[1]

Chimpanzees can live more than fifty years. Infants suckle and are carried by their mothers for five years. And then, even when the next infant is born, the elder child travels with his or her mother for another three or four years and continues to spend a good deal of time with her thereafter. The ties between family members are close, affectionate and supportive, and typically endure throughout life. Learning is important in the individual life cycle. Chimpanzees, like humans, can learn by observation and imitation, which means that if a new adaptive pattern is "invented" by a particular individual, it can be passed on to the next generation. Thus we find that while the various chimpanzee groups that have been studied in different

---

1. J. Goodall, *Through a Window: My Thirty Years with the Chimpanzees of Gombe* (Houghton Miflin, Boston, 1990).

parts of Africa have many behaviours in common, they also have their own distinctive traditions. This is particularly well documented with respect to tool-using and tool-making behaviours. Chimpanzees use more objects as tools for a greater variety of purposes than any creature except ourselves and each population has its own tool-using cultures. For example, the Gombe chimpanzees use long, straight sticks from which the bark has been peeled to extract army ants from their nests; 100 miles to the south, in the Mahale Mountains, there are plenty of the same ants, but they are not eaten by the chimpanzees. The Mahale chimpanzees use small twigs to extract carpenter ants from their nests in tree branches; these ants, though present, are not eaten at Gombe. And no East African chimpanzee has been seen to open hard-shelled fruits with the hammer and anvil technique that is part of the culture of chimpanzee groups in West Africa.

The postures and gestures with which chimpanzees communicate—such as kissing, embracing, holding hands, patting one another on the back, swaggering, punching, hair-pulling, tickling—are not only uncannily like many of our own, but are used in similar contexts and clearly have similar meanings. Two friends may greet with an embrace and a fearful individual may be calmed by a touch, whether they be chimpanzees or humans. Chimpanzees are capable of sophisticated cooperation and complex social manipulation. Like us, they have a dark side to their nature: they can be brutal, they are aggressively territorial, sometimes they even engage in a primitive type of warfare. But they also show a variety of helping and care-giving behaviours and are capable of true altruism.

The structure of the chimpanzee brain and central nervous system is extraordinarily like ours. And this appears to have led to similar emotions and intellectual abilities in our two species. Of course, it is difficult to study emotion even when the subjects are human—I can only guess, when you *say* you are sad and *look* sad, that you *feel* rather as I do when I am sad. I cannot know. And when the subject is a member of another species, the task is that much harder. If we ascribe human emotion to nonhuman animals we are, of course, accused of anthropomorphism. But given the similarities in the anatomy and wiring of the chimpanzee and human brains, is it not logical to assume that there will be similarities also in the feelings, emotions and moods of the two species? Certainly all of us who have worked closely with chimpanzees over extended periods of time have no hesitation in asserting that chimpanzees, like humans, show emotions similar to—sometimes probably identical to—those which we label joy, sadness, fear, despair and so on.

Our own success as a species (if we measure success by the extent to which we have spread across the world and altered the environment to suit our immediate purposes) has been due entirely to the explosive development of the human brain. Our intellectual abilities are so much more sophisticated than those of even the most gifted chimpanzees that early attempts made by scientists to describe the similarity of mental process in humans and chimpanzees were largely met with ridicule or outrage. Gradually, however, evidence for sophisticated mental performances in the apes has become ever more convincing. There is proof that they can solve simple problems through process of reasoning and insight. They can plan for the immediate future. The language acquisition experiments have demonstrated that they have powers of generalisation, abstraction and concept-forming along with the ability to understand and use abstract symbols in communication. And they clearly have some kinds of self-concept.

It is all a little humbling, for these cognitive abilities used to be considered unique to humans: we are not, after all, quite as different from the rest of the animal kingdom as we used to think. The line dividing "man" from "beast" has become increasingly blurred. The chimpanzees, and the other great apes, form a living bridge between "us" and "them," and this knowledge forces us to re-evaluate our relationship with the rest of the animal kingdom, particularly with the great apes. In what terms should we think of these beings, nonhuman yet possessing so very many human-like characteristics? How should be treat them?

Surely we should treat them with the same consideration and kindness as we show to other humans; and as we recognise human rights, so too should be recognise the rights of the great apes? Yes—but unfortunately huge segments of the human population are *not* treated with consideration and kindness, and our newspapers inform us daily of horrific violations of human rights in many countries around the world.

Still, things have got better in some Western-style democracies. During the past 100 years we have seen the abolition of enforced child and female labour, slavery, the exhibiting of deformed humans in circuses and fairs and many other such horrors. We no longer gather to gloat over suffering and death at public hangings. We have welfare states so that (theoretically) no one needs to starve or freeze to death and everyone can expect some help when they are sick or unemployed. Of course there are still a myriad of social injustices and abuses, but at least they are not publicly condoned by the government and, once public sympathy has been aroused, they are gradually addressed. We are trying, for example, to abolish the last traces of the old sadism in mental institutions.

Finally, there is a growing concern for the plight of nonhuman animals in our society. But those who are trying to raise levels of awareness regarding the abuse of companion animals, animals raised for food, zoo and circus performers, laboratory victims and so on, and lobbying for new and improved legislation to protect them, are constantly asked how they can devote time and energy, and divert public monies, to "animals" when there is so much need among human beings. Indeed, in many parts of the world humans suffer mightily. We are anguished when we read of the millions of starving and homeless people, of police tortures, of children whose limbs are deliberately deformed so that they can make a living from begging, and those whose parents force them—even sell them—into lives of prostitution. We long for the day when conditions improve worldwide—we may work for that cause. But we should not delude ourselves into believing that, so long as there is human suffering, it is morally acceptable to turn a blind eye to nonhuman suffering. Who are we to say that the suffering of a human being is more terrible than the suffering of a nonhuman being, or that it matters more?

It is not so long ago, in historical perspective, that we abolished the slave trade. Slaves were taken from "savage" tribes that inhabited remote corners of the earth. Probably it was not too difficult for slave traders and owners to distance themselves, psychologically, from these prisoners, so unlike any people their "masters" had known before. And although they must have realised that their slaves were capable of feeling pain and suffering, why

should that matter? Those strange, dark, heathen people were so *different*—not really like human beings at all. And so their anguish could be ignored. Today we know that the DNA of all ethnic groups of humans is virtually the same, that we are all—yellow, brown, black and white—brothers and sisters around the globe. From our superior knowledge we are appalled to think back to the intelligent and normally compassionate people who condoned slavery and all that it entailed. Fortunately, thanks to the perceptions, high moral principles and determination of a small band of people, human slaves were freed. And they were freed *not* because of sophisticated analysis of their DNA, but because they so obviously showed the same emotions, the same intellectual abilities, the same capacity for suffering and joy, as their white owners.

Now, for a moment, let us imagine beings who, although they differ genetically from *Homo sapiens* by about 1 percent and lack speech, nevertheless behave similarly to ourselves, can feel pain, share our emotions and have sophisticated intellectual abilities. Would we, today, condone the use of those beings as slaves? Tolerate their capture and export from Africa? Laugh at degrading performances, taught through cruelty, shown on our television screens? Turn a blind eye to their imprisonment, in tiny barren cells, often in solitary confinement, even though they had committed no crime? Buy products tested on them at the cost of their mental or physical torture?

Those beings exist and we *do* condone their abuse. They are called chimpanzees. They are imprisoned in zoos, sold to anyone who cares to buy them as "pets," and dressed up and taught to smoke or ride bicycles for our entertainment. They are incarcerated and often tortured, psychologically and even physically, in medical laboratories in the name of science. And this is condoned by governments and by large numbers of the general public. There was a time when the victims in the labs would have been human; but thanks to a dedicated few who stood up to the establishment and who gradually informed the general public of the horrors being perpetrated behind closed doors, and insane and other unfortunates are now safe from the white-coated gods. The time has come when we must take the next step and protect our closest living relatives from exploitation. How can we do this?

If we could simply argue that it is morally wrong to abuse, physically or psychologically, any rational, thinking being with the capacity to suffer and feel pain, to know fear and despair, it would be easy—we have already demonstrated the existence of these abilities in chimpanzees and the other great apes. But this, it seems, is not enough. We come up, again and again, against that nonexistent barrier that is, for so many, so real—the barrier between "man" and "beast." It was erected in ignorance, as a result of the arrogant assumption, unfortunately shared by vast numbers of people, that humans are superior to nonhumans in every way. Even if nonhuman beings are rational and *can* suffer and feel pain and despair it does not matter how we treat them provided it is for the good of humanity—which apparently includes our own pleasure. They are not members of that exclusive club that opens it doors only to bona fide *Homo sapiens.*

This is why we find double standards to the legislation regarding medical research. Thus while it is illegal to perform medical experiments on a brain-dead human being who can neither speak nor feel, it is legally acceptable to perform them on an alert, feeling and highly intelligent chimpanzee. Conversely, while it is legally permitted to imprison an innocent chimpanzee, for life, in a steel-barred, barren laboratory cell measuring five foot by five foot by seven foot, a psychopathic mass murderer must be more speciously confined. And these double standards exist only because the brain-dead patient and the mass murderer are *human*. They have souls and we cannot, of course, prove that chimpanzees have souls. The fact we cannot prove that *we* have souls, or that chimps do not, is, apparently, beside the point.

So how can we hope to procure improved legal standing for the great apes? By trying to prove that we are "merely" apes, and that what goes for us, therefore, should go for them also? I see no point in altering our status as humans by constantly stressing that we differ from the apes *only* in that our brains are bigger and better. Admittedly at our worst we can outdo the Devil in wickedness, but at our best we are close to the angels: certain human lives and accomplishments vividly illustrate the human potential. As we plod from cradle to grave we need all the encouragement and inspiration we can get and it helps, sometimes, to know that wings and halos *can* be won. Nor do I think it useful to suggest reclassifying the great apes as *human*. Our task is hard enough without the waving of red flags.

Fortunately there are some heavy-duty people (like the editors of this book) out there fighting for the rights of the great apes, along with those fighting for the rights of humans. If only we could march under one banner, working for apes and humans alike, and with our combined intelligence and compassion—our humanity—strive to make ever more people understand. To understand that we should respect the individual ape just as we should respect the individual human; that we should recognise the right of each ape to live a life unmolested by humans, if necessary helped by humans, in the same way as we should recognise these rights for individual human beings; and that the same ethical and moral attitudes should apply to ape beings and human beings alike. Then, as the thesis of this book proposes, we shall be ready to welcome them, these ape beings, into a "moral community" of which we humans are also a part.

Let me end with a combined message from two very special members of this moral community. The first is a chimpanzee being named Old Man. He was rescued from a lab when he was about twelve years old and went to Lion Country Safaris in Florida. There he was put, with three females, on an artificial island. All four had been abused. A young man, Marc Cusano, was employed to care for them. He was told not to get too close—the chimps hated people and were vicious. He should throw food to the island from his little boat. As the days went by Marc became increasingly fascinated by the human-like behaviour of the chimps. How could he care for them if he did not have some kind of relationship with them? He began going closer and closer. One day he held out a banana—Old Man took it from his hand. A few weeks later Marc dared step on to the island. And then, on a never to be forgotten occasion, Old Man allowed Marc to groom him. They had become friends. Some time later, as Marc was clearing the island, he slipped, fell and scared the infant who had been born to one of the females. The infant screamed, the mother, instinctively, leapt to defend her child and bit Marc's neck. The other two females quickly ran to help their friend; one bit his wrist, the other his leg. And then Old

Man came charging towards the scene—and that, thought Marc, was the end. But Old Man pulled each of those females off Marc and hurled them away, then kept them at bay while Marc, badly wounded, dragged himself to safety.

"There's no doubt about it," Marc told me later, "Old Man saved my life."

The second hero is a human being named Rick Swope. He visits the Detroit zoo once a year with his family. One day, as he watched the chimpanzees in their big new enclosure, a fight broke out between two adult males. Jojo, who had been at the zoo for years, was challenged by a younger and stronger newcomer—and Jojo lost. In his fear he fled into the moat: it was brand new and Jojo did not understand water. He had got over the barrier erected to prevent the chimpanzees from falling in—for they cannot swim—and the group of visitors and staff that happened to be there stood and watched in horror as Jojo began to drown. He went under once, twice, three times. And then Rick Swope could bear it no longer. He jumped in to try to save the chimp. He jumped in despite the onlookers yelling at him about the danger. He managed to get Jojo's dead weight over his shoulder, and then he crossed the barrier and pushed Jojo on to the bank of the island. He held him there (because the bank was too steep and when he let go Jojo slid back to the water) even when the other chimps charged towards him, screaming in excitement. He held him until Jojo raised his head, took a few swaggering steps, and collapsed on more level ground.

The director of the institute called Rick. "That was a brave thing you did. You must have known how dangerous it was. What made you do it?"

"Well, I looked into his eyes. And it was like looking into the eyes of a man. And the message was, 'Won't *anybody* help me?'"

Old Man, a chimpanzee who had been abused by humans, reached across the supposed species barrier to help a human friend in need. Rick Swope risked his life to save a chimpanzee, a non-human being who sent a message that a human could understand. Now it is up to the rest of us to join in too.

Discussion and Assignments

1. What is anthropomorphism? Why has Goodall sometimes been accused of anthropomorphism? Locate three anthropomorphic terms in Goodall's article, for example, *swagger* and *despair,* and evaluate how effectively the terms apply to both chimps and humans. Is her use of the terms appropriate?

2. Can you always identify when a term is used as an anthropomorphic term, and when it is not? What difficulties do you have in deciding whether a term is anthropomorphic? Give examples to illustrate your points.

3. In the case of chimps, if you believe an anthropomorphic term is being legitimately applied, for example, they *grieve* at the loss of a loved one, do you need to refer to it any longer as anthropomorphic?

4. Goodall draws an analogy between the slave trade and our current treatment of great apes. How similar or dissimilar do you believe our treatment of the great apes is to the slave trade of the past? Offer specific treatments or practices to illustrate your point, for example, slaves were sold as property, the same as apes. Be sure to refer to the *Declaration of Great Apes* (article 10.1) to gather some of your comparative material. Do you believe Goodall's analogy is strong or weak? If Goodall is correct, is the *Declaration of Great Apes* an Emancipation Proclamation?

5. According to Goodall, what double standards exist in medical research with respect to great apes and humans? Do you agree with Goodall on this point? How effective is this aspect of her argument in supporting her overall argument for bringing great apes into a common moral community with humans?

6. Goodall offers several chimpanzee behaviors or abilities (e.g., they're capable of altruism; they learn by imitation and observation; they experience suffering and

despair) to establish her case for including chimps in a common moral community with humans.

a. Which three behaviors or abilities do you believe are the most important to establishing her case for including chimps in a common moral community with humans? In a paragraph on each explain *why* the behaviors or abilities are important by comparing and contrasting them with the behaviors or abilities of other animals and humans.

b. Which behavior or ability offered by Goodall as evidence to support her case for including chimps in a common moral community with humans is least important? In a paragraph explain why you think the behavior or ability is weak as evidence by comparing and contrasting it to the behavior or abilities of other animals and humans.

7. A common criticism of TGAP is that it focuses on protecting and conferring rights on great apes when there are millions of people in the world in need of food, basic medical care, who work for wages that will not sustain a minimum standard of living, or live under repressive governments that don't respect human rights—that many people do not actually enjoy the rights Goodall wants to secure for great apes.

a. How does Goodall respond to this criticism? Explain why you believe her response is or is not convincing.

b. Imagine you live in an equatorial African country where there is much poverty, little quality education, great suffering and loss of life from AIDS, foreign companies are logging your forests at an alarming rate, and your government's human rights record is problematic at best. You open the daily newspaper and notice that a group of scientists and philosophers will be gathering at your university to discuss and elicit support for TGAP. The public is invited. Would you go? What would you say?

8. Reconstruct Goodall's argument for including the great apes in our moral community using the following argument form: Issue, Definitions, Premises, Conclusion. Use only clear, declarative statements, and remember to list your premises in the most logical order.

Issue: Whether the great apes should be granted rights that would include them in our moral community as equals.

Definitions: (You might want to define *moral community* or *moral equals*.)

Premises:

Conclusion:

9. a. Construct an argument *opposed* to Goodall's argument for including the great apes in our moral community using the following argument form: Issue, Definitions, Premises, Conclusion. Use only clear, declarative statements, and remember to list your premises in the most logical order.

Issue: Whether the great apes should be granted rights that would include them in our moral community as equals.

Definitions: (You might want to define *moral community* or *moral equals*.)

Premises:

Conclusion: The great apes should not be included with humans in a common community as moral equals.

b. Now write a 300 word essay arguing against Goodall's position using the argument you constructed as source material.

10.3 Why Darwinians Should Support Equal Treatment for Other Great Apes

James Rachels

A FEW YEARS AGO I set out to canvass the literature on Charles Darwin. I thought it would be a manageable task, but I soon realised what a naive idea this was. I do not know how many books have been written about him, but there seem to be thousands, and each year more appear.[1] Why are there so many? Part of the answer is, of course, that he was a tremendously important figure in the history of human thought. But as I read the books—or, at least, as many of them as I could—it gradually dawned on me that all this attention is also due to Darwin's personal qualities. He was an immensely likeable man, modest and humane, with a personality that continues to draw people to him even today.

Reflecting on his father's character, Darwin's son Francis wrote that "The two subjects which moved my father perhaps more strongly than any others were cruelty to animals and slavery. His detestation of both was intense, and his indignation was overpowering in case of any levity or want of feeling on these matters."[2] Darwin's strong feelings about slavery are expressed in many of his writings, most notably in the *Journal of Researches,* in which he recorded his adventures on the *Beagle* voyage. His comments there are among the most moving in abolitionist literature. But it was his feelings about animals that impressed his contemporaries most vividly. Numerous anecdotes show him remonstrating with cab-drivers who whipped their horses too smartly, solicitously caring for his own animals and forbidding the discussion of vivisection in his home.[3] At the height of his fame he wrote an article for a popular magazine condemning the in-famous leg-hold trap in terms that would not seem out of place in an animal-rights magazine today.

For the most part, however, Darwin avoided moralising in his scientific books. Earlier students of nature had viewed the natural order as a kind of moral laboratory in which God's design was everywhere evident, and so they found all manner of moral lessons there. Darwin believed it is a mistake to think about nature in this way. Nature is "red in tooth and claw." Rather than embodying some great moral design, nature operates by eliminating the unfit in ways that are often cruel and that do not conform to any human sense of right.

Nevertheless, Darwin did think that something can be learned about morality from the scientific study of human origins. The third chapter of his great work *The Descent of Man* is an extended essay on morality, "approached," as he put it, "from the side of natural history."[4] In that chapter Darwin discusses among other things, the nature of morality, its biological basis, the extent of our moral duties, and the prospects for moral progress. It is the work of a moral visionary as well as a man of science.

Darwin's remarks about moral progress are especially striking. We are moral beings because nature has provided us with "social instincts" that cause us to care about others. (The social instincts are, of course, produced by natural selection, as are almost all our traits.) At first, though, the reach of the social instincts does not extend very far—we care only about our near kin and those whom we can expect to help us in return. Moral progress occurs over time as the social instincts are extended ever more widely, and we come to care about the welfare of more and more of our fellow beings.

1. My own contribution to the deluge is James Rachels, *Created from Animals: The Moral Implications of Darwinism* (Oxford University Press, Oxford, 1990), which provides a more detailed account of the matters discussed in this [article].
2. This statement, from an unpublished reminiscence in the Cambridge University Library's collection of Darwiniana, is quoted in Ronald W. Clark, *The Survival of Charles Darwin* (Random House, New York, 1984), p. 76.

3. Darwin did, however, defend the practice of vivisection "for real investigations on physiology." For details concerning his ambiguous attitude on this subject, see Rachels, *Created from Animals*, pp. 212–16.
4. Charles Darwin, *The Descent of Man, and Selection in Relation to Sex* (John Murray, London, 1871), p. 71.

The highest level of morality is reached when the rights of all creatures, regardless of race, intelligence, or even species, are respected equally:

> [T]he social instincts which no doubt were acquired by man, as by the lower animals, for the good of the community, will from the first have given to him some wish to aid his fellows, and some feeling of sympathy. Such impulses will have served him at a very early period as a rude rule of right and wrong. But as man gradually advanced in intellectual power and was enabled to trace the more remote consequences of his actions; as he acquired sufficient knowledge to reject baneful customs and superstitions; as he regarded more and more not only the welfare but the happiness of his fellow-men; as from habit, following on beneficial experience, instruction, and example, his sympathies became more tender and widely diffused, so as to extend to the men of all races, to the imbecile, the maimed, and other useless members of society, and finally to the lower animals—so would the standard of his morality rise higher and higher.[5]

The virtue of sympathy for the lower animals is "one of the noblest with which man is endowed."[6] It comes last in the progression because it requires the greatest advancement in thought and reflection.

What are we to make of this? One possibility is to say that Darwin's moral attitudes were separate from, and independent of, his strictly scientific achievement. In opposing slavery, he was properly sympathetic to one of the great moral movements of his times. In opposing cruelty to animals, he showed himself to be kind-hearted, as we all should be. But no more should be made of it than that. On this way of thinking, the moral views expressed in *The Descent of Man* are just extra baggage, having no more to do with the theory of natural selection than Einstein's reflections on war and peace had to do with special relativity. Like other nineteenth-century writers, Darwin could not resist presenting his thoughts about ethics alongside his scientific work. But we, at least, should keep the two things separate.

There is, however, another way of thinking about Darwin's life and work. Perhaps his scientific work and his moral views were connected, as he apparently believed they were, in a significant way. If so, then we may have reason to view them as one piece, and it may not be so easy to embrace the one without the other. Asa Gray, the Harvard botanist who was Darwin's leading defender in America, took this view. Speaking before the theological faculty at Yale in 1880, Gray declared that

> We are sharers not only of animal but of vegetable life, sharers with the higher brute animals in common instincts and feelings and affections. It seems to me that there is a sort of meanness in the wish to ignore the tie. I fancy that human beings may be more humane when they realize that, as their dependent associates live a life in which man has a share, so they have rights which man is bound to respect.[7]

Asa Gray had identified the essential point. Darwin had shown that all life is related: we are kin to the apes. If this is true, then if we have rights, would it not follow that they have rights as well?

Let me try to explain this point in a little more detail. A fundamental moral principle, which was first formulated by Aristotle, is that like cases should be treated alike. I take this to mean that individuals are to be treated in the same way *unless there is a relevant difference between them*. Thus if you want to treat one person one way, and another person a different way, you must be able to point to some difference between them that justifies treating them differently. Where there are no relevant differences, they must be treated alike.

Aristotle's principle applies to our treatment of nonhumans as well as to our treatment of humans. Before Darwin, however, it was generally believed that the differences between humans and nonhumans are so great that we are almost always justified in treating humans differently. Humans were thought to be set apart from the rest of creation. They were said to be uniquely rational beings, made in God's image, with immortal souls, and so they were different in kind from mere animals. It is this picture of humankind that Darwin destroyed. In its place he substituted a picture of humans as sharing a common heritage, and common characteristics, with other animals.

5. Ibid., p. 103.
6. Ibid., p. 101.

7. Asa Gray, *Natural Science and Religion: Two Lectures Delivered to the Theological School of Yale College* (Charles Scribner's Sons, New York, 1880), p. 54.

If we take the Darwinian picture seriously, it follows that we must revise our view about how animals may be treated. It does not follow that we must treat all animals as the equals of humans, for there may still be differences between humans and some animals that justify a difference in moral status. It would make no sense, for example, to argue that clams should be given the right to live freely, because they lack the capacity for free action. Or perhaps the members of some species, such as insects, lack even the capacity for feeling pain, so that it would be meaningless to object to "torturing" them. Other examples of this type may come easily to mind.

Nevertheless, when we turn to the "higher" animals, such as the great apes, it is the similarities and not the differences between them and us that are so striking. These similarities are so widespread and so profound that often there will be no relevant differences that could justify a difference in treatment. Darwin argued that such animals are intelligent and sociable and that they even possess a rudimentary moral sense. In addition, he said, they experience anxiety, grief, dejection, despair, joy, devotion, ill-temper, patience, and a host of other "human" feelings. Ethological studies since Darwin's day have confirmed this picture of them. The moral consequence is that if they have such capacities, then there is no rational basis for denying basic moral rights to them, at least if we wish to continue claiming those rights for ourselves. Chief among those rights are the right to life, the right to live freely and the right not to be caused unnecessary suffering.

It would be easy to overstate this conclusion and to misrepresent its basis. The conclusion is not that the great apes should be granted *all* the rights of humans or that there are *no* important differences between them and us. There may still be some human rights that have no analogues for the apes. In an enlightened society, for example, humans are granted the right to higher education. Because reading is essential for acquiring such an education, and not even the most intelligent nonhumans can read, it makes no sense to insist that they be given this right. But the right to live freely and the other basic rights mentioned above do not depend on the ability to read or on any other comparable intellectual achievement, and so such abilities are not relevant to eligibility for those rights. Aristotle's principle requires equal treatment where, but only where, there are no relevant differences.

Partisans of the animal rights movement sometimes represent such conclusions as based on the genetic similarity between humans and other apes. But the importance of this fact is easily misunderstood. Shared DNA is further proof of our kinship with other animals, it confirms the Darwinian picture, but it is not the bare fact that we share genetic material with the chimps that forces the moral conclusion. What forces the moral conclusion is that the chimps, and other great apes, are intelligent and have social emotional lives similar to our own. Genes are important, to them and to us, only because they make those lives possible.

Before Darwin, the essential moral equality of the great apes—a category that, of course, includes us as well as the chimps, gorillas and orangutans— would have been a surprising claim, difficult to defend. But after Darwin, it is no more than we should expect, if we think carefully about what he taught us. Every educated person has now learned Darwin's lesson about the origins of human life and its connection with nonhuman life. What remains is that we take its moral implications equally seriously. Darwin himself was optimistic:

> Looking to future generations, there is no cause to fear that the social instincts will grow weaker, and we may expect that virtuous habits will grow stronger, becoming perhaps fixed by inheritance. In this case the struggle between our higher and lower impulses will be less severe, and virtue will be triumphant.[8]

8. Darwin, *Descent of Man,* p. 104.

Discussion and Assignments

1. Rachels contrasts how we looked at animals and ourselves before Darwin and after Darwin. What are the differences, and what implications can be drawn from them according to Rachels?

2. Rachels claims Darwin's moral thought is connected to his scientific thought. According to Rachels, how are these two aspects connected to each other?

3. Darwin speaks to the evolution of sympathy or moral sentiments as well as the evolution of species, in a strictly scientific sense. How does the development of sympathy occur, according to Darwin? According to Darwin, what implications has the development of sympathy had on (a) humans with respect to humans, and (b) humans with respect to other animals?

4. Explain the fundamental moral principal that Aristotle formulated. (a) Give an example of how humans might treat humans according to this principal, and (b) give an example of how humans might treat animals according to this principal.

5. Rachels claims if we take the Darwinian view seriously, then "we must revise our view about how animals may be treated." Why does Rachels make this claim? Do you agree with Rachels? Why or why not?

6. Why specifically should great apes be granted rights, according to Rachels, and what does this have to do with Aristotle's moral principal? Do you agree with Rachels? Is it possible we could be "kin" to other animals—great apes included— but argue against them having rights?

7. Which animals does Rachels discuss to illustrate his case that great apes should be treated as moral equals? Select two distantly related animals, for example, koala bears and deep sea bass, and using the criteria Rachels employs, what kind of rights would you grant each of them? Illustrate your conclusions with examples of treatment, for example, could you restrict the bass's movement by putting it in an aquarium? Could you kill and eat the bass? Could you cage the koala bear and put it in a zoo? Could you kill and eat the koala bear?

8. According to Rachels's interpretation of Darwin, the development of our moral sympathies has been connected with our evolution as a species. Do you agree that this development has occurred in the way Darwin claims? Does the development of moral sympathy necessitate a revision of the way we treat animals to the degree Rachels argues?

10.4 Keeping It in the Family

ROBERT WOKLER

WHAT HAS BEEN GAINED by the human race for all our pious declarations of the rights of man? Originally conceived in Reformation and Counter-Reformation Europe to justify the freedom of conscience and worship of religious minorities, natural rights and the rights of man have seldom been extended with good grace and real conviction by the powerful and predominant to the oppressed. Are we now more compassionate, more resolved to combat persecution, than immediately prior to the 1948 Universal Declaration of Human Rights?

Perhaps this is not a propitious moment for extending the rights of man to other species, but the eternal hope shown in defiance of experience by the authors of *The Great Ape Project* is inspired by compelling enthusiasm and goodwill. In these times of despair, it refreshes parts other moral philosophies fail to reach. The Declaration on Great Apes (including human beings) which it embraces is modest, articulating only three basic principles—the right to life, the protection of liberty and the prohibition of torture. These are elaborated by the editors, Paola Cavalieri and Peter

From TLS, *September 17, 1983, pp. 5–6. Reprinted by permission of Robert Wolker.*

Singer, in such a way as to seem unobjectionably sound common sense. Although most of the book's thirty chapters are too short to carry sufficient conviction, and some contributors, particularly those with greatest primatological expertise, show precious little interest in the rights, as distinct from the behaviour, of apes, their collection pursues some sensible arguments which both underlie and illustrate the editors' central theme.

Who can doubt that the human race has been grievously inattentive to the welfare of other species? In our commercial exploitation of Nature and our conduct of scientific experiments on animals, we have too often regarded the world we inhabit as fit only for our own use, its other life forms our property, over which we have an absolute title, irresponsibly exercised. Two of the contributors, Roger and Deborah Fouts, rightly observe that in such disregard for other creatures modern man has been influenced by the Cartesian portrayal of the rest of brute creation as mindless and insensate machines, but many societies spared such a doctrine have been similarly indifferent to the suffering of animals. We can only share Jane Goodall's bewilderment at the illegality of medical experiments on brain-dead human beings while they are tolerated on alert, feeling and intelligent chimpanzees.

The editors are also right to stress that it is because great apes are so often used in laboratory experiments that they need special protection, all the more because they are unable to fight for themselves. Slaves, we are reminded, did not generally win their freedom for themselves either. Christoph Anstötz's suggestion that apes should be entitled to rights on the same grounds as handicapped persons raises more questions about our perception of their nature than about their licence to share some of the benefits of ours, but plainly if human rights have any validity, they do not belong only to those who can always secure them unaided. Above all, perhaps, in their focus on the nexus of ethology and ethics, the editors rightly emphasize the normative and even radical character of their enterprise, which seeks to extrapolate to other species the equal respect we owe indiscriminately to all persons. Where sociobiologists have sought to subsume human nature into a determinist world whose patterns leave little room for moral choice or kindness to strangers, Cavalieri and Singer proceed instead from the righteousness of humans to our responsibility for other creatures. Instead of plumbing the darker depths of our animal nature, they would, by their unspecific benevolence, have apes join the ascent of man. Theirs is an uplifting spectacle of inexhaustible solicitude.

It is, of course, also a political campaign, which aims at "freeing all imprisoned chimpanzees, gorillas and orangutans and returning them to an environment that accords with their physical, mental and social needs." The editors appeal for others to join them in this enterprise, but such exhortations create mistrust at least as often as they gain friends. To some radicals, the law of the conservation of energy entails other priorities, and in pleading the rights of apes while thousands of our fellow humans are being slaughtered or tortured, animal liberationists, like stalking groupies at Crufts, seem oblivious to greater harm. Marx himself, in *The Communist Manifesto,* judged the animal rights activists of his day conservative, antirevolutionary and bourgeois. Primatologists are also sometimes unsettled by advocates of the rights of apes, as was evident at the *Pithecanthropus* centennial symposium held at the end of June in Leiden, to commemorate the fossil discovery of the ape-man now most commonly termed *Homo erectus.* To its critics, including those, with no less concern for the welfare of animals, the uniquely human language of rights is inappropriately anthropomorphic when applied to other animals, which ought not to be encumbered, even for their own apparent benefit, with the moral accoutrements of cosmopolitan civilization. The rights of man might be attributed to all the members of our species, but if this peculiarly modern, individualist and Eurocentric conception of humanity has so little purchase even throughout the civilized world, how can it be supposed to apply to other animals as well? In projecting a community of equals across species, the abolitionists of ape slavery appear, at least to some of their detractors, to form the exoteric and theosophical wing of Amnesty International.

Sociobiologists, having appropriated much of the language of the social sciences to which they object in order to make their explanations of animal life intelligible and coherent, all too characteristically lose their way when confronting the great apes, most especially the orangutan, which is as remote in its behaviour from the invertebrates they know best as any other creature apart from man. Would-be liberators of apes risk making equally mistaken transpositions in the opposite direction, for the projection of essentially human rights to chimpanzees, gorillas and orangutans on the presumption that they are our nearest relatives grants them a status they neither want nor need (from the available evidence), and out of the best of motives thereby does them a disservice. The editors' Declaration on Great Apes is fundamentally flawed for that reason alone, the weakness of their case most apparent from the ways they attempt to draw apes closer to mankind in order to partake of the same rights—above all in the imputed manner of their communication with us, and in contributors' claims about the similarity of their genes to ours.

As this work shows, the intelligence of apes has been well established by research undertaken over the past thirty years. Apes have quite distinctive personalities, and whatever we might imagine to be the role of the individual in human history, particular chimps, Jane Goodall argues, make a difference to chimp history. They embrace one another, they swagger, they grieve for their dead and are capable of altruism. Francine Patterson and Wendy Gordon report that Koko the gorilla chuckled when an inattentive researcher accidentally sat on a sandwich. After eleven years of separation from them, Washoe, now in semi-retirement in Washington but still very much the *grande dame* among the recent subjects of primatological studies, recognized and signalled to her first tutors, the Gardners. There is reason to believe that apes themselves classify other animals, and when grooming their young they have appeared to berate bad behaviour for its brutishness. But are apes more intelligent, affectionate or distinctive in their personalities than dolphins or cats? No one can tell. Are they more numerate, or do they have a better grasp of language, than parrots? Patient experts of psittacine cognition doubt it.

Of course, because they resemble us physically apes have, for very much longer than any other creatures, been the subject of investigations to establish that language is not unique to mankind. That interest alone merits critical scrutiny, since wild apes in their communication with one another show no sign of having developed a natural language, while the symbolic representations and incipient grammatical forms of their laboratory exchanges with investigators sometimes seem contrived to turn apes into children rather than to draw man back to Nature. Like La Mettrie and Lord Monboddo, who in the eighteenth century imagined that properly trained apes might eventually come "the length of language" under the tuition of the Chevalier de l'Épée in Paris or in Dr. Braidwood's classes for the deaf in Aberdeen, the Kelloggs in the 1930s and then the Hayes in the 50s tried to coax chimpanzees to speak in an agreeable domestic environment. More recent experiments since the 1960s have been based mainly on American Sign Language or a variety of lexigraphical markers, but the numerous trials thus far conducted by the Gardners, Premacks and Rumbaughs, and by Francine Patterson and Herbert Terrace, have all proved at best inconclusive, with researchers who hold more rigorous standards of linguistic competence (the Premacks and Terrace) generally disappointed at mature apes' apparent lack of conceptual inventiveness beyond that of a two-year-old child, and the less exacting (most notably Sue Savage-Rumbaugh, among current researchers) finding expressive creativity within an ape repertoire of natural gestures which do not just imitate their tutors' signs. Before they can fly, apes must jump, insist commentators who believe that the linguistic gulf between man and beast has already begun to vanish. To jump is not to embark on flight, the doubters retort, responding to experimental apes' brittle progress like anxious financiers of a stillborn Hollywood block-buster misled by their own publicity.

Since rights are conceptual abstractions intelligible only within a reasonably sophisticated language, these questions have a profound bearing on any rights-based imputation of moral equality to apes. They are here largely ignored, however, by editors and contributors alike. The mentally disabled, and perhaps human foetuses as well, may have rights without any command of language, but that can only be true with reference to abilities they once possessed, or with better fortune could have been expected to possess, or shall in time acquire or regain. Setting aside the alarming evidence of contemporary history which threatens to confirm it, the hypothesis that all of mankind might be mentally handicapped would be difficult to sustain and, if true with respect to language, would render our rights unintelligible, except to gifted aliens or God.

If apes are to have rights, moreover, then their right to remain silent and aloof from excessively solicitous linguistic researchers ought to be one of them. Is their detention for the sake of eliciting utterances not a deprivation of their liberty and a form of mental torture comparable to other experiments at their expense? No one is more sensitive to such matters than Roger Fouts, whose uniquely patient resolve to allow chimpanzees to sign (an admittedly borrowed) language on their own initiative has begun to show striking, if still modest, results in Washoe's self-appointed instruction of her adopted son, Loulis. In the Enlightenment, scientific commentators on human nature were already convinced that language forms the crucial divide between mankind and all other species, and they speculated about its origins and history, and about the physical or moral reasons for its absence among apes. "Parle, et je te baptise," dared the Cardinal de Polignac to the chimpanzee at the Jardin du Roi in Paris. Small wonder, Rousseau reflected in a letter to Hume, following widespread reports of ape political assemblies in the forest, that it was a trick of monkeys that they wisely pretend to be mute. If she wishes later generations of apes to remain free, Koko ought to feign her own stupidity instead of chuckling at the blunders of her human companions.

In support of the editors' contention that our "fellow apes" are our "closest relatives," some contributors lay stress on evidence drawn from molecular biology and evolutionary genetics to the effect that the biological distance separating us from the chimpanzee is only 1.6 percent, with a 2.3 percent divergence from the gorilla and a fraction more from the orangutan. It is, above all, the alleged evidence of DNA sequences which justifies their embrace of the chimpanzee, pygmy chimpanzee, gorilla and orangutan, together with humans, within a single family of apes, since it suggests a common ancestry to all these species some 12 to 16 million years ago, with our divergence from the chimpanzee perhaps occurring only in the past 7 million years. In connection with the same putative family tree, Richard Dawkins observes that "there is no natural category that includes chimpanzees, gorillas and orangutans but excludes humans."

One might have supposed that testimony drawn from the House of Atreus or from domestic violence throughout human history would make proponents of an interspecific confraternity of the righteous look elsewhere than to our immediate relatives for good reasons to bind us to perform our duties. But as presented here, the case for our equal treatment of other beings which share our ancestry is grossly misleading. If the research on DNA hybridization (by Sibley, Ahlquist, Yunis, Prakash, Koop and others) which informs it is borne out by palaeo-anthropological findings, then the orangutan, whose first appearance is on this evidence supposed to predate the common ancestry of the gorilla, chimp and human phylum, will, like the poor gibbon and siamang (otherwise regarded as great apes but ignored throughout this collection), have to be cast out of our family. If on the same DNA evidence we elect to invent an even more recent common ancestor, gorillas will also have to go the way of all flesh—deprived, by their loss of an imputed consanguinity, of their membership of our select club. Through such genetic conjectural history, the identity of our most remotely acceptable precursor in effect depends upon our choice of relatives.

But what is the point of emphasizing crude transcriptions of complex nucleotide sequence data in the absence of behavioural similarities across species which that evidence can be held to explain? Are we to suppose that our mere 1.6 percent genetic divergence from the chimpanzee, as distinct from the 98.4 percent identity, holds the key to the neurological differences between our species and to the development, in humans, of the sublaryngeal vocal tract which, on alternative suppositions, have made language possible? Or that it must therefore be culture after all and not our genes which determine our nature? The simplest invertebrates also share much of our genetic material; on the DNA criteria offered as the fount of our moral equality, we might as well recommend that a few fruit-flies join together to claim the rights of one man.

It is plain from their epilogue that the editors are reluctant to demarcate new boundaries between animal species which would leave mankind with obligations only within the great ape family as they define it. Yet that is precisely what their project achieves, with the flimsiest justification, threatening the identity and damaging the needs of species on either side of their fresh cleavage. Outside, abandoned in the wilderness, will be tigers, whales and other endangered species whose lack of the requisite genetic material in an arrangement sufficiently similar to that of humans must exclude them from that great ark of the righteous, the ape community of equals. Inside, chimpanzees, gorillas and orangutans will be greeted as our disabled brethren, endowed by their Creator with equal rights, albeit not as equal as ours. The editors suggest that, released from captivity to their African and other homelands on the model of slaves to Liberia, apes will henceforth be as free as the rest of us, perhaps not quite fit to enjoy all our rights, Steve Sapontzis adds helpfully, but at any rate free to enjoy all the rights fit for them.

There must be a better way to demonstrate goodwill to animals. Utilitarians in particular, like Peter Singer, ought to find the language of needs more congenial in an account of the moral status of apes than the language of rights. In abandoning their Declaration of the rights of apes, its authors might at least begin with the alternative principle that membership of another species is not of itself a warrant for subjection to maltreatment. If we wish to protect apes from human abuse and enable them to lead lives more in accord with their own preferences, we ought first to ensure that we do not make it our business to recast their nature in the image of man.

Discussion and Assignments

1. Wokler claims there is a "linguistic gulf" between the great apes and humans. What does he mean by this? What evidence does he cite to support his claim a gulf exists? How is this gulf connected to the discussion of rights for great apes?

2. Why does Wokler insist that teaching apes language is an infringement of their liberty? Do you believe this is a legitimate criticism? Why or why not?

3. What is Wokler's position on the high percentage of identity of DNA between great apes and humans? How does he relate the identity of DNA to the *differences* found between humans and apes? What is of most importance for Wokler with respect to the discussion of rights for great apes, the identity of DNA between apes and humans, or the observable differences between the species?

4. If great apes had a closer identity of DNA to humans, say, 99.99 percent, but still differed in all other respects as they do now, do you believe this would change Wokler's opinion on bestowing rights on great apes? What do his comments on gibbons, siamongs, and orangutans tell you about his views on TGAP's efforts to group humans with the great apes?

5. In closing his article Wokler states the "language of needs" would be preferable to the language of rights in demonstrating our goodwill toward animals. What does he mean by this? Is he clear on this point? Does he imply the language of needs might benefit *all* animals? How about humans?

6. According to Wokler, if we grant rights to great apes and welcome them into a common moral community, what does this imply for our relations with other animals? How would our relations with other animals be affected?

10.5 Rights for *Homo Sapiens*

AS TOLD TO JOHN BIGNALL

DON'T GET ME WRONG, I'm as tolerant as the next ape, but some notions human beings come up with make me want to scratch. Still, was it not the poet Schiller who said "Mit der Dummheit kampfen Gotter selbst vergebens"? We heard it, earwigging down the anthropologists' camp, me and Eric.

From Lancet *353, no. 9153 (1999): 610. Reprinted with permission.*

There's this Great Ape Project (GAP) in New Zealand (*New Scientist,* Feb. 13, 1999, pp. 20–21), which wants the New Zealand government to pass a law giving rights to apes—the right to life, the right not to suffer cruel or degrading treatment, and the right to take part in only "benign" experiments. Because us apes are intelligent, sensitive, humorous, literate, and all that, just like them.

We worked it out, me and Eric, what these GAP people were up to. Nothing to do with apes. All to do with a subspecies of *Homo sapiens* having a fit of bad conscience. It's them that kills us, locks us up, tortures us. If they want to give themselves rights to stop doing so, then they ought to go ahead, and not pretend they're giving us something. And whilst they're at it, would they leave off chopping down the places we live in and—this is Eric's—give over snooping on our private lives?

Phylogenetically and philosophically, though, there are deeper waters. Why rights only for great apes (gorillas, chimpanzees, bonobos, and orangutans)? Why not gibbons too? Maybe gibbons don't know their Schiller from their Schubert, but it doesn't seem right. And what about monkeys? Just because they've got tails (and are a darned sight easier to catch than apes), is it okay to lock them up and give them AIDS?

So, when we got back up and had a laugh with the others, we decided to grant *Homo sapiens* some rights (full text on http://www.unchr.ch/udhr/lang/eng.htm). Article 1 is "All human beings are born free and equal in dignity and rights. They are endowed with reason and conscience and should act towards one another in a spirit of brotherhood." Some hope.

Discussion and Assignments

1. Bignall argues TGAP is not about apes at all but rather about humans experiencing a fit of bad conscience about the way the great apes have been treated. If humans want to stop killing and mistreating the great apes, they can, without giving rights to apes. What role do you believe conscience plays in TGAP?

2. Bignall asks why TGAP doesn't include gibbons and monkeys in their project. What is the rationale for his objection? Is this an effective objection?

Concluding Questions and Observations

1. Wokler closes his article with an eloquent objection to The Great Ape Project. He cautions the reader that in trying to help the great apes we may actually be doing them, and by implication, ourselves, a disservice by recasting their nature in the image of man. What does he mean by this? What implications do you see coming from such a mistake if Wokler's appraisal is accurate? Do you think a similar objection can be made with respect to how we view other animals besides apes, and perhaps other humans? When we view humans or other species, do we refashion their characters or identities in our own image, instead of understanding and appreciating them for what they are in themselves?

2. If roughly the same state of affairs can be achieved for great apes, with or without rights, would conferring rights be preferable in any way to not conferring rights?

Chapter 11

Zoos

Background

OF THE MANY FUNCTIONS modern zoos perform for their communities, there are three basic goals they strive to keep in balance: (1) educating the public about animals; (2) preserving species and helping conserve the habitats of animals; and (3) attracting visitors to the zoo in a fashion that makes the outing enjoyable. But zoos have found the challenge of living up to diverse expectations can be difficult since education, preservation and conservation, and entertainment, are not always the most compatible goals. Once taken for granted as recreational mainstays of local city governments, zoos have often been on the defensive over their treatment of animals and lack of clearly defined goals. Often criticized for their substandard facilities, many modern zoos have come late to more sophisticated preservation, conservation, and education efforts. The difficulties in keeping animals in environments where their psychological and physical needs can be met have led some critics to question whether we need zoos at all.

What is the *purpose* of a zoo? Are we justified in caging wild animals in zoos? What exactly do we *mean* when we say an animal is a *wild* animal, and how are we to understand *wildness* in the context of a zoo? In an age where television and movie documentaries invite us to view animal behavior we would never experience in person, can we justify keeping animals in enclosures for us to observe? How can zoos justify keeping certain animals, like bears, in barren enclosures where they have little room to move about, forever pacing back and forth? Can children acquire a genuine understanding and develop a sense of respect, an affinity, for other species in the context of a zoo? In response to such inquiries defenders of zoos claim it's possible to adapt their environments to the needs of the animals they keep, and to make important contributions to conservation and preservation as well. For example, many zoos have created *enrichment* environments for their animals, enclosures tailored specifically for their physical and psychological needs.

The most radical critics advocate the eventual closing of all zoos. More moderate critics tend to focus on eliminating what they believe to be the worst abuses—the keeping of whales and polar bears, for example—and improving conditions for the animals that remain in zoos. The following two papers focus on various ethical issues, pro and con, that arise from keeping animals in zoos.

Both contributions to this study section were written especially for *The Thinking Reader* by Holly Penfound and Steven St C. Bostock.

Readings

Article 11.1 Holly Penfound is a cofounder of Zoocheck Canada, a registered charity that monitors the welfare of animals in zoos. Penfound has extensive experience in assessing animal behavior within the context of zoos. She is also an authority on the keeping of animals in large-scale aquariums. In *Rattling the Cage: Protecting Wild Animals from Zoos,* Penfound raises numerous animal welfare issues associated with keeping animals in zoos. She claims zoos have not been particularly successful in breeding endangered species and returning them to the wild. She also claims educational programs of zoos have done a poor job in raising the awareness of children about animals and their habitats. Many animals in zoos, she insists, live in impoverished conditions, within the limited confines of cement and gunite enclosures, their instincts suppressed by their artificial surroundings. Penfound recommends zoos refocus their efforts on three basic goals: habitat protection, the elimination of the wildlife trade, and other field conservation strategies. She closes her article by offering suggestions on how zoos might formally evaluate their efforts at keeping animals. For those zoos that do not adhere to rigorous standards for keeping animals in accordance with their special needs, her recommendation is clear: they should be closed down.

Article 11.2 Stephen St C. Bostock earned his Ph.D. in philosophy from Glasgow University. He teaches at Glasgow University and is the education officer at Glasgow Zoo. Among his publications are *Zoos and Animal Rights: The Ethics of Keeping Animals,* and the article "Zoos and Zoological Parks" in the *Encyclopedia of Applied Ethics.* Bostock sees zoos playing several important roles. Among the most important, zoos educate us in the ways of animals and habitats we would otherwise not experience, and they conserve endangered species at times with the assistance of computer technology to maximize diversity in gene pools. Bostock's definitions of what it means to be a *wild* animal, and what it means to be a wild animal in a zoo, help set the stage for his discussions concerning the justifiability of keeping animals in zoos, and how best to care for their needs. Central to Bostock's argument for keeping animals is creating *enrichment* environments to compensate for the lack of natural habitats. A created environment, though it need not replicate the animal's natural habitat, must be natural and complex enough to accommodate the animal's physical and psychological needs. If this can be accomplished, then a fundamental requirement for keeping the animal in a zoo will have been met.

11.1   Rattling the Cage: Protecting Wild Animals from Zoos

Holly Penfound

A ONCE VENERABLE INSTITUTION, zoos are increasingly the subject of controversy. Theories such as animal rights, utilitarianism and environmental holism are invoked to assess the morality of incarcerating wild animals in zoos. Depending on one's ethical stance, zoos may be justified on the basis of helping individual animals (rescue and rehabilitation), conserving species, educating the public or simply entertaining people.

The purpose of this paper is not to debate the ethical issues surrounding captivity, nor to debunk the conservation and education rationale used to defend zoos, although these issues are touched upon. Rather, this essay focuses on the animal welfare aspects of captivity. It argues that vast numbers of zoo animals endure lives of misery and deprivation, the captive environment failing—or being unable—to satisfy their most basic biological and behavioural needs. The poor track record of the zoo industry, even by its own standards, is exposed. The reader is provided with tools for assessing captive wildlife facilities. The zoo industry is challenged to act now to protect wild animals from the harmful aspects of captivity, or to be dragged kicking and screaming into the new millennium.

Conservation and Education Myths

Captive propagation in zoos is often touted as the saviour of the world's threatened or endangered species. Yet, with more than 10,000 zoos in existence worldwide, a minuscule percentage of threatened or endangered species—especially reptiles, amphibians, fish and invertebrates—are represented in less than 100 captive breeding programs. Of these, the success stories are few and far between. Little more than a dozen released species have established self-sustaining populations in the wild. And most of these were *not* the result of zoo-based initiatives. Beyond captive breeding, with one or two exceptions, the zoo industry has failed to allocate a significant

level of resources to what should be the real target of species preservation efforts: habitat protection, elimination of the wildlife trade and other field conservation strategies.

Equally questionable is the efficacy of education programs delivered by zoos. Despite years of claiming to impart knowledge about animals and their ecosystems, and to establish a conservation ethic in the public that translates into direct action to protect wild animals and their habitats, there is scant empirical evidence that zoos achieve these goals; in fact, some studies refute those claims.

In a 1989 study that included a review of the scientific literature, Dr. Stephen R. Kellert (Yale University) and Dr. Julie Dunlap (The Humane Society of the United States) noted that even at the largest zoos a "relatively small proportion of available personnel, resources and status are typically allocated to the educational function." They concluded that the "actual educational impact of the modern zoological park may be quite limited." At one zoo, Kellert and Dunlap found "a significantly greater negativistic and dominionistic attitude to animals among visitors . . . , particularly following the zoo visit." They failed to observe any appreciable increase in either factual or conceptual knowledge of animals and their ecosystems, nor in wildlife conservation. They concluded that education is regarded by zoo visitors as an arduous form of work. People go to the zoo to be entertained.[1]

Although surveys have shown that Americans, especially children, increasingly rely on zoos as their main contact with nature, this doesn't appear to translate into increased knowledge about the natural world around them. According to David Hancocks, a former director of the Woodland Park Zoo in Seattle and the Arizona-Sonora Desert Museum (a zoo featuring wildlife

---

1. Dr. Stephen R. Kellert & Dr. Julie Dunlap, *Informal Learning at the Zoo: A Study of Attitude and Knowledge Impacts* (Report to the Zoological Society of Philadelphia of a Study Funded by the G.R. Dodge Foundation, July 1989).

This article was written especially for this text.

of the southwestern United States), a study conducted by the science staff of the museum found that children in southern Arizona were profoundly ignorant about the natural world around them, a condition which Mr. Hancocks speculates is universal.[2] Sadly, only one-third of the children in that study had ever spent even half an hour alone in a wild place. Considering the mounting environmental crisis we face, there seems to be something foolish, if not immoral, about zoos and aquariums convincing an unsuspecting public that they are a reasonable facsimile of wild nature, and then failing to deliver the goods.

Setting aside the conservation/education debate, there is one issue about which there appears to be widespread agreement—at least in principle. So long as wild animals are kept in captivity, they ought to be treated humanely. This reflects a broadly held value enshrined in the statutes of many nations that animals have a right to protection from cruel treatment. How, then, we define humane or cruel treatment of wild animals becomes a pivotal point in this debate.

The Way Zoos Keep Animals

The view that many species of animals have the ability to suffer physically, mentally and emotionally is well established in the animal sciences. There is a developing body of literature regarding the requisite conditions for properly keeping certain species of animals in captivity. Taking the natural history of the species into consideration, a captive environment should be complex enough to compensate for the lack of natural freedom and choice, and to evoke the expression of the biological and behavioural nature of the wild captive.

This principle has been widely espoused by the modern zoo community in various articles, books, television documentaries and conferences, many of which have brought together zoo leaders and animal protectionists in an effort to find common ground.

It also seems to have popular support. A public opinion poll conducted in the United Kingdom showed that 82% of respondents agreed that

"more people are worried about keeping animals in zoos compared with 10 years ago," and 80% of respondents agreed "they are concerned about the welfare of animals kept in zoos." Sixty-two percent agree that "animals kept in zoos suffer physically or psychologically."[3]

A 1999 study conducted by Dr. Kellert found that "90% of Americans object to captive display of marine mammals in zoos and aquariums unless the animals are well cared for, and demonstrate results in education and scientific benefits."[4]

Yet despite the best of intentions or claims, *most* animals in captive wildlife exhibits throughout North America are still consigned to miserable lives, in small, impoverished enclosures that fail to meet their biological and behavioural needs. The fact that a largely uninformed public fails to recognise the characteristics of suffering these animals display and continue to flock to zoos and aquaria in large numbers (reportedly more than 350 million people visit zoos worldwide annually, more than 100 million of these in the United States) is no excuse for the zoo industry to hide or tolerate the abuse of animals.

Many in the zoo community will bristle at the above characterization as they point to the numerous improvements in the zoo field today. The mounting crisis of wildlife extinction and habitat loss, coupled with a growing awareness of the natural history of wild animals, has led to an evolution in zoos and zoo animal husbandry over the past half century. With a shift from entertainment as the primary purpose, some zoos have reinvented themselves as "zoological" or "conservation" centres with an emphasis on conservation, education and scientific study. In some cases, the display of animals in barred, sterile cages, grouped haphazardly with no biological or geographic relevance,

2. David Hancocks, "Adieu to the Zoo?" (Proceedings of Conservation and Animal Welfare—A New Era in Europe?, London School of Economics, 1995), p. 5.

3. *The Zoo Inquiry* (London, UK: World Society for the Protection of Animals & Surrey, UK: The Born Free Foundation, 1994), p. 11.
4. Excerpt from a press release dated June 21, 1999, issued by The Humane Society of the United States entitled "Study reveals American perceptions of marine mammals; Most Americans favor preservation over commercial exploitation," in reference to a study by Dr. Stephen R. Kellert, Yale University School of Forestry and Environmental Studies, *American Perceptions of Marine Mammals and Their Management* (Washington, DC: The Humane Society of the United States, May 1999).

has been replaced by more naturalistic, multi-species "habitats" and "landscape immersion environments" allowing both animal and visitor a more natural experience. But do they really?

Setting aside the ethical debate about whether or not wild animals ought to be kept in zoos in the first place, it is true that some facilities provide exhibits in which the inhabitants quite likely wouldn't know they're in captivity, for example, some of the well-designed enclosures for some invertebrates, fish and small mammals. It is also true for other species whose activities are inherently limited by captivity, some zoos provide adequate, even excellent, environments. The 8,000 acres, replete with woods, fields and streams, of the multispecies exhibit for bears, bison and other animals at the St. Felicien Zoo in Quebec (Canada) comes to mind.

But these positive stories are few and far between. Indeed, high-profile institutions with multimillion dollar exhibits like San Diego Zoo, New York Wildlife Conservation Park (formerly the Bronx Zoo), National Zoo in Washington, D.C. and Toronto Zoo in Canada mask the many underlying animal welfare problems within the zoo industry.

Naturalistic enclosures have their own problems. Many features of these exhibits are cosmetic, with no biological or behavioural function for the animal. They contain many artificial surfaces and "greenery" composed of moulded concrete, gunite, epoxy resin, plastic or metal. Animals are kept away from live vegetation with electrified wires, often reducing their real living space to barely larger than the sterile, rectangular, barred cages of days gone by. These, in fact, are still used in the off-display service areas where many zoo animals spend the majority of their lives after the zoo closes down for the day.[5]

If not all is well behind the invisible bars of North America's more luxurious zoos, a more transparent problem is found in the majority of captive wildlife exhibits that continue to keep animals in blatantly impoverished conditions using the old-style, menagerie format of displaying animals in small, barred or wire-meshed, rectangular or round, concrete-based enclosures, with little or no provision for the biological or behavioural needs of the species.

Typical of these clearly substandard zoos, investigators have observed tigers lying prostrate from the full glare of the hot summer sun, with no protection from the elements; monkeys with no branches to climb or swing from; dozens of black bears begging for marshmallows as they sit in a moat of dirty water, scarred and wounded from fighting in their overcrowded conditions; a small monkey in a parrot-cage, his tail a bloody stump from stress-derived self-mutilation; a pop-drinking polar bear, swaying back and forth in a monotonous, psychotic dance, housed for years in a small cage, with nothing but a bathtub to dip in instead of the vast Arctic Ocean; a cougar kept in a tiled, monotonous rectangular enclosure, the space broken only by a mural of trees painted on the wall for the viewing pleasure of the zoo visitor; predator and prey species kept in close proximity, with no opportunity for sensory escape.[6]

Indeed by the zoo industry's own standards (which in the author's view do not necessarily constitute adequate standards) close to 90% of captive wildlife exhibits fail to make the grade. Of the estimated 200 or 300 public display facilities in Canada, only 29 or slightly more than 10% have been deemed to meet the standards of the Canadian Association of Zoos and Aquariums (CAZA).

In the U.S., out of the 1,800 to 2,000 licensed exhibitors of wild animals (which includes small exhibitors, travelling shows, educational programs using live animals, zoos and aquariums), about 183 are accredited by the American Zoo and Aquarium Association (AZA), equivalent to less than 10% of all facilities.[7] Not to mention the hundreds, if not thousands, of unregistered, unregulated situations throughout North America in

---

5. Hancocks, p. 4.

6. The situations described are factual accounts based on numerous zoo visits conducted by Zoocheck Canada Inc., a Canadian wildlife charity which has monitored zoos for 15 years. Similar conditions have been found by others including The Humane Society of the United States, the Born Free Foundation, the World Society for the Protection of Animals and author Peter Batten in his book *Living Trophies: A Shocking Look at the Conditions in America's Zoos* (New York: Thomas Y. Crowell Co., 1976) and in an unpublished manuscript he coauthored entitled *Living Trophies Revisited* (Peter Batten & Suzanne Batten, [Lincoln City, Oregon: n.d.]).

7. Telephone conversation with Richard Farinato, Director, Captive Wildlife Protection Program, The Humane Society of the United States, February 1, 1999.

which small numbers of wild animals are kept for personal amusement or commercial gain.

That animals in both modern and outmoded captive wildlife facilities suffer profound psychological and physical distress has been demonstrated through numerous observations of stereotypic behaviours in zoo animals. Usually a sign of mental disorder, these are aberrant, functionless, often self-destructive, repetitive behaviours such as pacing, weaving, head-bobbing, bar-licking, self-mutilation, tongue-playing, paw-sucking, copraphagy (eating of feces or vomit) and so on.

In her book *The Modern Ark—The Story of Zoos: Past, Present and Future*,[8] Vicki Croke describes an assessment of the San Diego zoo made in 1994 by Dr. Nicholas Dodman, a brain chemistry expert at Tuft's University School of Veterinary Medicine. Croke writes: "Dodman visited the San Diego Zoo in 1994 with his family. While everyone else was awed by the vast array of spectacular creatures, the scientist says he was shocked by this 'sterotyper's heaven.' Everywhere he looked, he saw bears pacing, elephants swaying and giraffes bobbing their heads. This man, who is unlocking the chemical mysteries of such behavior in domestic and zoo animals, claims at least 30 percent and perhaps as much as 50 percent of the animals he observed at the San Diego Zoo were indulging in this disturbing activity."

For some species, reproductive problems, premature death and high mortality rates suggest either poor quality of care in individual facilities, or the inappropriateness of keeping certain species in captivity when contrasted to wild conspecifics. Take, for example, orca whales: worldwide at least 134 orcas were taken into captivity between 1961 to 1997. One hundred and three of those whales, or 77%, are now dead. The average survival time in captivity was under 6 years. Most died before they reached their early twenties. In the wild, female orcas live an average of 50 years, but can live to the age of 80. Males live an average of 29 years, but can live to the age of 50. Since 1968, there have been 50 known pregnancies in captivity of which only 19 calves survived.[9] Shouldn't this tell us something about the inability of marine parks to

meet the biological and behavioural needs of these large, far-ranging, deep-diving, highly intelligent and social animals?

Zoos also produce a predictable livestock surplus annually through uncontrolled and inadvertent breeding. What happens to those animals? In a newspaper exposé, reporter Linda Goldston found that each year roughly 1,000 prized zoo animals from AZA accredited facilities in the United States, many of them endangered or threatened species, end up as victims of the multibillion-dollar-a-year exotic animal trade.[10] Many are sold to private collectors or substandard roadside zoos, auctioned off to the highest bidder or shot as trophies in what are tellingly called "canned hunts." Alarmingly, Goldston found that the largest numbers of animals disposed of in this manner came from facilities such as the renowned San Diego Zoo and its sister institution, the San Diego Wild Animal Park, as well as zoos in Buffalo, New York; Baton Rouge, Louisiana; Omaha, Nebraska; Fort Worth, Texas; Cincinnati and Cleveland, Ohio; Miami, Florida; and Denver, Colorado.

Clearly Some Animals Should Not Be Kept in Zoos

The fact that some species just don't do well in captivity is widely known and ignored. David Hancocks argues that "elephants should not be kept in zoos . . . and neither should other big, active, intelligent and inquisitive animals such as whales, dolphins, and bears. We simply cannot meet their behavioral and social and psychological needs adequately."[11]

Can we adequately accommodate the complex needs of chimpanzees in zoos, let alone meet any reasonable moral test, to justify incarcerating animals who are our evolutionary next of kin, known to share 98.4% of human DNA? Dozens of scientific studies have demonstrated that chimpanzees, by human standards, have the intelligence of

---

8. (New York: Avon Books, 1997).
9. Whale and Dolphin Conservation Society Web site, http://www.wdcs.org, August 18, 1999.

10. In the article, "Americas zoos have a little secret: They breed animals with no intention of keeping them" (*San Jose Mercury News*, February 7, 1999), reporter Linda Goldston published her investigation of the disposition of animals at 183 U.S. zoos accredited by the AZA and covering the period of 1992 to mid-1998.
11. Hancock, p. 9.

human youngsters. They have been shown to have rich emotional lives, self-awareness, language and culture, and many other attributes previously thought to be uniquely human.

Is it reasonable to think a small, sterile, concrete tank can provide a humane living environment for intelligent, social whales evolved to travel many miles in a day, migrate vast distances, dive to deep depths, socialize in large numbers, and generally experience the complex ocean environment with its vast array of life forms, varying weather conditions and ever-changing topography?

Fix Them, or Close Them

By using a mixture of common sense and knowledge of the animal sciences we can draw conclusions about the inappropriateness of keeping many species of wild animals in captivity from an animal welfare perspective. And we can prescribe meaningful standards of care and accommodation for those animals that will continue to be incarcerated. Many facilities should be closed down.

Numerous indicators can be evaluated such as the physical design and construction of enclosures, the physical and mental condition of the animals, mortality rates, and facility services and policies. The starting point is knowledge of the animal's wild habitat, physiology, behaviour and social organization. A better captive environment will be designed with biologically/behaviourally functional features that facilitate the natural expression of the animal's wild nature.

An assessment of the exhibit itself will be a strong indicator of the quality of animal care and housing. Relative to the natural history of the species being held, is the exhibit well designed? How much "usable" space, both horizontal and vertical, does the animal actually have? Are natural, behaviourally stimulating substrates provided for animals to burrow, forage, play and hide, or are animals exhibited on hard concrete or gunite surfaces? Are environmental conditions such as temperature, humidity, and ventilation controlled to satisfy the animals' needs? Is enrichment built into the exhibit (e.g., appropriate space, climbing apparatus, high grasses and ground cover, earth and sand pits, objects for manipulation and play, pools, etc.) and husbandry regime (e.g., food hide-and-search activities, simulated hunting, socialization activities, visual and olfactory stimulation, etc.)?

Are the exhibits sturdy and well maintained, or ramshackle and flimsy? Are safety measures (e.g., public stand-off barriers, double-gate entryways into cages, perimeter fencing, emergency first aid stations, etc.) in place to protect animals, staff and visitors?

The physical condition of the wild captives may provide clues to their well-being. Obvious signs of ill-health might include obesity or excessive loss of weight, appetitive disorders, skin conditions, wounds or scars, tumours or cysts, hair loss, limps or broken bones, and so on. Unfortunately, many symptoms of physical deterioration are invisible to the human eye or may take many months or years to manifest themselves. These include disease, loss of muscle tone, organ deterioration, abnormal hormone levels, ulcers, and old bone fractures. The responsible zoo keeper would be able to detect many of these conditions. Ironically, the irresponsible captive wildlife operator, who allows the problem to occur in the first place, is the least likely candidate to investigate or reveal the negative results of his/her actions. Reproductive problems, premature death and high mortality rates are also indicators of either poor quality of care in individual facilities, or the inappropriateness of keeping certain species in captivity.

A good captive environment should produce a high percentage of natural behaviours in captive charges similar to those seen in wild conspecifics. These might include characteristic forms of locomotion, feeding and appetitive behaviour, grooming and other maintenance activities, behaviours establishing social hierarchies and territories, breeding and play. Catalogues of naturally occurring behaviours, called ethograms, should be developed for species in the wild. Captive behaviour can then be measured against the ethogram benchmark to evaluate enclosure success. In fact, ethograms have been developed for very few species, let alone utilized to measure the behaviour of captive wildlife.

Conversely, the presence of abnormal behaviour is a strong indicator of an inadequate captive environment. Symptoms might include apathy, hyperactivity or abnormal aggression. Stereotypic behaviours referred to earlier in this essay are common in captive wild animals. Like the canaries in the mine shafts, these bobbing, weaving, self-mutilating captive animals are telling us something is very wrong in the zoo world.

It is mystifying that the more responsible zoo industry has not come to its senses and acknowledged the obvious. Our ever-increasing knowledge of the animal sciences and the expansion and accessibility of high-tech forms of communication are gradually creating an ever-sophisticated public on wildlife issues. Zoos can either voluntarily adopt humane policies and practices, push for the closure of substandard facilities and advocate for laws to improve conditions, or be dragged kicking and screaming into the new millenium.

Once the cage is rattled, and the hidden truth about the appalling way we incarcerate and treat the other beings that inhabit this earth is revealed, the zoo profession will be forever tarnished for its betrayal of public trust as the protector and conservator of wild animals and their environments.

Discussion and Assignments

1. In her third paragraph Penfound claims zoos have virtually failed in their captive breeding, conservation programs. She recommends that species preservation efforts of zoos instead focus on "habitat protection, elimination of the wildlife trade, and other field conservation strategies."

   Imagine for a moment that, instead of captive breeding programs and the exhibition of animals for zoo visitors, zoos shift their focus to conservation efforts on "habitat protection, elimination of the wildlife trade, and other field conservation strategies," as Penfound recommends. How might this shift in priorities affect the average zoo patron when he or she visits the zoo on an afternoon out? What practical advantages or disadvantages do you see for visitors to the zoo with such a shift in priorities? Do you see any implications for zoos, and their patrons, if zoos extend their reach to participate in conservation programs that take them beyond the confines of the zoo itself?

2. Penfound claims that education efforts of zoos are underfunded and ineffective, and that children don't experience an appreciable increase in knowledge of the natural world around them after a visit to the zoo. Does your personal experience coincide with Penfound's claims? Does Penfound state what she believes the educational goals of a zoo should be? What do you believe the educational goals of a zoo should be? How do think a zoo could best define its educational goals?

3. According to Penfound, of the thousands of animal exhibits in Canada and the United States, what percentage are accredited by the Canadian Association of Zoos and Aquariums or the American Zoo and Aquarium Association? What implications does she draw from these statistics?

4. What is *stereotypic* behavior? According to Penfound, how frequently is it found in animal exhibits? Are stereotypical behaviors also found in zoos that enjoy accreditation of the Canadian Association of Zoos and Aquariums or the American Zoo and Aquarium Association? What implications can you draw from the prevalence of stereotypical behaviors in zoo animals?

5. Penfound mentions some animals that, on occasion, are successfully kept in zoos. What animals are they? What criteria does she employ when making her judgment about their care?

6. Penfound claims there are some animals that should not be kept in zoos and aquariums.
   a. What animals does she offer as examples of those that should not be kept in zoos? What reasons does she give to support her claim that they should not be kept? How strong a case does she make for not holding them in captivity?
   b. Now answer the same questions for marine mammals (e.g., orca whales and dolphins) kept in aquariums. What reasons does she give to support her claim

they should not be kept? How strong a case does she make for not holding them in captivity?

c. What implications can you draw from *a* and *b*?

7. Many animals—other than large animals like bears, elephants, or whales—use quite a bit of space living in the wild, much more than most zoos can offer. Birds fly through the open sky, wolves hunt over sizable distances, penguins dive in the expanse of Antarctica. Even skunks use a fair bit of space wandering about. Judging from Penfound's criteria for assessing how well zoos care for their animals, do you think it's possible to employ such standards for the well-being of the animals—and still have a zoo or aquarium to visit?

8. Penfound offers criteria to assess a zoo's success in keeping animals. Briefly describe this criteria and how, according to her, it should be employed. Does her suggestion sound reasonable to you? Why or why not?

9. The term *wild animal* is used in the title of Penfound's article. Does she anywhere define what she means by *wild*? What example does she use to illustrate wildness? Do you find her use of the term adequate?

11.2 Defending Zoos

STEPHEN ST C. BOSTOCK

A RECENT AND ENTERTAINING correspondence in *The Times* (of London) concerned the surprising homing abilities of garden snails. The initial correspondent had marked a snail before throwing it out of his garden and across a road, and so could prove it kept coming back. There were serious comments from other letter-writers (e.g., comparing limpets' similar homing behaviour) or more frivolous ones (e.g., that snails come back for the ride). But everybody seemed to quite like snails. All except one woman correspondent who couldn't see why everyone didn't do the sensible thing she did whenever she found a snail in her garden— stamp on it. This upset me. Even if her concern for her plants impelled her to do this, I thought she should tell us apologetically, not blame others for lacking her callousness. Then it struck me how her attitude of complete nonappreciation of a living creature was unlikely to be that of anyone involved in zoos. For whatever zoos' faults, they exist in the end to show us animals. And there is no point in doing this except on the assumption that animals are worth looking at, that they are something to appreciate and enjoy having around rather than (where possible) grind under foot. True, zoos go

in usually for bigger animals than snails, but many zoo educators must have shown snails—probably African giant snails—to children as I have and received ample confirmation that to find a snail a thing of wonder is normal, not eccentric.

Some may object that the motivation behind zoos is not to admire animals but to make money. Most people, including those who run or work in zoos, have to earn money to live, but can still have a deeper motivation for choosing a particular way of earning a living. Indeed, if no one liked looking at animals, it would be impossible to make money out of running a zoo. It's also significant that jobs with animals rarely make a lot of money, but this doesn't lessen the demand for them—zoos receive numerous applications for jobs, and for work as volunteers also. And then think of the thousands of people who keep animals through choice, despite the work involved. Obviously animal keeping offers other satisfactions than making money, satisfactions likely to be experienced by those working professionally in zoos as well as by those keeping animals privately.

Several writers claim, however, that there's a quite different motivation underlying animal

This article was written especially for this text.

keeping—the showing of domination over them. This seems to me highly unlikely as an explanation of all animal keeping, if only because plenty of the animals kept, whether by private people or zoos, are small, gentle ones—mice or rabbits or budgerigars. Who on earth would want to dominate over these, and why? Keeping gorillas or lions or the like may carry a message about your superiority, and this may be a factor historically in the keeping of powerful animals by those who wanted to appear powerful. This wouldn't itself, incidentally, make any difference to the animals provided they were kept properly. Sometimes though the asserting of such superiority or dominance may involve explicit bullying of the animals—as perhaps illustrated by Assyrian kings fighting with their lions, perhaps by bullfighters today, or by rodeo riders. But the keeping of (say) gorillas or lions in first-rate enclosures (and I wouldn't defend any other way of keeping them) to me demonstrates respect for the animals, or at least has nothing to do with explicit bullying of them. I don't doubt that animals can function as status symbols; almost anything humans go in for can too—cars or country houses or Rolex watches. But this again does no harm in itself to the animals concerned provided they are looked after properly. So I wouldn't deny that a desire for dominance—but dominance over other humans rather than over animals—may play a part in some animal keeping. But it can hardly be the main motivation, not least because keeping animals usually involves a lot of trouble. If you're *just* interested in status symbols, why not choose some other kind which doesn't involve so much bother?

The question of how animals are looked after brings us to what to me are much more serious challenges to my picture of zoos as benign places for admiring animals. Our motivation may be fine. But isn't zoo-keeping unacceptable in itself? Isn't it impossible to look after *wild* animals—such as zoos go in for—acceptably, and indeed cruel to deprive them of their freedom and their natural lives? And aren't zoos a betrayal of such animals' *rights*?

I think myself that animals do have rights, rights to proper treatment, and not to be hurt or killed, unless for a very serious reason. But *how* serious is serious? And why stop there? Why not grant animals the right to be left alone—except, say, where they endanger our lives? It would follow that we

shouldn't keep any animals at all, which is indeed the position of some supporters of animal rights. According to the philosopher Tom Regan, any animals that can "feel pain and pleasure, . . . anticipate the future," and so on, "should be treated as ends in themselves, never merely as means"; "human benefits are altogether irrelevant for determining how animals should be treated" (Regan, 1998, pp. 42–43). Think what granting animals such strong rights would involve. Here's one real life example. A population of mink in the Hebrides (the Scottish islands) is at present threatening the survival of much island wildlife, including various bird species. Haven't the islanders a right to try to exterminate the mink to save these other species? I think they'd be wrong to kill the mink cruelly (e.g., with painful poison). But wouldn't they be justified in killing the mink humanely (though I hope with more regret than the lady with the snails)?

In practice, I think we're bound to grant other animals less strong rights than we grant our fellow humans. Isn't it reasonable to allow the humane keeping of domestic animals: dogs and cats certainly, but also farm animals in good conditions? (In fact many domesticated animals—battery hens and some pigs, for example—are kept in very bad conditions, bad in particular because they are allowed almost no opportunity to show much of their natural behaviour.)

But is it wholly wrong to keep wild animals? And are zoo animals in fact wild animals? A fully wild animal is one living its natural life, wholly uninterfered with by man. Obviously that doesn't apply to zoo animals. But they are "relatively wild," to varying degrees, depending on whether they've been born in captivity (and if so, how many generations they are away from the wild), and also how tame, and well adjusted to the presence of humans they are. They may be to some extent selectively bred—perhaps unintentionally.

There is, I suggest, no simple "yes or no" answer to the question of whether or not a zoo animal is wild, and similarly there isn't to the question of whether it's in a state of well-being in a zoo. It depends on the conditions in which it's kept, and of course on what sort of animal it is. Can we judge? I think we can, using various criteria, primarily the degree of natural behaviour the animal shows. We should use the same criteria to judge the satisfactoriness of conditions for domestic animals. By the way, dogs still share a lot of behaviour with wolves, their wild ancestors, and other domestic animals similarly. So again there is no absolute distinction between wild and domestic animals.

But then, it may be said, the animals in zoos still shouldn't have been taken from the wild, or their ancestors shouldn't. The (fully) wild animals should surely be left there. I agree, normally speaking. As it happens, there isn't, I suggest, very much clash here between the position of the director (say) of a reputable zoo and an animal rights supporter, both of whom would agree that wild animals are normally better off in the wild. It's true zoos have in the past helped themselves unhesitatingly to animals from the wild, but that's not the position now. Most zoo mammals are captive bred. And according to the World Zoo Conservation Strategy, *no* animals should be taken from the wild except for serious conservational reasons, which would be decided on by zoo authorities in consultation with other conservation bodies such as IUCN. (I would think also that where particular wild animals—e.g., baboons—are regarded as a pest in their natural country and are being (say) exterminated, their being moved to a good zoo would be justifiable; it would be in the animals' own interests.)

As well as the degree of natural behaviour shown (including the animals' readiness to breed), the criteria I think we should use to judge animals' state in captivity would be the degree of unnatural behaviour such as stereotyped "weaving" (such as has often been seen in polar bears in zoos), the animals' physical health, and certain "direct indications"—such as some animals showing signs of well-being such as friendliness with their keepers, perhaps indulging in play, and also what I've called "theoretical assessment"—anything else that seemed relevant.

I would only defend the keeping of animals where they can be judged, by such criteria or similar ones, to be in a state of well-being. Some animals may well be ruled out by such criteria as unsuitable for being kept—polar bears may be an example.

I'd say that some animals, such as big herbivores, are fairly easy to keep satisfactorily. Marwell Zoo in England specialises in antelopes, zebras, and so on, keeping them in large enclosures. I don't think most people would be upset by this, though they may well be by giraffes (for example) in restricted enclosures in city zoos. Perhaps they're right. Animals such as big (or smaller) cats, bears, apes, monkeys and so on most obviously need conditions very different from the old-fashioned barred, concrete cages so many of us have seen, if they are to be kept. There is great attention now to enrichment, as it's often called, of enclosures for such animals particularly. Some may doubt that bears or gorillas, say, can possibly be kept satisfactorily. An example of how bears should be kept is the black bear enclosures at Glasgow Zoo, which include a wooded area, as well as an enclosure with a good deal of "enrichment"—climbing frames, a "honey tree," providing occasionally a trickle of honey or the like from a high branch, and food often provided in such a way that it has to be searched for—so that the bears (intelligent, exploratory animals) have frequent occupations not unlike what they'd have in the wild. An example of how gorillas should be kept is their enclosure at Howletts Zoo in Kent, England, which although not naturalistic (it doesn't look like a bit of rainforest) provides so much to do that it's like a gorilla holiday camp. Above all, it allows the gorillas to live there in a natural group. The essential guide for good conditions is that they should be based, so far as possible, on a knowledge of the animals' natural behaviour in their natural habitat. The best source of information on the latest in enrichment is *Second Nature* (Shepherdson et al. 1998). The American Zoo and Aquarium Association (AZA) is making great efforts (not least with this book, which they've helped to sponsor) to encourage all American zoos to put enrichment techniques into practice, and indeed this may be made a legal requirement in America for the running of a zoo.

But even if many animals can be kept satisfactorily, is there any real point in or justification for our keeping them? I would argue that there are considerable possible gains for humans (and perhaps even some for nonhuman animals too), which I want to look at briefly.

First, conservation. There are numerous possible problems with zoos' function of assisting conservation, even moral ones, such as the need to cull "surplus" individuals which don't fit into breeding programmes (zoos' capacity being severely limited), as well as practical problems, such as whether particular kinds of animals can be successfully reintroduced to the wild. Zoos' own special contribution of conservation by captive breeding is a supplement to the saving of habitats, not least because this saves thousands, even millions, of species—including innumerable invertebrates, instead of the few hundred "charismatic megavertebrates" which zoos can have much chance of saving. But conservation is so massively important, with the dangers of extinction arising from human population growth, as well as human greed causing poaching of rare animals, that any help is desirable. And zoos have impressive machinery at their disposal to help them to overcome the problems, most obviously genetic expertise supported by computer technology, making it possible to manage captive animals as genuine captive populations in which the gene pool is regulated so as to at least approach the diversity of the wild gene pool. There is also a striking range of ways in which zoos can assist conservation—so diverse, that it would seem foolish to disregard such possible assistance to a vastly important enterprise.

First there is captive breeding itself with the possibility of reintroduction, perhaps hundreds of years in the future after human populations have levelled out. The development of ISIS—International Species Information System—in the 1970s was a major step; there have been many further developments since then. Then the educational role of zoos, whether with the public, or with schools, is to a great extent conservationally useful in stimulating people to care about threatened species—on the principle that what they see and experience they care about much more, which seems reasonable enough. Many zoos also fundraise for the conservation of wild places, not least the rainforests. Just as ancient or fine archaeological sites or fine buildings have to be protected from being visited by too many people, so have actual wild places to be protected also. Here zoos, the better they become and the more naturalistic their enclosures, can do a useful job of fulfilling a lot of people's urge to visit wild places themselves. The famous Bronx Zoo of New York has long carried out many conservation projects in the field. But now many of the 180 or so zoos which are members of the AZA are beginning to do this too.

Zoos sometimes perform a useful scientific role, and a much more diverse one than at least one critic of zoos maintained in an article (Jamieson 1985). To a great extent now their scientific expertise is important as an underpinning of their conservational work. One remarkable, if exceptional, example of what can be learned scientifically in a zoo is Frans de Waal's *Chimpanzee Politics* (1982), which is based on observations at a marvellous enclosure in Arnhem Zoo in the Netherlands.

The educational role of zoos is now seen as very much a conservational role also, as I mentioned above. However the value of the educational opportunities in zoos has often been denigrated, never more so perhaps than by Randy Malamud recently, who argues, for example, that you don't only get a misleading view of a giraffe in a zoo, you don't get a view at all—the giraffe, by being in a zoo, ceases to be such (Malamud 1998, p. 29). Probably giraffes shouldn't be kept in zoos in the way they often are, or shouldn't be kept at all in zoos with restricted space. And perhaps the view we get of a giraffe in a zoo *is* seriously misleading compared to the view the African tourist gets of the animals in their natural habitat. But to go as far as Malamud does is absurd (interesting and disturbing though his literary study of zoos is); it would mean that those giant snails observed at close quarters in a zoo are not really snails at all (or similarly any other zoo animals you care to pick). In fact all animals have many aspects (remember the story of the elephant and the four blind men?), and much can be learned from the first-hand observation a zoo offers.

Remarkably it is computers, above all, which have made it possible for zoos to turn isolated groups of any particular species into a sort of virtual integrated population, and have thus made zoos' claims to be able to save many species an almost certain reality. But in another way zoos remain a bulwark against the sea of computerisation which threatens to divorce many of us from almost any contact with real life, in the way incidentally that E.M. Forster foresaw remarkably in his pre-1914 short story "The Machine Stops." Zoos keep (in some sense, pace Malamud) real animal—which have to be fed and coped with in all kinds of ways, and which you can sometimes touch (or of course smell). Some zoo critics look forward to the "virtual zoo," where there'll only be computerised animals. Such a zoo will be interesting. But it won't provide the satisfactions of being in the presence of real, live animals which "real" zoos offer—and I think acceptably, provided we can show the animals themselves not to be losing out by being in a zoo.

Further Reading

Bostock, S. St C., *Zoos and Animal Rights: The Ethics of Keeping Animals*, Routledge, London and New York 1993.

Bostock, S. St C., "Zoos and Zoological Parks," in R. Chadwick (ed.), *Encyclopedia of Applied Ethics*, Vol. 4, Academic Press, San Diego 1998.

Croke, V., *The Modern Ark*, Scribner, New York 1997.

de Waal, F., *Chimpanzee Politics*, Cape, London 1982.

Jamieson, D., "Against Zoos," in P. Singer (ed.), *In Defence of Animals*, Blackwell, Oxford 1985.

Malamud, R., *Reading Zoos: Representations of Animals and Captivity*, Macmillan, London 1998.

Norton, B.G., M. Hutchins, E.F. Stevens and T.L. Maple (eds.), *Ethics on the Ark: Zoos, Animal Welfare, and Wildlife Conservation*, Smithsonian Institution Press, Washington and London 1995.

Regan, T., "Animal Rights," in M. Bekoff (ed.), *Encyclopedia of Animal Rights and Animal Welfare*, Greenwood Press, Westport, USA 1998.

Shepherdson, D.J., J.D. Mellon and M. Hutchins, *Second Nature: Environmental Enrichment for Captive Animals*, Smithsonian Institution Press, Washington and London 1998.

Tudge, C., *Last Animals at the Zoo*, Oxford University Press, London 1992.

Discussion and Assignments

1. What is Bostock aiming to achieve with the first two paragraphs of his article? How effective is he in making his point, and how closely related are these introductory paragraphs to issues he raises throughout his paper?

2. a. How, according to Bostock, is domination over large, powerful animals related to domination over other humans? Do you agree or disagree with this assessment?

   b. Bostock claims domination over large powerful animals isn't necessarily bad. What must be done to make it acceptable for Bostock? In light of his comments about domination over animals, what do you think he would say about American rodeos? Taking Bostock's comments on domination of animals and humans into account, do you approve of American rodeos? Why or why not?

3. What *rights* does Bostock endorse for animals? How does he contrast his view of animal rights with the philosopher Tom Regan's view of animal rights?

4. How does Bostock define a *wild* animal? Do you find Bostock's treatment of *wildness* satisfactory? How does he define a *domesticated* animal? Is there a clear dividing line between a wild animal and a domesticated animal for Bostock? Are you satisfied with Bostock's definitions of the terms *wild* and *domesticated*, and how they apply to animals in zoos? Why or why not?

5. Study paragraph 7 where Bostock discusses wild animals in zoos. According to his criteria for judging *wildness,* could *any* animal in a zoo ever be considered completely wild? Is wildness in zoos, then, a matter of degrees? What factors does Bostock look for to determine how wild a zoo animal is?

6. What is *enrichment* in zoos and how has it been applied at the Glasgow Zoo? What is the goal of enrichment? From Bostock's description, do you believe the aims and accomplishments of enrichment are adequate to accommodate the needs of zoo animals?

7. Study Holly Penfound's section entitled "Clearly Some Animals Should Not Be Kept in Zoos" and other relevant comments she makes about not keeping certain animals in zoos. Compare her position on bears, chimpanzees, and other animals to Bostock's position on similar animals. Are their views similar? Different? What

role does *enrichment* play in each of their arguments about these types of animals?

8. Are there any animals Bostock claims should *not* be kept in zoos?

9. Penfound claims zoos accomplish very little in the way of educating children when they visit the zoo. What is Bostock's view on the educational function of the zoo? Can you find any common ground between the two on this point?

10. a. What are the two strongest pieces of evidence Bostock offers in the defense of zoos? Explain in a paragraph on each why each point is important in supporting his overall argument.

    b. What is the weakest piece of evidence he offers in defense of zoos? In a paragraph explain why you think it's weak.

Concluding Questions and Observations

1. a. Penfound sometimes uses the terms *incarcerate* and *held captive* to describe wild animals being kept in zoos. Provide a few examples of how we use these terms in everyday language. What kind of emotive value do you attach to these terms in everyday language? Do you think Penfound's use of these terms, in the context of animals and zoos, is effective for the purposes of her argument? Do you think it's an appropriate use of the terms?

    b. Bostock prefers to say animals are *kept* in zoos. Provide a few examples of how we use this term in everyday language. What kind of emotive value do you attach to the use of this term in everyday language? Do you think the use of this term, in the context of animals and zoos, is effective for the purposes of his argument? Do you think it's an appropriate use of the term?

2. Compare and contrast Bostock's views on species conservation efforts with Penfound's. Do you detect any important similarities or differences? Who do you believe makes the more convincing case, Penfound or Bostock?

3. Compare and contrast Bostock's and Penfound's use of the term *wild animal.*

4. Compare a visit to a zoo or zoological park to a visit to a museum or other cultural institution, for example, an art museum, a museum of anthropology, an aircraft and space flight museum, the local playhouse or symphony. Do the educational goals of zoos have anything in common with the educational goals of other cultural institutions you are familiar with? To what degree have zoos been successful in their efforts to educate the public? What specifically makes zoos more or less successful than other cultural institutions? What might they do to improve upon their educational missions? What might we reasonably expect a zoo to accomplish with its educational mission?

5. Imagine the following. Fast-forward twenty-five years. Great strides have taken place in creating enrichment environments for animals in zoos. Bears no longer pace in tiny enclosures, chimpanzees no longer self-mutilate, large cats have the room and luxury to hunt prey (though not always to the pleasure of zoo patrons). Enrichment, at least on appearance, seems to have satisfied the physical and psychological needs of the animals. What would such success mean in the overall equation of keeping or phasing out zoos? Should we have zoos, even if all the animals can be well cared for? Or should animals have a right to not be kept in zoos?

Chapter 12

Boxing

Background

IN THE JANUARY 14, 1983, issue of the *Journal of the American Medical Association* (*JAMA*), Dr. George Lundberg, editor of *JAMA,* and a colleague, Dr. Maurice W. Van Allen, declared that "boxing should be banned in civilized countries" (articles 12.2 and 12.3). Armed with new evidence that boxing presents great potential for eye injury and brain damage in boxers, they set their sights on nothing less than the complete abolition of the sport in the United States. While there was much discussion immediately after the appearance of their articles, they soon found they had not won enough converts outside the medical community. Nevertheless, the cause of the *JAMA* editor became a cause of the American Medical Association as well with its endorsement of a ban just over a year and a half later. The war on boxing, encouraged by continued research and reports of the medical establishment, continued into the 1990s, and gained an increasing body of supporters.

Doctors point out that boxing is a collision sport based on blows to the head and body. Unlike other collision sports, it's the aim of the boxer to render his opponent defenseless and "knock out" his opponent, to actually injure the brain of his opponent. A growing body of medical literature confirms what many boxing observers had suspected all along, that the frequency of brain and eye injuries to boxers is significant, the damage permanent and often devastating. The brain injury rate alone, not including eye and other types of injury, among boxers who box many fights is estimated at between 60 and 87 percent (article 12.4). And then there is the hardship often silently endured by families of boxers who live in anxiety and often care for their loved ones when their careers are over.

While boxing has always had its opponents, it has many supporters as well. An understanding of boxing and its mysterious attraction is found as much in its fans who watch, read, feud, and commune amongst themselves, as in the boxers themselves. Defenders of boxing point out there are other sports where injury, even death, are not unknown. Still, with boxing we have a unique blend of skill, isolation of combatants, savagery, and courage. Boxing can reach unusual heights by betraying that art and cruelty sometimes conspire, that the marriage of violence and grace can tell us as much about ourselves as those in the ring. In her book *On Boxing,* Joyce Carol Oates (article 12.9) argues that such physical, visceral experiences may be natural or essential expressions of the soul, and that we may be, in the end, as much informed by such expressions as we are repelled. Such experiences would seem to attest to the paradoxical nature of legitimizing boxing as a "sport." It is no surprise that the most effective arguments to be found for boxing are those that strive to balance a belief in personal rights and dedication to a kind of primal passion, with the stark realities of such a savage enterprise: ill health, brain damage, eye injury and blindness, possible death, and the ever present anxiety the families of boxers experience. Oates claims there is more than a trace of voyeurism in the act of watching a boxing match, a kind of vicarious participation in the forbidden. Even its long intimate relationship with the unsavory elements of society tells us the logic of boxing is not quite the same as with other sports.

If the perplexities of boxing inform us about ourselves, so also does boxing betray the secrets of others, institutions and the shaping of our collective preferences and prejudices. Ask any respected boxing trainer why boxing is good for the boxers he trains and you would be hard pressed to distinguish his voice from that of a Boy Scout leader extolling the virtues of scouting, or a minister attesting to the virtues of a religious life. If the boxer listens to his trainer he will stay off drugs, learn the importance of establishing goals and accept the sacrifices required to attain them, learn self-discipline and self-respect, cultivate an increased sense of self-confidence and self-esteem, and, as important as all the prior, learn to respect others. Aberrations like Mike Tyson aside, boxing, it is claimed, builds character.

For many youth and young men, especially minorities from poorer neighborhoods, boxing offers an accepted cultural path to personal virtue, societal acceptance, even self-realization. The danger and sense of forbiddenness, complete isolation of its combatants, the physical construction and placement of the ring for viewing of the combatants, the realization that a fight well executed is a personal victory no matter the outcome—all of this and more yields a continual process of personal overcoming for the boxer. And though fame and money are no doubt fundamental driving forces for the boxer and the overall equation of boxing, only the critic with blinders mistakes these ingredients as exclusive. Boxing is as much a testament to our culture as it is a sport, if indeed it can be regarded as a sport at all. Former heavyweight champion George Foreman characterized both boxing's uniqueness and its commonality with other sports when he said all other sports aspire to be like boxing. But though boxing may share some family resemblances with other sports, its relationship to them is closer to distant cousins than sisters, boxing's nourishments often being different in kind. It's not just the sociology of poverty that must be traversed for the critic to understanding boxing. Any boxer will insist that understanding is attained by intimating a passion deep inside, something simultaneously dark and light. Among boxing's many functions, metaphor is its most compelling.

Boxing is not practiced by so many on account of stupidity, inertia of the past, or ignorance of medical statistics. Few experienced boxers are persuaded to quit by statistics on eye injuries and brain damage. Indeed, with brain damage so intimately conjoined with the history and practice of the sport, the boxer might well retort that doctors would be better off studying football and race car driving. It is rare for an experienced boxer to claim he is ignorant of risk. It is unusual for participants from other sports to acknowledge risks rarely discussed in open, like race car drivers who sustain significant impacts to the head and body, and football players—even high school students—who sustain concussions and resume play with little or no time set aside for recovery. In his essay where he announced the AMA's formal opposition to boxing, Dr. Lundberg (article 12.4) extended an invitation to the sports medicine community to "examine scientifically the brains of current or former football players" to investigate whether there is a prevalence of chronic brain damage among them. His request, which was really more of a challenge, was issued fifteen years ago. As yet little research has been conducted on the brains of America's favorite collision sport athletes.*

In spite of the AMA's opposition, boxing has many supporters. Further, the medical community lacks complete agreement in its opposition to boxing. While Dr. Russel H. Patterson (article 12.8) does not dispute the dangers inherent in such a violent sport, he does argue that an individual should have the right to box if he wishes. To keep an individual from fighting, he reasons, would only encourage other, more dangerous restrictions on behavior for all of us. For other commentators boxing is an expression of the self, a primal drive within the individual, a passion. John Schulian (article 12.10) tells us that to try and ban boxing would be foolish. Such proposals are made by those who don't understand the sport or the meaning it holds for boxers and their patrons. Boxers know all too well the dangers of their occupation. If banned, Schulian insists boxing would continue anyway, further out of sight from those who object.

Although the sport continues in the United States—indeed, recently women have entered the ring—there have been countries that have successfully banned boxing. In 1969 Sweden outlawed professional boxing, and amateur boxing continues under strict medical supervision. It was Sweden's Ingemar Johansson, a 7-1 underdog, who beat Floyd Patterson in 1959 to take the world heavyweight title. In 1980 Norway also banned boxing. It is illegal to take money for a fight in Norway; it is even illegal for a pro boxer to train in Norway. If you come from either country and want to be a professional boxer, you have to leave the country.

In a 1994 editorial in *JAMA*, Dr. Lundberg called for the elimination of boxing at U.S. military academies, and U.S. participation in boxing in the Olympics. In 1995, in response to Dr. Lundberg's request, the Air Force surgeon general's medical operation's agency issued the following statement: "The risks of participation [in boxing] far outweigh any potential benefits." The Air Force academy has eliminated boxing as a mandatory activity.

---

*The research (and literature) is just beginning to accumulate on not only football but many other sports as well. In 1977 the American Academy of Neurology and the Brain Injury Association published guidelines to follow for assessing and acting on concussions (a bruised brain) sustained in sporting events. Football is responsible for 100,000 concussions each year in the United States. Soccer presents similar dangers to the brain. A recent study indicates that "heading" the ball (in soccer) without a helmet means the head is sustaining 160 to 180 percent greater force than routine impacts from helmeted football and hockey players.

Readings

Article 12.1 *A Life on the Ropes* is a portrait of Jerry Quarry, top heavyweight contender in the late 1960s and early 1970s. William Plummer chronicles Quarry's life and career in a boxing family, and how he kept fighting when his skills had left him more vulnerable to punches. At his peak he fought Muhammad Ali and Joe Frazier. Quarry was suffering from dementia pugilistica at the time the article was written. His brain cells were dying as a result of repeated blows to the head. He died in 1999 at the age of fifty.

Articles 12.2 and 12.3 *Boxing Should Be Banned in Civilized Countries* and *The Deadly Degrading Sport* represent the opening rounds by members of the medical profession to end boxing in the United States. The short articles appeared as editorials by Drs. George D. Lundberg and Maurice W. Van Allen in the *Journal of the American Medical Association* (*JAMA*). At the time their articles appeared, Dr. Lundberg was the editor of *JAMA,* and Dr. Van Allen was at the University of Iowa Hospitals and Clinics. Brain injuries are cited by both as reason for a ban. They criticize the savage nature of the sport by portraying it as a throwback to uncivilized man. Boxing, Lundberg insists, is an "obscenity" and should join the ranks of cockfighting and privately staged dogfights.

Article 12.4 In *Boxing Should Be Banned in Civilized Countries–Round 3,* Dr. Lundberg announces the American Medical Association's decision to support a ban on the sport. The article also includes an impressive list of additional medical organizations that advocate the same. It is interesting to note that Lundberg also discusses the broader issue of whether boxing and violence on TV encourage people to commit violent acts (a subject Joyce Carol Oates brings up in article 12.9). Lundberg closes his article with an optimistic prediction that most states in the United States will ban boxing by the end of the 20th century.

Article 12.5 Daved Kindred, a contributing writer for *The Sporting News,* wrote *Prescription for Murder* soon after flyweight Jimmy Garcia was killed in a match with Gabriel Ruelas. Kindred recalls how he once wrote favorable articles on boxing, but states that he now thinks differently. He now claims boxers are symbols of helplessness and hopelessness. They know no way out of their lives, except to give them up to a sport that wants to kill them. Like Lundberg before him, Kindred advocates banning boxing if it cannot be reformed.

Article 12.6 Hugh Brayne is a solicitor and a professor of law at Sunderland University, England. His books include *Law for Social Workers, The Legal Skills Book,* and *Clinical Legal Education* (all coauthored). He has published numerous articles in the area of legal education. Lincoln Sargeant is a medical doctor with specialties in internal medicine and epidemiology. He is currently a lecturer in clinical epidemiology at the University of the West Indies, Jamaica, where he is affiliated with the Epidemiology Research Unit, Tropical Medicine Research Institute. In *Could Boxing Be Prevented If Doctors Withdrew Cover? An Ethical Perspective,* Brayne and Sargeant argue medical associations may be justified in preventing doctors from participating as ringside physicians. The Hippocratic oath requires doctors to do no harm to their patients. By participating as a ringside physician, the doctor allows the fight to commence and gives the boxer the false impression that he is safer because of the doctor's presence. In fact, the doctor can do little to aid boxers and mitigate injury. Such participation, these authors conclude, is contrary to the vows a doctor takes when he or she enters the profession. If a medical association has good reason to lobby for banning the sport, why should it not change its own code of ethics to prohibit doctors from participating as ringside physicians? Brayne and Sargeant have previously been active in the effort to ban boxing in England. In an article published in the *British Medical Journal* (June 13, 1998, p. 1813) they argued that boxing, if tested in the British courts, may actually be declared illegal owing to the fact that the sport relies on the intentional infliction of injury for a match to take place. Brayne and Sargeant authored the article in this text especially for *The Thinking Reader.*

Article 12.7 Concerned with the dangers of the popular new collision sports of ultimate fighting, extreme fighting, and toughman fighting, Dr. Lundberg calls on the AMA to formally oppose these new sports as well as reaffirm its opposition to boxing. In *Blunt Force Violence in America–Shades of Gray or Red,* Dr. Lundberg details the types of injuries likely to result from the new violent sports, and requests that the AMA lobby for laws that would prohibit all forms of consensual unregulated fighting.

Article 12.8 In the same issue of *JAMA* where Dr. Lundberg announced the AMA's position on abolishing boxing, Dr. Russel H. Patterson published an article entitled *On Boxing and Liberty,* endorsing an individual's right to box. Patterson doesn't dispute the medical evidence concerning injuries to boxers; rather, his concern is with the fundamental liberties of boxers and, by extension, the liberties of all. He invokes John Stuart Mill, Isaiah Berlin, and Immanual Kant in defending an individual's right to box. As long as an individual is aware of the risks, and as long as he does not infringe on the freedom of others, the state has no right to prevent him from pursuing his interests, even when it believes that person's behavior is self-destructive. The state should intervene only to prevent an individual from harming another. So are the limits of freedom, Patterson insists, even with respect to sustaining brain damage.

Article 12.9 Joyce Carol Oates is one of America's premier contemporary poets and novelists. In an excerpt from her book *On Boxing,* Oates explores the nature of boxing as a sociological and psychological phenomenon, as an expression of the self, for both boxers and spectators, and as an enactment of modern American Tragedy. She accuses boxing critics of hypocrisy in not attacking other dangerous sports—football, thoroughbred horse racing, and auto racing—where injury rates are more frequent, and for singling out a sport where minorities, and the poor, dominate. The blunt, savage nature of boxing cannot be assimilated by many people who are opposed to boxing. On the one hand we have the destructive power of nuclear weapons, yet many people cannot accept the aggressive display of natural violence in the ring.

Article 12.10 John Schulian covered boxing as a sports reporter for the *Chicago Sun Times. Death in the Ring Is a Fact of Life* is taken from his popular book of essays on boxing entitled *Writers' Fighters and Other Sweet Scientists.* He wrote the article after Cleveland Denny died of injuries suffered in a match with Gaetan Hart. Schulian argues that it's in the nature of man to fight, and it would be foolish to think the sport could be banned.

12.1 A Life on the Ropes

WILLIAM PLUMMER

AT HOME IN THE HILLS north of Los Angeles, a mother and son are seated for dinner. The son is picking at his food. "If you don't eat the pizza," says the mother reprovingly, "you don't get to drink the Coke." The son looks up, his fingers on a slice. "Hey," he barks, "I'm eating the pizza. Don't give me no lip." Then he extends a hand, playfully punching his mom in the shoulder.

At this particular dinner table, though, the hand belongs not to a smart-aleck kid but to a 50-year-old man. It is big and beefy and battered around the knuckles from the glory days when heavyweight fighter Jerry Quarry was the latest Great White Hope. Now his memory of those days is lost in a haze caused by too many punches from the likes of Muhammad Ali and Joe Frazier.

The fog that has enveloped Quarry is known as dementia pugilistica, a progressive condition caused by repeated blows to the head resulting in severe brain damage. Quarry has the mentality, says neuropsychologist Dr. Peter Russell, of a person with advanced Alzheimer's disease. "If he lives another 10 years, he'll be lucky," says Russell, who has likened Quarry's dying brain cells to sugar dissolving in water.

Quarry has already lost nearly everything. The more than $2 million he made in purses is gone, along with his three wives, two of them the mothers of his three kids. To round out the family tragedy, his younger brothers, and fellow boxers, Mike, 44, and Bobby, 32, are also showing signs of brain damage. Only Jimmy, 51, the oldest brother, is in good health.

Until recently, Jerry lived with Jimmy, a loan officer, in Hemet, Calif. Jimmy started the Jerry Quarry Foundation in 1994, purportedly to raise funds for dementia pugilistica. But Jerry's father, Jack, 73, and his sister, Dianna, 49, say the foundation is a ruse—that Jimmy was using Jerry for his own book and movie deals. Jimmy denies the charges. "My dream," says Jimmy, "is to help fighters."

That may be, but the family became alarmed last October when Jerry was inducted into the World Boxing Hall of Fame. Quarry sat like a stone among the honorees. When it came time for autographs, he could not sign his name. Three weeks later, Jerry's son Jerry Lyn Quarry, 29, went to Jimmy's house and spirited his father away to live with his mother, Arwanda. She discovered Jerry had been overmedicated. "He was like a zombie," says Arwanda, 69, who, under Dr. Russell's supervision, weaned him from the drugs. "But as Jerry's dad used to say, 'There is no quit in a Quarry.'"

Maybe there should have been. Maybe then, Jerry would not be slurring his words, pounding his stomach, and picking absently at his pizza.

The Quarrys have boxing in their blood. Jack Quarry weathered the Great Depression by picking cotton during the week and fighting on weekends. "When I was 14, I chopped cotton for $1 a day in Roswell, N. Mex.," says Jack, who was divorced from Arwanda in 1972. "You could go out on Sunday and fight three rounds for $3—that was three days' work!"

Like a character out of *The Grapes of Wrath*, Jack came to California riding a freight car. Soon he and Arwanda were rearing a family in the migrant-labor camps. Jerry was born in Bakersfield in 1945 and first put on boxing gloves at age 3—though nowadays no one in the family wants to take credit for it. Arwanda says her husband took the boys to a gym in L.A. Jack says that Arwanda "wanted me to get the boys out of her hair."

One thing is certain: Jack, who had HARD tattooed on his left hand and LUCK on his right, did not abide sissies. The lesson that left the most lasting impression, according to Jimmy, came in a camp in Shafter, Calif., after a softball game. "The umpire called me out on strikes," says Jimmy. "I disagreed. He hit me, and I wouldn't hit him back. My dad saw that. He called me into the bungalow and had my mother put a baby bonnet and a diaper on me, and he made me suck a bottle laying on my bed. I was humiliated." Jerry was impressed too. Jimmy recalls his saying, "I will never let that happen to me."

From People Weekly 45, No. 7 (1996): 64. *Reprinted with permission.*

Jack denies the incident ever occurred, but there is no question his boys learned to hit back. "We fought in barrooms to please my father's friends," says Jimmy. "Jerry never wanted to be a fighter. He did it for the attention of my father." Sadly, Jerry can't remember. Asked when he began fighting, he says, "At 12."

Mike Quarry, now living in Diamond Bar, Calif., is more lucid than his big brother. A light-heavyweight contender who won 35 fights in a row, he says no one pushed him into the game. He says he became a boxer "because I looked up to Jerry."

Back in Jerry's fighting days, that was easy to do. Quarry, as *Sports Illustrated* noted in 1969, was "a man bred for the ring." He had a 17½-inch neck, muscles like knotted rope, coordination and ferocity. Quarry beat ex-heavyweight champ Floyd Patterson and in 1973 KO'd contender Earnie Shavers. But he lost his only title shot—to Jimmy Ellis in 1968.

Then came Ali and Frazier. Quarry earned his biggest purse, $338,000, against Ali in 1970, and it was after that fight that Jack reportedly told him to quit and buy a gas station. But Ali sliced Jerry up again in 1972. Fighting on the same card, Mike took a terrible beating from light-heavyweight champion Bob Foster. "I told his managers there was something wrong with Michael," says Arwanda, "and that he should get out of boxing. They thought I was just a mother out to protect her child, which I was."

Jerry and Mike both kept on fighting. In 1974, Frazier tore Jerry up so badly that Jerry promised to retire, but he came back nine months later to absorb more punishment from Ken Norton. In 1975, Mike was hurt so badly that Jerry—though incapable of recognizing his own plight—begged his brother to quit. But Mike fought five more years. Jerry, too, refused to hang up the gloves, even after a 1983 CAT scan showed signs of dementia. "Unfortunately," says Arwanda, "none of us believed it. Jerry was so normal. He always had a photographic mind. He never wrote down a phone number."

It was in 1987 that Arwanda first started to worry as Jerry's short-term memory began to go. But the decisive blow came in 1992, when he was talked into making a comeback in Aurora, Colo. For $1,050, Quarry, 47, was battered for six rounds by a no-name pug who knocked out two of his teeth. "When he came home from the fight in Colorado," says Jimmy, "he couldn't remember the night before."

Bobby Quarry, 32, never more than a journeyman fighter and currently in jail in San Luis Obispo, Calif., where he has been charged with receiving stolen property, appears to be in the early stages of dementia. About four years ago, says Arwanda, the California Athletic Commission tested Bobby and deemed him mentally fit but found that he had diminished reflexes in his left arm. A year later, Bobby got kayoed by heavyweight Tommy Morrison. Recently he was diagnosed with Parkinson's disease, the illness that afflicts Ali. But, insists Arwanda, "none of Bobby's brainpower is gone."

Mike's brain still works pretty well, too, despite a fling with cocaine during the '80s. Mike lives in Diamond Bar, Calif., with his wife, Ellen, a marriage and family counselor. By his count, he has had 20 jobs in the last dozen years, ranging from athletic trainer to landscaper. "I've never missed a day," he says. "But I've been subject to forgetting what I was told to do."

Mike also loses his balance sometimes, and he occasionally wakes up screaming, punching holes in the wall. Mike admits that he "took too many punches." But then he says, "Life is lived forward, learned backwards."

Jerry, meanwhile, is just where he wants to be. He basks in the attention of his mother and sisters. Leaning back in a chair beside the stereo one afternoon, Jerry looks older than his 50 years. Then his sister Brenda Martino thrusts a microphone into his paw, and his blue eyes become electric. Jerry stands up and unleashes a deep rich baritone: "Treat me like a fool/Treat me mean and cruel . . ." Brenda says she knew that Jerry was out from the spell of the prescription drugs when he began singing again.

His mother and sisters—Brenda, 46, manages a grocery, and Dianna a restaurant—tend to Jerry in shifts. They take him on walks and help him carry out the trash. They also help him entertain his kids (Jerry Lyn, Keri, 25, and Jonathan, 9) when they visit and join him in songfests at a social club for Alzheimer's patients.

But the news from Dr. Russell is not good. Recent MRI scans indicate that the damage in

Jerry's frontal lobe is increasing. Jerry's brain, says Russell, looks like the inside of a grapefruit that has been dropped dozens of times.

Occasionally even Jerry seems able to recognize the damage. At one point his mother and sisters tease him about the "girls" flirting with him down at the Alzheimer's club. "I can't have a girlfriend at this given time," Jerry suddenly says. "My situation has been very bad, and you know that."

Then the fog rolls in, and he is back in his own world. Until the family moves into the parlor and Brenda hands him the mike and he bursts into song: "Treat me like a fool/Treat me mean and cruel/But love me. . . ."

"Jerry was always good to his mom," says Arwanda when he finishes. "Now I'm taking care of him."

There is no quit in a Quarry.

12.2 Boxing Should Be Banned in Civilized Countries

GEORGE D. LUNDBERG

THE PRINCIPAL PURPOSE of a boxing match is for one opponent to render the other injured, defenseless, incapacitated, unconscious. No caring person could have observed the events in professional prizefighting in the past few months and not have been revolted. No prudent physician could have watched the most recent debacle/mismatch on Nov. 26, 1982, between Larry Holmes and Randall "Tex" Cobb and believe that the current boxing control system is functioning. The fact that this massacre came on the immediate heels of even more tragic fights serves to accentuate the uncontrolled situation.

The American Medical Association recognized this problem some time ago, and its Council on Scientific Affairs commissioned a panel to study the problem and to make recommendations. The report . . . is the official AMA position. It is solid, balanced, and reasonable. It operates with the assumption that boxing cannot be stopped, so it recommends ways in which it should be controlled better. To continue its interest in the safety and medical care of boxers, the AMA is cosponsoring a conference with the Association of Ringside Physicians on "Medical Aspects of Boxing" at Caesar's Palace Hotel in Las Vegas on Feb. 18, 1983. Eleven faculty members will discuss the duties and responsibilities of the ring physician, emergency medical procedures in the management of severely injured boxer, and several other important topics.

Since the Council report was approved by the House of Delegates in 1982, two other major studies have appeared. Kaste et al,[1] writing in a recent issue of *The Lancet*, studied 14 boxers who had been national champions in Finland and who had been carefully screened and found not to have other known reasons for brain atrophy. They report computed tomographic (CT) evidence of brain injury in four of six professional and one of eight amateur boxers. Also, two of the professionals and eight of the amateurs had EEG abnormalities that may have been caused by brain injury. Kaste and colleagues state, "The most predictable and permanent reward . . . is chronic brain damage," and "The only way to prevent brain injuries is to disqualify blows to the head." . . . Ross et al report a study of 38 boxers with CT scans, 24 of whom had a complete neurological examination and EEG as well. They report a significant relationship between the number of bouts fought and brain damage detected by CT scan and demonstrate no significant relationship with neurological symptoms or findings or number of knockouts or technical knockouts. This is additional strong evidence of chronic brain damage with cerebral atrophy in many fighters.

Some have argued that boxing has a redeeming social value in that it allows a few disadvantaged or

1. Kaste M, Vilkki J, Sainio K, et al; Is chronic brain damage in boxing a hazard of the past? Lancet 1982; 2:1186–1188.

From Journal of the American Medical Association *249, no. 2 (1983): 250. Reprinted with permission.*

minority individuals an opportunity to rise to spectacular wealth and fame. This does occur, but at what price? The price in this country includes chronic brain damage for them and the thousands of others who do not achieve wealth, fame, or even a decent living from the ring. Others argue that man must fight and that surreptitious fights will occur if boxing is outlawed, producing an even worse situation. I suggest that such is equivalent to arguing that gunfighter duels should be instituted, tickets sold, and betting promoted since, after all, homicide by gunshot is also common in our society.

This editor believes personally that boxing is wrong at its base. In contrast to boxing, in all other recognized sport, injury is an undesired byproduct of the activity. Boxing seems to me to be less sport than is cockfighting; boxing is an obscenity. Uncivilized man may have been bloodthirsty. Boxing, as a throwback to uncivilized man, should not be sanctioned by any civilized society.

12.3 The Deadly Degrading Sport

MAURICE W. VAN ALLEN

HOW STRANGE THAT, in this climate of preoccupation with health and physical fitness and with near-hysterical concern for every conceivable deleterious factor in the environment, so few raise their voices again boxing. How strange, when strident voices urge equality for all and promote and make capital of support for equal rights, that poor and minority youth are recruited and rewarded for sacrificing themselves to a spectacle for the more favored of whatever ethnic or fiscal group.

What factors contribute to this continued public spectacle of brutality, and the literal sacrifice of minority youth for the profit and delectation of self-styled sportsmen?

In fairness to the boxing game and its proponents, let us review the widely shared ignorance about the effects of trauma on the brain and the implications of being knocked unconscious.

Head injury from falls and blows is a common incident in the animated cartoons of children's shows. The hero or villain, whether animal or human, is often momentarily stopped in his action by a blow to the head—the circumstances are entertaining, and the victim quickly recovers and it is as fast and effective as before. This may happen repeatedly to the same character with no harmful effect. Children can grow up with the belief that head injury is amusing, recoverable, and of little consequence. Novels and television shows bludgeon their private eyes, heroes, and villains with never a suggestion of post-traumatic symptoms lasting more than a few minutes.

The football player who is stunned or senseless has had his "bell rung" or is "shaken up on the play." That he can walk off the field with help or even reenter the game is ample evidence of the triviality of the incident and its apparent short-lived consequences. No matter that memory of the incident may be lost and confusion be present for several days afterward. The sports commentators, whose own fortunes are invested heavily in the game, never allude to and are probably only vaguely aware of the implications of these brain injuries—hence, their prattle of euphemisms to cover only vague discomfort.

With this kind of folklore about brain injury, small wonder that those who enjoy and profit from regulated brawling and violence easily convince themselves that little harm is done in boxing. The "punch-drunk" fighter is an amusing oddity, seldom the object of pity and not, it seems, a catalyst of guilt.

The fight game provides an opportunity for ambitious youths to climb from scandalous social circumstances, through a disgraceful "sports" opportunity to some kind of fame or hero status. We are told this in different terms by those who justify boxing and who find the bashing of others to be financially and emotionally rewarding.

In boxing, we are reassured by the concern of the announcers for facial cuts and by the referee,

From Journal of the American Medical Association *249, no. 2 (1983): 250–251. Reprinted with permission.*

who will stop a fight when superficial hemorrhage may obscure the fighter's vision, or perhaps offend some in the audience and remind them of their involvement in the guilt of promoting a vicious and deadly game. At the end, some functionary will appear in formal evening attire to announce the winners. His ruffled shirt and black tie attest to the dignity of the proceedings, and to the gentlemanly way in which they are conducted.

Perhaps you will say that, with human nature as it is, some important societal needs are served by this vicarious outlet of violence for the viciousness hidden in all of us and that a good fight by others relieves tensions and lubricates communal living. Others, in defending the recruitment of children to the fight game, will point to the advantages of the discipline that comes from preparation for fighting and to the moral benefits of fighting within a set of rules. They will emphasize the opportunity for the otherwise hopeless to achieve fame, no matter what the price to the brains of the unsuccessful and successful alike. No matter the basic degradation of those who fight for the entertainment of others even when victorious. The owners and managers of a "stable" of fighters recall those who solved the energy crisis created by the cotton gin.

We are assured by the television networks responsible for bringing us a boxing spectacle that an ambulance will be available throughout the bout, and of course that physicians are present at ringside—a flattering faith in the ability of modern medicine to repair irreversible damage to the nervous system. We are not so reassured when clearly mismatched fighters are paired in the ring and one

game but less-talented gladiator is finally unmercifully beaten while the referee, for reasons of his own, allows a bout to proceed when the outcome is clear to all. The physical and mental consequences are smothered in euphemisms and suppressed by announcers, promoters, and audience.

We are reassured again, when we reflect on the respectability given to the sport by the Olympic Committee, since these self-appointed guardians of sportsman's virtues endorse fighting (under careful jurisdiction), suggesting that well-regulated sin is perhaps not very sinful after all.

Heroes usually arise from sacrifice, often in hazardous circumstances and at high cost. The high cost that is paid by the fighters in boxing is buried in emotional bookkeeping.

When a human or animal is struck on the head so that consciousness is lost, pathological changes—minute or larger hemorrhages—contusions often at the base, and tearing of nerve fibers that may not be easily identified, are all consequences of a blunt flow of sufficient force to render the subject unconscious. Detectable symptoms of a beating may not be apparent to a victim preoccupied by the pursuit that caused the injury, but have been admitted by the more introspective who go on to other occupations.

The accumulative destructive effects of repeated blows, even when consciousness and posture are not lost, are well known and accepted.

Is now not the time to suppress exposure of this fragment of our savagery by the mass media and leave boxing to those who enjoy privately staged dogfights?

Discussion and Assignments

Note: This material applies to the two preceding articles.

1. What evidence does Lundberg offer to support his case against professional boxing? Is the evidence convincing?
2. How does Lundberg distinguish boxing from other sports? How critical is the distinction to building his case against boxing?
3. Lundberg supports his case for banning boxing by anticipating two opposing arguments. What are the two arguments, and how does he reply to them? Do you think his replies are adequate?
4. Lundberg claims boxing should not be accepted in civilized society, and calls it an "obscenity." Look up the word *obscenity* in your dictionary. Do you think Lundberg's characterization of boxing is fair or accurate? See if you can employ examples to illustrate how strong or weak his characterization is.

5. According to Lundberg boxing is no more a sport than cockfighting. Why do you think Lundberg picked cockfighting as his example? How effective is the comparison?

6. Van Allen speaks of folklore concerning brain injury that we find in cartoons, TV, novels, and in sports like football. What function does folklore play in our assessment and acceptance of boxing, according to Van Allen? How important are his views on folklore to understanding his overall argument for banning boxing? Do you agree with Van Allen in his assessment of folklore and brain injury?

7. Both Lundberg and Van Allen argue against the view that boxing offers youth an opportunity to climb out of poverty and achieve financial success and fame. How do they argue against this view? Do you believe they make strong or weak arguments?

8. If professional boxing were to ban headshots, and the incidence of brain injury declined, where would Lundberg and Van Allen be with their arguments?

12.4 Boxing Should Be Banned in Civilized Countries— Round 3

GEORGE D. LUNDBERG

I am going to punish him. . . . I am going to beat him so badly that he'll need a shoehorn to get his hat on again.

> Cassius Clay prior to World Heavyweight Championship fight with Floyd Patterson (Time, Dec. 3, 1965, p. 73)

THE ORGANIZED BRUTALITY of boxing has become widely recognized for what it is since we published our pioneering articles on Jan. 14, 1983.[1-4] Most noteworthy have been the changes in the policies of organized medicine. Four years ago, the American Medical Association (AMA) had no policy on boxing. As the new information became widely known, the AMA went from calling for many safety measures recommended by its Council on Scientific Affairs and expert panel in December 1982[4] to a much more aggressive posture in June 1983.[5] Data from four research groups in three countries[2, 6–8] have documented the high frequency of chronic brain damage in boxers who have had many fights, and a series of strong editorials has argued that boxing is wrong medically and morally.[2, 3, 5, 9] We have seen the development of a broad international medical consensus that boxing should be abolished. Among the many medical groups that have taken official positions are the national medical associations of Britain, Canada, Australia, and the United States, the World Medical Association, specialty societies such as the American Academy of Pediatrics, the Canadian Psychiatric Association, and the American Academy of Neurology, and the state medical associations of California and New York.

In December 1984, the AMA House of Delegates, reflecting the new scientific data and

1. Ross RJ, Cole M, Thompson JS, et al: Boxers—computed tomography, EEG and neurological evaluation. *JAMA* 1983;249:211–213.
2. Lundberg GD: Boxing should be banned in civilized countries. *JAMA* 1983;249:250.
3. Van Allen MW: The deadly degrading sport. *JAMA* 1983;249:250–251.
4. Council on Scientific Affairs: Brain injury in boxing. *JAMA* 1983;249:254–257.
5. Lundberg GD: Boxing should be banned in civilized countries—round 2. *JAMA* 1984;251:2696–2698.
6. Kaste M, Vikki J, Sainio K, et al: Is chronic brain damage in boxing a hazard of the past? *Lancet* 1982;2:1186–1188.
7. Sironi VA, Ravagnati L: Brain damage in boxers. *Lancet* 1983;1:244.
8. Casson IR, Siegal O, Sham R, et al: Brain damage in modern boxers. *JAMA* 1984;251:2663–2667.
9. Richards NG: Ban boxing, *Neurology* 1984;34: 1485–1486.

From Journal of the American Medical Association 255, no. 18 (1986): 2483–85. *Reprinted with permission.*

clinical experience, extended its June 1983 opposition to boxing.[5] After substantial debate, the House passed Substitute Resolution 26, which stated as follows:

> RESOLVED, That the American Medical Association: 1. Encourage the elimination of both amateur and professional boxing, a sport in which the primary objective is to inflict injury; 2. Communicate its opposition to boxing as a sport to appropriate regulating bodies; 3. Assist state medical societies to work with their state legislatures to enact laws to eliminate boxing in their jurisdictions; and 4. Educate the American public, especially children and young adults, about the dangerous effects of boxing on the health of participants.

Twelve months later, in December 1985 in Washington, DC, after much less debate and with little dissent, the House of Delegates reaffirmed the December 1984 resolution.

Opposing Viewpoints

Three opposing viewpoints consistently appear, two represented in this boxing theme issue. One is that amateur boxing is not as bad as professional boxing, can be monitored and controlled, and has a low likelihood of harm. A description of such an approach to boxing in Sweden is contained in the commentary by Ludwig.[10] Another is the libertarian view that a person should be able to do anything he or she wishes as long as it doesn't hurt others or society. Such a view is presented by Patterson.[11] The third view is that poor and minority children have only one way to escape the ghetto in this and other countries and that way is fighting. Obviously, we disagree with these three views and have presented our reasons for disagreement many times. In addition, we have [provided information] on eye damage in boxing[12] and . . . on medical and public health aspects of boxing.[13]

Many people question why boxing (along with full-contact karate) has been singled out from all other sports for such major opposition by physicians. The data are clear: blows to the head in boxing damage the brain. While a few severe blows may kill acutely by cerebral contusion and edema and subdural hematoma, chronic brain damage results from repetitive subconcussive blows over multiple training sessions and matches. It is the high frequency of chronic brain damage (60% to 87%) among boxers who have had many fights that sets boxing apart medically. In comparing risk sports in regard to odds of death per unit of time of participation, mountain climbing, parachuting, and hang gliding are considered "high risk" while professional boxing and scuba diving are "medium risk."[14] Figures from 1983 for U.S. injuries by sport showing boxing leading the list at 50% of participants experiencing injury, followed by American football at 30%, baseball 3%, basketball 2%, and the others trailing.[15]

American football is violent. It results in many serious injuries, including cerebral concussions and fractured cervical vertebrae with paralysis. There may be a substantial prevalence of chronic brain damage in football players, but at this time no one seems to know. The peer review literature is apparently mute. One senses that the football enthusiasts, including the sports medicine establishment, may not want to know, since one does not hear of many people planning to do proper brain studies on football players. Can the football sports medicine community examine scientifically the brains of current or former football players prospectively, retrospectively, or epidemiologically cross-sectionally and send the reports of such studies for peer review and subsequent publication? We would welcome such at *JAMA*.

The other major difference between boxing (and full-contact karate) and all other contact or collision sports is the intent to win by deliberately harming the opponent. It is morally wrong for one human being to attempt intentionally to harm the brain of another. A major purpose of a sport event is to win. When the surest way to win is by dam-

10. Ludwig R: Making boxing safer: The Swedish model. *JAMA* 1986;255:2482.

11. Patterson RH: On boxing and liberty. *JAMA* 1986;255:2481–2482.

12. Maguire JI, Benson WE: Retinal injury and detachment in boxers. *JAMA* 1986;255:2451–2453.

13. Morrison RG: Medical and public health aspects of boxing. *JAMA* 1986;255:2475–2480.

14. Reif AE: Risks and gains, in Vinger PF, Hoerner EF (eds): *Sports Injuries*. Littleton, Mass, PSG Publishing Co Inc, 1981, pp 56–64.

15. *Accidental Facts.* Chicago, National Safety Council, 1984, p. 7.

aging the opponent's brain, and this becomes standard procedure, the sport is morally wrong. Many say that it is often the intent of American football players to harm their opponents, thereby removing them from the game, especially defensive linemen and linebackers going after the quarterback. This may be true, but such harm is not the intent of the game. Each football game continues to its conclusion, no matter how many injuries occur, by the use of substitutes.

Does Violence Beget Violence?

Yet another aspect of boxing's influence on society has recently been noted. Many people have suggested that boxing gives some men who may be naturally violent an opportunity to work off their aggressions in the ring. Others say that observers of boxing may rid themselves of the need to be violent by vicariously living such an experience. To my knowledge, no evidence exists to support such views. On the contrary, many believe that people who participate in and observe violence over the long haul become tolerant of it, as if violence were normal, and cease to find it abhorrent. There are articles in the psychology and sociology literature tying exposure of angered laboratory subjects to a filmed prize fight scene to an increase in aggressive behavior.[16, 17] Phillips[18] has presented evidence that there is a sharp, nontrivial increase in U.S. homicides after strongly publicized heavyweight championship prize fights. These and related observations that support the hypothesis that mass media portrayals of violence incite imitative responses among the public have recently been disputed on methodological grounds,[19, 20] and clarification of any cause-effect relationship awaits future research. The evidence supporting the view that violence shown on television produces additional actual violence was strong enough for the House of Delegates of the AMA in 1976 to pass a resolution on this subject, which reads as follows:

> RESOLVED, That the AMA: 1. Declare its recognition of the fact that TV violence is a risk factor threatening the health and welfare of young Americans, indeed our future society. 2. Commit itself to remedial action in concert with industry, government and other interested parties. 3. Encourage all physicians, their families and their patients to actively oppose TV programs containing violence, as well as products and/or services sponsoring such programs.

Support from Wide-Ranging Sources

There are many people out there who believe as we do about boxing. Support may come from surprising places. From the Roman Catholic Church, Jesuit theologian John Connery of Loyola University of Chicago makes a strong case against boxing on moral grounds. He points out that "there is no way you can justify doing damage to another unless you can show some compensating good." He says that the risk of cumulative brain damage rules out any blows above the collar bone as being moral.[21] Television sports reporter Howard Cosell, once one of the most influential spokesmen for boxing, ended many years of covering professional boxing in 1982 and has recently announced that he agrees with our position that professional boxing should be abolished in America and that he also has grave doubts about amateur boxing.[22] Of course, in our "age of litigation," the lawyers have also gotten into the act. The case of a young amateur fighter in West Virginia who died of brain damage shortly after his third bout was settled in favor of the plaintiffs (the boy's parents) after three days in a jury trial in 1986. This was apparently the first such court case in the United States.

16. Berkowitz L, Alioto JT: The meaning of an observed event as a determinant of its aggressive consequences. *J Pers Soc Psychiatry* 1973;28:206–217.

17. Berkowitz L, Rawlings E: Effects of film violence on inhibitions against subsequent aggression. *J Abnormal Soc Psychol* 1963;66:405–412.

18. Phillips DP: The impact of mass media violence on U.S. homicides. *Am Sociol Rev* 1983;48:560–568.

19. Baron JN, Reiss PC: Same time, next year: Aggregate analyses of the mass media and violent behavior. *Am Sociol Rev* 1985;50:347–363.

20. Phillips DP, Bollen KA: Same time, last year: Selective data dredging for negative findings. *Am Sociol Rev* 1985;50:364–371.

21. Bank J: Death and damage in the ring: The case against boxing. *St. Anthony Messenger,* March 1986, pp. 9–19.

22. Cosell H: *I Never Played the Game.* New York, William Morrow & Co Inc, 1985, pp 13, 217.

Where do we go from here? As scientists, we must continue to be responsive to new data, especially prospective and controlled, that will shed additional light on boxing's dangers and their possible elimination. As long as the data are there, we must resolutely stand by the position of the international medical community and do everything possible to abolish boxing. Until it is banned, we must support all reasonable efforts to improve safety in the ring. Many states, as well as the federal government, have moved toward improved safety, but none has yet abolished boxing.

Is there hope for amateur boxing? Generally speaking, the people who have come forth to defend amateur boxing seem well intentioned and responsibly motivated. It may be possible to develop rules that would allow this sport to continue to be one of speed, skill, enthusiasm, and discipline by simply abolishing blows to the head and having boxers win by points.

Unfortunately, blows to the head damage the brain,[23] whether or not the assailant and the recipient are paid for their efforts. If the highly vocal proponents of amateur boxing truly do not wish their fighters to win or lose by virtue of brain damage, they should be able to devise rules to prevent this. Society no longer sanctions sword duels in which one participant runs the other through; we now see skillful swordsmanship in the ritualized form of fencing. Amateur boxing could also be ritualized into safety if the responsible leaders so choose.

There is little support for the continuation of professional boxing, except from some of those with an obvious financial interest—some fighters and their entourages, promoters, the media, and various state officials who depend on regulating boxing for their livelihood. The final report of the State of New Jersey Commission of Investigation of Dec. 16, 1985, entitled "Organized Crime in Boxing," concluded that boxing should be abolished, that "the inherent problems of professional boxing—and most particularly its constant threat of bodily destruction, mentally and physically—cannot be effectively resolved at any governmental level," that the sport is "marred by official misconduct, promotional greed and matchmaking barbarism," and that "not even the sturdiest of statutory controls will reduce the brutality of the sport to any significant degree."[24] In response to this report, *The New York Times* (Dec. 16, 1985, p. 24) called on New Jersey to become the first state in the United States to outlaw boxing.

Professional boxing is hopeless and doomed to meet the same fate in the United States that it has met in Sweden and Norway: extinction. Some state will ban it in this decade. Most will ban it by the end of this century. Who will be first? Will it be a populous state with many citizen fighters to protect, such as New Jersey, Florida, New York, or California? Or will it be a state where boxing has little monetary influence, but where traditional morality runs high, such as Nebraska, Vermont, Arkansas, or North Carolina? Or might Oregon and Washington ban it regionally? Who will be first to abolish and who will be last to sanction this tragic obscenity?

We will see that hard scientific data, medical concern for the brains of all members of humanity, and the power of the pen are mightier than greed, human exploitation, and the fist.[25]

23. Lampert PW, Hardman JM: Morphological changes in brains of boxers. *JAMA* 1984;251:2676–2679.

24. Patterson HS II, Greenberg WS, Zazzali JR, et al: *Organized Crime in Boxing,* final boxing report. Trenton, State of New Jersey Commission of Investigation, 1985.
25. Lundberg GD: Brain injury in boxing. *Am J Forensic Med Pathol* 1985;6:192–198.

Discussion and Assignments

1. In this article Lundberg offers some of the strongest medical evidence he has against boxing. Is the evidence clear and understandable? Is it convincing?
2. Lundberg considers some opposing views to his position. Though he does not respond to every view in detail in this paper, he does consider a few of them in some length. Which objections does he consider, and how fairly does he represent them? How effective is he in meeting the objections?

3. Lundberg argues there may be a correlation between boxing on television and violent behavior in society. Do you agree with his position? What does boxing on television have to do with the immediate question of whether boxing should be banned? Could you object to other violent sports or programs on TV (e.g., tough-man competitions) for similar reasons?

4. In his 1986 article Lundberg predicted that most states in the United States would ban boxing by the turn of the century, like Norway and Sweden. He was wrong in his prediction. Why do you think boxing was not outlawed as Lundberg predicted?

5. Do you think it's appropriate that the American Medical Association has taken a position that boxing should be banned? In a 300 word essay, take a position, pro or con, on the American Medical Association taking a position on banning boxing. (Are there any implications you can see from taking such a position?)

12.5 Prescription for Murder

DAVE KINDRED

AN "IRISH KISS" is the swift application of one's forehead to another's nose bone. For such an egregious smooch, an English soccer player has been sentenced to three months in jail. His kiss was no kiss. It was a crime. Much the same assault was done in the United States recently when boxer Ray Mercer ran his forehead into the cheek of Evander Holyfield. The resulting cut caused Holyfield's face to take on the appearance of a tomato losing its juice.

Unlike the English kisser, Mercer stood not to be punished but to move near great rewards. Had the fight been stopped and Mercer declared the winner, a multimillion-dollar title fight might be in his future. That possibility existed because assaults are legal in the U.S. if they occur in a boxing ring where, after all, homicide is the standard of perfection.

A fighter's goal is a knockout. That's a concussion. That's an injury suffered by the brain when it is caused to slap up against the bone of the skull. The brain is traumatized; in shock it cannot function. Done with enough force, injury to a fighter's brain goes beyond bruising. The very best fighters deliver blows that cause the brain to slap the skullbone so hard as to rip the brain's tissue and its blood vessels. In which case the brain becomes a bleeding tomato.

What we see on Holyfield's face is what we don't see inside a man's skull. As Holyfield's face became a river of blood, so did Jimmy Garcia's brain. Only the latest fighter to die, Jimmy Garcia, a Mexican fighter of small renown, won't be the last. His death recently will be forgotten as "one of those things that happen" when, the truth is, he put his life at risk for the entertainment of barbarians.

Instead of that truth, we will hear Garcia's death prostituted by people who would have us believe his work in the ring was a symbol of man's courage and perseverance in rising above his life's barren beginnings.

Once upon a time, I wrote such blather. But, to quote Roberto Duran, no mas. No more. No sale here. Take your barbaric yappings somewhere else. The terrible truth is that anyone who steps into a boxing ring is a symbol of helplessness compounded by hopelessness. They are men with no way out of their lives except to give them up to a sport that wants nothing more than to kill them.

The late Howard Cosell once did television commentary on a Larry Holmes–Tex Cobb fight in which the champion all but butchered Cobb. The fight should have been stopped. "Doesn't that referee know," Cosell shouted, "that he is

From The Sporting News *219, no. 23 (1995): 6. Reprinted with permission.*

constructing an advertisement for the abolition of the very sport he is involved in?"

Cosell never worked another fight. He had done his crusading on the air. He had testified before the U.S. Congress about the need to regulate boxing for the protection of the men who fight. Nothing came of Cosell's pleadings. The people who run boxing know safety doesn't pay the bills. A boxing commissioner recently argued against headgear by saying, "This is the hurt business." It's the hurt that sells tickets.

Not that headgear is the answer, anyway. Headgear increases the impact of a punch by spreading it around the skull; headgear also gives a fighter a false sense of security that leads him to accept punches. When George Foreman advocates headgear, he reaffirms the obvious: He has been hit in the head so many times he has destroyed the brain cells that determine common sense.

At a memorial service for Cosell the other day, Muhammad Ali looked hale and prosperous in a cream-colored suit. Looks deceive. To be in Ali's company is to cry out for an end to boxing. The most beautiful athlete we'll ever see is now a shuffling, silent shell. Boxing did it.

The diagnosis of Ali's condition is Parkinson's syndrome secondary to pugilistic syndrome. That means he suffers symptoms of Parkinson's disease: tremors of the limbs, a shuffling gait, a masked face, slurred speech. It further means the symptoms are not the result of disease but of brain injuries suffered as a fighter.

To those of us fascinated by Ali, he seemed to be an artist who made the mean game palatable with his speed and grace. He was about magic, not brutality. We blathered on about Ali's footwork and defensive tactics. Blather it was, for in the end the cruelest game can be about only one thing: ripping apart the other guy's brain, or, to quote the child burglar who became an adult rapist Mike Tyson: "I deliver punches with murderous intentions. I want to drive a man's nose bone into his brain."

Irish featherweight Barry McGuigan lost the championship on a 100-degree day in Las Vegas. "You know," he once said, "I lost brain cells in that fight." He whispered the confession out of his wife's hearing, maybe the only fighter ever able to say those words. "I've heard about this my whole life," he said. "Now I know what it is."

He had killed a man in the ring, a Nigerian named Young Ali. "Both our wives were pregnant at the time," McGuigan said. "He never knew it, but he had a son, too. I still see that wee man in my dreams." As long as nothing is done to increase safety—bigger gloves, shorter rounds, shorter fights, rigorous physical standards, mandatory retirements—the simple answer is to make boxing illegal. Just get rid of it.

The usual argument against the abolition of boxing is that they'll do it illegally. Well, OK, go ahead. Let them take their fights onto cruise ships in international waters. Let them fight in underground rooms hidden from our sight. We cannot legislate away the bloodlust of human beings. Just don't bring boxing into our living rooms on television. Don't pretend it has a place in civilized life. It is beneath contempt.

This sport is no sport. It is murder for hire.

Discussion and Assignments

1. Kindred was once a boxing enthusiast, writing articles in favor of the sport. Now he declares boxing is not a sport at all, and supports its abolition. What changed his mind? What does he mean when he says, "This sport is no sport"?

2. Kindred insists that boxing has no place in civilized life, and says it should be abolished if it cannot be reformed. What specifically are his proposals to reform boxing? Do you think his proposals are realistic? Why or why not?

3. Kindred ends his article by speculating that if boxing is banned, it will continue anyway. But this is OK with him. What reasons does he offer to support this claim? Do you agree or disagree with him?

12.6 Could Boxing Be Prevented If Doctors Withdrew Cover? An Ethical Perspective

LINCOLN SARGEANT AND HUGH BRAYNE

THE BRITISH MEDICAL ASSOCIATION, like similar associations in the United States, Canada and Australia, has publicly stated its opposition to boxing and campaigned for legislation to outlaw the sport.[1] However, little attention has been given to other options that might be available to the profession for achieving the same result. Indeed, the Australian Medical Association concedes that "until such time as boxing is banned," it supports "steps designed to minimise harm to amateur and professional boxers" and "modifications in equipment and rules" to "reduce the morbidity and mortality rates associated with boxing."[2] The association then commits its members to participation in the sport in order to achieve the objectives of minimising harm.

While other medical associations do not explicitly advocate that their members be involved in providing medical supervision and care during boxing matches, they do not discourage this participation. It is widely accepted that this is responsible conduct as long as boxing remains legal. We will argue that such involvement by the medical profession conflicts with professional ethical standards. A change in the medical code of conduct to prevent doctors form participating in boxing would avoid these conflicts and would be an alternative option to the present position of collaboration with the sport while lobbying for legislation to ban it.

First, we will outline the alternative option to collaboration that the medical profession can adopt in order to force an end to boxing in its present form. We will then discuss the justification for adopting this option. In doing so we will examine the ethical principles that govern the practice of

medicine to see how participation in boxing may conflict with professional ethical standards. Finally, we will explore the implications that a ban on boxing may have for the sport, the medical profession and society in general whether brought about by legal means or medical activism.

A Change in the Code of Conduct Would Be Needed

Many individual doctors agree with the view of their medical association on boxing, but there are inevitably some who do not. Only bodies invested with the power to register and discipline doctors such as the General Medical Council in the United Kingdom or state medical boards in the United States can compel uniform behaviour. Despite the campaigns of the British Medical Association against boxing, a doctor who participates in boxing promotions does not violate the principles of Good Medical Practice as presently formulated by the General Medical Council.[3] If doctors were to uniformly withdraw from participation in boxing, a change in the code of conduct would be required. This would be a major undertaking and would have to be fully justified, since the position of the profession in society makes it a matter of public policy.

Principles of Medical Ethics

Two features are prominent in the professional ethics of medicine—the primacy of the patient-doctor relationship and the reliance on prima facie (binding unless in conflict with higher duties) ethical duties to guide practice. The most influential ethical system in medicine is based on four ethical principles—nonmaleficence, beneficence, respect

---

1. British Medical Association. *The boxing debate.* London: British Medical Association, 1993.
2. Australian Medical Association. Position statement on boxing, November 1997.

This article was written especially for this text.

3. General Medical Council. *Good medical practice.* London: General Medical Council, 1998.

for personal autonomy and justice.[4] These principles reflect the predominant concern of medicine with the individual patient.

Nonmaleficence (the duty not to inflict intentional harm) and beneficence (the duty to act in order to benefit the patient) are the two oldest of the principles and are expressed in the Hippocratic oath. In the 1960s concern with individual rights led to the conscious inclusion of the other two principles in medical ethics.[5] Autonomy refers to self-rule and implies freedom to make meaningful choices. The doctor has a duty to respect the patient's freedom to decide what is best for him or her given the necessary information and competence to make these choices. Justice encompasses the concept of fairness. The main concern has been with distributive justice, the duty to ensure that each individual has a fair share of health care opportunities and that any risk or cost is fairly shared.

However, in addition to his or her duty to the patient, the doctor has a duty to society as well. The doctor may experience conflict between these dual duties. The principle of justice deals most explicitly with the duty to society but cannot resolve these conflicts on its own.

A simple example illustrates the prima facie duty of respect for personal autonomy and its possible conflict with wider duties to society. A doctor employed by a company to provide health care for its employees may experience conflict in fulfilling his/her duty to the individual employee and to the company. The doctor, for example, may not reveal confidential information about the employee to the company unless permitted by him/her to do so. This duty of confidentiality (respect for personal autonomy) to the patient takes priority over the duty to the company (which is not encompassed within the four ethical principles we just listed, but is nevertheless a compelling contractual duty) unless there are compelling reasons to do otherwise. Compelling reasons may include a legal requirement or where concealing the information may lead to harm, for example, an employee with epilepsy who is hired to drive or operate machinery. In reporting this information, the doctor is acting to prevent injury to the employee and his colleagues (beneficence).

Medical Ethics and Boxing

When dealing with boxers we must determine how the principles of medical ethics apply. If the boxer is to be fully autonomous in deciding to box, he or she must have all the relevant facts. The doctor has a duty to ensure that the boxer is aware of the medical risks entailed in the sport.

However, participation by doctors may actually breach their duty of beneficence and inadvertently undermine the boxer's autonomy. When a doctor consents to involvement at a boxing match, that action contributes to making the match possible under the rules. The participation lends legitimacy to the match whatever the doctor's intent. This legitimacy stems from the implicit assumption that the match will be safer because of the doctor's involvement. The boxer may choose to take part because of the perception that the medical presence will minimise his or her risk of harm.

The example of Gerald McClellan who was seriously injured in the London Arena in 1995 illustrates the role of the ringside doctor.[6] The presence of medical personnel cannot prevent injury, although the doctor can advise that a match be stopped to prevent further injury. In the *Oxford Textbook of Sports Medicine* the observation is made: "In preventing injury, the ringside physician is about as effective as the priest at a judicial hanging."[7] The primary function of the doctor in the event of injury is damage control. McClellan was given oxygen, quickly transferred to a hospital and was on the operating table within two hours of the injury. The neurosurgeon credited ringside assistance for saving McClellan's life.

Recent reviews on the management of serious head injury indicate that the role of prehospital care should be basic resuscitation and rapid transfer to a

4. Beauchamp TL, Childress JF. *Principles of biomedical ethics*. 4th ed. New York: Oxford University Press, 1994.
5. Calman KC, Downie RS. Ethical principles and ethical issues in public health. In: Detels R, Holland WW, McEwen J, Omenn GS, eds. *Oxford textbook of public health*. 3rd ed Oxford: Oxford University Press, 1997, pp. 392–402.

6. Hoffer R. Enough. *Sports Illustrated* (3 June) 1995;82(9):24–29.
7. Schwartz ML, Tator CH. Head injuries in athletics. In: Harris M, Williams C, Stanish WD, Micheli CJ, eds. *Oxford textbook of sports medicine*. 2nd ed. Oxford: Oxford University Press, 1998, p. 897.

hospital for definitive treatment.[8, 9] This position reflects the finding that the prognosis is heavily determined by the type of injury and in many cases may not be significantly affected by prehospital care. The ringside doctor may be powerless to influence the speed of transfer in situations where emergency services do not function optimally.

The questions then are: how substantial is the reduction in risk to the boxer that can be achieved by participation of the medical profession in the sport and does this reduction justify the perception that boxing is made safer? The doctor must weigh the harm that may result from the false aura of safety his or her presence creates against the benefit he or she can provide to the injured boxer. It is possible that despite good intentions the overall result of medical collaboration with boxing is harm to the boxer. Actions by doctors that cause harm without apparent benefit clearly violate the principle of nonmaleficence.

In the practice of medicine, drugs or procedures may be prescribed that are harmful. They can only be ethically prescribed (even with informed consent) when the benefits are expected to outweigh the harm and there are no satisfactory alternatives. Clearly there is no intent to harm. Boxing is very different. Unlike other sports where harm is incidental, it is the intent to harm inherent in the sport that makes boxing objectionable.[10] Faced with the clear harm of the sport, the intent to cause injury and the limited ability of the ringside doctor to reduce the risk to boxers, the medical profession finds itself in an ethical dilemma.

8. Chesnut RM. The management of severe traumatic brain injury. *Emergency Medicine Clinics of North America* 1997;15(3):582–604.

9. Gruen P, Liu C. Current trends in the management of head injury. *Emergency Medicine Clinics of North America* 1998;16(1):63–83.

10. The Canadian Amateur Boxing Association, in noting the differences between amateur and professional boxing, states that the objective in amateur boxing is to win on points and that knock-outs are accidental. It observes that less than 1% of amateur matches are won by knock-outs compared to over 25% in professional bouts. If technical knock-outs are considered as well, over 50% of professional matches are won in this way. A professional boxer may earn more if he has a record of many knock-out victories. (Information from official Web site—http://www.boxing.ca/differen.html)

Approaches to Ban Boxing

We have shown that involvement of doctors in boxing may conflict with their ethical duties to boxers. The approach to dealing with the dilemma has been to advocate for legislation to ban it. In calling for changes in the law, the medical profession has consistently highlighted the harm, particularly to the brain, caused by boxing. The point has been made that boxing is distinct from other sports in that this harm is intentional and allowed within the rules of the game. The medical profession cannot eliminate this risk of harm.

These observations not only buttress the lobby for legislation but also bring into sharp focus the need to reform the profession's code of practice to avoid the ethical conflicts that result from participation in boxing. Consequently, if the arguments against boxing are robust enough to justify the medical profession calling for legislation to ban the sport, then they must also be compelling enough to justify a change in the code of medical practice to prevent doctors from participating in boxing matches.

Arguments Against Banning Boxing

One of the objections often raised against banning boxing in that this might result in the sport being driven underground. A well-regulated legal sport is safer and preferable to an unregulated illegal one. The same argument can be raised against an imposed ban by the medical profession. Those who hold this view do not allow for other possible outcomes that are equally plausible.

Boxing was banned in Norway without the negative sequelae suggested by those who raise this objection.[11] The sport may be forced to undergo reforms as a result of an imposed ban and may re-emerge as a sport of skill rather than knockout. Public opinion has led to many reforms of boxing over the years. Reforms in Sweden, for example, led to the elimination of head punches in amateur boxing. Public sensibilities may change once the veneer of safety is removed—boxers may be unwilling to accept the risk, and public interest may wane, making the sport unprofitable to promoters.

11. Cossell H, Bonventre P. *I never played the game*. New York: William Morrow, 1985.

The Role of the Medical Profession in Society

There are other objections that arise from the role of the medical profession in society. As noted earlier, for most of its history, the emphasis has been on the individual patient. The profession, though recognising a role in society at large, has never been able to articulate this in the same detail as it does for its duty to individuals. One area where this role is most prominent is in public health. Historically, actions recommended by the profession were justified on utilitarian grounds and were often backed by legislation. The practice of quarantine and mass infant vaccination are examples. Few objected to this paternalism because it was thought to be for the public good. Any harm to a few individuals was an acceptable price for the public's health.

Modern concerns with personal autonomy and individual rights have made paternalism objectionable. Citizens in a democracy accept restrictions to their autonomy in order to form societies but hold their leaders responsible to justify these restrictions. If the medical profession seeks to act in the interest of society, it must justify that it has a duty to do so and it must be accountable for such action.

Any group in society may lobby for legislation to address issues it feels are best handled in this way. In this context, the lobby by the medical profession may be acceptable, since the final decision rests with legislators who are the people's representatives. Actions by monopolies such as the medical profession are less under the people's control. We do not elect or remove our doctors as we do with politicians. We are therefore entitled to be concerned about their actions when they may impinge on our freedoms. A change in the code of conduct by the medical profession to prevent boxing by withdrawing medical cover can impair the boxer's choice to box and the spectator's choice to watch. One is justified in asking whether this is in the best interest of those affected.

We have argued that this action might be in the best interest of the boxer. Despite the potential benefits of physical fitness, enhanced self-esteem and financial gain from the sport, it is debatable whether these benefits outweigh the harm. There are other sports and pursuits where similar benefits may result without the risk associated with boxing. Boxing in its present form seems to have no compelling benefit to society at large that cannot be reasonably fulfilled by other activities or by modification of the sport to eliminate harm. The case of fencing suggests that reforms may be possible to retain the benefits of the sport without the associated harm.

Can the Medical Profession Justify Acting to Force a Ban of Boxing?

The question still remains: can the medical profession justify acting unilaterally in society even if the reasons for doing so are compelling and beneficial? Does it have a right to force changes in social behavior? The profession must first accept that it is granted special privileges by society in trust. The General Medical Council has noted that this is the central component in good medical practice. A doctor must give the patient the best medical advice, and the profession has a parallel duty to society. It must never betray the trust society places in it. The doctor must respect the competent decision of the patient, but if this decision involves action by the doctor that he or she for whatever reason cannot fulfill, the doctor cannot be forced to do so. A patient with terminal illness can request patient-assisted suicide, but this request does not compel the doctor to act even if inaction violates the patient's autonomy. Similarly, a gynaecologist who has a moral objection to abortion is not compelled to perform this procedure if a patient requests it. Good medical practice requires, however, that an appropriate referral be made so the woman may have the procedure done safely and competently.

Similarly, the wish of society should not compel the medical profession to act against its ethical principles when there is a genuine disagreement in what is best for the public's health. A strong public perception that the spread of HIV/AIDS should be controlled by isolating individuals with infection does not compel the medical profession to act in this way. In the case of boxing, society's "need" for the sport or the right of individuals to choose to watch or participate in it should not compel participation by the medical profession. The profession may also claim a right to autonomy in deciding the actions of its members.

In granting the medical profession the right of self-regulation, society also recognises the autonomy of the profession to fulfil this function. This autonomy is not absolute, as it is restricted by legislation and by the duty to act in the best interest of that society. While there are legitimate differences in defining what it means for a profession to act in the best interest of society, these do not diminish the status of the profession as an autonomous body in society.

Neither is the autonomous role of self-regulation an arbitrary function. The medical profession, in being accountable to the public and to its members, must be able to defend not only the ethical foundations of the positions it takes but also their scientific underpinnings. The relatively recent emphasis on evidence-based medicine illustrates the need to examine the scientific evidence pertinent to the practice of health care. Indeed, ethical practice relies on the best scientific evidence available. The evidence of the cumulative brain injury that results from boxing coupled with the inability of doctors to significantly ameliorate that risk by participating in the sport make a strong case for them to re-evaluate that participation.

Conclusions

One of the most recognised duties of the medical profession has been its role of self-regulation. Through codes of conduct, bodies such as the General Medical Council and the American Medical Association articulate for individual doctors the standards of ethical practice. These are followed because they are based on scientific evidence and generally accepted ethical principles. In addition, there is a long-standing relationship between doctors and their professional bodies that allows for resolution of conflicts that may arise. The public role of the profession is less clear.

The medical profession is expected to be an independent player in the formulation of public policy in areas pertinent to its expertise. That expectation should go beyond the mere provision of technical data. It involves interpreting those data in the wider context of the public good and offering its opinions about the best options for the society. Few would dispute this role.[12]

The medical profession, by virtue of its role in society and the autonomy it is granted to fulfil its functions, can be seen as a moral agent. As a moral agent it may act as an advocate for what it judges to be in the public good. This would be responsible behaviour. On the other hand, a moral agent is expected to act when it is within its power to bring about the desired outcome.

The problem of boxing illustrates the changing public role of the medical profession. It is one of the areas where the profession has chosen to play an activist role but has not given enough attention to the ethical issues inherent in adopting this stand. It also illustrates that besides advocacy the profession has another option at its disposal for influencing public policy. It may act on its convictions if this is consistent with its ethical principles and in the best interest of public health. The profession needs to articulate more clearly its role in public policy and the ethic principles involved in fulfilling that role.

12. This is well illustrated by the leading role the American Medical Association has taken for many years in influencing public policy against smoking interests.

Discussion and Assignments

1. What are the four ethical principals that guide doctors in their work? Which principal has special significance with regard to doctors and boxing? What makes this principal so important?

2. Explain how the principal of nonmaleficence is related to ringside doctors and boxers. Do you regard the ringside doctor and the boxers as being in a doctor-patient relationship?

3. The authors claim the principal of nonmaleficence may be violated by the ringside doctor. What are the two strongest pieces of evidence they offer to support this claim? In a paragraph on each, explain why you think they are strong. What is the weakest piece of evidence they offer to support this claim? In a paragraph explain why you think it's weak.

4. If the ringside doctor saved Gerald McClellan's life as the authors claim (paragraph 11), couldn't it be argued that doctors do help boxers, and that their presence is necessary to protect boxers' health? What is the authors' point in bringing up Gerald McClellan?

5. The authors claim ringside doctors give the false impression that they can do more to mitigate injury than is the case, that doctors are basically engaged in on-the-spot damage control. The authors further claim that such false impressions lead to further harm to boxers. Do you agree or disagree that ringside doctors give a false impression of increased safety to boxers?

6. Before claiming the ringside doctor cannot significantly reduce harm to the boxer, the authors claim in the previous paragraph (paragraph 10): "The boxer may choose to take part because of the perception that the medical presence will minimize his or her risk of harm." But a critic might respond that boxers are familiar with the dangers in boxing, and that they are well aware that ringside doctors can do little to mitigate their injuries. Do you think this is a reasonable response?

a. Do the authors need to convince you that fighters are mistaken about their safety in order to convince you that medical boards should prevent doctors from being ringside physicians?

b. Or would it be enough for the authors to convince you that doctors cannot prevent or mitigate injury (regardless of whether boxers are mistaken)?

7. The authors state the General Medical Council (in the U.K.) and the state medical boards (in the U.S.) would need to change their codes of ethics if they want to prevent doctors from participating in boxing matches. Do you agree or disagree that medical councils and medical boards should be involved in preventing doctors from participating at ringside during boxing matches? Explain why.

8. If medical councils in the United Kingdom and medical boards in the United States moved to prevent doctors from participating at ringside, do you believe it would be effective in bringing an end to boxing? What implications do you see arising from such actions?

9. The authors claim a changing public role for the medical profession, and offer nonparticipation in boxing as an example of this change in process. Can you think of other issues or situations in the past where doctors have taken positions, based on ethics and community health, that have affected public policy? Do you think such positions could be legitimately used to support the authors' position on boxing?

12.7 Blunt Force Violence in America—Shades of Gray or Red

George D. Lundberg

There is absolutely no limit to how revolting things can be.

Clifford B. Walberg, PhD,
Los Angeles, Calif., 1973.

THE ACTION OF ONE HUMAN striking another with the fists must date to about the time humans began to walk on two feet. Aggressive behavior is certainly a normal human trait. Defending oneself

From Journal of the American Medical Association *275, no. 21 (1996): 1684. Reprinted with permission.*

using any method available is at the top of Maslov's hierarchy, namely, survival. The use of a violent act to entertain others vicariously is also thousands of years old. Gladiatorial events, Christians being fed to lions, gunfights in the old American West, and other such events have been legendary. From time to time, however, society looks at its behavior in terms of both the effects on individual participants and the moral and ethical aspects of the events affecting society as a whole. Thus, Christians are no longer fed to lions, and gladiatorial combat, sword duels to the death, cockfights, dogfights, and gunfights have been outlawed and, to some extent, do not occur.

Over many decades, boxing has come under public scrutiny, which has led to numerous reforms. In 1743, Broughton's Rule put the testes off limits.[1] In 1838, new rules for the London prize ring eliminated holding, butting, gouging, kicking, and the wearing of shoes with improper spikes.[1] In 1866, the Marquis of Queensberry rules instituted gloves in all bouts and a 10-second count after a knockdown, and for the first time fighters were matched by weight. Such actions as limiting the number and length of rounds, having a referee with power, mandating medical evaluations, establishing athletic commissions, and requiring the wearing of mouthpieces have represented major efforts at reform.

January 14,1983, the *Journal of the American Medical Association* got the modern reform movement going with an Editorial entitled "Boxing Should Be Banned in Civilized Countries."[2] We stated that "the principal purpose of a boxing match is for one opponent to render the other injured, defenseless, incapacitated, unconscious." We pointed out that boxing was wrong medically because of the very high frequency of brain damage being experienced by boxers and that it was wrong morally because a boxer could win by intentionally damaging the brain of an opponent[3] Thus, we believe that there are many excellent reasons

why both professional and amateur boxing as we know them should be banned. The American Medical Association (AMA) has held a similar position since 1984,[4] and it has been reaffirmed several times.

There is a modern continuum from street fights to barroom brawls to domestic child, spousal, and elder abuse to ultimate fighting to extreme fighting to toughman fighting to professional boxing and to amateur boxing: shades of gray or shades of red. The first three are currently illegal, the legality of the second three is in question in various jurisdictions, and the last two are currently legal. Many people don't realize that even professional boxing as we know it today was illegal in New York, for example, until earlier in this century.[1]

Ultimate fighting is a throwback to the 19th century in this country and even to the 18th century in England. In ultimate fighting, fighters may be of any weight and any sex and can be very unevenly matched. There are neither headgear nor mouthpieces nor gloves. Any part of the body may be used as a weapon except the teeth—biting is banned. Blows may be struck to any part of the opponent's body. No holds are barred.

There are no rounds and no rest periods. It is literally a fight to the finish—be that death, incapacitation, or surrender. The more violent, destructive, and dangerous the events are, the more the promoters and some spectators seem to like it. Kicking is okay, as are head butting, gouging (not eyes), elbowing, kneeing, scratching, and piling on. Unnecessary roughness is necessary—even desirable. Holding with one arm and hitting with the other is okay, as are pounding the opponent's head to the floor while sitting on the opponent, choke holds, chops to the larynx, kidney punches, rabbit punches, chop blocks, and hair pulling. The more blood the better—on opponents, on ring officials, and on ringside spectators. This is one completely repulsive activity.

Potential injuries? Almost anything—brain concussions and hemorrhages; skin and scalp cuts and lacerations; broken and bloody noses; eye damage and blindness; fractures of various bones, including the cervical spine; damage to spinal cord and brain

1. Sammons JT. *Beyond the ring. The role of boxing in American society*. Champaign: University of Illinois Press; 1987.

2. Lundberg GD. Boxing should be banned in civilized countries. *JAMA*. 1983;249:250.

3. Lundberg GD. Boxing should be banned in civilized countries—Round 2. *JAMA*. 1984;251:2696–2698.

4 Lundberg GD. Boxing should be banned in civilized countries—Round 3. *JAMA. 1986;255:2483–2485.*

stem; brain damage or death from hypoxia from choke holds or from a fractured larynx; lost teeth; fractured hand bones; and exposure to blood-borne pathogens like hepatitis. This is a revolting event, utterly without redeeming social value.

Extreme fighting, as described by New York promoters, is a combination of boxing, kick boxing, wrestling, judo, and various martial arts. In order to escape the wave of legislation and regulation banning ultimate fighting, promoters of extreme fighting are scurrying to put in some safety measures (four weight classes, 5-ounce gloves, mouthpieces, groin protection, a referee with authority, HIV testing, computed tomographic scan and electroencephalogram if requested by physicians, and injury insurance for fighters). However, the marketing of extreme fighting for pay-per-view cable television on April 26, 1996, still emphasized its "brutal, barbaric" nature. This event was moved outside the United States to an Indian reservation near Montreal, Quebec. Television (a principal motivator), of course, can originate from anywhere.

Toughman fighting is a largely unsupervised activity. The contestants are usually untrained and may be unskilled. There may be rounds (three, each for 1 minute) and rest periods. Gloves are worn (light, without wrapping the hands inside the gloves). Rules are variable. Brawling is promoted.

Different U.S. jurisdictions are handling these relatively new U.S. activities in different ways. In March 1996, the Chicago City Council banned ultimate fighting from Chicago. The health department in Detroit has termed ultimate fighting "an imminent danger to health or lives" in order to prohibit a scheduled May 17, 1996, event.[5] In December 1995, after a fighter died of a subdural hematoma, the Kansas Athletic Commission in Kansas City banned toughman fighting. The New York State legislature is considering legislation to ban both ultimate and extreme fighting.

The House of Delegates of the AMA at its June 1996 meeting should reaffirm its opposition to amateur and professional boxing and should extend its call for a ban on these activities to explicitly include ultimate fighting, extreme fighting, and toughman contests.[6] Furthermore, because of the patchwork nature of state-by-state and city-by-city regulation of these activities (with many inconsistencies and gaps), the AMA should seek federal legislation banning all such now legal or unregulated barbaric variations of intentional blunt force trauma. Furthermore, we should all bring pressure to bear on cable and direct television companies not to telecast extreme or ultimate fighting or toughman contests in the United States. Just as they do not now telecast "underground" dogfights from Georgia or cockfights from Arkansas, legal bullfights from Juarez, Mexico, or human executions from prisons, they should not telecast these human fights. For a few activities, censorship (voluntary or mandatory) is all right.

5. Hearn W. Ultimate affront? *Am Med News.* May 6, 1996;39:19–20, 25–26.

6. Lundberg GD. Let's stop boxing in the Olympics and the United States military. *JAMA.* 1994;271:1790.

Discussion and Assignments

1. What evidence does Lundberg offer to support his case that the AMA should take a position against ultimate fighting, extreme fighting, and toughman fighting?

2. Lundberg wants the American Medical Association to take a position on ultimate fighting, extreme fighting, and toughman fighting. The conclusion to his argument might read: *The American Medical Association should extend its opposition to legalized boxing to include ultimate fighting, extreme fighting, and toughman fighting.* List the premises he offers to support his argument—just the premises—in clear declarative statement form, in their most logical order.

3. In paragraph 4 Lundberg claims: "There is a modern continuum from street fights to barroom brawls to domestic child, spousal, and elder abuse to ultimate fight-

ing to extreme fighting to toughman fighting to professional boxing and to amateur boxing: shades of gray or shades of red." What does Lundberg mean by *modern continuum?* What is he attempting to do by claiming such a continuum exists? Do you agree or disagree with Lundberg's claim? Why?

4. a. Lundberg believes the AMA should take a formal position against ultimate, extreme, and toughman fighting. Do you think the AMA should take such a position? Construct an argument, pro or con, for the AMA taking such a position using the following argument form.

Issue: Whether the American Medical Association should take a formal position against ultimate, extreme, and toughman fighting.
Definitions:
Premises:
Conclusion:

   b. Now that you have your argument, put it into essay form. Write a 300 word essay for or against the AMA taking a position on ultimate, extreme, and toughman fighting.

5. Lundberg would like to pressure television and cable companies to not televise extreme, ultimate, and toughman fighting. What do you think? (Note that bullfights have been off the air for many years, and cockfighting is nowhere to be seen on the tube.)

12.8 On Boxing and Liberty

RUSSEL H. PATTERSON

SHOULD A SPORT as brutal as boxing be allowed to exist in civilized society? Is a ban on boxing an excessive restraint of individual freedom? We perhaps could all agree that there should exist a certain minimal area of personal freedom that must not be violated or else the individual will be so confined that he is unable to develop his individuality even to the slightest degree. This means that a boundary or frontier must be defined between private life and public authority. The debate is on where that line should be drawn.[1]

John Stuart Mill wrote in his essay, "On Liberty," that there was only one circumstance under which society was entitled to use physical force, legal penalties, or moral coercion. He wrote:

That the only principle that is the sole end for which mankind are warranted, individually or collectively, in interfering with the liberty of action any of their number, is self-protection. That the only purpose for which power can rightfully be exercised over any member of a civilized community against his will is to prevent harm to others. His own good, either physical or moral, is not a sufficient warrant. He cannot rightfully be compelled to do or forbear because it will be better for him to do so, because it will make him happier, because, in the opinion of others to do so would be wiser or even right. These are good reasons for remonstrating with him, or reasoning with him, or persuading him, or entreating him, but not for compelling him or visiting him with any evil in case he did otherwise. To justify that, the conduct from which it is desired to deter him must be calculated to produce evil to someone else. . . .

1. Areen J, King PA, Goldberg S, et al: *Law, Science and Medicine.* Mineola, NY, The Foundation Press Inc, 1984, pp. 356–365.

From Journal of the American Medical Association *255, no. 18 (1986): 2481–82. Reprinted with permission.*

But neither one person, nor any number of persons, is warranted in saying to another human creature of ripe years that he shall not do with his life for his own benefit what he chooses to do with it.[2]

Why was Mill so rigid on drawing the line on public authority only at the point of self-protection? Certainly he understood that men are interdependent and that no one is so completely isolated as not to ever obstruct the lives of others in any way. Liberty for the pike is death for the minnows.[3]

Isaiah Berlin reasons in his "Four Essays on Liberty" that none of us is truly free because we are slaves to our passions and our habits, if not to another man. Besides our habits and pleasures, we also tend to pursue long-range goals of a higher level because we believe them to be for our best. Such goals might vary from honesty and charity to a set of religious beliefs. Often we extend these beliefs to something wider than ourselves, perhaps to our family, our tribe, our church, our country, or even to the rest of mankind. If our children or our friends seem unwilling to assume our beliefs as their own, we try to educate them, argue with them, or otherwise convert them. We believe them to be blind or ignorant. If only they understood themselves as we understand them, they would not resist. The use of logic and education to alter the ideas of others, we would all accept, still leaves the individual free to make the final decision for himself.[3]

However, it is but a small step to reason that because others fail to understand their own best interests and because they are not as rational and wise as we are, it is our duty to coerce them for their own sake and not for our own self-interest. If they understood their own inner spirit they would no longer resist. It is only their hidden inner self that we take into account. We are now in a position to ignore the actual wishes of men or society and to bully, or to oppress, or to torture them in the name and on behalf of their hidden, real self.

Therefore, the concept of liberty or freedom changes from a freedom that an individual actually feels he wishes and needs to a freedom buried within the individual and not dreamed of by his empirical self. This kind of freedom is then easily translated into some superpersonal entity, a state or a class or a nation or even to the march of history. The lessons of the last 50 years show us that this issue is more than academic.[3]

Kant wrote that "no one can tell me to be happy in his own way."[3] Paternalism is the greatest despot imaginable. This is so because it is to treat men as if they were not free but human material for one man, the "benevolent protector," to mold in accordance with his own purpose. This manipulation of men to propel them toward goals that only the social reformer sees and they do not is to deny them their human essence, to treat them as objects without wills of their own, and therefore to degrade them. To drive men toward a goal not conceived by them, even if it is for their own benefit, is in effect to treat them as subhuman, to behave as if their ends are less sacred than one's own. It is not enough to say that it is in the name of some value higher than themselves, because as Kant pointed out all values are the creation of men and consequently there is no value higher than the individual. All forms of tampering with human beings, shaping them against their will, all thought control denies them their freedom and deprives them of their most basic right.[3]

Boxing lasted 1,000 years at the time of the Greek and Roman empires, when Western Civilization as we know it was thriving. It ended in about 400 AD, probably because it had become thoroughly corrupt and professionalized and also because it was banned by a Christian emperor who had a dislike to heathen spectacles. The Greek temple to Zeus at Olympia was razed, the magnificent statue of Zeus was moved to Constantinople, and Christianity became dominant. Western Civilization entered the Dark Ages. Man's spirits soared again during the Italian Renaissance, and again boxing briefly flowered. But society became more restrictive, boxing and also learning disappeared, and the Renaissance faded. In the first part of the 18th century, with the industrial revolution and the rise of individual freedom, boxing again began to flourish. Art and science flowered during the first part of the 20th century, and boxing prospered as well.

2. Mill JS: On liberty, in *Utilitarianism, Liberty and Representative Government*. New York, EP Dutton & Co, 1947, pp. 65–170.
3. Berlin I: Four essays on liberty, in *Two Concepts of Liberty*. London, Oxford University Press, 1969, pp 118–172.

The association between man's highest intellectual accomplishments and boxing is no accident as I see it. Arts, letters, and science only thrive in a time when the government and the church remove the hobbles from individual creativity. If the government becomes an arbiter of moral standards and personal safety, it does so at the price of individual freedom, whether the curbs are on boxing or on the scholar. How much better to educate, cajole, inform, entreat, then let the individual make his own decision. I personally have great concerns about any restriction of an individual and his freedom. The banning of boxing could be looked on as telling boxers that their desires and their values do not count. They are not competent to decide for themselves, and the choice is better left in the hands of other individuals who are more educated and know better what they need. This modest tyranny, to me, is an early sign of repressive authority. I am against it.

Discussion and Assignments

1. Patterson quotes John Stuart Mill in making his case against banning boxing. Study the quotation from Mill. What does Mill have to say about self-protection and individual liberty?
2. Suppose I do not know my own best interests. According to Mill and Isaiah Berlin, should a person or the state have a right to force me to act in my own best interest? Why or why not?
3. How does Patterson relate Mill's and Berlin's views on liberty to boxing? (Note the issues raised in questions 1 and 2.)
4. Patterson invokes the ethics of Immanual Kant to support his case against banning boxing. According to Patterson, what are Kant's views on paternalism? How does Patterson relate Kant's views to banning boxing?
5. Patterson draws a parallel between the times when man attained his highest intellectual achievements, and when boxing flourished. What is Patterson's point in making this distinction? What is the relationship between cultural decline and the decline of boxing, according to Patterson? Might a critic respond to Patterson that just the reverse is the case—that by banning boxing (and other uncivil practices as bullfighting), culture will have a better chance to flourish?
6. Patterson is making a slippery slope argument. He doesn't claim boxing is necessary for culture to flourish; rather, it's the restriction of liberty, and what it may hold for the future, that concerns him. The slow erosion of liberties in all other areas of life might well ensue. It's not so much about boxing; it's about preserving liberty. How strong an argument for boxing, for liberty, is this? Is it likely that sacrificing the liberty to box will lead to the sacrificing of more cherished rights? Do the lessons of history teach us that dramatic sacrifices will issue from a willingness to ban activities such as boxing?

12.9 Excerpt from *On Boxing*

JOYCE CAROL OATES

NO AMERICAN SPORT or activity has been so consistently and so passionately under attack as boxing, for "moral" as well as other reasons. And no American sport evokes so ambivalent a response in its defenders: when asked the familiar question "How can you watch . . . ?" the boxing *aficionado* really has no answer. He can talk about boxing only with others like himself.

In December 1984 the American Medical Association passed a resolution calling for the abolition of boxing on the principle that while other sports involve as much, or even more, risk to life and health—the most dangerous sports being football, auto racing, hang gliding, mountain climbing, and ice hockey, with boxing in about seventh place—boxing is the only sport in which the objective is to cause injury—the brain is the target, the knockout the goal. In one study it was estimated that 87 percent of boxers suffer some degree of brain damage in their lifetimes, no matter the relative success of their careers. And there is the risk of serious eye injury as well. Equally disturbing, though less plausible, is sociological evidence that media attention focused on boxing has an immediate effect upon the homicide rate of the country. (According to sociologists David P. Phillips and John E. Hensley, the rate rises by an average of 12 percent in the days following a highly publicized fight, for the hypothetical reason that the fight "heavily rewards one person for inflicting violence on another and is at the opposite end of a continuum from a successfully prosecuted murder trial, which heavily punishes one person for inflicting physical violence on another.") Doubtful as these findings are in a culture in which television and movie violence has become routine fare, even for young children, it does seem likely that boxing as a phenomenon *sui generis* stimulates rather than resolves certain emotions. If boxing is akin to classic tragedy in its imitation of action and of life it cannot provide the *katharsis* of pity and terror of which Aristotle spoke.

The variegated history of boxing reform is very likely as old as boxing itself. As I mentioned earlier, in the day of Pierce Egan's *Boxiana* the Prize Ring was in fact outlawed in England—though the aristocracy, including the Prince Regent, regularly attended matches. Boxing has been intermittently illegal in various parts of the United States and campaigns are frequently launched to ban it altogether. Like abortion it seems to arouse deep and divisive emotions. (Though activists who would outlaw abortion are not necessarily those who would outlaw boxing: puritanical instincts take unpredictable forms.) The relationship between boxing and poverty is acknowledged, but no one

suggests that poverty be abolished as the most practical means of abolishing boxing. So frequently do young boxers claim they are in greater danger on the street than in the ring that one has to assume they are not exaggerating for the sake of credulous white reporters.

It is objected too that boxing as a sport is closely bound up with organized crime. Investigations on the federal and state level, over the decades, but most prominently in the fifties, have made the connection unmistakable, though the situation at any time is problematic. One wonders about "suspicious" decisions—are they fixed, or simply the consequence of judges' prejudices? As in Michael Spinks's second, highly controversial win over Larry Holmes, for instance; and the Wilfredo Gomez–Rocky Lockridge match of May 1985 (when judges gave a world junior-lightweight title to a Puerto Rican hometown favorite). And recent televised performances by former Olympic Gold Medalists and their handpicked opponents have struck the eye of more than one observer as not entirely convincing . . .

Not long ago I saw a film of a long-forgotten fixed fight of Willie Pep's in which Pep allowed himself to be overcome by an underdog opponent: the great featherweight performed as a boxer-turned-actor might be expected to perform, with no excess of zeal or talent. It occurred to me that boxing is so refined, yet so raw a sport that no match can be successfully thrown; the senses simply pick up on what is not happening, what is being held back, as a sort of ironic subtext to what is actually taking place. You can run but you can't hide.

Not boxing in itself but the money surrounding it, the gambling in Las Vegas, Atlantic City, and elsewhere, is the problem, and a problem not likely to be solved. I have made an attempt to read the 135-page single-spaced document "Organized Crime in Boxing: Final Boxing Report of the State of New Jersey Commission of Investigation" of December 1985 and have come to the conclusion that the Commission, which has moved to abolish boxing in New Jersey, was wrongheaded in its initial approach: it should have been investigating organized crime in New Jersey, in which Atlantic City boxing/gambling figures. That the Commission would vote to abolish boxing altogether because of criminal connections suggests a naïveté shading into sheer vindictiveness: one would then be required to abolish funeral parlors, pizzerias, trucking firms, some labor unions. And if gamblers can't gamble on boxing they will simply gamble on football, basketball, baseball—as they already do.

Since boxing has become a multimillion-dollar business under the aegis of a few canny promoters—the most visible being Don King—it is not likely that it will be abolished, in any case. It would simply be driven underground, like abortion; or exiled to Mexico, Cuba, Canada, England, Ireland, Zaire . . . Boxing's history is one of such exigencies, fascinating for what they suggest of the compulsion of some men to fight and of others to be witnesses.

The 1896 heavyweight title match between Ruby Robert Fitzsimmons and Peter Maher, for instance, was outlawed everywhere in the States, so promoters staged it on an isolated sandbar in the Rio Grande River, four hundred miles from El Paso. (Can one imagine?—three hundred men made the arduous journey to witness what was surely one of the most disappointing title bouts in boxing history when Fitzsimmons knocked out Maher in ninety-five seconds.) During Jack Dempsey's prime in the 1920s boxing was outlawed in a number of states, like alcohol, and, like alcohol, seems to have aroused a hysterical public enthusiasm. Dempsey's notorious five minutes with the giant Argentinian Firpo was attended by eighty-five thousand people—most of whom could barely have seen the ring, let alone the boxers; both Dempsey's fights with Gene Tunney were attended by over a hundred thousand people—the first fought in a downpour during which rain fell in "blinding sheets" for forty minutes on both boxers and onlookers alike. Photographs of these events show jammed arenas with boxing rings like postage-sized altars at their centers, the boxers themselves no more than tiny, heraldic figures. To attend a Dempsey match was not to have seen a Dempsey match, but perhaps that was not the issue.

When Jack Johnson won the heavyweight title in 1908 he had to pursue the white champion Tommy Burns all the way to Australia to confront him. The "danger" of boxing at that time—and one of the reasons worried citizens wanted to abolish it—was that it might expose and humiliate white men in the ring. After Johnson's decisive victory over the White Hope contender Jim Jeffries there were in fact race riots and lynchings throughout the United States; even films of some of Johnson's fights were outlawed in many states. And because in recent decades boxing has become a sport in which black and Hispanic men have excelled it is particularly vulnerable to attack by white middle-class reformers (the AMA in particular) who show very little interest in lobbying against equally dangerous Establishment sports like football, auto racing, thoroughbred horse racing.

The late Nat Fleischer, boxing expert and founder of *The Ring* magazine, once estimated that tens of thousands of injuries have occurred in the ring since the start of modern boxing in the 1890s—by "modern" meaning the introductions of the rules of the Marquis of Queensberry requiring padded gloves, three-minute rounds, one minute's rest between rounds, continuous fighting during rounds. (The bare-knuckle era, despite its popular reputation for brutality, was far less dangerous for fighters—fists break more readily than heads.) Between 1945 and 1985 at least three hundred seventy boxers have died in the United States of injuries directly attributed to boxing. In addition to the infamous Griffith-Paret fight there have been a number of others given wide publicity: Sugar Ray Robinson killed a young boxer named Jimmy Doyle in 1947, for instance, while defending his welterweight title; Sugar Ramos won the featherweight title in 1963 by knocking out the champion Davey Moore, who never regained consciousness; Ray Mancini killed the South Korean Duk Koo-Kim in 1982; former featherweight champion Barry McGuigan killed the Nigerian "Young Ali" in 1983. After the death of Duk Koo-Kim the World Boxing Council shortened title bouts to twelve rounds. (The World Boxing Association retains fifteen. In the era of marathon fights, however—1892 to 1915—men often fought as many as one hundred rounds; the record is one hundred ten, in 1893, over a stupefying seven-hour period. The last scheduled forty-five-round championship fight was between the black title-holder Jack Johnson and his White Hope successor Willard in 1915: the match went twenty-six rounds beneath a blazing sun in Havana, Cuba, before Johnson collapsed.)

To say that the rate of death and injury in the ring is not extraordinary set beside the rates of other sports is to misread the nature of the criticism brought to bear against boxing (and not against other sports). Clearly, boxing's very image is repulsive to many people because it cannot be assimilated into what we wish to know about civilized man. In a technological society possessed of incalculably refined methods of mass destruction (consider how many times over both the United States and the Soviet Union have vaporized each other in fantasy) boxing's display of direct and unmitigated and seemingly natural aggression is too explicit to be tolerated.

Which returns us to the paradox of boxing: its obsessive appeal for many who find in it not only a spectacle involving sensational feats of physical skill but an emotional experience impossible to convey in words; an art form, as I've suggested, with no natural analogue in the arts. Of course it is primitive, too, as birth, death, and erotic love might be said to be primitive, and forces our reluctant acknowledgment that the most profound experiences of our lives are physical events—though we believe ourselves to be, and surely are, essentially spiritual beings.

Discussion and Assignments

1. What does Oates think will happen to boxing if it is banned in the United States? Does her view of human nature affect her opinion? How? Do you agree or disagree with her? Why?

2. Why is race relevant to Oates in understanding boxing and its critics? Does she think boxing critics are fair in their assessment of boxing when it comes to issues of race?

3. Oates points out that many young boxers say it's more dangerous on the streets than in the ring. According to Oates, do critics of boxing understand this observation? If not, what is it they are they missing?

4. Oates claims the image of boxing is "repulsive" to many people. Why is it repulsive? Does she think there is an inconsistency in peoples' reaction to boxing's violence? What is the moral relevance of the claim that something is repulsive?

5. Oates discusses the AMA position on banning boxing, including the statistics on brain damage. Considering this is the AMA's main issue in advocating the abolition of boxing, do you think she addresses the issue sufficiently? Does she take a position on the issue of brain damage to boxers?

6. What is the relationship between boxing and human nature for Oates? According to Oates, what does this relationship tell us about ourselves? What does this relationship tell us about efforts to abolish boxing?

12.10 Death in the Ring Is a Fact of Life: Chicago, July 9, 1980

JOHN SCHULIAN

FIGHTING IS NOT A COWARD'S BUSINESS, no matter how much the air is polluted by cries that this pug is gutless and that one has no heart. To lace on a pair of eight-ounce gloves and climb into the square circle, face to face with a man intent on relieving you of your senses, is to give the world irrefutable proof of your courage before a punch is thrown. The hope here is that somehow, some way, this

From Writer's Fighters and Other Sweet Scientists, *by J. Schulian (Kansas City, KS: Andrews and McMeel,* 1983), pp. 115–118. *Reprinted with permission.*

provides at least an ounce of solace for the wife and child that Cleveland Denny left behind.

Surely he could not have bequeathed them much in the way of diamonds and gold, for he was of the genus club fighter. When his day at the factory was done, he had more long hours ahead of him at the gym, and if he didn't like the idea, he had an option that never varied: He could quit.

It is easy to say now that Denny should have done just that. But such a retreat would have been foreign to the instincts that made him what he was and to the impulses that sent him charging up to Gaetan Hart, the Canadian lightweight champion, screaming with the profane wrath born of their first two fights. "I'll kill you!" Hart shouted back. And how was anyone at an otherwise innocuous weigh-in to know that when the two of them battled under a weeping Montreal sky, Hart would lay the groundwork for his threat to come true?

Sixteen days later, Cleveland Denny was dead at the age of twenty-four. He had been in a coma from just before the Duran-Leonard fight until just before the Holmes-LeDoux fight, and then he became part of boxing's tragic history. The Associated Press sent word immediately that his was the fight game's fifth death in the last seven months, and in the instant it took to read that statistic, the word "game" became as bitter as a mouthful of bile.

Now we await the cries of rage and indignation that are sure to follow. They will show up on the editorial pages of our newspapers and on the commentary segments of the television news. They will bemoan the fate of our fighters and beleaguer the slice of society that lives off exhibitions of man's inhumanity to man. They will do everything except provide workable solutions for a breed of athletes beyond the comprehension of great thinkers who seldom descend into stinking arenas.

Too bad, for in those arenas dwell a precious few men made stronger by their surroundings, men with too much pride to peddle flesh guilelessly and too much savvy to assume that boxing can be policed like any other sport. The one who comes to mind immediately is Angelo Dundee, trainer of Sugar Ray Leonard and passing acquaintance of Cleveland Denny. "I said hello to the kid when we was getting our pictures taken for our credentials up in Montreal," Dundee was saying Tuesday. "When I heard he was dead, right away my mind flashed back to the way he looked that day—healthy, smiling, happy. And now he's gone, you know. It just leaves you empty."

On the heels of the emptiness is frustration. It has its basis in the extensive tests that every fighter underwent to become part of the evening that saw Roberto Duran win the World Boxing Council's welterweight championship. The malevolent Duran himself was called back to the hospital repeatedly to make sure an irregular heart beat was not hazardous to his health.

"They were giving these guys everything," Dundee said. "The electrocardiogram. The electroencephalogram, where they put the needles in your scalp. Everything. And then this poor kid dies. I'm tellin' you, it drives you outta your mind. What else can we do?"

Assuming that the medical profession has done its all, perhaps the answer is nothing. Protective head gear, so popular in the amateurs, has earned the professionals' disdain because it creates a blind spot and promotes a false sense of security. Gloves with thicker padding are dismissed with equal alacrity because they encourage fighters to stay on their feet longer, thereby inviting more sustained beatings. "Maybe bare knuckles is the answer," Dundee said. "A kid would get flattened out and that would be it." You can imagine how that would go over with faint hearts and pacifists. Most likely they would just start another futile campaign to legislate boxing out of existence.

Simply put, there isn't an emptier dream anywhere. Even if the law did dictate against fisticuffs, men would fight for prizes in cow pastures, on riverboats, and in the back rooms of saloons, the way they have done in the past. They would fight because it is their nature, because it is as much a part of them as painting was a part of Van Gogh and writing was a part of Hemingway. And they would pay no more heed to the possibility of being hurt, maimed, or even killed than any of the tough guys presently marching into combat.

"If something bad's gonna happen, it's gonna happen," Johnny Lira said Tuesday, and his shrug spoke as loudly as his fists have while making him *Ring* magazine's eighth-ranked lightweight. "Hey, people get hit by cars, you know. People fall down stairs, you know. I can't worry about dyin' when I'm trying to put some guy to sleep."

There will be those, of course, who will laugh off Lira's pronouncement as the posturing of a fighter who has known no pain worse than a split eyebrow. In that case, it would be wise for the doubters to remember Davey Moore, who lost his life in 1963 three days after losing his featherweight championship to Sugar Ramos.

After leading the fight for the first nine rounds, Moore walked into Ramos' right hand and toppled backwards, striking his head on the bottom ring rope. Though he climbed off the canvas, Moore was finished, destined to be knocked out seconds later and sent into a world where the pounding in his skull didn't stop until his heart ceased beating. But before he lost consciousness, before he so much as left the ring, he sought out Angelo Dundee, Ramos' trainer, and asked a question that should stand as a memorial to what boxers are made of: "Angie, you're gonna give me a rematch, ain'tcha?"

Discussion and Assignments

1. According to Schulian, do the critics of boxing understand the sport? Do they understand the men who choose to box?

2. What is it that drives a man to enter the ring? What analogies does Schulian use to make his point? Do you think these analogies are effective? Why or why not?

3. Does Schulian believe it is possible for boxing to be abolished? Why or why not? Do you agree with him?

4. According to Schulian, what would happen if boxing were outlawed? Why is he so sure of his views on this issue?

Concluding Questions and Observations on Boxing

1. Critics like Brayne and Sargeant note that fencing has evolved into a safe sport of skill and argue that boxing could change too, becoming a sport of skill rather than knockout. In effect, the winner of a boxing match would have to win on points, with headshots prohibited. Do you think banning headshots would be supported by people involved in boxing and by the public? Do you think it would be enough to silence boxing's critics?

2. Many critics who advocate the abolition of boxing claim it's likely it will continue illegally if it is outlawed. Do you think this is so? Could this mean that more fighters might be injured on account of *illegal* boxing?

3. It could be argued that boxers not only consent to fights that may result in injury, but that they are well informed of the dangers of boxing as well; that is, the possibility of injury is not *concealed* from them in any way. Indeed, the more medical data on boxing injuries, the more informed they become. Yet few choose to quit, and many more take up the sport. Do you think these factors are important in deciding whether to allow boxers to continue in their occupation? Explain your reasons.

4. What do you think would happen if boxing were outlawed? Would the sport go underground, or onto ships in international waters? Would the rules be changed to make it safer? Or do you think it's so popular that outlawing it will never happen?

5. In recent years women have taken to boxing in amateur and professional prizefighting. Does the fact that women have entered the ring affect your views on the movement to ban boxing?